THE CAMBRIDGE COMPANION TO

PHILO

The works of Philo of Alexandria, a slightly older contemporary
of Jesus and Paul, constitute an essential source for the study
of Judaism at the turn of the eras and of the rise of Christianity.
They are also of extreme importance for understanding the Greek
philosophy of the time, and they help to explain the onset of new
forms of spirituality that would dominate the following centuries.

This handbook presents, in an unassuming format, an account
of Philo's achievements. It contains a profile of his life and times,
a systematic overview of his many writings, and survey chapters
of the key features of his thought, as seen from the perspectives
of Judaism and Greek philosophy. The volume concludes with
chapters devoted to Philo's influence and significance.

Composed by an international team of experts, *The Cambridge
Companion to Philo* gives readers a sense of the current state of
scholarship and provides depth of vision in key areas of Philonic
studies.

Adam Kamesar is Professor of Judeo–Hellenistic Literature at
Hebrew Union College, Cincinnati.

The Cambridge Companion to
PHILO

Edited by Adam Kamesar

CAMBRIDGE UNIVERSITY PRESS
Cambridge, New York, Melbourne, Madrid, Cape Town, Singapore,
São Paulo, Delhi

Cambridge University Press
32 Avenue of the Americas, New York, NY 10013-2473, USA

www.cambridge.org
Information on this title: www.cambridge.org/9780521678025

First published 2009

Printed in the United States of America

A catalog record for this publication is available from the British Library.

Library of Congress Cataloging in Publication data
    The Cambridge companion to Philo / Edited by Adam Kamesar.
        p.   cm.
    Includes bibliographical references and index.
    ISBN 978-0-521-86090-1 (hardback) – ISBN 978-0-521-67802-5 (pbk.)
    1. Philo, of Alexandria.   I. Kamesar, Adam.   II. Title.
    B689.Z7C29   2009
    181'.06–dc22   2008045260

ISBN 978-0-521-86090-1 hardback
ISBN 978-0-521-67802-5 paperback

CONTENTS

CONTRIBUTORS

ADAM KAMESAR is Professor of Judeo–Hellenistic Literature at Hebrew Union College, Cincinnati.

CARLOS LÉVY is Professor of Roman Philosophy and Literature at the Université de Paris IV (Sorbonne).

ROBERTO RADICE is Professor of Ancient Philosophy at the Università Cattolica del Sacro Cuore, Milan.

JAMES R. ROYSE is Professor of Philosophy at San Francisco State University.

DAVID T. RUNIA is Master of Queen's College and Professorial Fellow in the School of Classics, Fine Arts and Archaeology at the University of Melbourne.

DANIEL R. SCHWARTZ is Professor of Jewish History at the Hebrew University, Jerusalem.

FOLKER SIEGERT is Professor of Jewish Studies and New Testament and Director of the Institutum Judaicum Delitzschianum at the Westfälische Wilhelms-Universität, Münster.

CRISTINA TERMINI teaches at the Pontificia Università S. Tommaso d'Aquino, Rome.

DAVID WINSTON is Professor Emeritus of Hellenistic and Jewish Studies at the Graduate Theological Union, Berkeley.

THE WORKS OF PHILO: EDITIONS
AND ABBREVIATIONS

The standard modern edition of Philo's works in English translation, which also includes a facing Greek text, is that of F.H. Colson, G.H. Whitaker, and R. Marcus. It appeared in the Loeb Classical Library in ten volumes and two supplementary volumes between 1929 and 1962. All contributors to this *Companion* acknowledge their debt to this translation. Some have employed it when citing Philo directly, on occasion with some alterations, while others have provided their own translations.

The standard critical edition of Philo's works in the original Greek is that of L. Cohn and P. Wendland, which appeared in six volumes between 1896 and 1915. A valuable set of indices constitutes volume VII, which was prepared by H. Leisegang and was published in two parts in 1926 and 1930. All major modern editions of Philo, including that of Colson and Whitaker, are based on this one. Among such editions, those in German and in French are especially important, and the French edition also contains a facing Greek text. These two editions, published in multiple volumes over long periods, often contain extensive and valuable annotations. Full details of the editions, which are cited in abbreviated form in this *Companion*, are as follows:

PCW   L. Cohn, P. Wendland, and S. Reiter (eds.), *Philonis Alexandrini Opera quae supersunt*, I–VII (Berlin 1896–1930)
PAPM   R. Arnaldez, J. Pouilloux, C. Mondésert et al. (eds.), *Les oeuvres de Philon d'Alexandrie*, 1–36 (Paris 1961–1992)
PCH   L. Cohn, I. Heinemann et al. (eds.), Philo von Alexandria, *Die Werke in deutscher Übersetzung*, I–VII (Breslau – Berlin 1909–1964)
PLCL   F. H. Colson, G. H. Whitaker, and R. Marcus (eds.), *Philo*, I–X, Supplements I–II (Cambridge, MA 1929–1962)

There are also other important editions and commentaries of single works or groups of works. These are listed at the appropriate place in chapter 2.

Philo's works are usually cited by their Latin titles, sometimes in short form; for example, *De congressu* is the short form for *De congressu eruditionis gratia* (= *On Mating with the Preliminary Studies*). There are also abbreviations for these Latin titles, which are often employed when specific references are given. The list of Philo's works, by alphabetical order of these abbreviations, is as follows:

Abr.	*De Abrahamo (On Abraham)*
Aet.	*De aeternitate mundi (On the Eternity of the World)*
Agr.	*De agricultura (On Husbandry)*
Anim.	*De animalibus (On Animals)*
Cher.	*De cherubim (On the Cherubim)*
Conf.	*De confusione linguarum (On the Confusion of Tongues)*
Congr.	*De congressu eruditionis gratia (On Mating with the Preliminary Studies)*
Contempl.	*De vita contemplativa (On the Contemplative Life)*
Decal.	*De decalogo (On the Decalogue)*
Det.	*Quod deterius potiori insidiari soleat (That the Worse Is Wont to Attack the Better)*
Deus	*Quod Deus sit immutabilis (On the Unchangeableness of God)*
Ebr.	*De ebrietate (On Drunkenness)*
Flacc.	*In Flaccum (Flaccus)*
Fug.	*De fuga et inventione (On Flight and Finding)*
Gig.	*De gigantibus (On the Giants)*
Her.	*Quis rerum divinarum heres sit (Who Is the Heir of Divine Things?)*
Hypoth.	*Hypothetica*
Jos.	*De Josepho (On Joseph)*
Leg.	*Legum allegoriae (The Allegories of the Laws)*
Legat.	*Legatio ad Gaium (Embassy to Gaius)*
Migr.	*De migratione Abrahami (On the Migration of Abraham)*
Mos.	*De vita Mosis (On the Life of Moses)*
Mut.	*De mutatione nominum (On the Change of Names)*
Opif.	*De opificio mundi (On the Creation)*
Plant.	*De plantatione (On Noah's Work as a Planter)*
Post.	*De posteritate Caini (On the Posterity of Cain and His Exile)*
Praem.	*De praemiis et poenis (On Rewards and Punishments)*
Prob.	*Quod omnis probus liber sit (Every Good Man Is Free)*
Prov.	*De providentia (On Providence)*
QE	*Quaestiones in Exodum (Questions on Exodus)*
QG	*Quaestiones in Genesim (Questions on Genesis)*

Sacr.	*De sacrificiis Abelis et Caini (On the Sacrifices of Abel and Cain)*
Sobr.	*De sobrietate (On Sobriety)*
Somn.	*De somniis (On Dreams)*
Spec.	*De specialibus legibus (On the Special Laws)*
Virt.	*De virtutibus (On the Virtues)*

OTHER ANCIENT SOURCES: EDITIONS AND ABBREVIATIONS

The pseudepigraphic literature related to the Old Testament, including the *Letter of Aristeas*, as well as the fragments of the minor Judeo–Hellenistic authors, such as Aristobulus, are cited according to J.H. Charlesworth (ed.), *The Old Testament Pseudepigrapha*, I–II (New York 1983–1985). Texts from Qumran and the *Damascus Document* are cited according to F. García Matinez and E.J.C. Tigchelaar (eds.), *The Dead Sea Scrolls Study Edition*, I–II (Leiden 1997–1998).

Books of the Bible are abbreviated as follows:

OLD TESTAMENT

Gen	Genesis
Exod	Exodus
Lev	Leviticus
Num	Numbers
Deut	Deuteronomy
Neh	Nehemiah
Ps/Pss	Psalm(s)
Prov	Proverbs
Isa	Isaiah
Jer	Jeremiah
Ezek	Ezekiel
Dan	Daniel
Zeph	Zephaniah

SEPTUAGINT (= LXX)

1–4 Macc	1–4 Maccabees
Sir	Sirach
Wis	Wisdom of Solomon

NEW TESTAMENT

Matt	Matthew
Rom	Romans
1–2 Cor	1–2 Corinthians
Gal	Galatians
Eph	Ephesians
Phil	Philippians
Col	Colossians
1–2 Tim	1–2 Timothy
Heb	Hebrews
Jas	James
1–2 Pet	1–2 Peter

Abbreviations of other ancient sources, such as Old Testament Pseudepigrapha, the Dead Sea Scrolls, the works of Greek and Latin writers, and rabbinic texts, follow P. H. Alexander et al. (eds.), *The SBL Handbook of Style* (Peabody, MA 1999).

ABBREVIATIONS OF PERIODICALS, REFERENCE WORKS, AND SERIES

ANRW	*Aufsteig und Niedergang der römischen Welt*
CPJ	V. A. Tcherikover and A. Fuks (eds.), *Corpus Papyrorum Judaicarum*, I–III (Cambridge, MA 1957–1964)
GCS	Die griechischen christlichen Schriftsteller der ersten Jahrhunderte
GLAJJ	M. Stern (ed.), *Greek and Latin Authors on Jews and Judaism*, I–III (Jerusalem 1974–1984)
GRBS	*Greek, Roman, and Byzantine Studies*
HThR	*Harvard Theological Review*
HUCA	*Hebrew Union College Annual*
JJS	*Journal of Jewish Studies*
JQR	*The Jewish Quarterly Review*
JSJ	*Journal for the Study of Judaism in the Persian, Hellenistic and Roman Period*
JSNT	*Journal for the Study of the New Testament*
JThS	*The Journal of Theological Studies*
NTS	*New Testament Studies*
PG	Patrologia Graeca
PRE	G. Wissowa et al. (eds.), *Paulys Realencyclopädie der classischen Altertumswissenschaft*
PRSt	*Perspectives in Religious Studies*
SBLSP	*Society of Biblical Literature Seminar Papers*
SC	Sources chrétiennes
StPhAnn	*The Studia Philonica Annual*
StPhilo	*Studia Philonica*
SVF	H. von Arnim (ed.), *Stoicorum veterum fragmenta*, I–IV (Leipzig 1903–1924)
VC	*Vigiliae Christianae*

INTRODUCTION BY ADAM KAMESAR

Philo of Alexandria (ca. 15 BCE – 45 CE) stands at the crossroads of three great civilizations of antiquity: the Judaic, the Greek, and the Christian. Philo's primary heritage was that of biblical Judaism, but in the form it had taken on in the Diaspora of the Hellenistic world. His chief literary medium was biblical exegesis, but he sought to interpret the Scriptures by reference to the most advanced and sophisticated systems of thought of the times, which were those of Greek philosophy. In theology and what was called 'physics', the system of primary importance for Philo was that of Platonism, and in ethics that of Stoicism. However, Philo's attempt to assimilate biblical and Greek thought often finds closer parallels in the Christian world than in a Jewish or a pagan environment. Indeed, Philo came to be appreciated more by the later Christian Fathers than by the Rabbis or the Greek philosophers of the Roman imperial age. In view of his background and influence, the writings of Philo are of fundamental importance for the understanding of Judaism, for the history of Greek philosophy, and for the study of early Christianity.

Within the context of the history of Greek literature as well, Philo appears to have lived across the span of the eras in more than simply a chronological sense. For in his writings he assumes many guises and, in a manner of speaking, emerges as a representative of different epochs. At times he is a man of science or a practitioner of the technical disciplines such as grammar and advanced literary study as they had developed in Hellenistic times. At other times, his moralizing diatribes and rhetorical displays have much in common with the popular philosophical literature of the early imperial age. And finally, his Platonistic religiosity and focus on the quest for the transcendent would appear to presage certain forms of spirituality that we encounter in later antiquity, in the Hermetic literature, in the Chaldean Oracles, and in Gnosticism. Of course, Philo's erudition was vast and he drew on an extraordinary array of sources. He knew not only secular Greek literature, but also owed much to a previous tradition of biblical exegesis, no doubt that of Greek-speaking Judaism, which he characterizes only in the most general of terms, without naming names. In fact, Philo's dependence on earlier authorities was such that some would study him, as A. D. Nock has put it, 'primarily as a source rather than as a man'.[1] Nevertheless, this circumstance alone cannot account for the great variety in the Philonic corpus. It must also be put down to the breadth of Philo's interests and horizons and to his versatility as a writer. His works represent a most interesting specimen of Greek literature.

Philo's bicultural heritage in Judaism and Hellenism, however, and even his proximity to Christian thought can make him a perplexing author to read. And the sheer bulk and variety of the Philonic corpus make it a difficult sea to navigate. Thus, the role for an up-to-date handbook of this sort. Of course, a handbook of moderate size cannot address all the aspects of Philo's works, nor can it be a substitute for reading those works directly, which, it may be acknowledged, is not always an easy or pleasant experience. But this *Companion* endeavors to supply some essential introductory information in a clear and unassuming format that can turn that experience into less of a struggle. While it is introductory, the *Companion* goes beyond the elementary level. The chapters are intended to provide not only a sense of recent progress in the scholarship on Philo, but also a certain vision of the topics under consideration.

As just indicated, the structure of the volume is meant to be very straightforward: Part I: Life and Writings; Part II: Thought; and Part III: Influence and Significance. With any author, it is necessary to have some appreciation of his or her life and times. In the case of Philo, while we possess few details about him personally, there is a good deal of data concerning his family, social position, and historical setting. He played a key role in the events related to the violence between Greeks and Jews in Alexandria in 38 CE, and wrote about them in two surviving works. All of this material, to be reviewed in chapter 1, allows us to gain concrete insights into some of his positions and attitudes. The corpus of Philo's writings is especially large and complicated, and consequently may appear somewhat intimidating to the novice. Not only did Philo write in a variety of genres and for a variety of audiences, his writings have suffered some modifications and corruptions in the course of their transmission, in manuscript form, through the ages. This circumstance has led to further difficulties in understanding the structure and organization of the corpus, which seems to have been anything but haphazard. The survey in chapter 2 provides an introduction and a reasoned guide to the catalogue of Philo's writings. The majority of those writings, about three-fourths of the corpus, are dedicated to the exegesis of

---

1   *Essays on Religion and the Ancient World* (Cambridge, MA 1972), II, p. 559.

Scripture. That is, for the most part, Philo does not set out his ideas in schematic treatises but proceeds according to the biblical text. His philosophy and religious beliefs emerge in the course of his exposition. Thus, the path to understanding Philo's thought must go through his biblical exegesis, because this is his primary mode of discourse. The objective of chapter 3 is to provide some background on Philo's approach to the Bible and on the basis and orientation of his exegesis, so that the reading of the exegetical works might prove less disconcerting.

Part II of the *Companion* is concerned with Philo's thought and its background. Chapter 4 is designed to provide a broad survey of Philo's biblical faith as understood in the setting of Second Temple or 'Middle' Judaism. There are a variety of contemporary sources that help us understand the Jewish context for Philo, and these include the deutero-canonical and pseudepigraphic works, the writings of Josephus, and the Dead Sea Scrolls. These sources often allow us to better appreciate the specific character of Philo's Jewish thought. In the view of some theorists, Judaism can be well described in terms of the threefold scheme, 'God, Torah, and Israel', and a close variation of this scheme provides the structure of chapter 4. The remaining two chapters in Part II are more in-depth treatments of the two chief spheres of Philo's thought as seen from the perspective of Greek philosophy. From the time of Xenocrates (396–314 BCE), it had been customary to divide philosophy into three branches: logic, physics, and ethics. In his treatise *Quod omnis probus liber sit*, § 80, where he is discussing the Essenes, Philo mentions these three parts of philosophy, and outlines the Essenes' attitude toward them. He indicates that they are completely unconcerned with logic, on the view that it is a kind of verbal sparring unnecessary for the attainment of virtue. With regard to physics, they focus only on the questions of God and creation, and disregard those parts of it that they consider to be beyond the grasp of man. To the ethical branch of philosophy, on the other hand, they devote intense study. This description of the primary interests of the Essenes could apply, with some nuancing, to Philo himself. Indeed, it is not improbable that he imposed his own perspective on them.[2] Accordingly, chapters 5 and 6 of the *Companion* will cover, respectively, Philo's theology and his views on creation, and his ethics. In both of these chapters, full attention is given to the primary philosophical sources of Philo's thought, namely, Platonism and Stoicism.

Finally, Part III of the *Companion* is dedicated to Philo's influence and significance. As indicated above, while Philo is a figure worthy of study for his own sake, his writings are often read for the light they may

---

2   This perspective seems to have been derived from a source related to Ariston of Chios, *SVF* I.352.

shed on other areas of inquiry. In the present volume, those areas are defined by reference to literary *corpora*. Our contributors consider the relationship of the Philonic corpus to three other quite distinct *corpora* of ancient literature: the New Testament, the works of the Church Fathers, and the rabbinic writings. From a chronological perspective, the New Testament is the closest to Philo. While one perhaps cannot speak of a direct influence of Philo's written works on the New Testament authors, it is highly probable that Philo's ideas, possibly spread through the medium of the Hellenistic synagogues, did have some influence on the New Testament. In any case, it is beyond doubt that the Philonic corpus is one of the most important sources parallel to the New Testament and that it can illuminate many of its central ideas. The first chapter of Part III, chapter 7, will provide a convenient and systematic survey of some of the key points of contact between Philo and the New Testament. In the case of the Church Fathers, one may speak of an actual reception of Philo. Especially from the time of Clement of Alexandria (ca. 150–215 CE) onward, the Christian writers adopted Philo almost as one of their own. It is through the Church Fathers, and especially through Origen and the 'Alexandrian' brand of exegesis and theology, that Philo exercised a massive influence on Western religious philosophy. For the Fathers also attempted to combine biblical revelation with Platonic philosophy, and it was therefore almost inevitable that they would take full advantage of the Philonic legacy. If Philo helps us understand patristic literature and thought, the reverse is also true. For the Fathers were Philo's readers in antiquity, and their understanding of his works has much to contribute to our own. Chapter 8 of the *Companion* illustrates in a detailed fashion how Philo's writings came to be a part of the early Christian tradition, and also looks at the question of why this was the case. Paradoxically, the rabbinic corpus stands at a greater distance from Philo. The Rabbis do not mention him at all, and any influence he may have exerted upon them seems to be indirect. Nevertheless, one should not suppose because of this that the works of Philo are not relevant for the understanding of rabbinic literature or vice versa. Quite the contrary. And one should be especially wary of the notion that the rabbinic writings are of too late a date to be of significance for the understanding of the Philonic corpus. While the contemporary critical approaches to the rabbinic writings are certainly in order, the fact remains that these writings preserve earlier traditions and, perhaps more importantly, modes of exegetical thinking. Indeed, the respective exegetical projects of Philo and the Rabbis have enough in common that the Philonic corpus and rabbinic literature may illuminate each other reciprocally. The great difficulties that one sometimes encounters in attempting to understand either Philo or the Rabbis make that possibility a welcome circumstance. Such reciprocal illumination is based on points of similarity, and also on points of contrast. Chapter 9 of this *Companion* provides a survey of the entire question, both with regard to the general issues and with regard to some specific points of comparability.

The study of Philo is vibrant in many countries, as the list of contributors to the present volume attests, and is carried out in many languages. While there has been an effort to direct attention to bibliographical resources in English, there has also been reference, of necessity, to contributions in other languages.

I. Philo's Life and Writings

1   Philo, His Family, and His Times

As might be thought appropriate for a philosopher who frequently expressed disdain for life in this world and its fleeting events, relatively little is known of Philo's life. Philo tells us little about himself,[1] and unfortunately, there is not much else in the dossier of ancient sources about him. Josephus gives him a few lines in his *Jewish Antiquities* (18.259–60), but beyond stating that he was highly respected, a philosopher, and led an Alexandrian Jewish delegation to the Roman emperor Gaius Caligula, they hardly tell us anything we could not learn or infer from Philo's own writings. The bits of information about Philo offered sporadically in early patristic literature beginning with Eusebius and Jerome (the latter of whom devoted, in his biographical compendium *De viris illustribus*, a brief entry to Philo [ch. 11]), add little, apart from Christian myth, to what we can learn – as they did – from Philo and Josephus.[2]

However, if we move out from the inner circle, that is, about Philo himself, which we shall address in section I, we find a good bit of information about the next two circles: his family and the historical context within which he lived. Both are relatively well-documented and of import for any proper understanding of Philo. Above we enumerated the data Josephus supplies and underlined how little they actually are; now we may add that Josephus gives one more datum, unparalleled elsewhere, that is a treasure: Josephus gives us the name of Philo's brother. As we shall see in section II, this datum allows us to locate Philo in the context of a family that was very affluent and among the most prominent in Alexandria, and that enjoyed special relationships with the Roman

---

1 For collections of his statements about himself, see D. Winston's edition of Philo of Alexandria, *The Contemplative Life, the Giants, and Selections* (New York 1981), pp. 75–8, and D.M. Hay, 'Philo's View of Himself as an Exegete: Inspired but not Authoritative', *StPhAnn* 3 (1991), pp. 40–52.
2 On 'Philo Christianus', see D. T. Runia, *Philo in Early Christian Literature: A Survey* (Assen 1993), pp. 3–7. The relevant passages from Eusebius and Jerome are conveniently accessible (along with others) in PCW I, pp. LXXXXV–CXIII.

imperial family and also with the Herodian dynasty of Judea. Members of the family appear several times in Josephus' writings, there are some ostraca that document the family's import-export business, and one member of Philo's family, his nephew, had quite a successful – and well-documented – career in service of Rome. As for Philo's broader historical context – whether we look at the Roman Empire in general (the days of the Julio–Claudian emperors) or the Jews in particular (the days of the Herodian epigones, anti-Roman agitation, incipient rabbinic Judaism and nascent Christianity) – here too we have rather full dossiers, on the basis of which we will concentrate in section III on one central issue.

I. PHILO

Given the fact that Philo terms himself 'old' at the time of his participation in a Jewish delegation to Gaius Caligula in 38/39 CE (*Legat.* 1), his birth is usually placed around 20–10 BCE. This fits well with his dialogue *De animalibus*, in which he represents himself as a mature adult in an argument with a much younger Tiberius Julius Alexander.[3] The latter, Philo's nephew, to be discussed in section II, who was old enough to be an *epistratēgos* (sub-governor) of the Thebaïd in Upper Egypt in 42 CE but still young enough to be on Titus' staff at the siege of Jerusalem in 70 CE, was probably born around 15 CE. As for Philo's death, the only plain *terminus post quem* is given by his allusion to an event under Claudius (*Legat.* 206), which means that he did not die before Gaius' death and Claudius' accession to the throne in January of 41 CE. This may also be extrapolated from Philo's promise, in the same work (*Legat.* 373), to tell the 'palinode' of the Gaius story. This promise seems clearly to imply that Philo, in the lost ending of the *Legatio ad Gaium*, narrated how the story worked its way back to a happy ending, which certainly entailed the death of Gaius.[4] We have no way to determine precisely how long Philo lived after that, although several of his writings appear to have been written after that date,[5] implying that he lived at least a few more years.

3   See A. Terian in his edition of Philo Alexandrinus, *De animalibus* (Chico, CA 1981), p. 31.
4   On that episode in general, see P. Bilde, 'The Roman Emperor Gaius (Caligula)'s Attempt to Erect His Statue in the Temple of Jerusalem', *Studia Theologica* 32 (1978), pp. 67–93. For the possibility that Josephus used the lost ending of the *Legatio*, as also extant parts of the book, see D. R. Schwartz, *Agrippa I: The Last King of Judaea* (Tübingen 1990), pp. 18–23, 180–2.
5   See Terian in his edition of *De animalibus*, pp. 33–4; also D. R. Schwartz, 'Philonic Anonyms of the Roman and Nazi Periods: Two Suggestions', *StPhAnn* 1 (1989), pp. 64–5.

Jerome asserts that Philo was born in Alexandria (*Vir. ill.* 11). Whether he had that on good authority or it was only an inference, it is a very reasonable assumption. Certainly all that we hear from and about Philo points no where else. Jerome's entry on Philo also states that he was of priestly descent (*de genere sacerdotum*), that is, a *kohen*. There is no particular reason to doubt this statement, and if it were merely legendary hyperbole, *high*-priestly descent would have been expected. Moreover, it may be bolstered by some evidence of a pro-priestly slant in Philo's writings. Particularly telling is his explanation that the biblical law that prohibits non-priests from eating sacred things (Lev 22:10–16) is 'in order that the privileges not be tainted with bastardy (!) but remain the securely guarded possessions of the priestly order' (*Spec.* 1.124). It seems difficult to imagine that a Jew who was not a priest would phrase the matter that way.[6] However, Philo himself never claims such lineage. The contrast with Josephus, who repeatedly refers to his own priestly pedigree and builds upon it (see, e.g., *BJ* 1.3, 3.352; *Vita* 1–2, 198; *C. Ap.* 1.54), indicates either that Philo was not a priest or that his religion, the temple-less religion of an Alexandrian Jew, was very different from that of Josephus, the Jerusalemite priest, a fact that may easily be established on its own, as we shall see in section III.

We hear nothing of Philo's private life – nothing of a wife, of children, of how he made a living. Concerning the latter, we may note that Philo not infrequently voices contempt for life in the city, which stupefies, corrupts, and defiles.[7] We do not know whether this reflects his personal experience or, rather, his observation of others, but it does resonate like aristocratic prejudice against the *hoi polloi*. Given that Philo mentions no literary patrons who supported him, and that his own family was very affluent, we may rightly tend to view such statements as the snobbish remarks of a wealthy pensioner, tucked away in his study in one of the family's residences.

It is to that type of leisurely and scholarly life that Philo indeed refers, wistfully, as once having been his until he was wrenched out of it and forced to deal with 'worries of state' (*Spec.* 3.3). As usual he is not specific. In the absence of other direct evidence for Philo's public involvement, it is usual to link this up with the only political involvement of his of which we know – his role in the Alexandrian Jewish

---

6 For more on this, see D.R. Schwartz, 'Philo's Priestly Descent', in F.E. Greenspahn et al. (eds.), *Nourished with Peace: Studies in Hellenistic Judaism in Memory of Samuel Sandmel* (Chico, CA 1984), pp. 155–71.

7 See F.H. Colson, PLCL IX, p. 105 n. a, and D.T. Runia, 'The Ideal and the Reality of the City in the Thought of Philo of Alexandria', *Journal of the History of Ideas* 61 (2000), esp. pp. 370–5.

delegation to Gaius Caligula in 38/39 CE, to which we shall turn in section III. This would require a late date for the composition of *De specialibus legibus*, or at least of that portion of it, and therefore it might be preferable to infer that Philo's public life began earlier, which would not be unnatural given what we know of his family.[8] For the present, suffice it to say that, while Philo's own long account of that episode in the *Legatio ad Gaium* does not indicate that his role was *ex officio* or that he headed the delegation, Josephus specifically terms Philo the leader of the delegation, and we may assume that that did not happen *ex nihilo*. Rather, if Philo was asked to head the delegation, it was probably not only because his family connections might enable him to find willing ears in the imperial capital while his writings and bearing would grant him respect as an advocate of the Jewish religion, but also on the basis of some track record in public service. The delegation went to Rome in the winter of 38/39 CE (so it seems),[9] and may have stayed there as long as a year or even two, due to the long delays between meetings with Gaius.

II. PHILO'S FAMILY

As noted, there is much more evidence concerning Philo's family, the main figure being Philo's brother, Alexander the Alabarch. The term 'Alabarch' probably derives from 'Arabarch', and was the title of a tax official responsible for customs on produce imported to Egypt via Arabia.[10] In the nature of things, it was a lucrative position. Moreover, Alexander ran an import-export business (in which his position may have given him some special advantage), known to us today from several ostraca.[11] His wealth and prestige, and also his close ties with the Roman imperial family, are evident in the pages of Josephus. In *Jewish War* 5.205, Josephus reports that Alexander donated the gold and silver plating for nine of the gates of the temple enclosure; in *Antiquities* 18.159, he reports that Alexander once lent the then indigent Agrippa I (a grandson of Herod the Great and later king of Judea) a huge sum of

---

8 See esp. E. R. Goodenough, *The Politics of Philo Judaeus* (New Haven 1938), pp. 66–8. On Philo's family and its involvement in public life, see below, section II.

9 There are some problems with the sources concerning this point. See P. J. Sijpesteijn, 'The Legationes ad Gaium', *JJS* 15 (1964), pp. 87–96; Schwartz, *Agrippa I*, pp. 196–9.

10 See F. Millar in E. Schürer et al., *The History of the Jewish People in the Age of Jesus Christ (175 B.C. – A.D. 135)*, III.1 (Edinburgh 1986), pp. 136–7; M. Stern, *GLAJJ* II, pp. 96–7.

11 See A. Fuks, *CPJ* II, pp. 197–200.

money; in *Antiquities* 19.276, we learn that Alexander was important enough to be imprisoned by Gaius, and, in the same passage, we learn that Alexander was the *epitropos* (administrator) of the Egyptian properties of no less a personality than Antonia Minor – the daughter of Mark Antony and the mother of Claudius.[12]

Alexander's ties with the imperial house were paralleled, and reinforced, by those with Jewish royalty as well. We have already mentioned his loan to Agrippa, who, as Herod's grandson, was raised in Rome's highest circles and was a close friend of such personalities as Tiberius' son Drusus (*AJ* 18.143, 146) and Claudius (*AJ* 18.165). Now we add that Agrippa's daughter Berenice married Alexander's son Marcus, although the marriage was soon ended by Marcus' untimely death.[13] Against the background of such well-documented ties, we may also conjecture that, in the summer of 38 CE, when Agrippa I, then the new king of regions in northeastern Palestine, came to Alexandria, the 'host' he had lined up in advance (mentioned by Philo, *Flacc.* 27) was Alexander. This conjecture fits well with the fact that Philo records that, when Agrippa visited Alexandria, 'we' told him about the troubles with Flaccus and he promised to intervene on the Jews' behalf (*Flacc.* 103) – a formulation that again points to Philo's personal involvement in the community's affairs.

Much more famous than Alexander and Marcus, however, was another son of Alexander, Tiberius Julius Alexander. When, for example, Josephus refers to Alexander the Alabarch's contribution to the temple in *War* 5.205, he identifies him simply as 'Alexander, the father of Tiberius'. Indeed, this Tiberius was quite a successful character in the Roman Empire.[14] Above we mentioned him as Philo's partner in

---

12 The latter circumstance apparently explains how it happened that, with reference to the same loan, Josephus once says Alexander lent Agrippa money and once – that Antonia did (*AJ* 18.159–60, 165). Probably it was Antonia's money that Alexander lent Agrippa.

13 *AJ* 19.276–7. On this passage, which places the marriage in ca. 41 CE, and its coordination with the fact that ostraca mention Marcus between 37 and 43/44, and with *AJ* 19.354, which has Berenice married to her next husband by 44 CE, see A. Fuks, 'Marcus Julius Alexander', *Zion* 13–14 (1947–1949), pp. 14–17.

14 On him see Fuks, *CPJ* II, pp. 188–97; Stern, *GLAJJ* II, pp. 7–8, 15–16, 96; L. Petersen (ed.), *Prosopographia Imperii Romani Saec. I.II.III*[2] , IV.3 (Berlin 1966), pp. 135–7 (no. 139); S. Etienne, 'Réflexion sur l'apostasie de Tibérius Julius Alexander', *StPhAnn* 12 (2000), pp. 122–42; G. Schimanowski, 'Die jüdische Integration in die Oberschicht Alexandriens und die angebliche Apostasie des Tiberius Julius Alexander', in J. Frey et al. (eds.), *Jewish Identity in the Greco–Roman World* (Leiden 2007), pp. 111–135.

dialogue in the *De animalibus*, where he defends the view that animals have souls just as do humans; similarly, in *De providentia* he doubts the existence of divine providence. Given such anti-Judaic positions that, taken together, leave people just as far from God as animals, and given his father's ties with the imperial family, it is not surprising that he eventually crossed the line, or, as Josephus puts it, 'did not persevere in his ancestral practices' (*AJ* 20.100), and undertook what would eventually become a stellar career in the Roman hierarchy. From a regional governorship of the Thebaïd in Upper Egypt in 42 CE Tiberius went to the Judean governorship in 46–48,[15] to a military role alongside Corbulo in the Parthian war of 63 CE (Tacitus, *Ann.* 15.28.3), then to the governorship of Egypt under Nero, and he became Titus' chief of staff in the Judean war (Josephus, *BJ* 5.45–6, 6.237). Eventually, before dropping out of sight, Tiberius was to serve as praetorian prefect in Rome.

Given the illustrious ties of Philo's brother and nephews, it seems that while we might imagine Philo as the retiring, studious and respected resident of an upstairs suite of Alexander's palatial home in Alexandria or of some nearby residence, we should also imagine him emerging from his chambers now and then, as the opportunity arose, to share in the visits of wealthy businessmen, Roman officials, and members of the Herodian family. It is this type of contact that lies behind the nonchalant way in which he mentions that 'I once knew a member of the ruling class' (*Somn.* 2.123). Now and then, moreover, he would get into debates with his nephew Alexander (as in *De animalibus* and *De providentia*), or with other similarly-minded Jews (such as those he addresses in *Migr.* 89–93, see below), about the path they chose and why or why not a Jew should adopt such approaches to life in the Roman world. This brings us to the broadest of our three circles.

III. ALEXANDRIANS, ROMANS, JEWS, AND JUDEANS IN PHILO'S DAY

Alexandria underwent a massive change in status in the decade or two preceding Philo's birth.[16] From being the capital of the Ptolemaic kingdom that had held sway for three hundred years, ruled by heirs of Alexander the Great and symbolized by such wonders as the great lighthouse of Pharos in its harbor and the great library of the city, it had been reduced to the seat of a Roman governor, whose main mission was to maintain law and order and allow Egypt to be exploited as Rome's

---

15   It has also been suggested that he served as governor of Syria ca. 59 CE; see Etienne, 'Réflexion', p. 135.

16   In general, see D.I. Sly, *Philo's Alexandria* (London 1996).

granary. Moreover, this had not happened because of a war fought against heroic rivals such as Hannibal and Mithradates. Rather, the Ptolemies had the misfortune to have been represented in their final stage by – *horribile dictu* – a woman, someone the Romans typically recalled as a devious and seductive oriental whore who had corrupted Rome's best men and brought civil war and the collapse of the Roman Republic.[17] In revanche, the world's rulers now stereotyped Alexandrians – male and female alike – as 'soft, licentious, and undisciplined'.[18] Alexandria lost its kingdom, its prestige, and even its status as a *polis* (a city with a kind of *de iure* independence).[19]

The Jewish population of Egypt and Alexandria was massive, although the figures that we have are, of course, exaggerated – Josephus writes of 120,000 Jews in Egypt in the days of Ptolemy II (283–246 BCE) and of 50,000–60,000 Alexandrian Jews killed in 66 CE (*BJ* 2.497, 7.369), and Philo, who asserted that the Jews are the most numerous of all the world's peoples (*Virt.* 64), claimed the Jews of Egypt numbered a million in his day (*Flacc.* 43).[20] For these Jews, the Roman takeover of Egypt and concomitant humiliation of Alexandria had highly significant implications, and these were already evident in Philo's own day. But before we examine that situation in detail, it will be helpful to provide some broader background on Jewish life in Alexandria.

17 See J. W. van Henten, 'Cleopatra in Josephus: From Herod's Rival to the Wise Ruler's Opposite', in A. Hilhorst and G. H. van Kooten (eds.), *The Wisdom of Egypt: Jewish, Early Christian, and Gnostic Essays in Honour of Gerard P. Luttikhuizen* (Leiden 2005), esp. pp. 116–17.

18 See inter alia Quintilian, *Inst.* 1.2.7; Frontinus, *Strategmata* 1.1.5; and Julius Caesar, *Bell. civ.* 3.110.2. The phrase 'soft, licentious, and undisciplined' is from J. M. Carter's explanation of Caesar's reference in the last-named passage to the 'ill-disciplined ways of Alexandrian life'; see his edition of Julius Caesar, *The Civil War, Book III* (Warminster 1993), p. 230. As Carter adds, 'the catalogue of moral deficiency went on to include, among other failings, over-cleverness, cowardice, homosexuality, lack of principle, and an interest in philosophy.' This is all based upon the identification of the Alexandrians as Greeks; see N. Petrochilos, *Roman Attitudes to the Greeks* (Athens 1974), pp. 17–21.

19 See P. M. Fraser, *Ptolemaic Alexandria* (Oxford 1972), I, pp. 94–5; H. A. Musurillo (ed.), *The Acts of the Pagan Martyrs: Acta Alexandrinorum* (Oxford 1954), pp. 83–8 (on the 'Boule Papyrus').

20 See Sly, *Philo's Alexandria*, pp. 44–6, and P. van der Horst, *Philo's Flaccus: The First Pogrom* (Leiden 2003), pp. 136–7. Sly concludes, on the basis of a papyrus (*P Giss. Univ.* V 46; see D. Delia 'The Population of Roman Alexandria', *Transactions of the American Philological Association* 118 [1988], pp. 286–8) that the Jewish population of Alexandria was perhaps 180,000, while Van der Horst tends somewhat lower.

Jews had been a fixed part of Alexandria from its earliest years.[21] Josephus has them settling in the city upon its foundation (*BJ* 2.487; *AJ* 12.7–9, 19.281;[22] *C. Ap.* 2.35). A pseudepigraphic work known as the *Letter of Aristeas*, which tells us about the Greek translation of Torah (= the Septuagint) undertaken at the initiative of Ptolemy II, reports a thriving Jewish population in Alexandria in his time.[23] The Book of 3 Maccabees focuses on the Jews of Alexandria under Ptolemy IV (221–204 BCE), and a story in Josephus focuses on debates between Jews and Samaritans in Alexandria in the mid-second century BCE (*AJ* 13.74–9). As for the first century BCE, Egyptian Jews played a significant role in the course of Julius Caesar's 'Alexandrian War' in 48/47 BCE (Josephus, *AJ* 14.131–2),[24] and an Alexandrian stele recorded the rights granted to them by Caesar (Josephus, *AJ* 14.188; *C. Ap.* 2.37; see also *BJ* 2.488). In Philo's day, it was said that two of the city's five quarters were called 'Jewish' because of the great numbers of Jews that dwelt in them.[25]

The Jewish residents of Alexandria had acquired in very early times the status of a recognized independent political community, called in technical language a *politeuma*.[26] This afforded them legal rights, the most important of which was a certain measure of autonomy, or the privilege of living according to their 'ancestral laws'. According to the *Letter of Aristeas* 310, this *politeuma* was in existence already in the days of Ptolemy II. In the time of Philo, the *politeuma* was governed by a council, called a *gerousia*, which may have had as many as 71 members, and over which a group of leaders or archons may have presided. Just before Philo's time, however, the community had been

---

21   For surveys, see J. Mélèze Modrzejewski, *The Jews of Egypt: From Rameses II to Emperor Hadrian* (Philadelphia 1995); E.S. Gruen, *Diaspora: Jews amidst Greeks and Romans* (Cambridge, MA 2002), pp. 54–83.

22   For the Jewish nature of this edict ascribed to Claudius, see my *Agrippa I*, pp. 99–106.

23   On the *Letter of Aristeas*, see M. Goodman in Schürer et al., *History*, III.1, pp. 677–87.

24   See A. Kasher, *The Jews in Hellenistic and Roman Egypt* (Tübingen 1985), pp. 13–18.

25   *Flacc.* 55. It is not quite clear whether Philo means here that most of their inhabitants were Jews or, rather, that most of the city's Jews dwelt in them; see Van der Horst, *Philo's Flaccus*, p. 156. For a separate Jewish quarter in Alexandria, see also Josephus, *BJ* 2.488, 495, and *AJ* 14.117 ('a large part' of Alexandria was set aside for the Jews).

26   On *politeumata*, see esp. A. Kasher, *JQR* 93 (2002/2003), pp. 257–68 – a review of J.M.S. Cowey and K. Maresch, *Urkunden des Politeuma der Juden von Herakleopolis* (Wiesbaden 2001).

governed by an ethnarch, who, according to Strabo, ruled the Jews of the city 'as if he were the ruler of an autonomous city'.[27]

Strabo's remark confirms that the Jews enjoyed a considerable amount of autonomy. This was possible because the Ptolemaic kingdom recognized the validity of different judicial systems within a single state, applicable to different classes of the population. The law of Moses, which had been translated into Greek by royal initiative (at least according to the *Letter of Aristeas*), was likely to have been the actual basis of Jewish autonomy. For it appears that the Greek Torah attained a status analogous to that of the 'civic laws', or *politikoi nomoi*, which served as the law for the Greek-speaking immigrants, alongside the Egyptian law that was in force for the indigenous population. At the same time, however, as the papyrological evidence indicates, Jews seem to have been free to follow Hellenistic common law, especially in the realms of business and of family arrangements. This may have been a kind of anticipation of the talmudic dictum, 'the law of the land is the law.'[28]

The primary institution of Jewish religious life in Alexandria was the synagogue. In fact, inscriptions from Egypt are the oldest concrete evidence of the existence of synagogues anywhere. There is epigraphic and papyrological evidence for synagogues in and around Alexandria and in eight other places in Ptolemaic Egypt beginning in the third century BCE.[29] The usual term for synagogue is *proseuchē*, which means '(place of) prayer'. The most detailed information about a synagogue service comes from Philo himself. He does not provide extensive direct descriptions of synagogal prayers, but one can learn a great deal from his various casual remarks. He puts much more emphasis on the formal reading of Torah, and the expositions of it, usually undertaken by the senior members. This activity was, in Philo's eyes, so central that he refers to the synagogues as 'schools' of wisdom and the other virtues (*Mos.* 2.215–16; *Spec.* 2.62–3). According to Philo's testimony, there were 'many' synagogues in all parts of the city, although there seems to have been one that was particularly grandiose (*Legat.* 132, 134). The synagogues were no doubt the focal points of Jewish communal life in Alexandria, as is confirmed by the fact that they were among the chief

27   Strabo's testimony is reported by Josephus, *AJ* 14.117. On the governance of the *politeuma*, which seems to have undergone changes over time, see Millar in Schürer et al., *History*, III.1, pp. 92–4.

28   For all of this, see V. A. Tcherikover, *CPJ* I, pp. 32–6; Mélèze Modrzejewski, *The Jews of Egypt*, pp. 107–19.

29   See Tcherikover, *CPJ* I, p. 8.

targets of attack by anti-Jewish rioters when conflict erupted between Greeks and Jews in 38 CE.[30]

Despite the fact that the Jews had such a highly developed communal life, they were quick to adapt themselves to Hellenistic culture. At a very early stage, the use of Hebrew seems to have declined and the language of the Jews of Alexandria came to be Greek exclusively. The translation of the Torah (and in time the other books) allowed Greek to be a vehicle for Jewish culture. Indeed, there developed a very rich Jewish literature in Greek already in the second century BCE. By the time of the era of Philo, it is hardly surprising that he was a highly accomplished Greek stylist, and probably knew little to no Hebrew.[31]

In fact, the level of literary sophistication that we find in much Judeo–Greek literature, and especially in Philo, allows us to conclude that Jews must have been able to frequent Greek schools, and in particular the gymnasium, where one acquired the necessary level of 'secondary education'. The gymnasium combined physical education with training in 'liberal arts', such as literary study (called 'grammar') and rhetoric, about which Philo himself provides a great deal of important information.[32] That Jews participated in this form of education can be confirmed by some inscriptions from Cyrene, for a long time a Ptolemaic province, in which boys with characteristically Jewish names are listed among the ephebes, that is, the youth enrolled in the gymnasium.[33] Completion of the ephebic training also allowed one to take part in the civic affairs of the *polis*. It can hardly be doubted that Philo attended a gymnasium, especially in light of his rhetorical capabilities and his fondness for athletic imagery.[34]

What all of this shows is that, although the Jews retained a strong national identity, they came to be well integrated into Hellenistic Alexandria, both as a community and at the individual level. Indeed, the three hundred years of Jewish life under the Ptolemies seem to have been remarkably quiet and irenic in contrast to the next one hundred fifty years of Roman rule. Anyone looking for 'the Jewish question', or

30 On the synagogues in Egypt and Alexandria, see L.I. Levine, *The Ancient Synagogue: The First Thousand Years* (New Haven 2000), pp. 74–89; and on synagogal life, see J. Leonhardt, *Jewish Worship in Philo of Alexandria* (Tübingen 2001), esp. pp. 74–95.

31 For this, see below, ch. 3, pp. 65–72.

32 See A. Mendelson, *Secular Education in Philo of Alexandria* (Cincinnati 1982).

33 See M.H. Williams, *The Jews among the Greeks and Romans: A Diasporan Sourcebook* (Baltimore 1998), pp. 107, 113–14.

34 See Mendelson, *Secular Education*, p. 31; Sly, *Philo's Alexandria*, pp. 8–9, 149–54; and esp. H.A. Harris, *Greek Athletics and the Jews* (Cardiff 1976), pp. 51–95.

even just for Jewish troubles, in Ptolemaic Alexandria, will find precious little. The most we can come up with is some doubtful evidence for a special anti-Jewish animus on the part of Ptolemy VIII (145–116 BCE) due to the notion that the Jews had supported Cleopatra II against him (Josephus, *C. Ap.* 2.51–6). But the evidence itself is doubtful and points to a specific political constellation that was soon to pass in any case.[35] The story of 3 Maccabees does refer to specific anti-Jewish hostility and measures by a Ptolemaic king – but that story is widely recognized to be fiction and in its current version may indeed reflect the changed climate of the Roman period, to which we shall turn below.[36] In general, Josephus' statement that the Jews of Egypt were 'doing well' (*eupragein*) in the late second century BCE (*AJ* 13.284) seems to be a fitting summary of the entire Ptolemaic period.

By the first century CE, however, that world had turned upside down. First of all, we note the appearance of a whole corpus of anti-Jewish literature in Greek coming out of Egypt. As Josephus was to put it, 'badmouthing of the Jews began with the Egyptians' (*C. Ap.* 1.223). As the context shows, by 'Egyptians' he means *Hellenized* Egyptians or Greeks of Egypt, such as those whose writings he assembled thereafter (1.227–2.144), culminating with Apion, who was an Alexandrian gymnasiarch in the first century. But those writings were only harbingers, or reflections, of a real atmosphere of hatred, that was to find its expression in real events. Large-scale anti-Jewish violence broke out in 38 CE and is documented in Philo's *Legatio ad Gaium* and *In Flaccum*. The year 66 CE was to see, parallel to the start of the Jewish rebellion in Judea, a violent outbreak of Jewish rebelliousness in Alexandria that was put down heavy-handedly by Tiberius Julius Alexander (*BJ* 2.487–98). And by the second decade of the second century CE, a Jewish rebellion – the so-called *tumultus Judaicus*[37] – would engender such widespread death and destruction that the Jewish community of the city would more or less disappear.[38] If, for four hundred years Jewish Alexandria had been

---

35   See Mélèze Modrzejewski, *The Jews of Egypt*, pp. 146–7, 152–3; M. Stern, *Yehudah ha-hasmonait ba-olam ha-hellenisti* (Jerusalem 1995), pp. 126–7.

36   See F. Parente, 'The Third Book of Maccabees as Ideological Document and Historical Source', *Henoch* 10 (1988), pp. 143–82.

37   See M. Pucci Ben Zeev, *Diaspora Judaism in Turmoil, 116/117 CE: Ancient Sources and Modern Insights* (Leuven 2005).

38   See V. A. Tcherikover, 'The Decline of the Jewish Diaspora in Egypt in the Roman Period', *JJS* 14 (1963), pp. 1–32. A perusal of *CPJ* beginning with no. 447 will give a plain impression of the poverty of our evidence for Jews in Egypt following the rebellion.

the Jewish New York of the ancient world, the capital of Jewish life in the Diaspora, from that point on it would hardly be on the map.

To understand what caused this massive turnabout, it seems we must recall the Roman humiliation of Alexandria.[39] For if the irenic situation of the Jews in Ptolemaic Alexandria was predicated upon the understanding – by Jews, Alexandrians, and Ptolemies alike – that the Jews were 'foreigners in a foreign land' (3 Macc 6:3), guests in the city who knew their place and therefore should be well treated by their hosts, the Romans swept that aside. Because the Greeks were now no longer masters of Alexandria, the Jews were no longer their guests, and the Greeks could no longer go on being gracious hosts. Or, to put it another way, if during the Ptolemaic period there had been three social strata in Alexandria – Alexandrians, Hellenized foreigners (including Jews), and Egyptians (non-Hellenized 'natives') – the addition of a fourth stratum on top of the pile, Romans, squashed the others together and required them to scramble to protect their differential status.

Some primary documents bespeak this process quite eloquently. One is a papyrus of 5/4 BCE (CPJ II, no. 151), when Philo was a youth. It is a draft of a petition from one Helenos, son of Tryphon, to the Roman governor of Egypt, in which Helenos, now over sixty years old, complains that although he had always lived in Alexandria and had acquired a Greek education, he was now being denied Alexandrian citizenship and treated as if he were a 'native' and required to pay the laographia – the tax paid by laoi, 'natives'.[40] What is eloquent here is the fact that Helenos first characterized himself as 'an Alexandrian', but the scribe crossed that out and substituted 'a Jew from Alexandria'. Presumably, the first formulation was the one Helenos wanted, while the second was forced upon him by the scribe who wrote up the petition or by the official called upon to accept it. Another document makes the motivation clear: in one of the papyri of the corpus known as the *Acts of the Pagan Martyrs* (or: *Acts of the Alexandrians*), literature of the first and second century that combines anti-Roman Alexandrian patriotism with anti-Semitism,[41] a spokesman for the Greeks of Alexandria insists that the Jews should pay the laographia because 'they are not of the same nature as the Alexandrians, but live rather after the fashion of the

---

39   For what follows, compare D. R. Schwartz, 'Antisemitism and Other -isms in the Greco–Roman World', in R. S. Wistrich (ed.), *Demonizing the Other: Antisemitism, Racism, and Xenophobia* (Amsterdam 1999) pp. 73–87.

40   On this text, see esp. Mélèze Modrzejewski, *The Jews of Egypt*, pp. 164–5.

41   These texts are easily accessible, with translation and commentary, in Musurillo, *Acts of the Pagan Martyrs* and *CPJ* II, pp. 55–107.

Egyptians; are they not on a level with those who pay the poll-tax?'.[42] In other words, the imposition of Romans above them created for the Greeks of Alexandria a situation of relative deprivation that forced them to try to demote those beneath them, thus collapsing – in their minds – the Jews and the 'natives' into one category.

How were the Jews to respond to this? One obvious route was to embrace Roman rule and respond to the Alexandrians' hostility by asking the Romans to defend them. That amounted to asking the Romans to view the Jews and the Greek Alexandrians as equals: now they were all guests (or subjects) of the Romans and should be treated equally. This is what lay, fundamentally, at the bottom of the Jewish demand for *isopoliteia* ('equal political status') and the like that surfaces a few times in first-century texts.[43] And it went hand in hand, of course, with demonstrative Jewish acceptance of Roman rule, such as the Alexandrian stele mentioned above, the display in the synagogues of shields, crowns, and inscriptions honoring the emperor (*Legat.* 133), public mourning by the Jews of Alexandria upon the death of members of the imperial family (*Flacc.* 56), and the like along with various moves by Philo, underlined by M.R. Niehoff, that amount to adoption of Roman values and of Roman anti-Greek stereotypes.[44]

But of course that approach by the Jews only exacerbated bad feelings between Jews and Alexandrian Greeks. Thus, for the main example close to Philo: it was evidence of Roman graciousness to the Jews, and Jewish celebration thereof, that touched off the anti-Jewish rioting in Alexandria in the summer of 38 CE – the events that engendered Philo's participation in the Alexandrian Jewish delegation to Gaius. As Philo tells the story in *In Flaccum*, the rioting was touched off by King Agrippa I's visit to the city. Although Philo denies that Agrippa was in any way ostentatious, and indeed claims that Agrippa visited the city only at the 'suggestion' of Gaius (§ 26) and tried to hide the very fact of his presence in the city (§ 27), it is clear that Philo misrepresented matters in order to blame the Alexandrians for the sequel.[45] For it is clear that Agrippa, the new monarch of part of Palestine, paraded about with all the trappings of monarchy, that the Jews of Alexandria (or enough of them to arouse

---

42 Translation from *CPJ* II, p. 79 (no. 156c).

43 See Kasher, *Jews in Hellenistic and Roman Egypt*, pp. 278–97.

44 Niehoff, *Philo on Jewish Identity and Culture* (Tübingen 2001), esp. pp. 111–58.

45 This is the case that elicited H. Willrich's comment, 'Philo has not the least respect for the facts' (*Klio* 3 [1903], pp. 402–3 n. 1 [my translation – D.R.S.]). For a recent study of these events, focusing on how Philo skewed his account in the Jews' favor, see A. Kerkeslager, 'Agrippa and the Mourning Rites for Drusilla in Alexandria', *JSJ* 37 (2006), pp. 367–400.

notice) welcomed him with enthusiastic demonstrations, and that it was this that aroused the jealousy of the Alexandrians – 'as if the good fortune of others were their own misfortune' (*Flacc.* 29). Here Philo clearly states the issue: with the establishment of Roman hegemony, which knocked the Alexandrians off their pedestal, Alexandrians and Jews were in competition, and any points won by the Jews, such as the coronation of a Jewish king, were, in effect, lost by the Alexandrians. If the Alexandrians could not express their resentment toward the Romans, they could do so by attacking those who were perceived as Rome's protégés – the Jews.[46]

Accordingly, just as the visit of a Jewish king by the grace of Rome sparked Alexandrian resentment toward Rome and Jews, and Alexandrian violence toward the latter, so too would any other demonstrative acceptance of Roman rule by Alexandrian Jews.

Moreover, adoption of such an approach by Alexandrian Jews was problematic from their own point of view and not only from that of the Greeks of the city. For Alexandrian Jews were not only Alexandrians, they were also Jews, but the Greek term *Ioudaioi* implied they were Judeans.[47] This had had the advantage, during the Ptolemaic period, of clarifying that they were guests, foreign residents in the city. True, there was some movement toward understanding this term in the sense that we mean it today – 'Jews' are defined by a relationship to something a-territorial, they are a people or a religion. Thus, we find the term 'Judaism' appearing several times in a Jewish Hellenistic work, 2 Maccabees (2:21, 8:1, 14:38), which is of Ptolemaic origin,[48] just as later it will recur in Paul (Gal 1:13–14). In large measure, however, the Jews of Egypt, including Alexandria, still understood themselves, and were still understood by their neighbors, as Judeans; this

---

46 For the Alexandrians' perception of Rome as intractably and unfairly protective of the Jews, note especially the *Acta Isidori* (*CPJ* II, no. 156d), where the Alexandrian hero, about to be executed by Claudius, complains that the emperor is in fact the cast-off son of a Jewess. For more of the same, see *CPJ* II, no. 157, col. 3, where an Alexandrian spokesman complains to Trajan that his council (= the Senate?) is full of Jews.

47 That *Ioudaioi* basically means 'Judeans', i.e., people from Judea, is said clearly by Clearchus of Soli *apud* Josephus, *C. Ap.* 1.179 (= *GLAJJ* I, no. 15). In general, cf. S. Mason, 'Jews, Judaeans, Judaizing, Judaism: Problems of Categorization in Ancient History', *JSJ* 38 (2007), pp. 457–512.

48 For the Ptolemaic origin of 2 Maccabees, see 2:23, where the work is said to be an epitome of a much larger work by one Jason of Cyrene (in Lybia, which was part of the Ptolemaic kingdom). See also D. R. Schwartz, *2 Maccabees* (Berlin 2008), pp. 541–3, on Ptolemaic elements in the account of Antiochus Epiphanes' decrees against Judaism in 2 Macc 6.

is the point of view Philo bespeaks by terming them 'colonists' from the Judean homeland, of which the capital was the 'metropolis' of all Jews.[49]

But to the extent that Alexandrian Jews were Judeans, embracing Roman rule – although an obvious move insofar as the Romans defended the Jews' status in Alexandria – was far from an obvious move. This is because half a century before Philo's birth, the Romans had destroyed the sovereign Jewish state in Judea, and in 6 CE, when Philo was a young man, they had established – after a long intermediate period of rule by middlemen (Hyrcanus II and Herod) – direct Roman rule in Judea.[50] If the Romans were protective of the Jews but predators vis-à-vis the Judeans, where did that leave the *Ioudaioi* of Alexandria?

There were three consistent ways of dealing with this, and several middle positions as well. One obvious option was the one taken by Philo's nephew, Tiberius Julius Alexander. He accepted Roman rule in Egypt but also abandoned his status as *Ioudaios*,[51] and 'did not persevere in his ancestral practices' (Josephus, *AJ* 20.100). As governor of Judea he executed Jewish rebels against Rome (*AJ* 20.102), bloodily put down Jewish rebels in Alexandria when serving as governor there (*BJ* 2.487–98), and then, to ice the cake, was chief of Titus' army at the destruction of Jerusalem. We can imagine Tiberius telling his father, Alexander the Alabarch, the donor of huge sums of money to the temple (*BJ* 5.205), that he was only being more consistent in the latter's pro-Roman stance. Josephus does claim that Tiberius Alexander eventually voted with Titus to preserve the temple (*BJ* 6.242; so it was only by divine intervention that it was destroyed – § 252, 7.331–2). But this – even if true, and not simply part of Josephus' orchestration of the destruction – does not change anything fundamental or the implication that, in fact, Tiberius Alexander had first voted to destroy it.

The diametrically opposite option would be to reject Roman rule in Egypt as in Judea, which would entail rebellion. While there does not seem to be any specific evidence of any Alexandrian Jews taking this route, or (for example) moving to Judea and joining one of the rebellious groups that flourished there in the first century until the final struggle and catastrophe in 70 CE, there may have been some. Certainly we may

---

49 See esp. *Flacc.* 46 and *Legat.* 281–2; Van der Horst, *Philo's Flaccus*, pp. 140–2; Kasher, *Jews in Hellenistic and Roman Egypt*, pp. 236–8.

50 On this process and the irresistible power that made it happen, see I. Shatzman, 'The Integration of Judaea into the Roman Empire', *Scripta Classica Israelica* 18 (1999), pp. 49–84.

51 Tacitus terms him an 'Egyptian', ignoring his Jewish roots (*Hist.* 1.11.1); see Stern, *GLAJJ* II, pp. 7–8.

wonder if Philo is completely truthful, and not perhaps 'protesting too much', when he insists in *In Flaccum* 90–4 that no arms were found in all the searching of Jewish Alexandrian homes in 38 CE.[52] Similarly, one may doubt that only non-Jews were to blame for the violence that broke out in Alexandria in 66 CE; and there is no doubt that the Jews of Alexandria were warlike and aggressive during the rebellion in the time of Trajan.

The third obvious and consistent option would be effectually to sever 'being a *Ioudaios*' from Judea, link it instead with a transcendent Judaism, and then embrace Roman rule in Alexandria while – at least in theory – making irrelevant, from a 'Judaic' point of view, the Roman takeover of Judea.

For clear and consistent and even polemical expressions of this latter option, our first-century evidence leads us slightly outside of the Jewish world to the New Testament. Here we find the evangelists claiming Jesus believed one could render both to Caesar and to God (Matt 22:21 and parallels). Here we find Stephen – said to be a 'Hellenistic' Jew (Acts 6:1–5), just as his Greek name would suggest – underlining that God was with Abraham in Mesopotamia (Acts 7:2), with Joseph in Egypt, and with Moses in Midian (Acts 9:9–10, 30ff.[53]), but that He does not reside in the so-called Holy Land and especially not in the temple which, like idols, was 'made by hands'.[54] Here we find Luke artistically allowing Paul to reinterpret Jesus' reference to evangelizing 'unto the end of the land' (Acts 1:8) into 'unto the end of the earth' (13:47).[55] Here we find Paul insisting that one should be a citizen of the Jerusalem above, not that which is below (Gal 4:26; cf. Phil 3:20: 'our commonwealth is in heaven').

However, it seems that Philo too should be viewed as leaning in the same direction, albeit inconsistently and without the polemics. And we can also see that such a point of view was natural. We should remember, first of all, that the facts of Jewish life in the Diaspora, any Diaspora,

---

52 Note, in this connection, that although Philo's long account of the Jews' response to Gaius Caligula's attempt to erect a statue in Jerusalem portrays only unarmed Jewish protesters, unwilling to fight but willing to be martyrs (see esp. *Legat.* 229–42, echoed closely – see above, n. 4 – by Josephus [*BJ* 2.187, 196–7; *AJ* 18.264–72]), Tacitus specifically says the Jews 'resorted to arms' (*Hist.* 5.9.2 = *GLAJJ* II, no. 281).

53 And note that Acts 7:33 pointedly quotes Exod 3:5 to the effect that the site of God's revelation to Moses in Midian was 'holy land'.

54 'Made by hands' is a standard Jewish adjective meaning 'idolatrous'. For the interpretation of Stephen's speech summarized above, see D.R. Schwartz, *Studies in the Jewish Background of Christianity* (Tübingen 1992), pp. 117–22.

55 See D.R. Schwartz, 'The End of the ΓΗ (Acts 1:8)', *Journal of Biblical Literature* 105 (1986), pp. 669–76.

create a pressure for God to be conceived of as transcendent, universally available. For if that is not the case, and God rather resides in what the Bible usually and plainly terms 'the house of God', in Jerusalem, Jews of the Diaspora are second-class and far from God, which no Jew wants (or, at least, wants to admit that other Jews are closer to Him). Accordingly, we should not be surprised to discover, via a glance in a concordance to the Hebrew Bible, that almost all evidence for the use of 'God of heaven' begins with the Persian period, that is, with the period in which the Diaspora entered the Jewish world.[56]

But beyond that which is natural for any Diaspora, the Hellenistic Diaspora made its own special contribution to undercutting the importance of Judea (and hence allowing Jews to make their peace with Rome). I refer to the Greek tendency to view everything important dualistically, distinguishing between form and matter. This engendered a devaluation of real things and places: what made something important was its *logos*, which is something abstract.

Thus, if we look at the type of literature produced by Alexandrian Jews in the generations preceding Philo, we find such examples as:

(1)   The author of 2 Maccabees pounds on the table at 5:19 that 'the people was not chosen because of the place,[57] but, rather, the place was chosen because of the people,' so if the people is sinful the place too will suffer.

(2)   The author of the *Letter of Aristeas* emphasizes in §§ 143–69 that it is not the case that certain animals and birds are impure while others are pure. Rather, the former symbolize bad behavior and the latter good behavior, and the laws that forbid eating the former are simply pedagogical measures intended to inculcate appropriate values. That is, the physical things of this world are of religious significance only as symbols, as pedagogical tools. A well-known Philonic passage (*Migr.* 89–93) indicates that, by Philo's days, there were Alexandrian Jews who were applying that approach to Jerusalem as well.

(3)   Pseudo-Hecataeus claims that Jewish priests were chosen among the most excellent people.[58] This shows that what is important is

56 See my *Studies in the Jewish Background*, p. 7 n. 15.
57 Here 'the place' (*topos*) means primarily Jerusalem, as is shown by the preceding verse; but the term implies the temple as well, as is shown by 2 Macc 3:2 and 8:17.
58 See Diodorus Siculus, *Bibl. hist.* 40.3.4 (= *GLAJJ* I, no. 11). For the ascription of this text to a diasporan Jewish Pseudo-Hecataeus, see D.R. Schwartz, 'Diodorus Siculus 40.3 – Hecataeus or Pseudo-Hecataeus?', in M. Mor et al. (eds.), *Jews and Gentiles in the Holy Land in the Days of the Second Temple, the Mishnah and the Talmud* (Jerusalem 2003), pp. 181–97.

to be excellent – although for the Bible being a priest was a matter of descent alone.

(4)   The author of the Wisdom of Solomon retells a biblical story about Aaron offering up incense and thereby putting an end to a plague (Num 16:41–8). Although no prayer is mentioned in the biblical text, the author of Wisdom claims that Aaron prayed and even gives details of his prayer, insisting that he overcame the plague with his *logos* (18:20–5). But praying is something Jews could do in Alexandria, too, while offering up incense was not allowed outside of the temple. Similarly, Aaron is characterized here (v. 21) as a 'blameless man'; that is, for the author of this book as for Pseudo-Hecataeus, what characterizes him is something available to all men, not only to those of a particular seed.

Thus, given the nature of diasporan circumstances, Hellenistic culture, and Alexandrian Jewish precedents, it would have been quite natural for Philo to develop a point of view undermining the importance of Judea (and, accordingly, avoiding the need to oppose Rome). Indeed, he seems to have done so. True, there was nothing that forced him to be polemical or consistent about this, and so it is understandable that, just as his brother Alexander straddled the fence, cultivating ties with Romans of the highest level and nonetheless gilding the gates of the temple of Jerusalem, so too Philo had it both ways. Nevertheless, just as Alexander's main impact upon the world, via his son Tiberius, was in the former direction, so too did Philo's main tendency and importance seem to have been in that same direction – which is why his works were preserved by Christians, not by Jews.

Thus, although we can find Philo writing positively about the temple of Jerusalem, and he even once mentions that he visited it (*Prov.* 2.107), that allusion is quite low-key and incidental (it comes only apropos of some pigeons Philo saw at Ashkelon on his way to Jerusalem). Very frequently his references to the temple actually undercut it by spiritualizing it.[59] In the first place, even when he refers to worship in the temple,

59   See V. Nikiprowetzky, 'La spiritualisation des sacrifices et le culte sacrificiel au temple de Jérusalem chez Philon d'Alexandrie', in his collected studies, *Études philoniennes* (Paris 1996), pp. 79–96. Cf. Leonhardt, *Jewish Worship*, p. 219, who is more sanguine about enthusiasm of Jews of the Hellenistic Diaspora for the temple cult despite their inability to participate in it (as a rule) and their tendency, pronounced for Philo, to spiritualize it. I tend to believe that many or most of the enthusiastic statements about the temple cult that can be found in Diaspora literature were made because the Bible and keeping up appearances require them, and could be made because they did not 'cost' their authors anything.

he – as the author of the Wisdom of Solomon – first mentions prayer, and only thereafter (if then) mentions sacrifice, although that was what was especially characteristic of worship in the temple.[60] Again, when he begins his detailed discussion of the laws of the temple, he first begins by noting that there are in fact *two* temples, of which the first is the whole universe (*Spec.* 1.66). Only thereafter does he mention the temple 'made by hands', in Jerusalem. Indeed, when in a non-legal context nothing requires him to focus on the real temple in Jerusalem, he does not. Rather, in explaining 'city of God' in Ps 46:5 he has no problem in proclaiming that there are two temples, of which neither is a man-made building in any particular place in this world: one is the world itself and the other is the soul of the sage (*Somn.* 2.248). That, quite naturally, leads to the conclusion:

> Therefore do not seek for the city of the Existent among the regions of the earth, since it is not wrought of wood or stone, but in a soul, in which there is no warring, whose sight is keen. … For what grander or holier house could we find for God in the whole range of existence than the vision-seeking mind, the mind which is eager to see all things and never even in its dreams has wish for faction or turmoil?[61]

When we note that Philo ends the latter discussion with the admonition that the wise man should yearn to depart from this world, just as elsewhere he says that he who would see God must depart from this world (which is why God took Abraham 'outside' [Gen 15:5]), we realize that no particular place could mean much for him, much less be 'the Holy Land'. As S. Sandmel put it, 'It cannot be over-emphasized that Philo has little or no concern for Palestine.'[62]

True, Philo reports that, during his mission to Rome on behalf of the Jews of Alexandria, when he learned that Gaius had in the meantime ordained the erection of a statue in his honor in the temple of Jerusalem, he and his fellow Alexandrian Jewish delegates became terribly upset. He explains to his readers that, from that point on, the troubles of the Jews of Alexandria took a backseat to threats to the temple of Jerusalem (*Legat.* 186–94). Similarly, when called upon to explain the nature of the Jews' connection to Judea, he has, as mentioned above, no problem applying the Greek category of 'colonists', explaining that *Ioudaioi*

---

60 See, for example, *Spec.* 1.97, 229, 2.17; *Somn.* 1.215; Schwartz, 'Philo's Priestly Descent', p. 162.

61 *Somn.* 2.250–1 (trans. Colson – PLCL V, p. 555).

62 *Philo's Place in Judaism: A Study of Conceptions of Abraham in Jewish Literature* (augmented edition; New York 1971), p. 116. Cf. B. Schaller, 'Philon von Alexandreia und das "Heilige Land"', in G. Strecker (ed.), *Das Land Israel in biblischer Zeit* (Göttingen 1983), pp. 172–87.

all over are colonists from Judea, and Jerusalem is their *metropolis*.[63] Again, when explaining what is wrong with allegorizing the Torah's commandments to the exclusion of actually fulfilling them, his trump argument is that going down that road could lead to the abandonment of the temple cult (*Migr.* 89–93). This seems to be, for him, a *reductio ad absurdum* because no one could imagine going that far.

In fact, however, we know that going that far was not at all impossible, and it was happening around the same time Philo wrote (see, for example, 1 Cor 3:16–17 and 2 Cor 6:16). Indeed, Philo himself, in this passage from *De migratione Abrahami*, was arguing with others, and it may be that among these others there were some willing to adopt the logical conclusion from their views, even if Philo thought it was absurd.[64] But Jews in Alexandria did not, usually, need to be polemical about the temple cult; it was far away and could safely be ignored or disposed of with appropriate lip service and an occasional donation.[65]

A clear view of Philo's true position is afforded, I believe, by his account of the incident that touched off Gaius' decree to erect a statue in the temple of Jerusalem. Philo tells the story in detail and with surprising candor (*Legat.* 200–3), but nevertheless with some highly significant reserve. Namely, although many modern writers portray Gaius' decree as another indication of the emperor's oft-claimed insanity, Philo tells a story which makes Gaius' decision perfectly reasonable from a Roman point of view. According to Philo, non-Jewish inhabitants of the coastal town of Jamnia (Jabneh), seeking to provoke the Jews, built an altar in honor of Gaius, and 'when the Jews saw the altar and were greatly incensed at the effectual destruction of the sanctity of the Holy Land, they gathered together and pulled it down.'[66] When this was reported to Gaius, he decided to ordain the erection of a colossal statue in the temple in the 'metropolis' (§ 203). Gaius' move was perfectly logical, and the logic of it is indicated by Philo's use of the term 'metropolis'. For if the Jews of Jamnia destroyed the altar because they viewed it as a defilement of the Holy Land, Gaius' advisors on Jewish affairs could easily tell him that the temple – what the Bible calls the 'house of God' – was the linchpin, the axis, of the Jewish notion of 'holy land'. That is, the

63   *Flacc.* 46. See Van der Horst, *Philo's Flaccus*, pp. 142–4.
64   See D.M. Hay, 'Putting Extremism in Context: The Case of Philo, *De Migratione* 89–93', *StPhAnn* 9 (1977), pp. 126–42.
65   On the latter, see *Spec.* 1.76–8 and *Legat.* 216, 312, along with Stern, *GLAJJ* I, pp. 198–200, II, p. 129, and S. Mandell, 'Who Paid the Temple Tax When the Jews Were under Roman Rule?', *HThR* 77 (1984), pp. 223–32.
66   *Legat.* 202, in the translation of E.M. Smallwood in her edition of Philo Alexandrinus, *Legatio ad Gaium* (Leiden 1970²), p. 104.

Jamnia incident meant that Jews in that coastal town viewed it as part
of a country whose capital ('metropolis') was in Jerusalem, not in Rome,
and that the law of the sovereign Who dwelled in His house (palace) in
Jerusalem was the law of the land. While Gaius could tolerate Jewish
houses of worship, he could not be expected to tolerate the continued
existence of the palace of an unconquered king. Accordingly, because
the Jamnia incident showed that many Jews viewed the temple in that
way, Gaius moved, quite logically, to complete the Roman conquest of
Judea by taking over the temple.

What is interesting for us here is Philo's reserve: Philo says only that
the Jews of Jamnia did what they did because *they* were greatly incensed
by the 'effectual destruction of the sanctity of the Holy Land'. Although
the drift of his narrative clearly justifies them, Philo abstains from
signing on to the logic that explained the Jews' action. Note, especially,
that while he condemns those who erected the altar, portraying them
as villainous provocateurs, he makes no effort to justify the Jews' reaction, so his condemnation of the others simply means that those whose
neighbors have special sensitivities should be considerate.

As scholars have noticed, the issue this episode raised is whether
Jamnia was part of the Diaspora and whether, accordingly, the Jews of
Jamnia should have acted as they did or, rather, as was normal in the
Diaspora, should have abstained from showing disrespect for their neighbors' cults.[67] Philo, who was used to the Diaspora, and who (as we saw
in *Somn.* 2.248–51) had in his heart of hearts little use for the terrestrial
Jerusalem, could not bring himself to adopt as his own the Jamnians'
notion of the Holy Land. But neither could he condemn them, just as he
was totally upset and distraught by the threat to the temple that they
engendered (*Legat.* 189–90).

Such inconsistency is human; we often retain affinity for things with
which we grew up even after our values have changed in ways that
undermine their importance. This inconsistency is also useful, because
it allows us to postpone conflicts, but there are limits. For the Jews
of Alexandria, a clear status in the Ptolemaic period had deteriorated
to unclarity in the Roman period, beginning in 30 BCE. When no new
modus vivendi was found, one hundred forty-five years punctuated by
a few major outbreaks of violence culminated in a major catastrophe.
Similarly, in Judea, the Roman conquest of the Hasmonean temple-
state in 63 BCE had given rise to a series of attempts to find a *modus*

67 See Smallwood in her edition of the *Legatio*, pp. 263–4; Schwartz, *Agrippa I*,
    p. 82 n. 59. On the relevant diasporan principle, see P.W. van der Horst,
    ' "Thou Shalt not Revile the Gods": The LXX Translation of Ex. 22:28 (27),
    Its Background and Influence', *StPhAnn* 5 (1993), pp. 1–8.

vivendi, to allow the Jews to render both unto Caesar and unto God, but it too ended with a catastrophe. That happened because too many Judeans were unwilling to go on being inconsistent, accepting Rome's sovereignty in the Holy Land alongside of God's, which was supposed to be exclusive, or to allow a reinterpretation of the latter in a way that would leave room for the former.[68]

Philo, in his manifold writings, shows us a Jew who, when free of responsibility for actually leading a response to Rome, bespoke a position that could have allowed for a *modus vivendi* with Rome by doing just that – making 'being Jewish' a matter of no-place but within the heart and the mind. Such a position indeed allows easily for rendering unto Caesar as well as unto God. How could this not be so for a Jew so at home in a Diaspora environment, where one imbibes such separation of religion from state along with one's mother's milk? And how could this not be so for someone for whom Plato was 'the greatest of all' and 'the most holy'?[69] However, Philo also shows us a Jew who was so bound up with his people that when he was called upon to leave his ivory tower and serve them, he steadfastly defended his flesh and blood. He, in his own way, in Alexandria and Rome, just as the Zealots and the Sicarii in theirs, in Judea, proclaimed his allegiance to Judea, and to its capital – Jerusalem.

Views may vary on Gaius Caligula and his treatment of the Jews in general and of Philo in particular.[70] However, it is difficult not to have some sympathy for a Roman emperor who was forced to realize that even this most philosophical and Platonic of Jews, who was the brother of such a Romanized Jew as Alexander the Alabarch and uncle of such a Roman as Alexander's son Tiberius, insisted on – could not bring himself to accept the consequences of his own ideas and abandon – the preservation of the sanctity of their shrine in what they saw as *their holy* city. Every subsequent Roman emperor, up to and including Vespasian, will have learned the lesson well, and after one more generation of attempts to live inconsistently, history eventually insisted on a showdown. As in 39–41 CE, that crisis too broke out around the temple, as Jews proclaimed

---

68 For this interpretation of the rebellion of 66–73, which culminated in the destruction of the temple in 70 CE, see my *Studies in the Jewish Background*, pp. 29–43; also below, n. 71.

69 For the former, see *Prov.* 2.42 (translation in Winston's anthology [above, n. 1], p. 184); for the latter, *Prob.* 13 (but others read 'most musical' or 'most clear-voiced'; see Colson, PLCL IX, p. 16 n. 2).

70 Contrast Philo's portrait of Gaius (*Legat.* 349–73) with Gruen's (*Diaspora*, pp. 66–7: 'levity rather than animosity'; 'frivolity by the mischievous monarch'); cf. P. McKechnie, 'Judaean Embassies and Cases before Roman Emperors, AD 44–66', *JThS* 56 (2005), pp. 340–1.

that the sanctity of the temple required them to reject Roman rule.[71] But, as opposed to 39–41, in 66–70 even the death of three emperors could not postpone the end anymore, and the issue was resolved by the victory of the side with the most legions.

Those interested in 'what-if?' exercises may wonder whether, if Philo had chastised the Jews of Jamnia in 39 CE, a process would have begun that might have prevented the chain of events that was to bring his nephew, a generation later, to preside over the burning down of the temple his own father, Philo's brother, had so extravagantly funded.

---

71 See Josephus, *BJ* 2.409–10. On this episode, which pitted consistent defenders of the temple as God's house against moderates who were willing to equivocate so as to avoid a crisis, see my *Studies in the Jewish Background*, pp. 102–16.

2   The Works of Philo

(With the Collaboration of Adam Kamesar)[1]

Philo of Alexandria has left an extensive body of works that have influenced a vast range of subsequent biblical, historical, philosophical, and theological studies. But, like the works of other writers of antiquity, the preservation of Philo's works has been far from straightforward.

The majority of Philo's works have come down to us in the original Greek. Some, however, have been preserved in Armenian translations dating from the sixth century. Much more limited in scope is a Latin version, which retains some importance, however. The process of textual transmission, both in Greek and in translation, has to a certain degree obscured whatever principles of organization may have been established by Philo himself or by early guardians of his corpus. However, through the losses and the corruption, scholars have been able to identify wider structures and superior manuscripts. What is presented here is an overview of the current consensus regarding Philo's works, and an indication of some of the problems involved in the reconstruction of what Philo originally wrote.[2]

---

1   Kamesar bears primary responsibility for the following: the section on 'the classification of Philo's works' (pp. 33–4); the lead paragraph(s) of the sections on the *Quaestiones* (pp. 34–5), the *Allegorical Commentary* (pp. 38–9), and the 'Exposition of the Law' (pp. 45–6). Royse and Kamesar bear joint responsibility for the section on the philosophical works (pp. 55–8).

2   The structure of Philo's corpus has been the subject of much discussion. Important earlier surveys include: L. Massebieau, 'Le classement des oeuvres de Philon', *Bibliothèque de l'École des Hautes Études: Sciences religieuses* 1 (1889), pp. 1–91; L. Cohn, 'Einteilung und Chronologie der Schriften Philos', *Philologus: Supplementband* 7 (1899), pp. 387–436; J. Morris, 'The Jewish Philosopher Philo', in E. Schürer et al., *The History of the Jewish People in the Age of Jesus Christ (175 B.C. – A.D. 135)*, III.2 (Edinburgh 1987), pp. 813–70. Besides these studies, the prefaces to the edition of Philo by L. Cohn and P. Wendland (PCW) contain much valuable material, as do the various introductions to the English (PLCL), German (PCH), and French (PAPM) translations of Philo's works. The Cohn–Wendland edition, along

I. THE CLASSIFICATION OF PHILO'S WORKS

Despite some complexities and uncertainties, it is clear that many of Philo's works belong to a few larger groups. In fact, most of his writings belong to three great exegetical series: (1) the *Quaestiones* and (2) the *Allegorical Commentary*, which follow a verse-by-verse format, and (3) the 'Exposition of the Law', which has a more thematic structure. All of these works comment on and explain the Pentateuch, as known to Philo from the Greek translation called the Septuagint. The *Quaestiones* covers much of Genesis and Exodus, and consists of short explanations of biblical verses in the form of questions and answers. Philo discusses both the literal and the allegorical meaning of the text. The *Allegorical Commentary*, on the other hand, at least in the form that we now have it, treats only Genesis. As the name suggests, Philo is concerned with the allegorical meaning of the text. Many consider this to be the work in which his most character-istic form of exegesis comes to the fore. It consists of very involved and sophisticated discussions of the biblical verses, in a much more developed and expanded form than we find in the *Quaestiones*. Indeed, it is possible that the *Quaestiones* represents Philo's elementary instruction, whether in a school or in a synagogal setting, whereas the *Allegorical Commentary* represents his more advanced instruction. Both of these works, and espe-cially the latter, are often termed *esoteric*, in that they presuppose a cer-tain knowledge of the Greek Pentateuch. They were no doubt aimed at an audience of readers within Greek-speaking Judaism and, in the case of the *Allegorical Commentary*, a very well-informed and even 'initiated' audience (*Cher.* 42, 48; cf. *Leg.* 3.219). The 'Exposition of the Law', on the other hand, is often termed *exoteric*. In this work, Philo summarizes and presents the Pentateuch in a more structured and thematic form and in such a way that 'general readers', including non-Jews, might be able to get a sense of Moses' literary and legislative achievements. He does not follow a verse-by-verse format, and employs allegorical interpretation to a lesser degree. E. R. Goodenough went so far as to claim that the 'Exposition' was aimed primarily at a Gentile audience.[3] Although the view has not found wide acceptance, it is certainly true that the 'Exposition' gives a more basic and systematic overview of the Pentateuch. It has a clearer literary structure than the other two series, and would be accessible to a broader circle of readers.[4]

---

with the editors' various concomitant studies, made many aspects of earlier research obsolete or at least in need of revision.

3 'Philo's Exposition of the Law and His De vita Mosis', *HThR* 26 (1933), pp. 109–25.

4 An alternative view, that the *Allegorical Commentary* and the 'Exposition' form one series, has been proposed by V. Nikiprowetzky, *Le commentaire*

Two other groups of writings have been discerned. One group, the so-called apologetic and historical writings, reveal that Philo was not simply a reclusive philosopher, but was also fully engaged in contemporary issues related to Judaism and in the political problems facing the Jewish people. The apologetic works include the *De vita Mosis* (*On the Life of Moses*), an encomiastic biography of the Jewish legislator, the *Hypothetica* or *On the Jews*, and the *De vita contemplativa* (*On the Contemplative Life*), a treatment of a contemporary Jewish sect with monastic tendencies known as the Therapeutae. The 'historical' writings include the *In Flaccum* (*Flaccus*) and the *Legatio ad Gaium* (*Embassy to Gaius*). Both of these works are concerned with the violent clashes between Greeks and Jews in Alexandria that took place in the year 38 CE and the events of the immediate aftermath.

The third and final group consists of philosophical works that treat traditional themes of Greek philosophy. These are the two treatises *Quod omnis probus liber sit* (*Every Good Man Is Free*) and *De aeternitate mundi* (*On the Eternity of the World*), and the two dialogues preserved completely only in Armenian translation: *De animalibus* (*On Animals*) and *De providentia* (*On Providence*). These texts demonstrate that Philo was fully at home discussing Greek philosophy, with little or no reference to the Bible and Judaism. Let us now turn to a more detailed presentation of all of these works, and of other works that are preserved only in fragments or are completely lost.

II. THE *QUAESTIONES*

The origin of the genre known as *Zētēmata kai lyseis*, 'Questions and Answers', or perhaps better, 'Problems and Solutions', goes back to pre-classical times. As early as the sixth century BCE, philosophically oriented critics began raising questions and finding 'problems' with the theological and moral views found in the Homeric poems. In time, critics came to be concerned with inconsistencies and aesthetic infelicities. Others, however, took upon themselves the task of explaining or 'solving' the difficulties, in a kind of defense of Homer, who had become the 'educator of Greece' (Plato, *Resp.* 606e). Aristotle dedicated chapter 25 of his *Poetics* to 'problems and solutions', and in the Hellenistic era, which was the great age of Homeric scholarship, many works with this or similar titles were written. Other authors in addition to Homer came

de *l'Écriture chez Philon d'Alexandrie* (Leiden 1977), pp. 202, 241–2. For a defense of the traditional view, see A. Terian, 'The Priority of the *Quaestiones* among Philo's Exegetical Commentaries', in D. M. Hay (ed.), *Both Literal and Allegorical: Studies in Philo of Alexandria's Questions and Answers on Genesis and Exodus* (Atlanta 1991), pp. 30–1.

to be treated in a similar fashion, and the genre remained popular into the imperial age.[5]

The Bible, also composed in a remote era and based on oral tradition, naturally lent itself to a similar kind of treatment. Problems related to outdated theology and morality, as well as to inconsistency, were readily noted. Moreover, as time went by, writers of *zētēmata* commentaries came to be concerned with more general exegetical issues, and not simply those that involved criticisms of or attacks on the biblical text.[6]

The first biblical commentary of this sort to have survived is Philo's *Quaestiones et solutiones in Genesim et in Exodum* (*Questions and Answers on Genesis and Exodus*).[7] Philo's overall approach is to begin each section (as we may call the pair of question and its answer) by posing some problem in interpretation in the biblical text, or by more generally asking simply what is the meaning of a word or phrase found in it. This question is then followed by an answer that typically refers to the literal meaning of the text (sometimes perfunctorily) and to the allegorical meaning. Often the answer is quite short, although on occasion Philo will present a more extended treatment, perhaps bringing in other biblical passages, perhaps referring to secular Greek authors (Homer and Plato are favorites), and perhaps referring to common philosophical issues or terminology. In any case, the sections follow the sequence of the biblical text quite carefully (but with a few departures).[8]

As an example, we may consider *Quaestiones in Genesim* 1.37, where Philo asks concerning Gen 3:6: 'Why does the woman first touch the trees and eat of its fruit, and afterwards the man also take of it?' Philo's answer is twofold. The literal meaning emphasizes the temporal priority of the woman. But the allegorical meaning is that woman

5 For a survey of ancient exegetical *zētēmata* literature, see A. Gudeman, s.v. Λύσεις, *PRE* I.13.2 (1927), cols. 2511–22.

6 For a recent work on *zētēmata* literature, see A. Volgers and C. Zamagni (eds.), *Erotapokriseis: Early Christian Question-and-Answer Literature in Context* (Leuven 2004).

7 For a recent discussion, see P. W. van der Horst, 'Philo and the Rabbis on Genesis: Similar Questions, Different Answers', in Volgers and Zamagni, *Erotapokriseis*, pp. 55–70, who notes (p. 57) that Demetrius the Chronographer (3rd century BCE) 'is the first traceable author' who applied the Greek form of questions and answers to the biblical text. The work of Demetrius survives in only a few fragments.

8 P. Borgen and R. Skarsten, '*Quaestiones et Solutiones*: Some Observations on the Form of Philo's Exegesis', *StPhilo* 4 (1976–1977), pp. 1–15, point out that Philo also uses the 'exegetical form of the question and answer' in the *Allegorical Commentary* and even in the 'Exposition of the Law'. See also Borgen, *Philo of Alexandria: An Exegete for His Time* (Leiden 1997), pp. 80–101.

symbolizes sense and man symbolizes mind, and objects are grasped first
by sense and then moved into the mind. At *QG* 1.83, where Philo asks
concerning Gen 5:21–3 why Enoch lived 165 years before his repentance
and 200 years after his repentance, the answer is devoted entirely to the
significance of the two numbers and their component numbers. And
at *QG* 3.3, an exceptionally long section devoted to the animals that
Abraham sacrificed according to Gen 15:9, Philo ranges widely among
moral, physiological, and cosmological points in his answer, citing both
Plato and Homer.

Regrettably, this work (actually a series of books) survives incom-
pletely. The original Greek books have been lost; the primary source
is the ancient Armenian translation, which contains four books on
Genesis and two books on Exodus, and was published by J.B. Aucher
in 1826.[9] For much of the biblical text (Gen 2:4–28:9; Exod 12:2–23,
20:25, 22:21–28:34 [LXX; MT 28:38]), this Armenian version provides
a more or less continuous discussion. There also exist several hundred
Greek fragments that are found in various later Christian writers, and
derive ultimately from the original Greek books.[10] A comparison of the
Armenian translation with the extant Greek fragments shows that the
Armenian is, in general, a literal rendering of a Greek text that was
identical with or very close to Philo's original text.

While the overall plan is fairly clear, many of the details of this work
are obscure owing to the disparate nature of the remains. Besides the
Armenian and the Greek fragments, there exists an ancient Latin translation of one portion of the *Quaestiones in Genesim* (*QG* 4.154–245,
according to the Armenian numbering, apparently the original *QG* book
6). Moreover, the Latin contains twelve sections (following *QG* 4.195),
covering Gen 26:19–35, that do not have a correlate in the Armenian,
which jumps from 26:19 (*QG* 4.195) to 27:1 (*QG* 4.196). It would thus
appear that the Armenian is lacunose at that point, as indeed is confirmed by the fact that three Greek fragments can be located within
those twelve sections. One thus wonders whether there are other lacunae within the Armenian, which has several substantial gaps. Such gaps
might have contained some of the Greek fragments that are attributed

9   Philo Judaeus, *Paralipomena armena* (Venice 1826).
10 For the fragments, see F. Petit's edition of Philon d'Alexandrie, *Quaestiones
    in Genesim et in Exodum: Fragmenta Graeca* (Paris 1978 = PAPM 33). Her
    collection can be supplemented by J. R. Royse, 'Further Greek Fragments of
    Philo's *Quaestiones*', in F. E. Greenspahn et al. (eds.), *Nourished with Peace:
    Studies in Hellenistic Judaism in Memory of Samuel Sandmel* (Chico, CA
    1984), pp. 143–53; 'Philo's *Quaestiones in Exodum* 1.6', in Hay, *Both Literal
    and Allegorical*, pp. 17–27.

to the *Quaestiones* but have not yet been located. And there are a few further texts that, although not attributed to the *Quaestiones*, are plausibly assigned to them.

The result, then, is that the bulk of our knowledge of the *Quaestiones* rests on the Armenian, into which almost all of the Latin version and most of the Greek fragments can be located (although often with textual differences). But the Armenian is clearly incomplete, and can be supplemented with some certainty from the Latin, and with more or less certainty from some of the Greek fragments. We thus meet many uncertainties and puzzles.[11]

There are two important exceptions to the fragmentary nature of the Greek evidence. One Greek manuscript provides the continuous text of *QE* 2.62–8.[12] These sections are, philosophically and theologically, a very rich discussion of the divine powers.[13] And another Greek manuscript contains excerpts from *QG* 2.1–7.[14] These excerpts preserve about one-half of the original text, and are of great textual value, although they do not provide the sort of straightforward transmission that we find for *QE* 2.62–8.

Thus, we have extensive evidence in Greek, Armenian, and Latin, and many scholars have attempted to define the original structure and extent of the books that made up the *Quaestiones*. An important clue to how Philo originally structured this work lies in the agreement found at many points between the divisions of the *Quaestiones* into books and the division of the Pentateuchal text into readings for synagogal services.[15] Utilizing this agreement it is possible to reconstruct the original structure of the *Quaestiones* as consisting of six books on Genesis and

11 For a recent survey of these issues, see J. R. Royse, 'Philo's Division of His Works into Books', *StPhAnn* 13 (2001), pp. 76–85.

12 These sections, so important for Philo's thought, have had an unsatisfactory fate. Although they exist in a Greek manuscript of very high quality and in a very literal Armenian version, they have never been, as I would judge, quite properly edited. Two excerpts are found in the Byzantine anthology called the *Sacra parallela*, and these are indeed well handled by Petit in her edition of the Greek fragments, pp. 274–5. But for her reasons for not including all of *QE* 2.62–8 in her edition, see her note on p. 273.

13 See now the translation and commentary by D. T. Runia, 'A Neglected Text of Philo of Alexandria: First Translation into a Modern Language', in E. G. Chazon et al. (eds.), *Things Revealed: Studies in Early Jewish and Christian Literature in Honor of Michael E. Stone* (Leiden 2004), pp. 199–207.

14 These have been edited by J. Paramelle with E. Lucchesi: Philon d'Alexandrie, *Questions sur la Genèse II 1–7* (Geneva 1984).

15 This idea was suggested independently by M. Gaster, *The Samaritans* (London 1925), pp. 76–7, and by R. Marcus in his edition of the *Quaestiones* (Cambridge, MA 1953 = PLCL Suppl. I), pp. xii–xv.

six books on Exodus, which are partially preserved in the Armenian, the Latin, and the many Greek fragments.[16]

The original six books of the *Quaestiones* on Genesis covered Gen 2:4b–28:9, and are preserved (with some lacunae) in the four books of the *Quaestiones in Genesim* as found in Armenian and (for book 6) in Latin. The original six books of the *Quaestiones* on Exodus, which have suffered even graver losses, covered Exod 6:2–17:16 and 20:25b–30:10, and are preserved in the two books of the *Quaestiones in Exodum* as found in Armenian.[17]

The original six books on Genesis are preserved much more fully than the original six (if that is the number) books on Exodus, although much of each series appears to have been lost entirely. Moreover, there is no persuasive evidence to show that the *Quaestiones* originally extended beyond the above bounds, let alone into subsequent books of the Pentateuch.[18]

III. THE *ALLEGORICAL COMMENTARY*

The work known by this title, for which Philo is probably most famous, is actually a series of exegetical commentaries on the Book of Genesis. These commentaries, preserved in the original Greek, are structured on the basis of biblical lemmata, that is, biblical verses cited according to the text of the Septuagint. Philo provides extensive discussion of the moral, philosophical, and spiritual meanings to be discerned beneath the surface of the literal biblical text. His method of allegorical interpretation in this work is not entirely dissimilar from that in the *Quaestiones*. The similarity may be seen especially at the beginning of a lemmatic unit in the *Allegorical Commentary*, where Philo may employ the logic of *zētēmata* literature in establishing the need for allegorical interpretation. In fact, in recent times V. Nikiprowetzky has taken the view that the *Allegorical Commentary* may, in fact, be a kind of expanded form of *quaestiones* or *zētēmata*.[19] Nevertheless,

---

16 For details and additional references see J. R. Royse, 'The Original Structure of Philo's *Quaestiones*', *StPhilo* 4 (1976–1977), pp. 41–78, and 'Philo's Division', pp. 76–85 (and see p. 76 n. 112 for some corrections to the former article).

17 For further details, see my 'The Original Structure', and esp. the overviews on pp. 52 (*QG*), 61–2 (*QE*).

18 It has been frequently argued (e.g., by Massebieau, 'Le classement', pp. 7–8; Cohn, 'Einteilung', p. 403) that the series extended, or at least was intended to extend, through all of the Pentateuch. But see my arguments in 'The Original Structure', pp. 42–3.

19 *Le commentaire*, pp. 170–80.

this view does not account for what might be termed the 'homiletical' features of the *Allegorical Commentary*. These are connected with both the Jewish and the Greek educational background of Philo. On the one hand, we find a highly imaginative and elaborate use of parallel Pentateuchal passages, which is characteristic of Palestinian midrash. On the other hand, this method is combined with the moralistic themes and tone of the Greek diatribe, often set out with sophisticated rhetorical technique. Both the exegesis of 'secondary texts' as well as the moralistic and philosophical digressions sometimes take Philo far away from the biblical lemma, to which he may return by a very circuitous route. For these reasons, many scholars have concluded that the *Allegorical Commentary* also contains synagogal homilies or parts of homilies, edited or revised by Philo to a lesser or greater degree.[20] However, the problem of the literary form and structure of the *Allegorical Commentary* is a complex one, and in more recent years many interesting hypotheses have been put forward.[21]

There seems to be no reason to think that this series extended past Genesis, although it is far from clear exactly how much of Genesis was originally covered. We can at least trace Philo's treatment from Gen 2:1 (cited in *Leg.* 1.1) to Gen 17:22 (cited in *Mut.* 270), and on to the dreams found in Gen 28, 31, 37, 40, and 41 (as discussed in *Somn.* 1–2). But there are many gaps within that sequence, and it is generally unclear whether Philo's treatment of a certain block of text has been lost or never existed at all (and, thus, in the following I mark such books non-committally as 'missing'). It is striking that Gen 1 is not treated in this series, nor in the *Quaestiones*.[22] However, as with the *Quaestiones*, what survives is extensive and complete enough to make clear what Philo's project was.

In his *Ecclesiastical History* 2.18.1, Eusebius describes Philo as commenting on 'the events in Genesis in connected sequence, in the books which he entitled *The Allegories of the Sacred Laws*'. The conventional general title *Allegorical Commentary* is derived from this phrase (Greek, *Nomōn hierōn allēgoriai*), which is applied in a strict sense in

---

20 See esp. I. Heinemann, PCH III, p. 5.

21 For a treatment of some of the recent theories, see D. T. Runia, 'The Structure of Philo's Allegorical Treatises', *VC* 38 (1984), pp. 209–56; 'Further Observations on the Structure of Philo's Allegorical Treatises', *VC* 41 (1987), pp. 105–38.

22 As with the *Quaestiones*, though, some have argued that the beginning of the series has been lost; see Massebieau, 'Le classement', pp. 14–16, and more recently T. H. Tobin, 'The Beginning of Philo's *Legum Allegoriae*', *StPhAnn* 12 (2000), pp. 29–43, who notes several remarks in the *Allegorical Commentary* that seem to refer to a missing allegorical treatment of Gen 1.

the modern editions only to the first three books of the series. However, Eusebius also mentions as separate works quite a few of the works that are now typically assigned to the *Allegorical Commentary*, beginning with the originally single book comprising *De gigantibus* and *Quod Deus sit immutabilis*. Presumably Eusebius was confused by the titles that he found, where perhaps four books were called *Legum allegoriae* (*The Allegories of the Laws*), into thinking that they formed a separate series from the other works.

The books within this series are:

> *Legum allegoriae* 1–2 (*The Allegories of the Laws* 1–2): Gen 2:1–17 (*Leg.* 1) and 2:18–3:1a (*Leg.* 2). This is the original first book of the *Legum allegoriae*.[23] Corresponding to the difference between the immaterial world and the material universe, Philo contrasts the creation of the heavenly man (in Gen 1:27) and the creation of the earthly man, Adam (in Gen 2:7). Spiritual significance is found in the various details of the garden of Eden.
>
> [Missing: original second book of the *Legum allegoriae*: Gen 3:1b–8a.]
>
> *Legum allegoriae* 3 (*The Allegories of the Laws* 3): Gen 3:8b–19. This is the original third book of the *Legum allegoriae*. Philo here interprets the fall of Adam and Eve as showing how the desire of pleasure leads to the rejection of God, which in turn results in conflict with true wisdom and happiness.[24]
>
> [Missing: original fourth book of the *Legum allegoriae*: Gen 3:20–3.][25]
>
> *De cherubim* (*On the Cherubim*): Gen 3:24–4:1. Philo here discusses the expulsion of Adam and Eve from Eden, and the significance of the Cherubim that God places at the gate of the garden. Then we are led to the significance of the birth of Cain (meaning 'possession') as illustrating the union of mind and sense-perception to produce the idea that man possesses things of his own accord rather than through God's gift.

23 The division into three books, as presented in the Cohn–Wendland edition, relies on part of the manuscript tradition. However, *Leg.* 1 and *Leg.* 2 are combined into one book in the Armenian translation and in one Greek manuscript, and together they are of roughly the length of *Leg.* 3. See J. R. Royse, 'The Text of Philo's *Legum Allegoriae*', StPhAnn 12 (2000), p. 2.

24 There is a full commentary on *Legum allegoriae* 1–3 by R. Radice, entitled *Allegoria e paradigmi etici in Filone di Alessandria* (Milan 2000).

25 It is likely that some Greek fragments of this work survive; see my 'The Text of Philo's *Legum Allegoriae*', pp. 2–3. For the possible missing books of the *Legum allegoriae*, see also Morris, 'Philo', pp. 832–3.

De sacrificiis Abelis et Caini (*On the Sacrifices of Abel and Cain*):
Gen 4:2–4. Philo analyzes the distinction in the sacrifices that
Abel (a true shepherd who loves God) and Cain (a type of the
lover of self) present to God. This discussion leads to comments
on other biblical mentions of sacrifices. At one point (§§ 20–32)
the difference between pleasure and virtue is depicted by images
of a courtesan and a virtuous woman; the latter is accompanied
by a long list of virtues and admirable qualities, while the former
brings with her some 150 despicable qualities.

[Missing: Gen 4:5–7. These verses are discussed in *Quaestiones in
Genesim*, but there is no apparent lacuna in either *De sacrificiis*
or *Quod deterius*. Might there have been a separate work?]

Quod deterius potiori insidiari soleat (*That the Worse Is Wont to
Attack the Better*): Gen 4:8–15. The conflict between Cain and
Abel is seen as an image of the conflict between love of self and
love of God. Although Cain appears to be the victor, in fact he has
brought upon himself the condemnation of God.

De posteritate Caini (*On the Posterity of Cain and His Exile*): Gen
4:16–25. The fate of Cain and his offspring is seen as illustrating
the results of impiety (as found later in the maxim of Protagoras
that 'man is the measure of all things').

[Missing: Gen 4:26–5:32. Genesis 5 is mostly names, and so an
extensive commentary the length of a book would be unnecessary. But we might expect treatment of Gen 4:26, which Philo
does discuss elsewhere.]

De gigantibus (*On the Giants*) – *Quod Deus sit immutabilis* (*On
the Unchangeableness of God*): Gen 6:1–4 (*Gig.*) and 6:4–12
(*Deus*). These two books originally formed one book, and there is
no reason to suppose that any portion is missing. The first book
discusses the enigmatic reference to the 'angels of God' in Gen
6:2 (LXX), the 'spirit of God' as found in 6:3, and the 'giants' of
6:4. The second book includes an attempt to reconcile the suggestion in Gen 6:6 that God repented with the view that God's
perfection excludes change of mind.[26]

[Missing: *De testamentis* (*On the Covenants*) 1–2: Gen 6:13–9:19.
In his discussion of Gen 17 in *De mutatione nominum* 53, Philo
cuts short his interpretation of 'covenant' at Gen 17:2 and states
that he has written two books *On the Covenants*. Scholars have
usually held that Gen 6:13–9:19 would be an appropriate place
for Philo to discuss such a topic. Presumably Philo would have

26 For this pair of works, see D. Winston and J. Dillon, *Two Treatises of Philo
of Alexandria* (Chico, CA 1983), which contains a commentary.

taken the occasion of the first covenant with Noah to discuss the various covenants that God makes with Abraham, Isaac, and Jacob.]

De agricultura (*On Husbandry*): Gen 9:20a. Philo illustrates the statement that Noah began to be a gardener with examples of the importance of tending the soul in contrast to the one who seeks pleasure. And of course a good beginning must be continued properly.

De plantatione (*On Noah's Work as a Planter*): Gen 9:20b (with a transition to Gen 9:21 in § 139). The end of this work (after § 177) is missing. Here Philo moves to the statement that Noah planted a vineyard. God's planting is presented as the model of human planting.

De ebrietate (*On Drunkenness*): Gen 9:21. Eusebius, *Hist. eccl.* 2.18.2, states that Philo wrote two books *De ebrietate*, but only one such book has survived. The usual view is that the extant book is the original *first* book of *De ebrietate*, and that the *second* book has been lost, apart from fragments. However, it is also possible that our *De ebrietate* is the *second* book, and that the *first* book has been lost, and some early evidence tends to support this view. The issue is complex and ultimately involves trying to reconstruct Philo's line of thought throughout *De agricultura*, *De plantatione*, the two books *De ebrietate*, and *De sobrietate*.[27]

[Missing: Gen 9:22–3. If the second book *De ebrietate* is missing, these verses could have been discussed there.[28] But perhaps whatever Philo wanted to say here (probably not much) was said in the *Quaestiones in Genesim* or in *De testamentis*.]

De sobrietate (*On Sobriety*) – *De confusione linguarum* (*On the Confusion of Tongues*): Gen 9:24–7 (*Sobr.*) and 11:1–9 (*Conf.*). *De sobrietate* is exceptionally short; it is likely that it and *De confusione linguarum* originally formed one book, and that Philo simply skipped treatment of Gen 10. The first book's title derives from the initial discussion of Noah's return to soberness, understood chiefly as soberness of the soul, after his drunkenness. The second book interprets the story of Babel allegorically, after raising some objections to a literal interpretation.

[Missing: Gen 11:10–32. It seems likely that Philo simply skipped this genealogical material.]

De migratione Abrahami (*On the Migration of Abraham*): Gen 12:1–6. Philo comments on the story of Abraham's journey from

---

27   For further details, see Morris, 'Philo', pp. 836–7.
28   As Massebieau, 'Le classement', p. 25, proposed.

Haran to the land of Canaan, on God's blessing of Abraham and through Abraham of others, and on Abraham's arrival at Shechem.

[Missing: Gen 12:7–15:1. In the opening words of the following treatise (*Her.* 1), Philo says that he has discussed rewards in the preceding book. We can imagine that Philo could have found relevant material for this topic in Gen 12:16, 13:2, 13:5, 13:14–15, 14:16, 14:21–4. But it is certainly possible that Philo devoted more than one book to this quantity of biblical text.]

Quis rerum divinarum heres sit (*Who is the Heir of Divine Things?*): Gen 15:2–18. This book, the longest of the *Allegorical Commentary*, takes the reference to division in Gen 15:10 as an occasion to discuss the role of the divine Logos in making divisions within the created world. Indeed, precise division into equal halves is possible only for God. (Presumably Gen 15:19–21 is skipped here since it was covered in the lost *De testamentis*.)

De congressu eruditionis gratia (*On Mating with the Preliminary Studies*): Gen 16:1–6. Philo finds in the story of Hagar and Sarah an allegory of the distinction between the so-called encyclical studies, or liberal arts, as found in the Stoic conception of education, and true philosophy, the goal of which is virtue.

De fuga et inventione (*On Flight and Finding*): Gen 16:6–14. The flight of Hagar leads Philo to a discussion of the various types of flight as found in the Bible. Then, the angel's finding her is the occasion for a treatment of finding and seeking. Finally, in reference to the spring of water Philo notes five meanings of 'spring' in the Bible.[29]

De mutatione nominum (*On the Change of Names*): Gen 17:1–22. The change of the name 'Abram' to 'Abraham' (Gen 17:5) provides an opportunity for an extended discussion of the significance of names and of other people whose names are changed (notably Sarah and Jacob). (Much of the material in 17:1–22 is not discussed, because presumably it was covered in the lost *De testamentis*.)

[Missing: Gen 17:23–7. From the sparse treatment in *Quaestiones in Genesim*, it seems likely that Philo skipped many, if not all, of these verses.]

---

29 Massebieau, 'Le classement', p. 28, notes that the extant works of the *Allegorical Commentary* skip Gen 16:15–16, and suggests that these verses were discussed in a lost final portion of *De fuga*. But it seems more likely that Philo simply omitted treatment here (perhaps having said what he wanted to in *QG* 3.37–8).

De Deo (On God): Gen 18:2.[30] This survives only in Armenian, and probably came from a missing book of the *Allegorical Commentary* that treated Gen 18:1ff. The surviving fragment is of great philosophical and theological interest.[31]

We are here almost at the end of what survives of the *Allegorical Commentary*. Eusebius, *Ecclesiastical History* 2.18.4, says that Philo wrote five books on 'dreams being sent from God' (*De somniis* [*On Dreams*]), but only two such books survive. The original five books must have discussed the reports of various dreams and visions that occur in the remaining chapters of Genesis (to Abraham, Jacob, Joseph, and the chief butler and chief baker of Pharaoh). The placement of the two surviving books within the original five books is controversial. It is clear that the surviving two books form a sequence (treating the second and third classes of dreams identified by Philo, respectively), and that some book or books have been lost at the beginning of the series. Perhaps most straightforward is the view that our two books are the original second and third books.[32] Thus, the original first book (now lost) discussed the 'first class of heaven-sent dreams, in which ... the Deity of His own motion sends to us the visions which are presented to us in sleep' (*Somn.* 1.1; cf. *Somn.* 2.2). The original second book, our *De somniis* 1, discusses the 'second kind of dreams ... in which our own mind ... seems to be possessed and God-inspired' (*Somn.* 1.2; cf. *Somn.* 2.2). And the original third book, our *De somniis* 2, discusses the 'third kind of dreams [which] arises whenever the soul in sleep, setting itself in motion and agitation of its own accord, becomes frenzied' (*Somn.* 2.1). It then remains obscure what the original fourth and fifth books covered.[33]

What we then would have is:

---

30   The title here is certainly not derived from Philo.

31   This text is the subject of extensive investigation by F. Siegert. See his edition of Philon von Alexandrien, *Über die Gottesbezeichnung 'wohltätig verzehrendes Feuer' (De Deo)* (Tübingen 1988). Siegert provides the Armenian original, a retroversion into Greek, and a valuable commentary. See also his article, 'The Philonian Fragment *De Deo*: First English Translation', *StPhAnn* 10 (1998), pp. 1–33.

32   So F. H. Colson, PLCL V, p. 285.

33   On the other hand, Massebieau, 'Le classement', pp. 29–31, supposes that Philo began the series with an extensive discussion in three books of earlier philosophical views on dreams, and that our two books are thus the original fourth and fifth books; Cohn, 'Einteilung', p. 402, finds this more probable. In any case, it seems plausible that Christian copyists of the works of Philo might more readily forego the task of copying books that were devoted to pagan views.

[Missing: original first book of *De somniis*. We may suppose that the dream of Abimelech in Gen 20:3–8 was treated in this missing book, because it fits the criteria for the first class of dreams.[34] Other possible contents would be the dream of Isaac in Gen 26:24–5, and of Laban in Gen 31:24.]

De somniis (*On Dreams*) 1: Gen 28:12–15 (Jacob's dream of the heavenly ladder), and 31:11–13 (Jacob's dream of the colors of his flock). This is the original second book. The opening words tell us that the preceding book treated the first class of dreams.

De somniis (*On Dreams*) 2: Gen 37:7 and 37:9 (Joseph's dreams of the sheaves and the zodiac), 40:9–11 and 40:16–17 (the dreams of the chief butler and the chief baker), and 41:11–17 and 41:22–4 (Pharaoh's dreams of the seven kine and the seven ears of corn). This book (the original third) ends abruptly in the middle of a sentence (§ 302), although the length of what survives shows that we must be near the end.

[Missing: original fourth and fifth books of *De somniis*.]

Whether Philo ever wrote more treatises in the *Allegorical Commentary* is unknown, although the works that survive and that are known to have once existed already form a substantial literary product. In fact, Philo covers much of the latter part of Genesis in his *De Josepho*, and doubtless covered yet more in the lost *De Isaaco* and *De Jacobo*, all treatises of the 'Exposition of the Law'. Moreover, it seems plausible that he had little motivation to give to this portion of Scripture the meticulous analysis that we find in the earlier books of the *Allegorical Commentary*.

IV. THE 'EXPOSITION OF THE LAW'

If in the *Quaestiones* and in the *Allegorical Commentary* Philo provides detailed exegesis of the biblical text, in the 'Exposition' he presents the Pentateuch in a broader and more systematic fashion.[35] Indeed, the very structure of the 'Exposition' is based on a sophisticated understanding of the genres of the Pentateuch that Philo puts forward in *De praemiis et poenis* 1–2. The Pentateuch has three genres or parts. There is a cosmological section, which deals with the creation of the world and allows us to understand that the legislation to follow is in harmony with the nature of the universe. There follows a genealogical or historical section

---

34 See Massebieau, 'Le classement', p. 30.
35 The title 'Exposition of the Law' is conventional, and does not derive from an ancient source. See Cohn, 'Einteilung', p. 405.

that recounts the lives of virtuous men, lives that constitute 'embodied laws', for the early men lived in accord with natural law, and provided a model for the written laws that were enacted later. Finally, there is the legislative section proper, which contains both general principles (the Ten Commandments), and the more specific or special laws that are based on them.[36] The primary treatises that make up the 'Exposition of the Law', the *De opificio mundi*, the set of *Lives* of the patriarchs, and the *De decalogo* and the *De specialibus legibus*, take up each of these sections of the Pentateuch in turn. Philo makes this structure clear by means of cross-references especially at the beginning of the treatises *De Abrahamo* (§§ 2–3), *De decalogo* (§ 1), and *De specialibus legibus* 1 (§ 1).[37]

Although Philo's discussion relates to the biblical text, he does not engage in the verse-by-verse exegesis that he practices in the other two series. And, in contrast to the *Allegorical Commentary*, he does not pursue secondary biblical texts. What is characteristic of the 'Exposition' is the constant endeavor to discover the logic and systematic basis of the Pentateuchal corpus, as it might be considered from a Greek perspective. This is seen, for example, in the framework he establishes for the *Lives* of Abraham, Isaac, and Jacob (*Ios.* 1). They are paradigms for the acquisition of virtue through, respectively, instruction, nature, and practice – a threefold scheme that belongs to Greek educational theory.[38] The attempt to discuss the Mosaic laws as they relate to the virtues as defined in Greek thought, undertaken at the end of the 'Exposition', represents a similar tendency.[39]

The first book in this series, *De opificio*, is typically printed at the head of Philo's works, which then continue with the *Allegorical Commentary*. According to the division generally accepted, however, *De opificio* would more appropriately come immediately before

---

36   For these characterizations of the Pentateuch, see also *Opif.* 1–3, *Abr.* 3–5, and the fuller discussion below, ch. 3, pp. 73–7.

37   Cf. Cohn, 'Einteilung', pp. 405–6; Royse, 'Philo's Division', pp. 63–4.

38   See F. H. Colson, 'Philo on Education', *JThS* 18 (1917), pp. 160–1.

39   Borgen, *Philo: An Exegete*, esp. pp. 63–79, has advocated the view that the 'Exposition' may be regarded as a kind of 're-written Bible', a designation often applied to originally Semitic works such as the *Liber antiquitatum biblicarum* or *Jubilees*, which 're-write' the Bible as opposed to commenting upon it. But the view has found little support. See A. Kamesar's review of Borgen in *JThS* 50 (1999), pp. 754–6, and D. T. Runia in the introduction to his edition of Philo of Alexandria, *On the Creation of the Cosmos according to Moses* (Leiden 2001), pp. 5–7.

De Abrahamo.[40] But Philo's presentation in *De opificio* certainly serves as a clear introduction to his method and thought in general. And Philo may have meant it to be such. For it is striking that (at least as we have them) the *Quaestiones* and the *Allegorical Commentary* are both missing any discussion of Gen 1:1–2:4a, which is precisely what Philo discusses in *De opificio*. Thus, although the style of *De opificio* is characteristic of the 'Exposition of the Law' rather than of the *Quaestiones* or the *Allegorical Commentary*, its contents may have been felt by Philo himself to be appropriate as an introduction to all three series. The 'Exposition' as a whole, as has been noted earlier, including the *De opificio*, has a more 'exoteric' character.

It should also be pointed out that there seems to be some relationship between the 'Exposition' and the *De vita Mosis*. It seems clear, on the one hand, that *De vita Mosis* is not properly part of the 'Exposition', but on the other hand, it may have been intended as a kind of introduction to it.[41] I have followed the current consensus in placing *De vita Mosis* among the apologetic and historical works.

The books in the 'Exposition' are:

> *De opificio mundi* (*On the Creation*). A fine treatise on the creation (Gen 1–3) and a clear introduction to many of Philo's characteristic philosophical ideas. The two biblical stories of creation (in Gen 1 and 2) correspond to two aspects of God's creative activity. Like an earthly architect who creates a plan before proceeding to the material construction, God first creates the incorporeal world of (Platonic) forms and then creates the material universe. God's creative power is mirrored by His providential care of His creation.[42]
>
> *De Abrahamo* (*On Abraham*). Philo here begins his discussion of those individuals who lived before the written law but were themselves embodiments of the divine law. These 'living laws' are grouped into two triads. The first consists of Enos, Enoch, and Noah, who embodied hope, repentance, and justice, respec-

---

40 A careful analysis of the external and internal evidence concerning the position of *De opificio* may be found in A. Terian, 'Back to Creation: The Beginning of Philo's Third Grand Commentary', *StPhAnn* 9 (1997), pp. 19–36. Note that of the modern editions of Philo, *De opificio* is at the head of the 'Exposition' in PCH I–II, and in the new Hebrew translation edited by S. Daniel-Nataf, vols. II–III (Jerusalem 1991, 2000).

41 See Goodenough, 'Philo's Exposition'; Morris, 'Philo', pp. 847 n. 137, 854–5.

42 See the recent edition and commentary of Runia mentioned just above (n. 39).

tively. The second and greater triad consists of Abraham, Isaac, and Jacob, and we find here stories from the life of Abraham, the model of one who acquires virtue through instruction.

[Missing: *De Isaaco* (*On Isaac*) and *De Jacobo* (*On Jacob*). At the beginning of *De Josepho*, Philo says: 'Since I have described the lives of these three, the life which results from teaching, the life of the self-taught, and the life of practice, I will carry on the series by describing a fourth life, that of the statesman.' This seems to imply that, corresponding to the work *De Abrahamo*, there were originally separate works discussing Isaac and Jacob. Eusebius does not mention them, however, and there is no trace of them elsewhere, unless one or more of the unidentified fragments derive from them. Thus they seem to have been lost very early. The *De Isaaco* would have treated the life of Isaac as a model of the 'self-taught' soul, and the *De Jacobo* that of Jacob as the model of the life of 'practice'.]

De Josepho (*On Joseph*). A treatment of Joseph as the paragon of the wise statesman. The events in the biblical narrative are presented in such a way so as to illustrate various virtues that are necessitated by involvement in political life. The positive depiction of Joseph here contrasts with the frequent negative remarks to be found in the *Allegorical Commentary*.[43]

De decalogo (*On the Decalogue*). Having discussed the patriarchs who serve as unwritten laws through their virtues, Philo turns to a discussion of the written laws. Chief among these are the Ten Commandments, which God Himself delivered while leaving the other laws to be spoken by Moses.

De specialibus legibus (*On the Special Laws*) 1–4. Philo now proceeds to organize the disparate laws found in the Pentateuch by considering them to be 'special [or specific] laws' subsumed under the headings of the various Ten Commandments, which thus serve as the 'generic laws' of the divine legislation.

De specialibus legibus 1. A discussion of the special laws that fall under the first and second commandments, which relate to the sovereignty of God. The corresponding laws thus deal with the nature and conditions of the worship of God, including the rules for priests, sacrifices, and offerings, and also with the requirement that the worshiper be pure in both body and soul.

De specialibus legibus 2. A treatment of the special laws that fall under the next three commandments. The third commandment occasions a discussion of the nature of swearing and oaths.

---

43   See Colson, PLCL VI, pp. xii–xiv.

Under the fourth, Philo subsumes the rules regarding not only the Sabbath but also the other feasts (which Philo conveniently counts in such a way so as to arrive at the number ten for the entire set). And the fifth leads to an encomium on the nature of parents and a comparison of their procreative activity to the creative activity of God.

De specialibus legibus 3. A treatise on the special laws that fall under the sixth and seventh commandments. Under these headings Philo considers laws relating to marriage and sexual activity generally, as well as laws concerning murder, homicide, accidental death, and even various sorts of violence.

De specialibus legibus 4. A discussion of the special laws that fall under the eighth, ninth, and tenth commandments. In relation to the eighth Philo treats laws concerning stealing, kidnapping (as the stealing of a person), and the theft of a deposit. Under the ninth are subsumed a variety of laws relating to deceit and the obligations of judges. And the tenth gives Philo the opportunity to emphasize the need to restrain desire of all sorts, and to state that Moses introduced the dietary laws as special cases of the need for self-control. In the second half of the book (*Spec.* 4.133–238 [end]), Philo shifts his approach and relates the laws to the virtues, beginning with justice, and the rest of the book concerns its exemplification in laws.

De virtutibus (*On the Virtues*). A discussion of individual virtues, as an appendix to *De specialibus legibus* 4, continuing the discussion of justice there.[44] Four apparently complete sections of this work survive, which discuss courage, humanity, repentance, and nobility.[45] An especially difficult textual problem is whether this book originally also contained a section on piety.[46]

De praemiis et poenis (*On Rewards and Punishments*). Having presented the creation, the unwritten laws, and the written laws in both the summary forms and the specific ordinances, Philo

44 Morris, 'Philo', p. 851, soundly suggests that Philo divided his discussion between *De specialibus legibus* 4 and *De virtutibus* in order to have books of a uniform length.

45 Although only one manuscript ('S' in PCW) presents these four sections in this order, the basic integrity and sequence are guaranteed by Clement of Alexandria's use of them in this same order; see J. R. Royse, 'The Text of Philo's *De virtutibus*', *StPhAnn* 18 (2006), pp. 80–1.

46 This is indicated by the title of the book in some manuscripts, and three fragments are ascribed to such a work in the *Sacra parallela*. See Colson, PLCL VIII, pp. xiii–xiv with note b, and my discussion of this work in 'The Text of Philo's *De virtutibus*', pp. 81–94.

completes the 'Exposition' by turning to what awaits the good and the bad. First we learn of the rewards given to individuals (Enos, Enoch, and Noah; Abraham, Isaac, and Jacob; Moses), and to the family of Jacob. Then the treatise turns to the punishments given to Cain and Korah and his followers, but is interrupted by a lacuna. When the text resumes (*Praem.* 79), Philo discusses the blessings and then the curses, as found especially in Lev 26 and Deut 28.

These last six books (*De specialibus legibus* 1–4, *De virtutibus*, *De praemiis*) have an especially complex manuscript tradition. Indeed, the different discussions of the various special laws and of the individual virtues have had bewilderingly different textual histories. The currently accepted text (as presented in the standard edition of L. Cohn and P. Wendland) is basically a construction by Cohn, but many problems remain. The structure and extent of *De virtutibus* are especially problematic. What may have happened (but this is far from certain) is that Philo himself introduced subtitles into these separate books to mark the separate sections.[47] And then during the textual transmission some scribes copied these sections more or less independently of other sections within the same book as sub-treatises. Subsequently, other scribes or editors attempted to organize these sections in some coherent way, thus adding to the confusion. In any case, Cohn arranged what is found in the manuscripts into a coherent series of books, utilizing Philo's own comments on the structure of this series, the divisions within the manuscripts, and the principle of the standard length of an ancient scroll (= a 'book').

V. APOLOGETIC AND HISTORICAL WORKS

If the 'Exposition of the Law' reveals that Philo did address himself to broader circles of readers, his apologetic and historical works go even further, and reveal him as an advocate of Judaism and of the Jewish people in its social and political struggles of the day. Indeed, these works may have been intended for a primarily Gentile readership. Philo employs a variety of literary forms in these works, and in general they make up a less homogeneous group. These writings have also suffered greater damages in the course of their transmission, and this has made it more difficult to ascertain what Philo's grander objectives may have been.

De vita Mosis (*On the Life of Moses*) 1–2. An extended discussion of Moses as the prophet, priest, and lawgiver in two books. This

---

47 Already Eusebius, *Hist. eccl.* 2.18.5, cites *De victimis* (= *Spec.* 1.162–256) as one of the works of Philo, as Cohn, 'Einteilung', p. 411, notes.

discussion fits chronologically (and rather naturally, it seems) between *De Josepho* and *De decalogo*, and editions include them in that position. However, as noted in the previous section, despite the evident close connection between these two books and the 'Exposition', the differences in style make clear that they are not properly part of it.[48] The current consensus is that *De vita Mosis* belongs among the apologetic and historical works, although it certainly differs from the other works included here in its concentration on events of the distant past. Moses is presented as superior to other lawgivers, chiefly because of his knowledge of God; he is the true philosopher.

Apologia pro Judaeis / *Hypothetica*. Eusebius, *Hist. eccl.* 2.18.6, cites as a work of Philo 'the treatise composed by him *On the Jews* (= *Peri Ioudaiōn*)'. And in his *Praeparatio evangelica* 8.11.1–18, he quotes a discussion of the contemporary sect of the Essenes as from the *Apology for the Jews* (*hē hyper Ioudaiōn apologia*). It seems likely that some confusion has occurred here, due either to Eusebius or later copyists, and that this extract in fact comes from the work that he also called *On the Jews*. Moreover, a little earlier (*Praep. ev.* 8.6.1–7.20), Eusebius quotes three extracts as from 'the first book of the work which he entitled *Hypothetica*, where, while speaking in defence of the Jews (*hyper Ioudaiōn*) as against' their accusers, he says as follows ...' (8.5.11). And these extracts indeed display Philo's intention to respond to various calumnies against the Jews, which could well occupy more than one book. The title *Hypothetica* bears no relation to any work of Philo that is otherwise mentioned by Eusebius or anyone else, but the subsequent phrase suggests that Eusebius is giving an alternative designation of the book that he cites later as the *Apology for the Jews*. Thus, there is general agreement that Eusebius provides four extracts from this one work, which would seem to have consisted of at least two books.[49] However, it remains obscure what the title *Hypothetica* might mean.[50] At any rate, what is preserved here is meant to serve Philo's apologetic interests in showing the superiority of the way of life and the thought of the Jews.

48 Cf. Cohn, 'Einteilung', pp. 409–10, 417; Morris, 'Philo', pp. 854–5.
49 See Cohn, 'Einteilung', pp. 418–19; Morris, 'Philo', pp. 866–8.
50 See the extended discussion by Massebieau, 'Le classement', pp. 57–9, as well as Morris, 'Philo', pp. 866–7. For a survey of issues related to the *Hypothetica*, see G. Sterling, 'Philo and the Logic of Apologetics: An Analysis of the *Hypothetica*', *SBLSP* 1990, pp. 412–30.

De vita contemplativa (*On the Contemplative Life*). This work
survives in a fragmentary form (it seems much too short to have
formed an original book by itself), and has generated a vast literature.[51] Philo describes a group of 'disciples of Moses' (*Contempl.* 63),
called the Therapeutae, who had retired to an isolated area near
Alexandria in order to follow a life of study and contemplation.
The work was extensively quoted by Eusebius as testifying to the
existence of early Christian converts near Alexandria (*Hist. eccl.*
2.16–17). While this view was frequently held by later Church
writers and by later scholars, the implausibility of such a description by Philo became evident. But then many scholars argued
that the work must be a forgery by a later Christian writer, who
wanted to present Philo as praising early Christians. However,
this view has been decisively refuted. Apart from the manuscript
evidence, which presents the work as one of Philo's, the language
and style are unmistakably Philonic. Thus, current scholarship is
unanimous in holding that this work is Philo's own description
of a sect of Jews. But there is little agreement beyond that. A few
have held that the work is a completely fictitious delineation of
what Philo views as an ideal theoretical life.[52] But others note that
it seems unlikely that Philo would have localized a fictional community so precisely, and so close to Alexandria, where it would
be evident to all that there was no such community. What we
most likely have, then, is a description of an actual group of Jews,
perhaps with idealized traits. But who were these Jews? There
are similarities with the Essenes, but there are also crucial differences. In fact, in the opening words of the treatise, Philo contrasts
the Essenes (as he has elsewhere described) and the Therapeutae:
the Essenes lead a practical life of work while the Therapeutae
live a theoretical life of study and contemplation. Of course, one
may doubt the accuracy of Philo's report (or of his information, if
he did not have first-hand knowledge), and there is no agreement
among scholars concerning what relation there might have been

51 See the recent study by J. E. Taylor, *Jewish Women Philosophers of First-
Century Alexandria: Philo's 'Therapeutae' Reconsidered* (Oxford 2003),
and P. Graffigna's annotated edition of Filone d'Alessandria, *La vita contemplativa* (Genova 1992), which contains references to earlier editions and
a bibliography. Of earlier literature, especially important is I. Heinemann,
s.v. 'Therapeutai', *PRE* II.5.2 (1934), cols. 2321–46.
52 See, for example, T. Engberg-Pedersen, 'Philo's *De Vita Contemplativa* as a
Philosopher's Dream', *JSJ* 30 (1999), pp. 40–64, who calls the description a
'utopian fantasy done for a serious purpose' (p. 43).

between the Essenes and the Therapeutae.[53] Furthermore, as is often noted, many small Jewish sects could have arisen and disappeared without attracting the attention of Greek and Latin writers. Thus, it may well be that the Therapeutae were an isolated group, with no connection to the Essenes, who have left no trace beyond this one work of Philo.

As detailed in the previous chapter, Philo was actively engaged in the contemporary political affairs involving the Jewish community in Alexandria, especially in relation to the anti-Jewish riots that took place in 38 CE and the events that followed. For after the violence, Philo went on an embassy to Rome as the leader of the Jewish delegation, in order to plead the cause of the community. Two of his extant works give detailed, and often first-hand reports of these events.

> *In Flaccum (Flaccus).* Philo describes various episodes in the conflicts between Jews and Greeks in Alexandria, centering on the activities and fate of Flaccus, who was the prefect of Alexandria and Egypt from ca. 32 CE.[54] As Philo tells it, political intrigues led Flaccus to feel threatened when Gaius (Caligula) became emperor in 37 CE, and he thus agreed to support the anti-Jewish Greek party in Alexandria in their opposition to the Jews if they in turn would support him from any antagonism from Gaius. The ensuing riots and outrages directed against the Jews (including attacks on their homes and synagogues) are vividly recounted. But Flaccus eventually met his downfall (for reasons that are not clear), as he was arrested and condemned to execution by Gaius.
>
> *Legatio ad Gaium (Embassy to Gaius).* Philo narrates the circumstances that led to the embassy of Jewish leaders to Rome in 38/39 CE.[55] The continuing tensions between the Jewish and Greek residents of Alexandria led the Jewish leaders to send a delegation to Rome. Philo, as an 'old man' (*Legat.* 1: the fixed point for discussions of the dates of Philo's life), thus played a leading role representing the Jews of Alexandria before the emperor. Although Gaius proved to be unreceptive to the Jewish petition,

---

53 For a summary of the key issues, see Schürer et al., *History*, II (1979), pp. 591–7.

54 There are two editions of this text with extensive commentary: one by H. Box (London 1939), and one by P. W. van der Horst (Leiden 2003).

55 For the date, see above, ch. 1, p. 12. There is also an edition of this text with commentary by E. M. Smallwood (Leiden 1970²). In the introduction, pp. 3–36, one may find a full history of the conflicts between Jews and Greeks in Alexandria.

no decision was made, and the *Legatio* ends with the Jewish delegation waiting in Rome. In fact, Gaius was assassinated in early 41 CE, and his successor, Claudius, was more receptive to the Jewish side in Alexandria, as shown by the famous letter to the Alexandrians (= *CPJ* II, no. 153). These events lie outside the *Legatio* proper, although it is possible that Philo and his associates remained in Rome to press their case with Claudius. The last words of the *Legatio* (§ 373) promise a 'palinode', which would presumably, as scholars have suggested, have given an account of the death of Gaius and the shift in policy by Claudius.[56]

Both of these books serve apologetic purposes by emphasizing the justice of the Jewish cause and the immorality of their opponents. And it has been suggested that the *In Flaccum* and the *Legatio* could have been written for Claudius and other Romans.[57]

Philo's historical works were originally parts of a wider series. Eusebius states that Philo wrote five books concerning 'what happened to the Jews in the time of Gaius', and his further description seems plausibly to include both *In Flaccum* and *Legatio ad Gaium* (*Hist. eccl.* 2.5.1). And elsewhere Eusebius refers to Philo's 'description of the impiety of Gaius, which he entitled, with fitting irony, *Concerning Virtues* (*Peri aretōn*)' (*Hist. eccl.* 2.18.8). Finally, he also mentions *Peri aretōn* as a work that described the vicissitudes of the Jews under Gaius (*Hist. eccl.* 2.6.3). One can thus reasonably infer that Eusebius knew five books entitled *Peri aretōn*, of which *Legatio ad Gaium* and *In Flaccum* are two. And in three manuscripts *Legatio ad Gaium* is called the 'first book of the virtues'. But what might this overall title mean, and what were the other three books?

S. Reiter, who edited *In Flaccum* and *Legatio ad Gaium* for the Cohn–Wendland edition, asserted that in the overall title 'virtues' (*aretai*) had not been used in an ironic sense, as Eusebius thought, but referred to demonstrations of power, miraculous acts, performed by God for the deliverance of the Jewish people. But this meaning could hardly be clear unless 'of God' (*theou*) were added, and so Reiter postulates that this word was lost in the archetype of our manuscripts.[58]

---

56 See Smallwood in her edition, pp. 324–5. The meaning of the word *palinōdia* is unclear here.
57 See Taylor, *Jewish Women Philosophers*, pp. 39–41.
58 'APETH und der Titel von Philos Legatio', in Ἐπιτύμβιον *Heinrich Swoboda dargebracht* (Reichenberg 1927), pp. 228–37. Reiter also notes that the title without *theou* would be even more striking since Philo wrote another book with *Peri aretōn* in the title, namely *De virtutibus*, where however the word *aretē* obviously has its usual ethical meaning.

As to the missing books, at the beginning of *In Flaccum*, Philo refers to his previous account of a persecution of the Jews by Sejanus, the commander of the praetorian guards who was very influential during the reign of Tiberius. It is possible that the account of Sejanus' persecution was in a preceding book. Similarly, we have seen that at the end of the *Legatio* Philo promises a 'palinode'. This could also allude to an additional book. To complicate the picture, however, the title of *De vita contemplativa* in most manuscripts includes the words 'the fourth book concerning the virtues'. The problems of reconstructing the layout of the work are very involved, and various configurations of the five books have been proposed. Unfortunately, we cannot go into greater detail in this context.[59]

VI. PHILOSOPHICAL WORKS

Several of Philo's works are devoted to problems that were treated by Greek philosophers. In these works Philo refers rarely, if at all, to biblical and Jewish teachings, although his characteristic views do emerge. The philosophical works also reveal Philo's gifts and versatility as a writer, for he employs a number of different genres: diatribe; *thesis*; dialogue. Regrettably this particular group of Philonic writings has also suffered much in transmission, probably because the contents of such works did not have as much interest for the Christian scribes who preserved Philo's works as did his exegetical works. In any case, of the philosophical works, one has been preserved intact in Greek (*Quod omnis probus*), another has been partially preserved in Greek (*De aeternitate mundi*), two have been preserved in Armenian (*De providentia, De animalibus*), and one has been completely lost (the companion to *Quod omnis probus*). The details are as follows:

> *Quod omnis probus liber sit* (*Every Good Man Is Free*). Here Philo presents a typical philosophical diatribe on the Stoic 'paradox' that all good men are free. True freedom is internal, and does not depend on external circumstances. Treatments of this same theme are found in a number of contemporary or near contemporary sources: Cicero (*Parad.* 5); Horace (*Sat.* 2.7); Dio Chrysosotom (*Orr.* 14–15); Epictetus (*Diatr.* 4.1). Philo develops the theme by means of arguments (§§ 21–61), as well as by

---

59 For surveys of the various proposals and recent discussion, see Smallwood in her edition of the *Legatio*, pp. 36–43; Morris, 'Philo', pp. 859–64; Taylor, *Jewish Women Philosophers*, pp. 31–46.

means of examples (§§ 62–136). Among the latter he cites the life
of the Essenes (§§ 75–91).

[Lost companion to *Quod omnis probus*: *Quod omnis malus servus
sit* (*Every Bad Man Is a Slave*). Philo tells us that he wrote such
a book (*Prob.* 1), and in fact it is listed by Eusebius (*Hist. eccl.*
2.18.6). This work would have considered the Stoic 'paradox' that
all bad men are slaves, in a way that must have been similar to
what we now have in the previous work.]

De aeternitate mundi (*On the Eternity of the World*). This book is
also striking for its almost total lack of reference to the Bible or to
Jewish thought, dealing rather with the philosophical issue of the
eternity (or, more precisely, the incorruptibility) of the world.[60]
The work's authenticity had been often disputed, but the major
modern editors have accepted it as Philonic. D. T. Runia's careful
analysis shows that this work belongs to the genre of philosophical literature known as *thesis*, in which an introduction stating
the problem to be considered is followed by two sets of arguments
presenting opposing viewpoints on the issue.[61] What we now
have are: an introduction (§§ 1–19), in which the problem of the
imperishability of the cosmos is stated; the first set of arguments
(§§ 21–149), supporting the view that the cosmos is uncreated and
indestructible; and a transitional statement (§ 150), referring to
the second set of arguments. The treatise ends at this point, however, and the second set of arguments has been lost. These lost
arguments would presumably have supported the view that the
cosmos is created and indestructible, and thus would represent
Philo's actual view. However, we could expect that Philo would
do more than make a quick appeal to biblical passages to support
that view, and thus that this lost second set of arguments might
be more or less of the same length as the existing first set. Because
De aeternitate mundi is already adequately long for a Philonic
book, I would suggest that the second set was contained in a separate book, which has been entirely lost.[62]

60 The only exception is *Aet.* 19, where Philo cites Moses as preceding Hesiod
    in the view that the world is created and imperishable. It is certainly pos-
    sible that more such references occurred in the lost portion of the work.
    However, this one citation gives Moses and the references to Genesis no
    greater status than various other authorities that Philo quotes.
61 'Philo's De aeternitate mundi: The Problem of Its Interpretation', *VC* 35
    (1981), pp. 105–51.
62 The loss of an entirely separate book is a common phenomenon. It of course
    would have been helpful if Philo had indicated more clearly that an entire
    book was planned. However, Philo seems never to make explicit that a book

As a second group of philosophical works we may consider the two dialogues that have been preserved in Armenian, which were first published by J.B. Aucher.[63] Philosophical dialogues are best known from Plato, of course, and we may have here another aspect of Plato's pervasive influence on Philo. But the dialogue form was also used by Aristotle (in now lost works), Cicero, Plutarch, and others. These two works by Philo are notable for their strictly philosophical content; there is no reference at all to the Bible or to Jewish teachings.[64] Rather, these dialogues reveal the depth to which Philo had absorbed and adopted for himself the ideas of Stoicism. Indeed, both texts provided source material to H. von Arnim when he put together his collection of Stoic sources.[65] Nevertheless, it has struck scholars that these works are at least consistent with Jewish teaching (as interpreted by Philo), and thus may still serve an apologetic purpose.[66] The two dialogues are:

> *De providentia* (*On Providence*) 1–2. Philo investigates the role
> of divine providence in the world.[67] From book 2, extensive
> excerpts, amounting to about one-quarter of the book, are cited
> by Eusebius in his *Praeparatio evangelica*. It is curious, however,
> that in *Hist. eccl.* 2.18.6, he cites *De providentia* as being extant
> in (only) one book. It seems likely therefore that he did not know
> of book 1 of *De providentia*. It is also to be noted that in the
> Armenian version, book 1 seems to have undergone some kind of
> abridgment, since it does not retain the original dialogue form.[68]
> The importance of the concept of divine providence emerged first
> in Stoicism, and Chrysippus, as well as Philo's slightly younger
> contemporary Seneca, wrote works with the title *On Providence*.
> Opposition to the idea of providence came from many circles:
> Peripatetic, Epicurean, and Neo-Academic. In the *De providentia*,
> Philo defends providence, and his apostate nephew Alexander

   is to follow, whereas he often makes explicit that a book has preceded (see
   my 'Philo's Division', pp. 62–4).

63 Philo Judaeus, *Sermones tres hactenus inediti* (Venice 1822). For a survey,
   see A. Terian, 'A Critical Introduction to Philo's Dialogues', *ANRW* II.21.1
   (1984), pp. 272–94.

64 However, we do find in *Prov.* 2.107 the only reference in Philo's works to
   his visiting Jerusalem. But even this is brought in to inform us of the status
   accorded to doves.

65 *Stoicorum veterum fragmenta* (= *SVF*), I–IV (Leipzig 1903–1924).

66 See Terian, 'Critical Introduction', p. 293.

67 On the topic in general, see P. Frick, *Divine Providence in Philo of
   Alexandria* (Tübingen 1999).

68 See Terian, 'Critical Introduction', p. 275 with n. 7

opposes it.[69] The primary themes that come under discussion are the cosmos, its creation and governance, and theodicy.

De animalibus (Alexander or Concerning Whether Irrational Animals Have Reason). Eusebius, *Hist. eccl.* 2.18.6, preserves the full title of this work, but other than that, only a few brief fragments in Greek have come down to us.[70] In *De animalibus* Philo takes up a theme closely related to that of divine providence. For the Stoics argued that man had a unique position in the world based on his possession, with God, of *logos* or reason. The Neo-Academics denied that man alone possessed *logos*, and argued that animals also had a share in it. In this dialogue, Philo is in conversation with Lysimachus, the nephew of Alexander and his own great nephew. A treatise of Alexander is read in which he sustains the view that animals have reason. Philo then argues for the opposite position. This topic was of continuing philosophical interest, as is shown by the fact that Plutarch wrote on this subject as well (*De sollertia animalium; Bruta animalia ratione uti*).

VII. ADDITIONAL LOST WORKS AND FRAGMENTS

De Numeris (On Numbers)

Philo refers explicitly to this work in *De vita Mosis* 2.115 (see also *QG* 4.110, 151; *QE* 2.87). In all his writings he displays an interest, doubtless a result of the influence of Pythagoreanism, in the special meanings of the numbers found in the biblical text. For example, it is not simply accidental that the creation of the world is said to have taken six days; rather, the number six is cited because it is a perfect number (it is the sum of its divisors: $1 + 2 + 3 = 6$; see *Opif.* 13). Philo appeals to other characteristics of numbers, especially in the *Quaestiones*. Such comments express Philo's belief that even the smallest, apparently irrelevant, details of the sacred text are divinely inspired and worthy of interpretation. What appears to be a fragment of this otherwise lost work has been preserved in Armenian.[71]

---

69 On the historical Tiberius Julius Alexander, see above, ch. 1, pp. 13–14.

70 For the text, translation, and commentary, see A. Terian's edition of Philo Alexandrinus, *De animalibus* (Chico, CA 1981).

71 This excerpt has been edited, translated, and discussed by A. Terian, 'A Philonic Fragment on the Decad', in Greenspahn et al., *Nourished with Peace*, pp. 173–82.

Fragments

There are more than a hundred Greek fragments, consisting usually of a few lines, that are ascribed to Philo in some source or another, but that cannot be placed within the extant works in Greek, Armenian, or Latin. Some of these may be spurious (see the following section), but many, perhaps most of them, may derive from the lost works or portions of works that have been noted above. Indeed, on occasion there is some feature of vocabulary or style that confirms that the fragment is genuinely Philonic.[72]

VIII SPURIOUS WORKS

While substantial portions of Philo's genuine works have perished, works from other sources have been assigned to him in both ancient and modern times.[73] Notable among these are two treatises extant only in Armenian, *De Jona* (*On Jonah*) and *De Sampsone* (*On Sampson*), which seem to be Jewish Hellenistic synagogue sermons, and the Latin *Liber antiquitatum biblicarum* (*Book of Biblical Antiquities*), an originally Hebrew work that may be assigned to the genre of 're-written Bible'.[74] Moreover, there are also several scores of Greek fragments that have been incorrectly assigned to Philo.[75] Unfortunately, we can hardly hope that all these puzzles will ever be resolved, for there are many lost works from antiquity, and an unidentified Greek text may, in principle, derive from any of them.

IX THE CHRONOLOGY OF PHILO'S WORKS

Two works, *In Flaccum* and *Legatio ad Gaium*, can be dated after the well-known events that they describe, and were thus written toward the end of Philo's life. But most of his works contain no such references, and

72 See J.R. Royse, 'Reverse Indexes to Philonic Texts in the Printed Florilegia and Collections of Fragments', *StPhAnn* 5 (1993), pp. 156–79, which includes 124 unidentified texts. Three of those have now been shown to be spurious; see Royse, 'Three More Spurious Fragments of Philo', *StPhAnn* 17 (2005), pp. 95–8.
73 See J.R. Royse, *The Spurious Texts of Philo of Alexandria: A Study of Textual Transmission and Corruption with Indexes to the Major Collections of Greek Fragments* (Leiden 1991), pp. 134–47.
74 For the sermons extant in Armenian, see F. Siegert, *Drei hellenistisch–jüdische Predigten*, I–II (Tübingen 1988–1992), and for the Latin work, see H. Jacobson, *A Commentary on Pseudo-Philo's Liber antiquitatum biblicarum*, I–II (Leiden 1996).
75 See my *Spurious Texts*, pp. 59–133.

attempts to fix a chronological sequence have been very controversial.[76] One sort of evidence that has been frequently utilized is the occasional cross-references in Philo's works to his earlier discussions of certain issues. For example, from a variety of references to it, A. Terian infers that Philo's lost work *De numeris* is the earliest of Philo's works.[77] We also find comments that are (or may be) relevant to the sequence of the great exegetical series. Cohn took the view that the most certain result concerning chronology was that the *Quaestiones* were written after the *Allegorical Commentary*, whereas Terian has argued forcefully that the sequence was *Quaestiones, Allegorical Commentary*, 'Exposition'.[78] However, the interpretation of the evidence is not always as straightforward as we might like.

At *Sobr.* 52, Philo refers to his having stated earlier that the name 'Shem' means 'good'. This would seem to refer to *QG* 1.88 and 2.79, although some scholars have held that the reference is to a lost treatise of the *Allegorical Commentary*.[79] Similarly, at *Sacr.* 51, Philo says that in earlier books he explained what is meant by a 'tiller of the soil', as found at Gen 4:2. This might be taken as referring to *Agr.* 21, which, however, comes after *Sacr.* 51 in the *Allegorical Commentary*. Perhaps, more plausibly, it refers to the discussions at *QG* 1.59 and 2.66.[80] Alternatively, though, one might think that Philo gave such an explanation when he discussed Gen 3:23 in the lost fourth book of the *Legum allegoriae*.[81] And there is an important piece of evidence that appears to

76 See, for example, the overviews by Cohn, 'Einteilung', pp. 426–35, and Morris, 'Philo', pp. 841–4. A completely different approach is taken by L. Massebieau and É. Bréhier, 'Essai sur la chronologie de la vie et des oeuvres de Philon', *Revue de l'histoire des religions* 53 (1906), pp. 25–64, 164–85, 267–89, who attempt to correlate, often very precisely, the works with events in history and in Philo's life; see the overview at p. 289.

77 'A Philonic Fragment', p. 182. In contrast, Massebieau and Bréhier, 'Essai', pp. 284–5, observe that Philo refers to this work at *QG* 4.110 and 4.151, but has extensive discussions of numbers at *QG* 2.5 and 3.56, and thus conclude that the lost treatise on numbers was written between books 3 and 4 of *QG*.

78 Cohn, 'Einteilung', pp. 431–2; Terian, 'Priority'; cf. his later article, 'Back to Creation' (in which he employs arguments of a broader character).

79 Terian, 'Priority', pp. 40–1, cites this as 'overwhelming evidence for the priority of the *Quaestiones*'. But he notes that M. Adler, PCH V, p. 93 n. 4, who was followed by Colson, PLCL III, p. 471 n. c, ascribed the reference to Philo's comment on Gen 9:23 in a missing book of the *Allegorical Commentary*.

80 See Terian, 'Priority', pp. 38–40.

81 See Cohn, 'Einteilung', p. 430, and D.T. Runia, 'Secondary Texts in Philo's *Quaestiones*', in Hay, *Both Literal and Allegorical*, pp. 71–2.

show that the *Quaestiones* are later than (at least some books of) the *Allegorical Commentary*. At *QG* 1.55 Philo states that he has already referred to the two 'highest principles' of Mosaic discourse as found in Num 23:19 and Deut 8:5. Indeed, besides *QG* 1.55, Philo relates these two verses at *QG* 2.54, *Sacr.* 94 and 101, *Deus* 53–4 and 69, *Somn.* 1.237, and in an unlocated fragment assigned to the (now missing) fourth book of *Legum allegoriae*.[82]

A few passages have been cited to show that the *Allegorical Commentary* preceded the 'Exposition'. At *Decal.* 101 Philo refers to his earlier allegorical treatment of the creation in six days, as is in fact found in *Leg.* 1.2–4, 20. At *Sacr.* 136 Philo seems to refer to a future discussion of sacrifices, as we now have in *Spec.* 1.212–19. And at *Somn.* 1.168, Philo seems to refer to the future *De Abrahamo*.[83]

Other types of considerations have sometimes been advanced. For instance, Cohn argued that the *Quaestiones* and the *Allegorical Commentary* give the impression that they were written when Philo's thoughts were devoted exclusively to interpreting the scriptural text, whereas the words of *Spec.* 3.1–6, in which Philo describes how he was pulled down from philosophical leisure into political cares, were written during a time of political unrest. Cohn concludes that the last books of the 'Exposition' were written during the time of Caligula, while the *Quaestiones*, the *Allegorical Commentary*, and the first books of the 'Exposition' belong to an earlier time.[84]

The dating of the philosophical works has also been controversial. Scholars have often asserted that these works were written by Philo early in his career, and perhaps even as academic exercises, before he turned to his characteristic exegetical works.[85] However, such a chronology faces many problems, in particular with the two dialogues preserved in Armenian. In fact, there are some textual clues that seem to show that *De animalibus* (at least) belongs to the end of Philo's life. At

---

82 On the fragment, see my *Spurious Texts*, p. 9, and Petit in her edition of the Greek fragments of the *Quaestiones*, p. 54 n. d. Note that of all these passages, *QG* 1.55 is the only one where Philo says that he has discussed these matters elsewhere. Moreover, in our extant *Quaestiones in Genesim* there seems to be no discussion that Philo could be referring to at *QG* 1.55, and there also does not seem to be any lacuna in the text prior to that point. The only conclusion seems to be that Philo is referring there to some discussion outside of the *Quaestiones in Genesim*, and indeed to the discussions in the *Allegorical Commentary* cited above.

83 See Cohn, 'Einteilung', p. 432.

84 'Einteilung', pp. 433–4; see, on the other hand, the comments of Colson, PLCL VII, pp. 631–2.

85 See Terian, 'Critical Introduction', pp. 275–6 with n. 12.

§ 27 there appears to be a reference to a celebration by Germanicus that can be dated to 12 CE. Yet more significant is Alexander's comment at § 54 ('When I went on an embassy to Rome'), which probably indicates that Alexander must have taken part in the embassy to Gaius (the subject of *Legatio ad Gaium*) in 38/39 CE.[86] Thus the dramatic setting of *De animalibus*, and hence the work itself, must be dated after 40. Because *De providentia* is similar in format and style, it should likely be dated to the same general period, that is, late in Philo's life.[87]

X. THE TRANSMISSION OF THE PHILONIC CORPUS

It is quite uncertain how Philo's works were transmitted through the crucial first few centuries, but it appears that they were known only within a fairly narrow stream of tradition. One must remember that Jewish culture in Alexandria was virtually extinguished after the revolt of 115–117 CE. Indeed, Philo's writings passed at some point into the hands of Christians, by whom he was considered to be virtually, if not actually, a Christian.[88] Clement of Alexandria is familiar with Philo's writings in the late second century CE, as is his successor, Origen, in the third century. Therefore, the Philonic writings had somehow been preserved, and apparently became the property of what is known as the Catechetical school in Alexandria.[89] When Origen moved to Caesarea in 233, he took a collection of Philonic writings with him, and this collection formed a portion of the library there, where they were utilized by the Church historian, Eusebius. In fact, Eusebius liberally cites many of Philo's works, including some portions that have not been otherwise preserved.[90] Indeed, he could still read in Greek several works that survive (apart from fragments) only in Armenian: six books of *Quaestiones*

---

86 On the two passages in *De animalibus*, see Terian in the introduction to his edition, pp. 30–1.

87 For the later date of the dialogues see already M. Pohlenz, 'Philon von Alexandreia', in his *Kleine Schriften*, I (Hildesheim 1965; this essay from 1942), pp. 308–11.

88 There was an early legend that Philo met Peter in Rome. On this and many other aspects of the reception of Philo by Christians, see D. T. Runia, *Philo in Early Christian Literature: A Survey* (Assen 1993), esp. pp. 3–33, but also the chapters devoted to Clement, Origen, and Eusebius. Furthermore, citations from Philo's works are sometimes said to be from 'Philo the bishop'; see my *Spurious Texts*, pp. 14–15.

89 See A. van den Hoek, 'The "Catechetical" School of Early Christian Alexandria and Its Philonic Heritage', *HThR* 90 (1997), pp. 59–87.

90 See H. J. Lawlor, *Eusebiana* (Oxford 1912), pp. 138–45; A. J. Carriker, *The Library of Eusebius of Caesarea* (Leiden 2003), pp. 164–77.

in Genesim, five books of *Quaestiones in Exodum*, *De providentia* 2, and *De animalibus*. He even cites an excerpt from *QG* 2.62 as well as about one-quarter of *De providentia* 2 (the bulk of the known Greek of *De providentia* 1–2). He also gives an excerpt from *Apologia pro Judaeis*, and another from the *Hypothetica*, apparently one work cited under two names; but in any case the original has otherwise disappeared entirely. Yet we can see from Eusebius' lists that his corpus was much the same as ours; the bulk of the works known to him is what we know as the works of Philo. And the later manuscripts of Philo seem to derive from the copies held in Caesarea.[91]

The principal sources of our knowledge of the text are several scores of Greek manuscripts dating from the tenth to the fourteenth centuries. But the oldest direct witnesses to Philo's works are two papyri from the third century. The first to be discovered was the Coptos Papyrus, published by V. Scheil in 1893, and thus utilized by Cohn and Wendland. This contained originally the continuous text of *De sacrificiis* and *Quis heres*, and has been quite well preserved. Fragments of another third-century codex discovered at Oxyrhynchus have been published in several different places, and preserve portions of *De sacrificiis*, *Legum allegoriae* 1–2, *De ebrietate*, *De posteritate Caini*, *Quod deterius*, and at least one or two lost works.[92]

However, it was not solely within the Greek tradition that the works of Philo had their influence, for, as was learned in the early nineteenth century, a corpus of Philonic works is preserved in ancient Armenian. These works of Philo, along with the Old Testament and New Testament and writings from various early Church Fathers, were translated in a very literal fashion from Greek manuscripts by what is known as the 'Hellenizing school' within early Armenian literature. The translation of Philo belongs to the earliest period of activity of this school, and may thus be dated to the latter part of the sixth century. This translation has been preserved in numerous later manuscripts. What we find there are, in the first place, several works of Philo that are known in Greek: *De vita contemplativa*, *De Abrahamo*, *Legum allegoriae* 1–2, *De specialibus legibus* 1.79–161, 285–345, 3.1–7, *De decalogo*, and *De specialibus legibus* 3.8–64.[93] Here the Armenian provides a valuable textual source,

---

91 As argued most notably by Cohn, PCW I, pp. III–IV.

92 See J.R. Royse, 'The Oxyrhynchus Papyrus of Philo', *Bulletin of the American Society of Papyrologists* 17 (1980), pp. 155–65.

93 I follow here the order of the edition, *P'iloni Hebrayec'woy čark'* [The Works of Philo the Jew] (Venice 1892). Between *De specialibus legibus* 3.1–7 and *De decalogo* appears the fragment of *De numeris*, as edited by Terian, 'A Philonic Fragment'.

and it was utilized in the Cohn–Wendland edition. But, as we have seen above, within the Armenian tradition we also find extensive works that have not survived in Greek: *Quaestiones in Genesim*, *Quaestiones in Exodum*, *De providentia*, and *De animalibus*. Here the continuous text of the Armenian translation provides a faithful version of Philo's thought, and also a context within which one can locate many Greek fragments (especially of the *Quaestiones*) that have been transmitted from antiquity. The Armenian also provides two brief fragments of its own that appear to come from otherwise lost works of Philo, namely *De Deo* and a fragment of *De numeris*. Moreover, attached to these undoubtedly genuine works of Philo are the two pseudo-Philonic sermons, *De Jona* and *De Sampsone*.[94]

Finally, there is a Latin version of Philo from the end of the fourth century, which contains *De vita contemplativa* 1–41, and *Quaestiones in Genesim* 4.154–245, as well as the pseudo-Philonic *Liber antiquitatum biblicarum*.[95]

94   For fuller information on the works preserved in Armenian, see F. Siegert, 'Der armenische Philon', *Zeitschrift für Kirchengeschichte* 100 (1989), pp. 353–69; A. Terian, 'The Armenian Translation of Philo', in C. Zuckerman, *A Repertory of Published Armenian Translations of Classical Texts* (Jerusalem 1995), pp. 36–44.

95   See Cohn, PCW I, pp. L–LII, and F. Petit, ed., *L'ancienne version latine des Questions sur la Genèse de Philon d'Alexandrie*, I–II (Berlin 1973), esp. I, pp. 7–15. Cohn edits the Latin of *De vita contemplativa* in PCW VI, pp. XVIII–XXIX.

3 Biblical Interpretation in Philo

As we have seen from the preceding chapter, the major part of Philo's works, about three-fourths of the surviving corpus, is devoted to the interpretation of Scripture. Both the individual treatises and the structure of the corpus as a whole reveal that Philo had a systematic approach to the biblical text, and that the primary aim of his endeavors as a writer was to present and perfect that approach. Indeed, it was as a biblical commentator that he made his greatest impact on the Greek (and Latin) literature of the following centuries. Eusebius sums up Philo's career in the *Ecclesiastical History* as follows: 'He reached a most sublime level in the study of the divine writings, and he produced a varied and sophisticated exposition of the holy texts' (2.18.1). Of course, Philo was also a philosopher and religious thinker of the utmost significance, but the medium through which he expressed his ideas is scriptural interpretation. Accordingly, it is necessary for anyone who would approach Philo directly, through his own writings, to gain some understanding of how he set about the exegetical task. It is the purpose of this chapter to facilitate this process, by surveying (I) his notions of text and canon and (II) some of the fundamental principles or characteristics of his biblical exegesis, specifically: (1) his conception of the Pentateuch as a literary document, (2) his rationale for the use of the allegorical method, and (3) the primary orientation of his allegorical interpretation.

In general, however, one must keep in mind that Philo stands at the end of a long tradition of Judeo–Hellenistic exegesis. What we know of this tradition is largely derived from what Philo himself says about it. Therefore, after the discussion of the question of text and canon, it will be necessary to consider his position within the tradition, before coming to the principles of exegesis proper.

I. PHILO'S BIBLE: THE GREEK PENTATEUCH

Philo read and studied the Bible not in Hebrew, but in Greek. The Hebrew text of the Torah or Pentateuch had been translated into Greek in Philo's native city of Alexandria about 250 years before his time.

According to the traditional account, which is preserved in a document called the *Letter of Aristeas* and, as well, in Philo's own *De vita Mosis* 2.25–44, the translation was made by seventy-two scholars who came to Alexandria from Jerusalem in the time of King Ptolemy Philadelphus (283–246 BCE). It is therefore called the Septuagint (= LXX), which means 'seventy'.[1] While many of the details of the story have been colored by later embellishment, most scholars accept the claim that the translation of the Pentateuch goes back to the middle of the third century BCE.[2] Over the course of the next 100 to 200 years, the remainder of the biblical books were translated into Greek. Moreover, by the beginning of the second century BCE, Jews were composing literature in Greek in a variety of genres. What all of this means is that in Philo's day, there was a significant body of Jewish literature, including the sacred books, that existed in Greek. In fact, the Hebrew language seems to have fallen into disuse in the Egyptian Diaspora. Judeo–Hellenistic culture in its golden age was, like Greek culture itself, monolingual for the most part.[3] Consequently, it is not surprising that Philo calls Greek 'our language' (*Congr.* 44; cf. *Conf.* 129), and goes so far as to claim that Moses himself had a partially Greek education (*Mos.* 1.23).

The most significant evidence of Philo's reliance on the Greek text of the Bible comes from his own explicit statements. In his account of the origin of the LXX, to which we have just alluded, he says that the Greek text is the equivalent of the Hebrew, thus implying that the use of the Hebrew is unnecessary. This may seem extraordinary for an exegete of his caliber, but the following passage from *De vita Mosis* speaks for itself:

(2.37) The translators, sitting in seclusion and with no one present ... as if possessed, prophesied, in the course of translating, not each one something different, but all of them the same nouns and verbs,[4] as if a prompter were invisibly giving them instructions. (38) Yet who does not know that every language, and

1   In the present essay, the Roman numeral 'LXX' will refer to the text of the Greek translation of the Bible, whereas the word 'Seventy' will refer to the seventy translators as persons.
2   See N. L. Collins, *The Library in Alexandria and the Bible in Greek* (Leiden 2000), pp. 6–7.
3   See V. A. Tcherikover, *CPJ* I, pp. 30–2; S. Schwartz, 'Language, Power and Identity in Ancient Palestine', *Past and Present* 148 (1995), pp. 38–43.
4   This is a phrase that reflects the division of the 'parts of speech' as known from Plato's writings. See Plutarch, *Quaest. Plat.* 10; cf. Quintilian, *Inst.* 1.4.17–20. It therefore indicates, in this passage, *all the words* in the translation, and should not be understood 'literally', as it is by F. Siegert, 'Die Inspiration der Heiligen Schriften: Ein philonisches Votum zu 2 Tim 3,16', in R. Deines and K.-W. Niebuhr (eds.), *Philo und das Neue Testament:*

Greek in particular, is rich in vocabulary, and it is possible to adorn the same thought in many different ways by metaphrasing and paraphrasing,[5] applying [to the thought] different words on different occasions? It is denied that this occurred in the case of the present translation, but words in their proper meanings corresponded to words in their proper meanings, the Greek to the Chaldean (i.e., Hebrew), with the same sense (*eis tauton*), perfectly suited to the external realities intended. (39) Just as, I suppose, in geometry and in dialectic the concepts intended (*sēmainomena*) do not allow for variety in expression, but rather the expression used at the outset remains unchanged, in the same way, so it appears, even these translators came up with words which fit the external realities, and which would alone or better than others make perfectly clear that which was intended. (40) There is a very clear proof of this. If Chaldeans learn the Greek language and Greeks Chaldean, and they read both texts, that is, the Chaldean and the translation, they are filled with wonder and revere them as sisters, or rather as one and the same, both in matters (*pragmata*) and in words, calling the authors not translators but hierophants and prophets. To them it was granted to be in communion, through sheer thought, with the most pure spirit of Moses.[6]

These paragraphs have been discussed many times, and the general import of Philo's position has often been recognized.[7] However, the precise significance of Philo's words needs to be more fully elucidated. For by examining the passage within the context of ancient translation theory and that of Stoic linguistic ideas, we can get a sense of the full extent of Philo's faith in the LXX. An important step in this direction has been taken by S. Brock, who has considered Philo's statements against the background of the ancient distinction between sophisticated 'literary translators' and *interpretes*, mechanical and unlearned hacktranslators. The former had an orientation toward the 'target text' or readers and rendered the overall *sense* of the original, while the latter

---

Wechselseitige Wahrnehmungen (Tübingen 2004), pp. 211, 213. Cf. also the use of the phrase in Ps.-Archytas, *De sapientia*, fr. 2 Thesleff.

5   It is difficult to say whether Philo is using these two words with different senses. They are often synonymous. See esp. Aelius Theon, *Progymnasmata* 15 (Armenian), available in French translation in the edition of M. Patillon and G. Bolgnesi (Paris 1997), p. 107. For a distinction in later Byzantine sources, see E. Stemplinger, *Das Plagiat in der griechischen Literatur* (Leipzig 1912), p. 118 n. 2.

6   The translation is my own.

7   In the present context, references must be limited to the following: K. Otte, *Das Sprachverständnis bei Philo von Alexandrien* (Tübingen 1968), pp. 36–43; Y. Amir, 'Authority and Interpretation of Scripture in the Writings of Philo', in M.J. Mulder (ed.), *Mikra: Text, Translation, Reading and Interpretation of the Hebrew Bible in Ancient Judaism and Early Christianity* (Assen/Maastricht 1988), pp. 440–4.

had an orientation toward the source text and rendered each *word*. The distinction is attested in Cicero, but probably goes back to even earlier times. Primarily on the basis of the prophetic powers that Philo attributes to the translators in § 37 and § 40, Brock thinks that Philo considered the Seventy to be 'literary translators', who had their minds on the finished product.[8]

If we turn to §§ 38–40, however, where Philo gives his detailed view of the mechanics of the translation technique, we will emerge with more complete results. In § 38, Philo appears to rule out the notion that literary, sense-for-sense translation is involved. For he raises the possibility of literary adornment, of paraphrastic translation (= expressing the same sense with different words),[9] and perhaps also of variety in translation, only to deny that they took place. And we know that all three of these – adornment, paraphrase, and variation (= Greek, *poikilia*, in § 39) – belonged to literary translation.[10] In addition, Philo goes on to state that the translation was word-for-word, when he says that the words corresponded to the words, the Greek to the Chaldean (§ 38). Yet he also says, in the same sentence, that the words corresponded with each other 'to the same effect' or 'with the same sense'. This is the most likely meaning of the two words *eis tauton*, even though they are often omitted or rendered weakly in translation.[11] To get a clear idea of what Philo is really saying, it is necessary to point out that his discussion here presupposes the distinction among words (*onomata*), which signify or are signifiers (*sēmainonta*), concepts, which are signified (*sēmainomena*, *dēloumena*), and things or external realities (*pragmata*). This distinction is Stoic, and it is attested elsewhere in the

8   'Aspects of Translation Technique in Antiquity', *GRBS* 20 (1979), pp. 69–72; 'To Revise or Not to Revise: Attitudes to Jewish Bible Translation', in G. J. Brooke and B. Lindars (eds.), *Septuagint, Scrolls and Cognate Writings* (Atlanta 1992), p. 320; cf. 326.

9   For the definition of paraphrase, see Theon, *Progymnasmata* 15 (Armenian), ed. Patillon and Bolognesi, p. 108. For a similar formulation in Greek, see John of Sardis, *Comm. in Aphth. Progym.*, ed. H. Rabe (Leipzig 1928), pp. 64–5.

10   For adornment, see Quintilian, *Inst.* 10.5.3; Jerome, *Ep.* 57.5.5; cf. H. Marti, *Übersetzer der Augustin-Zeit* (Munich 1974), pp. 86–7, 91. For paraphrastic translation, see Marti, *Übersetzer*, p. 72. As he points out, Quintilian, *Inst.* 10.5.4–11, discusses paraphrase immediately after discussing (literary) translation. So also Pliny, *Ep.* 7.9.2–6, where the two are not even clearly distinguished. For *varietas*, cf. F. Stummer, *Einführung in die lateinische Bibel* (Paderborn 1928), pp. 114–15.

11   So in F. H. Colson, PLCL VI, p. 469; H. St John Thackeray, in his translation of the *Letter of Aristeas* (London 1917), p. 99; R. Arnaldez et al., PAPM 22, p. 209.

Philonic corpus.[12] In the present passage Philo is primarily focused on the difference between the 'words' on the one hand and the 'concepts' and 'external realities' on the other, so he does not maintain a sharp differentiation between the latter two.[13] However, the basic scheme is present, and therefore, when, in § 40, Philo says that the version has been admired as one and the same 'in both matters and in words', he sums up his view in Stoic terms: The translation is both sense-for-sense and word-for-word!

That is not all, however. The Greek term *kyria*, which I have translated as 'words in their proper meanings', really means words in their non-metaphorical or etymological senses.[14] So what Philo is saying is that the Seventy produced a version in which there was not only word-for-word correspondence, but word-for-word correspondence at the non-metaphorical and even etymological level. This is a translation technique that is normally associated with Aquila, who produced another Greek version of the Bible around 135 CE. In fact, Origen characterizes Aquila as 'he who was zealous to translate *kyriōtata*', that is, 'by the use of *kyria*', or etymological equivalents.[15] Here again, Philo's statement may be explained as an explicit denial that the Seventy undertook a 'literary translation', for in paraphrase in any case, one technique was to substitute words in their proper sense for words in their metaphorical sense and vice versa.[16] In addition, although he does not state this so clearly, Philo appears to think, that rather than 'applying different words on different occasions' (§ 38), the Seventy maintained the same translation equivalents throughout the work. This was because they found words which 'alone or better than others' gave the sense, so there was no need to look for synonyms or variety in translation. This maintenance of the same translation equivalents is again a technique associated with the version of Aquila.[17]

This portrayal of the version of the Seventy is quite astonishing. One could say in Philo's favor, that the translation of the Pentateuch in the LXX might seem like the version of Aquila to someone accustomed to

---

12 See Sextus Empiricus, *Math.* 8.11–12 (= *SVF* II.133); Philo, *Leg.* 2.15. For a brief explanation of the Stoic theory, see M. Harl in her edition of Origène, *Philocalie, 1–20* (Paris 1983 = SC 302), pp. 275–9.

13 For a similar semi-assimilation of *sēmainomena* and *pragmata*, cf. Origen, *Cels.* 1.25.

14 For this concept, see C. K. Callanan, *Die Sprachbeschreibung bei Aristophanes von Byzanz* (Göttingen 1987), pp. 92–4.

15 *Philocalia* 14.1; cf. *Sel. Ps.* 4:5 (PG 12.1144a).

16 For this, see Theon, *Progymnasmata* 15 (Armenian), ed. Patillon and Bolgnesi, p. 108. Cf. Quintilian, *Inst.* 10.5.8.

17 See F. Field, ed., *Origenis Hexapla* (Oxford 1875), I, p. XX.

'literary translations'. However, to describe it as a kind of perfect Aquila, or a Platonic Idea of Aquila, as it were, is simply irreconcilable with the reality of the differences between the Hebrew and the LXX texts as they existed in Philo's time. Indeed, it is precisely because of such differences that the so-called predecessors of Aquila began to produce more literalist and 'Aquila-like' versions at the time of Philo or earlier.[18]

The more general assertion by Philo that the version of the Seventy was both word-for-word and sense-for-sense is even more extraordinary. For it is irreconcilable with translation theory as known to the ancients. As would be stated eloquently by Jerome, the translator's dilemma was the necessity to choose between one method and the other.[19] And the basic quandary is already implicit in Cicero's distinction between literary and word-for-word translation. Moreover, we have the testimony of the grandson of Ben Sira about the Greek Bible itself, including the Pentateuch. This man, who translated his grandfather's work into Greek while in Egypt, about a century before the birth of Philo, states that what is said in Hebrew 'does not have the same meaning' when rendered into another language.[20]

How, then, do we explain such an audacious view of the reliability of the LXX on the part of Philo? Well, he does say at the end of § 40 that the translation was inspired. And the miracle of a translation that was both word-for-word and sense-for-sense would be as great if not greater than the one accepted by the Church Fathers, that the 70 or 72 translators all produced the same version while working independently from each other.[21] In addition, it is likely that, as K. Otte has suggested, Philo understood the whole issue on a deeper level, as related to the ability of

18   The best evidence for this phenomenon is the Greek version of the Minor Prophets found near the Dead Sea, known by the siglum 8HevXIIgr. For a brief statement of its significance, see Brock, 'To Revise', p. 303.
19   See esp. the preface to his translation of Eusebius' *Chronicon*, ed. R. Helm (Berlin 1984³ = GCS 47), p. 2, which he quotes in *Ep.* 57.5.6–7. See also *Ep.* 84.12.
20   Sir, prol. 21–6; cf. Iamblichus, *De myst.* 7.5.
21   Scholars have often claimed that this version of events is also implicit in *Mos.* 2.37, where Philo says '[the translators] prophesied not each one something different, but all of them the same nouns and verbs.' A. Wasserstein, *The Legend of the Septuagint* (Cambridge 2006), pp. 44–5, has recently disputed this, and would attempt to understand the latter phrase with reference to what Philo says about the use of the same translation equivalents in §§ 38, 39. But this idea has no more to commend it than the more traditional interpretation. However that may be, one should note that Philo's own idea of a word-for-word and a sense-for-sense correspondence between the Hebrew text and the translation has been absorbed into the tradition about the agreement between the 70 or 72 separated translators. See Nicetas

the translators to match 'being' with language. Unfortunately we cannot pursue this matter in detail here.[22] However, the final sentence from the passage quoted above may give us a clue as to how Philo conceived of it: 'To them (the translators) it was granted to be in communion, through sheer thought, with the most pure spirit of Moses.' This may indicate, and so I have translated, that the Seventy were able to communicate with Moses (in his capacity as ever-living author of the Pentateuch) by means of *logos endiathetos* (internal speech), rather than *logos prophorikos* (enunicated, articulated speech). That is, they communicated with him, or with his ideas, on a thought-to-thought basis, without the use of verbal language. This would not be surprising, for we know that the Greek gods, and the angels of the Judeo–Christian tradition, communicated with each other in this fashion and not with their voices.[23] Accordingly, Philo may have believed that if the translators had achieved, perhaps by a kind of divine grace, a thought-to-thought communion with the Mosaic legacy, it would hardly have been difficult for them to reproduce it on the mere level of enunciated language. To put all of this more simply, we might say that Philo did have a very clear theory about how the Greek could match the Hebrew, and was able to express it in a sophisticated fashion based on Stoic teachings. If that theory did not fit with the actual state of disparity between the Greek and Hebrew texts, or with the more widespread ideas about translation as they came to be articulated by the masters of that art, it was just a matter of detail.

But whatever the explanation is for Philo's view, it allows us to understand quite easily why he treats the Greek text as if it were the original, and dispenses with the Hebrew. For in actual practice, in the course of his exegesis, Philo does not cite the Hebrew text, nor does he reveal a knowledge of Hebrew philology, except in one area – that of proper names. He will often give the Greek translation of a Hebrew proper name, and offer some interpretation connected with it. But his apparent competence in this area is easier to explain by assuming that he relied on pre-existing *onomastica*, or lists of biblical names with their corresponding Greek translation, although the lists that have come down to

of Heraclea, *Catena in Pss.*, praef. (PG 69.700c-d); cf. Ps.-Justin, *Cohortatio* 13.3; Cyril of Jerusalem, *Catech.* 4.34.

22 See Otte, *Sprachverständnis*, pp. 38–43; D. Winston, 'Aspects of Philo's Linguistic Theory', *StPhAnn* 3 (1991), pp. 117–22.

23 See Heraclitus the Allegorist, *All.* 72.17; Elias, *In Porph. Isag.*, ed. A. Busse (Berlin 1900 = Commentaria in Aristotelem Graeca 18.1), p. 95.29–30. For Philo's reliance on the concepts of *logos endiathetos* and *logos prophorikos*, see A. Kamesar, 'The *Logos Endiathetos* and the *Logos Prophorikos* in Allegorical Interpretation: Philo of Alexandria and the D-Scholia to the *Iliad*', *GRBS* 44 (2004), pp. 163–81.

us must be dated to a later era.²⁴ This was common practice among later Greek and Latin biblical scholars who had no knowledge of Hebrew. It should also be pointed out that this recourse to Hebrew knowledge was necessitated by the appearance of the Hebrew names in transliteration in the Greek text. It does not imply a reading of the Hebrew Bible, and indirectly confirms the fact that Philo felt no need for the latter. In short, his neglect of the Hebrew text in practice is in complete accord with his theory.

As far as canon is concerned, Philo's Bible is essentially the Torah, or Pentateuch. He comments on Pentateuchal books only, and even his citations of books from other parts of the conventional canon are proportionately few. This is most easily seen from an examination of the most complete index of Philo's biblical citations and allusions.²⁵ In this volume, the citations and allusions from non-Pentateuchal books take up about three pages, whereas those from the Pentateuch take up more than sixty-one. This circumstance probably reflects older Alexandrian tradition, as attested in Aristobulus and in the *Letter of Aristeas*, according to which the Pentateuch enjoyed an authority that was higher and more sharply distinguished from that of the other biblical books than was the case in Palestinian Judaism.²⁶ The survival of this older tradition in Philo may be attributable simply to more conservative tendencies surviving in the periphery. That is, Philo's nearly exclusive focus on the Pentateuch would be a kind of remnant of what E. Rivkin has called 'Aaronide Pentateuchalism', dominant in Palestine before the time of the Maccabean revolt.²⁷ In Palestine, this same tendency seems to have survived among the Sadducees, at least to some degree.²⁸

II. PHILO'S EXEGESIS

Philo within the Context of Tradition

Philo's name is nearly synonymous with allegorical exegesis, and it can hardly be denied that this is his more characteristic mode of

24 See D. Rokeah, 'A New Onomasticon Fragment from Oxyrhynchus and Philo's Etymologies', *JThS* 19 (1968), pp. 70–82 (the fragment was later published as *P Oxy.* 2745).
25 J. Allenbach et al. (eds.), *Biblia patristica: Supplément: Philon d'Alexandrie* (Paris 1982).
26 See N. Walter, *Der Thoraausleger Aristobulos* (Berlin 1964), pp. 31–2.
27 *A Hidden Revolution* (Nashville 1978), pp. 191–207, cf. 328–9.
28 See K. Budde, *Der Kanon des Alten Testaments* (Giessen 1900), pp. 42–3; E. Schürer et al., *The History of the Jewish People in the Age of Jesus Christ (175 B.C. – A.D. 135)*, II (Edinburgh 1979), pp. 408–9.

biblical interpretation. Indeed, the great Byzantine scholar Photius, in his general assessment of Philo in the *Bibliotheca*, codex 105, claims that allegorical interpretation in the Church had its origin in Philo's work. This claim is probably based on Antiochene sources, and in particular, Theodore of Mopsuestia (ca. 350–428). In a fragment of his *Treatise against the Allegorists*, preserved in Syriac translation, Theodore identifies Philo as the master of Origen, the most influential allegorical exegete of Christian antiquity.[29] However, in the course of his discussion, Theodore makes some other comments about Philo's exegetical stance that are quite revealing. He indicates that Philo, in contrast with Origen (or so it is implied), 'was nevertheless obliged to respect' *a part* of the historical sense of the text, because he felt shame in the face of, among other things, 'the truth, which was maintained among the people of his nation'. In these brief remarks, 'the blessed Interpreter' seems to have hit the mark in a colorful fashion. For he was apparently able to recognize a basic circumstance that emerges from the Philonic corpus itself as well as from comparative data. Philo was a man of tradition, and inherited from his predecessors various non-allegorical approaches to Scripture that permeate all through his writings. At the same time, however, as Theodore recognizes, Philo's own tendencies are allegoristic in the extreme. Consequently, in attempting to provide a brief summary of Philo's exegetical principles, it is necessary to take into account both the more traditional elements and those elements that are more characteristically Philonic.

II.1. Conception of the Pentateuch as a Literary Text

It has been said that in the Hellenistic period, Jewish study of the Torah in general was influenced or stimulated by the study of Homer among the Greeks.[30] This would be true especially with regard to Judeo–Hellenistic biblical interpretation, which, according to many, is closely modeled on Greek interpretation of the Homeric poems.[31] The educational role

29 For this important text, see L. Van Rompay's translation of Théodore de Mopsueste, *Fragments syriaques du Commentaire des Psaumes* (Louvain 1982 = Corpus Scriptorum Christianorum Orientalium 436), pp. 14–16. For a brief exposition, see D. T. Runia, *Philo in Early Christian Literature: A Survey* (Assen 1993), pp. 265–70.

30 See esp. E. J. Bickerman, *The Jews in the Greek Age* (Cambridge, MA 1988), p. 171; S. P. Brock, 'The Phenomenon of the Septuagint', in M. A. Beek et al., *The Witness of Tradition* (Leiden 1972 = Oudtestamentische Studiën 17), p. 16.

31 See F. Siegert, *Drei hellenistisch-jüdische Predigten*, II, *Kommentar* (Tübingen 1992), pp. 57–8; C. Blönnigen, *Der griechische Ursprung der*

that was played by both texts is cited, as is the extensive use of the allegorical method in interpreting them. These assessments are no doubt accurate, but require some further qualification. Concerning Judeo–Hellenistic biblical interpretation, one might say more broadly that it is based on Greek approaches to literary texts, among which the Homeric poems held the pre-eminent position. However, the notion that the Jewish Hellenistic interpreters themselves aimed at establishing an equivalence between the Pentateuch and Homer is not in accord with their more explicit statements on the nature of the Pentateuch as a literary text.

Such statements do exist, and they come from Philo himself. In two key passages, he discusses the literary format of the Pentateuch. In *De praemiis et poenis* 1–2, he indicates that it is made up of three genres or parts: *cosmopoietic* or cosmological, historical, and legislative. In a parallel passage, *De vita Mosis* 2.46–7, there is a slight variation, and Philo speaks of two genres or parts, a historical and a legislative. But the former he subdivides into two parts, the cosmological and the genealogical. The genealogical part, according to Philo, concerns the punishment of the wicked and the rewarding of the pious. It corresponds to the historical genre as described in *De praemiis*, and no doubt refers to the narrative segments of the Pentateuch, especially in the Book of Genesis (cf. *Abr.* 1, 3–6). The cosmological and legislative genres refer, of course, respectively, to the account of creation at the beginning of Genesis and the legal material in the remaining four books of the Pentateuch. Essentially, then, the structure of the Pentateuch is tripartite. There is a parallel to this idea in Josephus, who appears to allude to 'natural philosophy', 'deeds' (*praxeis* = the subject matter of history according to standard Greek terminology), and 'laws' as the components of Moses' work (*AJ* 1.18). The parallel probably allows us to conclude that we are dealing with a traditional Judeo–Hellenistic scheme, and not one that originated with Philo himself.

The true significance of this description of the Pentateuch emerges only when we compare it to a certain Hellenistic theory of literary genres, and take into account a claim made by a number of Judeo–Hellenistic authors, namely, that the Pentateuch contains no myth.[32] The Hellenistic theory in question is attested in a rather obscure source,

jüdisch–hellenistischen Allegorese und ihre Rezeption in der alexandrinischen Patristik (Frankfurt am Main 1992), pp. 57–8; G. Stemberger, in C. Dohmen and Stemberger, *Hermeneutik der Jüdischen Bibel und des Alten Testaments* (Stuttgart 1996), p. 64.

32   The following three paragraphs are based on A. Kamesar, 'The Literary Genres of the Pentateuch as Seen from the Greek Perspective: The Testimony of

the so-called *Tractatus Coislinianus*. This is a treatise or rather the outline of a treatise on literary criticism, which appears to be connected with the Peripatetic school. According to the *Tractatus*, all poetry may be divided into two main categories, non-mimetic and mimetic. This terminology is derived from Aristotle's *Poetics*. In that work, Aristotle made the claim that the essential component of poetry was *mimesis*, or imitation, and he excluded non-mimetic poetry from his discussions. Mimesis, in the way it is understood by Aristotle, denotes the fictional component of poetry. Thus, mimetic poetry includes works of epic, tragedy, and comedy, whereas non-mimetic poetry is didactic poetry. Didactic poetry is that which provides instruction to the reader on a given subject, and it is non-fictional. Much of it was written in the pre-classical age, and it again became popular in Hellenistic times. The *Tractatus* would 'correct' Aristotle, and make room for the didactic genres excluded by him. The didactic or non-mimetic genres identified in the *Tractatus* are the 'historical' and the 'paideutic' or educational, the latter of which is in turn divided into 'morally instructive' and 'theoretical'. From another source, Diomedes the grammarian, we learn that the historical rubric includes 'genealogy', whereas the theoretical genre comprises works about nature and cosmology. There is, then, a correspondence between the non-mimetic genres described in the *Tractatus* and the genres of the Pentateuch as described by Philo, for the cosmological genre of Philo corresponds to the 'theoretical' of the *Tractatus*, the historical/genealogical genre corresponds to the 'historical', and the legislative genre corresponds to the 'morally instructive'. This last correspondence is quite reasonable, because Jewish Hellenistic writers tend to portray the Mosaic legislation as a code of ethics. In general, that the Pentateuch, a prose work, might be compared to poetic works is not surprising, because in Hellenistic times it was thought that poetry was the more ancient literary mode, and categories concerning poetry could have been applied to ancient works in general.

We also read in Philo's *De opificio mundi* 1–2 the programmatic statement that Moses refrains from the use of 'myth' (*mythos*) in the Pentateuch. Josephus makes similar statements, and the same notion is also discernible in the fragments of Aristobulus and in the *Letter of Aristeas*.[33] Now, the term *mythos*, in Hellenistic literary criticism, is often a functional equivalent of the term *mimesis* as used in the Aristotelian tradition. Therefore, when the Judeo–Hellenistic writers say there is no myth in the Pentateuch, they are saying, in Aristotelian

Philo of Alexandria', *StPhAnn* 9 (1997), pp. 143–89, to which I refer for further detail and full bibliographic references.

33 Josephus, *AJ* 1.15, 22–3; Aristobulus, fr. 2: 10.1–2; *Let. Aris.* 168.

terms, that it is non-mimetic. For this reason, the fact that the genres of the Pentateuch specifically named by Philo line up with the non-mimetic genres given in the *Tractatus Coislinianus* is no mere casual coincidence. Rather, the correspondence of genres, when understood in light of the statement about the absence of myth from the Pentateuch, allows us to determine that Philo and his Judeo–Hellenistic predecessors developed a highly sophisticated literary critical theory. They believed that Moses employed genres that were similar to those of ancient Greek didactic literature. At least from the standpoint of an overall classification, the Pentateuch was non-mythical and non-fictional, even if it included the occasional mythical component.

This conception of the Pentateuch, as found in Philo's writings, is quite significant. For it indicates that in the view of Jewish Hellenistic scholars, the Pentateuch was not to be regarded as parallel to the Homeric poems. Rather, it was to be seen in the light of Greek didactic works. In all probability, the originators of the theory had literature from the archaic period in mind, such as semi-philosophical cosmological poems and semi-historical genealogies. For it is works of this sort that are mentioned by Diomedes the grammarian, and that have titles related to the genres of the Pentateuch named by Philo. Accordingly, the theory may entail the view or concession that the Pentateuch is, with all its wisdom, a work that contains primitive elements. This is not entirely surprising, because there was in Judeo–Hellenistic circles in the earlier period, a greater willingness to accept a kind of parity between Judaism and Hellenism than there was in the Roman age.

Of course, if the Pentateuch was viewed as something similar to Greek didactic literature, there would be no need to interpret it allegorically. For didactic literature, by its very nature, teaches its lessons in a straightforward literal fashion. Rather, it was the mythical literature that was the object of allegorical interpretation. As Theodore of Mopsuestia puts it, the pagans invented allegorical interpretation 'to do away with', or, from their own perspective, 'heal' the myths.[34] In other words, they sought to discover the meaning or 'lesson' of the myth by means of the allegorical method. The Pentateuch, on the other hand, as a non-mythical, didactic work by virtue of its genre(s), would not be interpreted allegorically. That is, the theory of genres that may be reconstructed on the basis of Philo's statements would entail a literalistic kind of exegesis. For all its sophistication, this theory would not be an unnatural development. For it would simply reflect a highly

---

34 Theodore, *Treatise against the Allegorists*, tr. Van Rompay, p. 11. For the expression 'healing of myth', see just below, p. 79.

Hellenized version of Aaronide 'Pentateuchal literalism' as it is attested in Palestine before the time of the Maccabean revolt.[35]

The structure and basic approach of Philo's own 'Exposition of the Law' is to a large degree in tune with this vision of the Pentateuch.[36] The *De opificio mundi* covers the cosmological part; the *Lives* of the patriarchs mentioned in *De Josepho* 1, but not all extant, cover the 'genealogical' part; and in *De decalogo* and *De specialibus legibus*, the legislative part is treated. While allegorical interpretation is not absent from these treatises, it does not determine their structure and plays a secondary role. It would appear, therefore, that the 'Exposition' represents the more traditionalist position. This suggestion would be in accord with the widely held view that this series of treatises is *exoteric*; that is, written for a wider circle of readers.[37]

II.2. *Rationale for Allegorical Interpretation*

A rather different approach to the Pentateuch is found in Philo's *esoteric* treatises, known under the comprehensive title of *Allegories of the Laws* or *Allegorical Commentary*. These treatises make up a verse-by-verse commentary on much of the 'historical' part of the Pentateuch. Here Philo's basic assumptions about the nature of the Pentateuch appear to be at odds with the vision that emerges from the presentation of its genres. For in the *Allegorical Commentary*, as we would expect from the title, he constantly insists on the need for allegorical interpretation, while often rejecting the literal meaning. To the extent that this insistence is out of tune with the idea of the Pentateuch as a didactic work in its literal sense, it is probably best to attribute it to Philo's own tendencies, which diverge here from, or go beyond, traditional teaching. However, the relentless focus on the allegorical meaning does not always disallow or discredit the literal sense. In fact, Philo's more common procedure, although this is best said of his exegetical works as a whole, is to piece together the allegorical meaning while accepting also the literal, even if he will nearly always give prime place to the former. In this way, we see that the conception of the Pentateuch that he inherited is to some extent maintained. But let us elaborate on these observations with reference to specifics.

---

35 For 'Pentateuchal literalism' in Ben Sira, see E. Rivkin's 'Prolegomenon' to the reprint of W. O. E. Oesterley et al. (eds.), *Judaism and Christianity*, I–III (New York 1969), pp. XXVII–XXVIII; see also his *Hidden Revolution*, pp. 203–4.

36 For the designation 'Exposition of the Law', see above, ch. 2, p. 45.

37 On this, see J. Morris in Schürer et al., *History*, III.2 (1986), p. 840.

In his *Allegorical Commentary*, Philo often indicates that allegorical interpretation is necessary, because the text does not make sense if it is understood literally; that is, it contains some difficulty that prevents us from accepting it in its literal meaning. J. Pépin, who has studied and collected the relevant passages, and has looked at the alleged bases for allegorical interpretation in pagan and Christian authors, is wont to characterize such difficulties in a blanket fashion as 'absurdities'.[38] This term, however, reflects the perspective of a somewhat later age. In the case of Philo and the Hellenistic period, it is perhaps preferable to follow the terminology of Aristotle's *Poetics*, ch. 25, and the subsequent tradition represented in the Homeric scholia, and refer more generally to 'problems' (*problēmata*) of the text or 'faults' (*epitimēmata*). A passage could appear to be 'absurd', but also 'impossible', 'morally noxious', or 'in contradiction' (with another passage).[39] A better general designation for these sorts of difficulties is probably *defectus litterae*, that is, defect(s) of the letter.[40] For when the 'letter' or literal sense is defective, one cannot accept it. Thus, for example, when one reads that God planted a Garden (Gen 2:8), or that Adam and his wife hid themselves from God (Gen 3:8), or that Potiphar, a eunuch, had a wife (Gen 39:1, 7), Philo believes that one must reject the literal sense in favor of the allegorical.[41]

In employing this procedure, Philo was following the theory and practice of Greek allegorical interpretation. As is well known, allegorical interpretation was developed by Greek scholars primarily as a means of explaining mythical narratives, especially those contained in the Homeric poems and in Hesiod.[42] This is in line with what has been said in the previous paragraph. For if because of the 'problems' noted, and especially 'impossibilities', a narrative could not be accepted in its literal sense, it could be called *myth*, since this was defined essentially as that

---

38 *La tradition de l'allégorie de Philon d'Alexandrie à Dante*, II (Paris 1987), pp. 167–86, cf. 70–5; and for Philo, 34–40.
39 For the specific Greek terminology, see A. Gudeman, s.v. Λύσεις, PRE I.13.2 (1927), cols. 2516–17.
40 This phrase is employed by M. Simonetti. See his *Lettera e/o allegoria* (Rome 1985), pp. 17–18 with n. 20; cf. 14–15.
41 *Plant.* 32–6; *Leg.* 3.4, 236. Other examples of this type may be found in Pépin, *La tradition*, pp. 35–40.
42 Cf. Theodore of Mospuestia, loc. cit. (n. 34). The allegorical interpretation of the 'historical data' (*historoumena*) in the poems was the exception. See Eustathius, *Commentarii ad Iliadem*, prooem., ed. M. van der Valk, I (Leiden 1971), p. 4.

which cannot happen and did not.[43] And Philo's own perspective is not too far removed from this. For he himself will sometimes acknowledge that a narrative in the Pentateuch is mythical, if it is taken exclusively in the literal sense. If, however, an allegorical meaning underlies the narrative, the myth is only apparent. As he phrases it when discussing the talking serpent in Gen 3 and the serpent of bronze in Num 21, 'when the allegorical interpretation is given, the mythical element vanishes away, and the truth emerges in full clarity' (*Agr.* 96–7; cf. *Leg.* 2.19ff.).

In putting forward this notion, and in formulating it is this way, Philo is again following Greek models. For in some currents of contemporary Greek interpretation, allegorical exegesis was viewed as a 'healing of myth', a *therapeia mythōn*. This particular phrase is known from Byzantine sources, but the idea is much older, as similar terminology is found in Heraclitus the Allegorist.[44] This author is probably an approximate contemporary of Philo, and even if he did live slightly later, he is certainly not dependent on the Jewish author's work. Heraclitus, in contrast to other allegorical interpreters of his era, employs the term 'myth' in what for him is an entirely negative sense. He appears to use the word in its 'Peripatetic' or literary critical sense, according to which 'myth' means just an unusual or scary story, told (usually by poets) for the purpose of entertainment or to cause astonishment and/or fear, not to teach any kind of lesson.[45] Thus, a tale with an underlying moral or philosophical meaning goes beyond mere 'myth'.

Nevertheless, even if Philo follows this usage, he would still be, *de facto*, acknowledging the presence of 'myth-like' material in the Pentateuch. Consequently, Theodore of Mopsuestia would appear to be on the mark when he intimates that Philo, in taking his allegorical interpretation from the Greeks, was indirectly 'mythologizing' the Scriptures. For he was applying to the biblical material a method of interpretation that had been applied to myth.[46] And to this extent, Philo would be rather out of tune with the idea implied in *De praemiis* 1–2 and in *De vita Mosis* 2.46–7, namely, that the Pentateuch in its basic literary format is a non-mythical work made up of didactic genres.

---

43 See Sextus Empiricus, *Math.* 1.263–5; *Schol. in Dion. Thr. Artem grammaticam*, ed. A. Hilgard (Leipzig 1901 = Grammatici Graeci I.3), p. 449; Isidore, *Etym.* 1.44.5.

44 *All.* 6.1, 22.1. For allegorical interpretation as a 'healing of myth', see Eustathius, loc. cit. (n. 42). See also my 'Literary Genres', pp. 168–9.

45 Cf. R. Meijering, *Literary and Rhetorical Theories in Greek Scholia* (Groningen 1987), p. 92.

46 Theodore, *Treatise against the Allegorists*, tr. Van Rompay, p. 15. Cf. A. Kamesar, 'The Bible Comes to the West', in J. F. Rowley (ed.), *Living Traditions of the Bible* (St. Louis 1999), p. 58.

For this idea, needless to say, entails the basic belief that Scripture is something fundamentally different from Greek myth. And it is hard to resist the conclusion that this inconsistency in Philo's own writings is the same disaccord that Theodore identified as existing between Philo himself and the 'truth', which was maintained among Philo's people. For if there was any 'truth' dear to the Antiochenes, it is essentially the same idea – Scripture is on an entirely different plane than Greek myth.

However, there is a second aspect of Philo's allegorical exegesis that is in accord with the concept of the Pentateuch as a non-mythical work. Often, and especially in the *Quaestiones* and in the 'Exposition', Philo will accept both a literal level of meaning and an allegorical level. Indeed, many scholars have recognized that this procedure character-izes Philo's approach and makes it distinct from Greek allegorical inter-pretation.[47] The use of the procedure implies that even where he does not regard the letter as 'defective' or mythological, he still sees the need to provide an allegorical interpretation. Why? In all probability, the answer to this question lies in his conception of the Pentateuch as a divinely inspired, didactic, and even 'super didactic' work, that is, every part of it is inspired and contains divine wisdom. If there are passages that seem either trivial, or even not sufficiently instructive, they must contain some hidden meaning. As Augustine would put it later, one must recognize as figurative 'any passage in divine Scripture which can-not refer, in its literal sense, to ethical rectitude or to doctrinal truth' (*Doctr. chr.* 3.10.14). Philo does not make this criterion as explicit as Augustine does, but he seems to implicitly follow it when he justifies an allegorical interpretation of a passage that is not 'defective' in its literal sense, but simply 'low' (*Leg.* 2.89; the Greek word is *tapeinon*). He also indicates in *Quod deterius potiori insidiari soleat* 13, that if one follows the allegorical method, one will never find anything 'low or unwor-thy of the greatness' of the Scriptures.[48] The assumptions that underlie these directives are well expressed in 2 Timothy 3:16, a passage which no doubt reflects Judeo–Hellenistic thinking: 'All Scripture is inspired by God and is beneficial (*ophelimos*) for teaching, for reproof, for cor-rection and for training in righteousness.' It is the notions expressed in

47   T.H. Tobin, *The Creation of Man: Philo and the History of Interpretation* (Washington, DC 1983), pp. 154–8; P. Carny, 'Dimuyim merkaziyim ba-teoryah ha-allegoristit shel Filon', in M. A. Friedman et al. (eds.), *Teuda*, III, *Studies in Talmudic Literature, in Post Biblical Hebrew, and in Biblical Exegesis* (Tel Aviv 1983), pp. 251–9; 'Ha-yesodot he-hagutiyim shel darsha-nut Filon ha-aleksandroni', *Daat* 14 (1985), pp. 5–19.
48   See P. Heinisch, *Der Einfluss Philos auf die älteste christliche Exegese* (Münster 1908), p. 80; and my forthcoming commentary on *Quod deterius*, § 13.

this verse that explain the need to interpret allegorically passages that are acceptable in their literal sense. The reference to 'benefit' has led scholars to refer to an 'opheleia criterion'.[49]

The term opheleia ('benefit') in a literary critical context is derived from a Greek view or a Greek formulation of matters, but the idea expressed by the term is also Jewish, and certainly the 'opheleia criterion', or perhaps better the pan-scriptural opheleia criterion came to be operative in a Jewish sense. In the Hellenistic period, scholars debated about whether the chief aim or telos of poetry and literature was benefit and instruction (Greek didaskalia) or entertainment (psychagōgia) and pleasure (hēdonē). In general, the Peripatetics and the Alexandrian critics tended to think it was the latter, whereas the Stoics usually thought it was the former. Also common was the view that some writers looked to achieve both objectives. What is important to emphasize in the present context is that even the 'didacticists', that is, those who believed that instruction was the primary aim of literature, for the most part allowed for the fact that even in Homer, the 'educator of Greece', there were 'psychagogic' elements.[50] In other words, they were not all-inclusivists in their didacticism and, allowing for 'psychagogic' intentions on the part of Homer, they did not feel compelled to find a didactic purpose in every line of the Iliad or the Odyssey.

In contrast, Philo explicitly denies that Moses aimed at psychagōgia 'without benefit' (Mos. 2.48). And the passage from 2 Timothy reveals that the Judeo–Hellenistic view of the Bible was not simply didacticist but pan-didacticist, and that this may be attributed to a belief in a more pervasive form of inspiration: 'All Scripture (pasa graphē) is inspired by God and is beneficial for teaching (didaskalia).' This notion was pressed to extremes, and it was believed that every detail of the biblical text conveyed some sort of meaningful lesson. As Philo himself puts it, Moses 'does not employ any superfluous word' (Fug. 54; cf. Leg. 3.147). The same principle finds expression in both rabbinic and patristic interpretation of Scripture, and it is not derived from Greek exegesis.[51]

Now, it may be conceded that we find glimmerings of a more general pan-didacticism on the part of some enthusiasts of Homer in the early

---

49   Esp. Simonetti, Lettera, pp. 79 with n. 43, 146–7.
50   See A. Kamesar, 'Philo, the Presence of "Paideutic" Myth in the Pentateuch, and the "Principles" or Kephalaia of Mosaic Discourse', StPhAnn 10 (1998), pp. 58–9. To the sources there cited, add Maximus of Tyre, Or. 4.5–6.
51   See R.P.C. Hanson, Allegory and Event (London 1959), pp. 24–5, 46; Heinisch, Einfluss, pp. 81–2 (the example he cites from 'the Stoics' is not based on the same principle); cf. L. Goppelt, Typos (Gütersloh 1939), p. 58 n. 7.

imperial age.[52] But the phenomenon is isolated, and its fuller form is a later development. And in any case, it is most unlikely that Greek influence is at the root of the pan-didacticism we find in Judeo–Hellenistic literature. For Philo knows of and even advocates himself a didacticism with regard to Greek epic, but it is only that of the moderate type. In *De providentia* 2.40–1, he praises the great wisdom of Homer and Hesiod, which can be appreciated by employing allegorical interpretation, but he also allows for 'error' on their part. That is, his position is similar to that of most Stoicizing interpreters in the late Hellenistic and early imperial age, who may have claimed that Homer was a very wise teacher, but did not claim that he had no concern to entertain or 'does not err'.

It may be concluded therefore that pan-didacticism is a more characteristically Jewish feature of Philonic exegesis. Consequently, the same may be said of the pan-scriptural *opheleia* criterion as an underlying motive for allegorical exegesis. However, what concerns us at the moment is not only the role of the pan-scriptural *opheleia* criterion as a stimulus to allegorism, but the fact that it allows us to account for the double nature of Philonic exegesis. For, as we have noted above, it is Philo's recognition of both the literal and the allegorical meaning of the text at the same time that distinguishes his exegesis from that of contemporary pagan allegorical interpretation. The latter was motivated primarily by a 'defective' literal text. But the pan-scriptural *opheleia* criterion is in force even when the letter is not defective, so the literal meaning remains valid, and the allegorical meaning is added to it.

Furthermore, the pan-scriptural *opheleia* criterion came to be operative not only breadthwise but also depthwise. That is, the notion of benefit or *opheleia* became multi-leveled, as expectations for biblical wisdom became greater and greater. In his discussion of Augustine, H.-I. Marrou has put it as follows: 'nothing in the Bible has no benefit, or *even minor benefit*'.[53] This same assumption was made by Philo. On the one hand, the literal sense of a text might appear to be trivial, or 'low', that is, without any didactic value whatsoever, and, as we have seen above, in such cases it is necessary to employ allegorical interpretation. However, there are other cases where Philo recognizes that the literal sense has

---

52   See Dio Chrysostom, *Or.* 53.11 (the passage is probably slightly hyperbolic in countering Plato's claim cited in § 2). Whether Heraclitus the Allegorist may be called a pan-didacticist is difficult to say. See *All.* 1.3, 3.2, 26.2 (transmitted text), with my 'Philo & Paideutic Myth', pp. 59–60. In *All.* 76.4, speaking more generally, he does acknowledge that one derives pleasure from Homer.

53   *Saint Augustin et la fin de la culture antique*⁴, Paris 1958, pp. 479–80; my italics.

value, but only to a certain degree. In these cases he indicates that it is necessary to progress from a literal interpretation of the text to an allegorical one.[54] He implies, therefore, that the literal sense has a didactic import, but not sufficiently so if one wishes to arrive at a truly correct understanding of the text. That Philo applied this reasoning in a generalized way to the Pentateuch as a whole is clear from the fact that he illustrates it with a favorite simile. He compares the literal sense of the text to the body and the allegorical sense to the soul. In his famous critique of the so-called 'extreme allegorizers', a designation for those persons who neglected the literal sense of the law and focused only on the allegorical meaning, Philo urges them to pay heed to the former, just as one takes care of the body as the house of the soul (*Migr.* 89–93). In another passage he attributes the use of the same simile to the Therapeutae, who made up a kind of monastic community living outside Alexandria around Lake Mareotis (*Contempl.* 78). But there he implies that focus on the 'soul' or allegorical meaning of the text is the true aim of the exegete, for it allows one to progress toward a kind of Platonic contemplation of intelligible realities. These remarks about the Therapeutae may suggest that he inherited the general conception from earlier Platonizing exegetes. However, on yet another occasion, Philo describes the literalists as 'micropolitans' or citizens of a small community, whereas those who look also to the allegorical meaning are citizens of the world or cosmopolitans (*Somn.* 1.39). The use of this imagery could point rather to Stoicizing predecessors.[55] Accordingly, the notion of two valid levels of meaning, one literal and one allegorical, both of which convey some form of instruction (*didaskalia*), need not have been originally tied to a Platonistic world view. In any case, that the *opheleia* criterion was operative even when a first level of instruction had been reached at the literal level seems to find confirmation in those keen readers of Philo, Origen and Gregory of Nyssa. Both of these Fathers refer explicitly to the *opheleia* of the biblical text at multiple levels.[56]

We see, then, that there were two different factors that led Philo to interpret the Pentateuch in an allegorical fashion. On the one hand, the apparent 'defects' in the literal sense of the text prompted him to treat the content of the Pentateuch as myth-like in nature. Following

54 See esp. *Conf.* 190; *Abr.* 200, 217.
55 See *SVF* III.336–7 (= Philo, *Opif.* 3, 142–3); and M. Pohlenz, *Die Stoa*, I⁷ (Göttingen 1992), p. 133. In *Opif.* 143, Philo uses the term 'megalopolitans', citizens of a large community, in the sense of 'cosmopolitans'.
56 Origen, *Princ.* 4.2.6; Gregory, *Vit. Mos.* 2.204, 207. On this latter text, cf. the comments of M. Simonetti in his edition of the text (Milan 1984), p. XXIII.

Greek procedure, he is able to 'heal' the myth-like matter by employing the allegorical method. On the other hand, Philo applies the allegorical method even when the literal sense of the text does not appear defective. In these cases, he accepts the literal sense and adds the allegorical one to it. In doing this, he seems to be motivated by what is best called 'pan-scriptural didacticism', a terminology that can be derived from 2 Tim 3:16: 'All Scripture (*pasa graphē*) is inspired by God and is beneficial for teaching (*didaskalia*).' This idea that the *entirety* of the text has a didactic intent seems to be derived from Jewish sources, although it is formulated in terms of Greek views about the aim or *telos* of literature.

These two different foundation points for allegorical interpretation are connected to, or in the case of pan-scriptural didacticism, came to be connected to, two different visions of the Pentateuch as a literary document. The two visions are largely inconsistent with one another, and this has led to no small confusion among readers and scholars of Philo. The appeal to the defects in the literal sense of the text as a basis for allegorical interpretation entails the notion that the Pentateuchal material is a kind of Jewish myth, similar to that contained in Homer and Hesiod. Theodore of Mopsuestia perceived this well, and accused Philo, if we may employ modern terminology, of 'mythologizing' the Scriptures. On the other hand, Philo seems to have inherited from his predecessors the view that the Pentateuch, by virtue of its literary genres, is a didactic non-mythical work. This view may have entailed the concession that it did contain occasional mythical elements, but not to the extent that it should be classified among the fictional genres. According to this conception, the Pentateuch – for all it had to teach – was nevertheless a primitive kind of work, parallel to early Greek didactic poetry. It contained simple lessons about cosmology, ancient history, and law. By the time one reaches the age of Philo, this level of instruction was seen as insufficient, at least in some circles. There developed the expectation that the *didaskalia* of the ancient texts reach a philosophical level of sophistication. It is this phenomenon that explains how the principle of pan-scriptural didacticism came to be operative in Philonic allegorical exegesis. Philo accepted from his predecessors the idea that the Pentateuch, or much of the Pentateuch, even at the literal level, was a didactic work. However, he was willing to accord to the literal sense only the inferior status of 'body'. The 'soul' of the text was its allegorical meaning, a higher or second level of *didaskalia*.[57] The literal sense was for the multitude, whereas the 'hidden' meaning was

---

57   For the specification of 'teaching' as the objective of the allegorical level of the text, when both letter and allegory are under discussion, see *Migr.* 91; *QG* 3.8. Cf. Strabo, *Geogr.* 1.2.7.

available only to the few (*Abr.* 147). Thus, at least in his exoteric works, he will engage in a double exegesis, literal and allegorical. While he may not have been the originator of this approach, he is certainly its most significant theorist and practitioner among Jewish Hellenistic writers. The procedure was to have a long and illustrious history, especially in the patristic age.

II.3. Orientation of Philo's Allegorism: The Human Soul and Its Progress

While in the 'Exposition of the Law' Philo deals with all three parts of the Pentateuch – the cosmological, the historical, and the legislative – in the *Allegorical Commentary* he treats only the historical. It is here, however, that we see the more characteristic form of his allegorical interpretation, and indeed, of his philosophical and spiritual quest. In the *Allegorical Commentary*, as Jerome might have said it, Philo 'unfurls the full sails of his brilliance to the blowing winds and, leaving dry land behind, makes for the open sea'.[58] Although he is, in this work, commenting on the 'historical' part of the Pentateuch, which means primarily the narratives in the Book of Genesis, he has very little interest in these narratives as historical record. In fact, he himself states this explicitly (*Congr.* 44; *Somn.* 1.52). Rather, in his eyes, the historical part of the Pentateuch constitutes an allegorical portrayal of the ethical and spiritual progress of the individual. In Philonic thought, the 'soul' of each person struggles with the body and the passions, in the effort to dominate them and advance toward a state of virtue. This process is conceived according to the model of the 'person who makes ethical progress', the Stoic *prokoptōn*. However, the aim of such a person is not merely the acquisition of virtue. Virtue is linked with an upward movement of the soul (*Her.* 241), and what the Stoics call progress is in Platonic terms a purification or *katharsis*, which allows an individual soul to penetrate the realm of the divine (Plato, *Phaed.* 67a-b). The ultimate objective of that penetration for Philo is vision or contemplation of God.

Philo sees this ethical and spiritual quest represented allegorically in the various *personae* of the Pentateuchal narrative. For him, the biblical *personae* most often represent 'souls', or more precisely, 'minds' or 'dispositions of soul'. For example, according to the most important Philonic scheme, the three patriarchs, Abraham, Isaac, and Jacob, symbolize three 'dispositions of soul', who acquire virtue by learning

---

58   In the *Preface to Origen's Homilies on Ezekiel*, Jerome says this of Origen, specifically of his commentaries as opposed to his other exegetical works.

(Abraham), by nature (Isaac), and by practice (Jacob).[59] Again, Hagar and Sarah are not women, but 'minds', the one which engages in the preliminary studies or liberal arts without moving beyond them, the other the mind which strives for virtue (*Congr.* 180). Other characters can represent more pronounced negative qualities. Cain, for example, symbolizes the 'self-loving' creed (*Sacr.* 3; *Det.* 32), whereas Laban represents the soul of the foolish person that values sense-perceptible objects (*Agr.* 42). In Philo's interpretation, the Pentateuch becomes a tale of the human soul and its vicissitudes and ascent. Modern scholars speak of an 'allegory of the soul', a phrase that can be justified on the basis of Philonic usage (*Praem.* 158). What is striking about this allegory is its systematic structure as it emerges in Philo's works, for Philo employs recurring allegorical equivalencies to put together a more or less systematic elucidation of the Pentateuch as a whole, and not just of individual episodes. S. Sandmel calls Philo's allegorical interpretation 'architectonic', to indicate that there is 'a completed edifice, and that the walls, the roof, and the floor and their component parts have been brought together into a unified structure.' This structure, as he puts it, may be called a 'grand allegory'.[60] Now, the notion of the 'allegory of the soul' itself may be traced back to earlier exegetes, whom Philo himself cites.[61] It is possible, however, that the creation of the overarching structure is Philo's own achievement.[62] What one can say with certainty is that the systematic nature of the allegorical interpretation in the Philonic corpus distinguishes it from other ancient Jewish allegorical exegesis.[63] Comprehensive allegorical readings of the Homeric poems are also absent from contemporary pagan exegesis, at least as far as we can determine, although they do appear in later Neoplatonist interpreters.[64] It may be that Philo and later Neoplatonists were inspired by a common source, perhaps Neopythagorean.

59   For representative sources, see *Abr.* 52–3; *Congr.* 35–6; *Somn.* 1.167–8.
60   *Philo of Alexandria: An Introduction* (New York 1979), pp. 23–4. In calling Philo's allegorical exegesis 'architectonic', Sandmel has no doubt been inspired by Philo himself, who refers to *allēgoria* as a 'wise architect' (*Somn.* 2.8). Cf. Isa 3:3 (LXX).
61   See É. Bréhier, *Les idées philosophiques et religieuses de Philon d'Alexandrie*³ (Paris 1950), pp. 59–61; E Stein, *Die allegorische Exegese des Philo aus Alexandreia* (Giessen 1929), pp. 30–1.
62   See H. Lewy in the introduction to his anthology, Philo, *Philosophical Writings: Selections* (Oxford 1946), pp. 13–14.
63   See Sandmel, loc. cit. (n. 60)
64   See R. Lamberton, 'The Neoplatonists and the Spritiualization of Homer', in Lamberton and J.J. Keaney (eds.), *Homer's Ancient Readers* (Princeton 1992), pp. 124–33.

All of this is not to say that we do not encounter other forms of allegorical interpretation in Philo. The ancients were wont to distinguish 'physical' allegory and 'ethical' allegory. The former refers especially to the figure whereby the gods and their activities represent physical or natural phenomena. The notion of 'ethical' allegory is somewhat more difficult to define. Originally this may have indicated something parallel to physical allegory, according to which divine *personae* symbolize moral states or virtues: Athena stands for wisdom, Aphrodite for desire, etc.[65] However, sometimes ethical allegorism is thought to include what is simply moralistic interpretation, even when the interpretation does not nullify the literal sense.[66] Philo himself employs the distinction between 'physical' and 'ethical' allegory. For example, in discussing Lev 19:24, where it is said that the fruit of the trees will be holy in the fourth year, Philo interprets this number in a double sense. In the physical sense, the number alludes to the four elements from which the world exists, but in the ethical sense, it alludes to the figure of a square, which in turn refers to 'right reason', the source of the virtues.[67] In general, however, there is a tendency in Jewish Hellenistic interpretation to prefer the ethical allegory.[68] That Philo's interpretation of the biblical *personae* as 'dispositions of soul' constitutes a variety of ethical allegorism may be confirmed from the terminology he employs. The word he uses to indicate these 'dispositions' is *tropoi* (*Abr.* 52, 217), and in Plutarch, *De sera numinis vindicata* 6, 551e-f, the word *tropos* is an equivalent of *ēthos* (= 'character', from which, 'ethics').[69]

The allegory of the soul, which stands at the core of Philo's understanding of the intent of the Pentateuchal narrative, despite all the abstract notions that it involves, may not be unrelated to more traditional and conservative forms of Judeo–Hellenistic interpretation. In particular, it may be descended from the view that the Pentateuch is a didactic work in its literal sense, which we have considered above. However, we need to examine that view as it relates to the specifically genealogical or historical part of the Pentateuch. In one key passage, Philo tells us that the historical part of the Pentateuch is 'a recording of lives, good and bad, and the punishments and rewards determined for both, in every

---

65 See J. Pépin, *Mythe et allégorie*[2] (Paris 1976), pp. 97–8
66 See F. Buffière, *Les mythes d'Homère et la pensée grecque* (Paris 1956), pp. 251–391.
67 *Plant.* 119–22. For other passages where Philo refers to the two principal types of allegory, see *Leg.* 1.39, 2.12; *Mos.* 2.96; *QG* 2.12, 3.3.
68 See Stein, *Exegese*, p. 5.
69 This use of the term *tropos* should not be confused with the use of phrases like *tropikai apodoseis* (*Conf.* 190) and *tropikōteron* (*Ios.* 151), when these point to allegorical interpretation more generally. Cf. Stein, *Exegese*, p. 30.

generation' (*Praem.* 2; cf. *Mos.* 2.47). Elsewhere he indicates that the men who have lived righteous lives, whose virtues are 'engraved' in the Scriptures, are to serve as instigation for others to follow a similar path (*Abr.* 4). These statements allow us to conclude that Philo saw history as a set of *exempla*, that is, examples that have prescriptive moral force. This view of history was common in the Hellenistic and early imperial period, and was taught in the schools.[70] Livy, in the introduction to his history, tells his readers that they will find in it good and bad examples: the former to imitate, the latter to avoid (*Ab urbe cond.*, praef. 10). The theme of reward for virtue and punishment for vice, to which Philo alludes, also plays a role in the compendium of *exempla* from Roman and 'foreign' history by Valerius Maximus.[71] In short, the portrayal of the historical component of the Pentateuch as a didactic work, concerned with 'what happened', but also with virtue and vice, is in line with standard Hellenistic ideas about historiography.

Also in tune with those ideas is the particular nature of the Philonic *exempla*. These are not the stories, or events, but the *personae* of the Pentateuch. The use of persons as *exempla*, while it goes back to the sophistic age, came to be very prevalent from the first century BCE onward, in Cynic–Stoic diatribe, and in Jewish and Christian preaching.[72] In the case of Philo and his immediate predecessors, this phenomenon may also be due to the influence of Posidonius. This philosopher, as we know from the testimony of Seneca, put forward a more practical kind of ethical instruction, in addition to theoretical principles. Within that system a certain value was placed on the highlighting of persons who could serve as *exempla*, and be the objects of imitation for those seeking to acquire virtue.[73] Seneca himself draws on Roman history for his *exempla*, Cato the Younger being among his favorites.[74] And we know from another source that Posidonius advocated the use of both positive and negative *exempla*, the former to be imitated, the latter to be shunned.[75] Now, of course we find reference to the ancestors of

---

70 See C. Skidmore, *Practical Ethics for Roman Gentlemen: The Work of Valerius Maximus* (Exeter 1996), pp. 7–12, esp. 11–12; cf. H.-I. Marrou, *Histoire de l'éducation dans l'antiquité*[6] (Paris 1965), pp. 413–14.

71 See *Facta et dicta mem.* 1, praef., and Skidmore, *Practical Ethics*, pp. 66–7, 79–82 (see also Ps.-Dionysius, *Rhet.* 11.2, cited by Skidmore on p. 12).

72 See F. Dornseiff, 'Literarische Verwendungen des Beispiels', *Vorträge der Bibliothek Warburg* 1924–1925, pp. 218–20.

73 See Posidonius, fr. 176 Edelstein–Kidd (= Seneca, *Ep.* 95.65–7), with the comments of Pohlenz, *Stoa*, II[6], p. 120. Cf also Quintilian, *Inst.* 12.2.28–31.

74 *Ep.* 95.69–73. Cf. *Tranq.* 16.1, where Cato is called 'virtutium viva imago'.

75 Clement of Alexandria, *Paed.* 1.2.1–2; see K. Reinhardt, *Poseidonios* (Munich 1921), pp. 56–7. Cf. Seneca, *Ep.* 104.21.

Israel as *exempla* in much other Jewish literature of the Second Temple period.[76] However, what is noteworthy in Philo is the characterization of the historical part of the Pentateuch as a whole as a repository of *exempla*, as explained in the previous paragraph, and the stress on their value for the acquisition of virtue on the part of the individual.[77] These features allow us to determine that the literalistic approach in question, present in Philo's writings, has been inspired by Greek models.

But how does one get from this conception of Pentateuchal history to the allegory of the soul? That is, how are the biblical characters transformed from historical persons who were regarded as ethical models into 'dispositions of soul' or 'minds'? The transformation may be connected with certain Platonistic tendencies that came to be influential in the later part of the Hellenistic period. In the first place, Plato, in *Alcibiades* I, 130c, defined man as 'nothing other than soul'. Probably Plato himself, and certainly those who came after him, took 'soul' in the sense of its rational element, the mind.[78] However, within the Stoa, the notion of the man as soul or mind alone was understood primarily in an ethical sense.[79] In other words, the soul or the mind is the entity that is engaged in the quest and struggle for virtue. This portrayal of the matter is found in Seneca, and is reflected in Philo's allegorical interpretations.[80] It is, consequently, the mind that would constitute the model to be imitated, and indeed, it is precisely this idea that is attested in the fragment of Posidonius to which we have referred in the previous paragraph. The person to be imitated is described as an 'outstanding mind', the characteristics of which one can learn to recognize and transfer to oneself (Seneca, *Ep.* 95.67). This fragment can help us understand how the representation of the biblical *personae* as ethical models could be reshaped, and an 'allegory of the soul' could emerge. This will especially be the case when one takes into account the fact that the definition of the 'true man' as mind was much beloved by Philo (*Plant.* 42; *Fug.* 71; cf. *Prob.* 111).

---

76 See A. Lumpe, s.v. 'Exemplum', *Reallexikon für Antike und Christentum* 6 (1966), cols. 1240–1.
77 Cf. H. Thyen, *Der Stil der jüdisch–hellenistischen Homilie* (Göttingen 1955), pp. 76–7, 111–12.
78 See J. Pépin, *Idées grecques sur l'homme et sur Dieu* (Paris 1971), pp. 73, 79; Cicero, *Somn. Scip.* 26.
79 See Pépin, *Idées grecques*, pp. 128–9.
80 Seneca, *Vit. beat.* 9.3; *Brev.* 20.5 ('profectus animi' = progress of the mind [sc. towards virtue]); *Ep.* 88.20; Philo, *Det.* 5; *Fug.* 202, 213; *QG* 4.137. Cf. the Cynic view as reported by Diogenes Laertius, *Vit. philos.* 6.70, and Plutarch, *Sera* 18, 561a.

There was a second factor, also connected with Platonism, which contributed to the high degree of abstraction inherent in the Philonic 'allegory of the soul'. Platonists were interested in the universal, not the particular. In the field of ethics, they put their focus on the forms or ideas of the virtues like justice, bravery, temperance, etc. The virtue of an individual man was important not so much in its own right, but in so far as it revealed a universal form of virtue. Accordingly, as Philo puts it, when an individual dies, the wise or temperate or brave component in him may die also. However, the wisdom or temperance, or the forms of these, in which the individual had a share, 'have been engraved on the undying nature of the universe', and in accordance with them others will become virtuous in the generations to come (*Det.* 75; cf. *Mut.* 79–80). Thinking of this sort transforms the conception of the biblical *personae* as historical examples. From being *exempla* they become, if we may use the language of Seneca, *exemplars*, existing beyond history.[81] In Greek as well, this transformation was facilitated by terminology. The word *paradeigma* was employed by the rhetoricians in the sense of historical *exemplum*, but the same term was used in Platonic philosophy to indicate the eternal forms or ideas. Philo often uses this and other Platonistic terminology when referring to the biblical *personae*. Both Joseph and Moses put forward their own lives of virtue as 'archetypal pictures or designs' (*graphai archetypoi*) to inspire others to pursue goodness.[82] And in *De vita Mosis* 1.158–9, where the Platonic context is completely apparent, Philo speaks of the life of Moses as a *paradeigma* and a *typos*.[83]

For Philo, that biblical *personae* indicate 'dispositions of soul' or minds is a defining feature of allegory as it is found in the Pentateuch. This is clear from his explicit statements, especially in the work *De Abrahamo*. For here he says that the text in its literal meaning is about the 'man', whereas in its allegorical sense it is about the virtue-loving

81 *Ep.* 95.66 (Posidonius, fr. 176 Edelstein–Kidd, cited above, n. 73). See the note of M. Bellincioni in her edition of Seneca, *Lettere a Lucilio Libro XV: Le lettere 94 e 95* (Brescia 1979), p. 324. See also the conclusion of the same letter (§ 73), where it is indicated that the example of virtue exhibited by Aelius Tubero would last forever, with Bellincioni, pp. 329–30.

82 *Jos.* 87; *Virt.* 51, 70. Cf. also *Prob.* 62, a possible allusion to the Jewish patriarchs, as described in *Abr.* 4–6, among others. For a parallel to these passages, see also Seneca's references to his own life in his dying hour, as recorded by Tacitus, *Ann.* 15.62.1 (the sense is clarified in 15.63.1), although the Platonistic coloring is less manifest.

83 On Philo's representation of Moses-as-exemplum in Platonic terms, see A.C. Geljon, *Philonic Exegesis in Gregory of Nyssa's De vita Moysis* (Providence 2002), pp. 67–8.

soul (§§ 68, 88). But that he also regarded this feature of Mosaic writing as tied closely to the notion that the 'dispositions of soul' were general and universal is clear from an interpretation of Gen 24:61. In this passage it is said that the servant of Isaac, on a mission to fetch his master's future wife, 'took Rebecca and departed'. Interpreting Rebecca according to the meaning of her name as 'constancy', and the servant as the 'mind progressing [sc. toward virtue]', Philo notes: 'it [must] be supposed that the progressive mind takes Constancy as (an object of) contemplation. For the inquiry of the theologian [i.e., Moses] is about characters and types and virtues, and not about persons who were created and born' (*QG* 4.137). Here Philo intimates that the allegorical and true meaning of the text is about ethics in general, and not about individual persons.

Nevertheless, in other passages Philo seems to allow that the interpretation of the biblical *personae* as 'men' is in line with the conception of them as 'dispositions of soul'. In *De Abrahamo* 47, when he discusses the first trio of biblical heroes, Enosh, Enoch, and Noah, he acknowledges that one may interpret them in a similar fashion whether they are viewed as men or dispositions of soul. This acknowledgment is in accord with the fact that in *De somniis* 1.120–6, it is the literal Jacob that is the 'athlete of virtue' (§ 126; cf. *Sobr.* 65; *Jos.* 26) and the 'lover of toil' (§ 127; cf. *Fug.* 14; *Mut.* 88). Therefore, he is here an *exemplum* of one who acquires virtue by practice, and not simply the symbol of a 'mind' with that characteristic.[84] From these passages, we can deduce that for Philo, biblical *personae-as-exempla* are on a kind of line of continuum with biblical *personae-as-minds*. This circumstance facilitates Philo's tendency to allow for both literal and allegorical interpretation. However, it also indicates the degree to which Philo's allegorical interpretation, even in its most characteristic form, is derived from, although it is not entirely consistent with, a more traditionalist vision of the Pentateuch

---

84   See above, pp. 85–6.

II. Philo's Thought

4 Philo's Thought within the Context of Middle Judaism[1]

For centuries, Philo was relegated to the margins of Judaism. This may be due to the Hellenistic spirit that pervades his works and the absence of any reference to him in the rabbinic corpus, especially as contrasted with the warm reception granted to him by the early Christians. In any case, his slight status was largely confirmed by the conception of Second Temple Judaism that was dominant through the first half of the twentieth century. According to that conception, there was a sharp distinction between the Hellenistic Judaism of the Diaspora and the normative Judaism of Palestine, and the former was often characterized as deviant or syncretistic, whereas the latter was thought to be pure and monolithic. Over the past decades this paradigm has gradually crumbled, both because of new discoveries (the Dead Sea Scrolls, papyri, archaeological finds) and because of more in-depth study of the literature of Middle Judaism that was previously available.[2] The current consensus seems to be that only after 70 CE did Judaism acquire a new identity, formulated by the Rabbis in reaction to the destruction of the temple in Jerusalem and characterized by a certain unity in outlook. The system of rabbinic Judaism, although it has real links with the past and did not spring up out of nothing, is based on new ideological constructs and should not be projected back onto the preceding period. Indeed, the Judaism of the Second Temple period, both in Palestine and in the Diaspora, displays considerable diversity both synchronically and diachronically. This diversity reflects different political settings and different social environments, and relates to doctrine and to way of life.

---

1 I would like to express my sincere gratitude to Prof. Adam Kamesar for the translation of my article and to the Classics Department of the University of Cincinnati for a summer fellowship that allowed me to complete my research.
2 G. Boccaccini, *Middle Judaism: Jewish Thought, 300 B.C.E. to 200 C.E.* (Minneapolis 1991), pp. 7–25, introduced the phrase 'Middle Judaism' as a designation for period that goes from the 3rd century BCE to the 2nd century CE.

Relations between Palestine and the Diaspora were constant and the meeting with Hellenism was common in both. We need not believe that Hellenism and Judaism were monolithic entities, constantly set in an antagonistic relationship. The interaction was more varied, and includes elements of assimilation, creative re-elaboration, and reaction. For many Jews, Philo among them, Hellenism did not constitute a threat to be rebuffed or something alien. Greek was their mother language and Hellenistic categories and modes of thought, as components of the dominant culture, furnished ideas and models that allowed for creative interpretation of the Jewish tradition. Those aspects of Hellenistic culture perceived as too dissonant could be left aside. At times, conflicts emerged. As in Rome in the second century BCE, when Cato the Censor held that the diffusion of Greek ways led to the corruption of venerable Roman mores, so in certain historical incidents and in some Jewish circles Hellenism was viewed with diffidence and hostility. However, the sharp opposition between *Ioudaismos* and *Hellenismos*, formulated in 2 Maccabees (2:21; 4:13–15), betokens an internal dispute within the Jewish community. Beyond the violent reaction, in the specific instance, against an external enemy viewed as a persecutor, there seems to have been a feeling of indignation against those Jews who, of their own free will, both in Palestine and in the Diaspora, were ready to follow the dominant culture and disavow their own faith.[3]

The figure of Philo may be set within this pluralistic galaxy that is Middle Judaism, and the goal of the present contribution will be to highlight the rich network of links that exists between Philo and contemporary Jewish literature. The subject of the relationship between Philo's writings and the rabbinic corpus will be taken up in a later chapter. Philo probably does not represent the typical Jew of the Diaspora. Rather, he seems to express the viewpoint of a cultured elite, and his writings may also reflect the acme of a Jewish Hellenistic tradition, in which exegesis and philosophy were deeply influenced both in form and in content by Greek models.

I. THEOLOGY

I.1. Monotheism

During the Hellenistic period, the Jewish religion continued to undergo transformation. Whether 'monotheism' is the correct term to describe

---

3   For recent discussion of some of the key issues regarding the relationship between Judaism and Hellenism, see J.J. Collins, *Jewish Cult and Hellenistic Culture* (Leiden 2005), pp. 1–43.

the complex configuration of the divine world that is reflected in the literature of the period is a subject of ongoing discussion.[4] Of course, the affirmation of the oneness of God is unalterable and is linked to an exclusive and aniconic cultic practice, but the negative corollary of this belief requires a more nuanced formulation. Aristobulus, a second-century predecessor of Philo, citing a passage of Aratus, substitutes the name 'Zeus' with the word *theos* (God), alluding to a concord between the philosophical teachings of the Greeks and the Jewish religion (fr. 4: 6–8). In the *Letter of Aristeas*, it is suggested that Greeks should view their own supreme deity and the Jewish God as one and the same (§§ 15–16), even if later in the text the superiority of Judaism in the ethical and cultic sphere is maintained (§§ 134–8). Philo follows a similar path; the best among the philosophers of both Greeks and barbarians acknowledged that there is one supreme principle from which all depends, as is attested in the Jewish legislation (*Spec.* 2.164–7; *Virt.* 65). Polytheism is for Philo a grave error that arises from the failure to recognize the difference between the first cause and the various beings that make up the material cosmos, even the most perfect among them such as the heavenly bodies (*Spec.* 1.13–20). Even more foolish is the adoration of images, because it involves the worship of inert material, whereas God is invisible and transcendent (*Decal.* 66–72). The height of delusion is the deification of irrational animals, typical of the Egyptian religion (*Decal.* 76–80).

On the practical side, however, Philo favors a respect of the religion of others. In fact, on the basis of the Greek text of Exod 22:27 ('Thou shall not revile the gods'), he notes that Moses forbade the cursing of those considered to be gods, even in error, by others.[5] Such caution no doubt betrays the experience of living in the multi-ethnic metropolis of Alexandria.

I.2. The Personified Attributes: Logos, Wisdom, Powers

Beyond these basic aspects of Jewish theology that came to be formulated in the encounter with the Greek world, there developed a concept of God that was consistent with the multiplication of various divine agents and intermediaries that occupy a subordinate position. This trend had its roots in the Persian period but became stronger in the

---

4   See L. W. Hurtado, 'First-Century Jewish Monotheism', *JSNT* 71 (1998), pp. 3–26.
5   *Mos.* 2.203–5; *Spec.* 1.53; *QE* 2.5; cf. Josephus, *AJ* 4.207; *C. Ap.* 2.237; P. W. van der Horst, ' "Thou Shalt not Revile the Gods": The LXX Translation of Ex 22:28 (27), Its Background and Influence', *StPhAnn* 5 (1993), pp. 1–8.

Hellenistic age. God continues to fulfill the role of creator, savior, king, and judge, as in the biblical texts, and, on the model of the Eastern monarchies, there is a further emphasis on His supreme sovereignty that is well expressed by the term *monarchia* (=absolute power). In addition, there is a great proliferation of divine titles.[6] The extravagance in the use of titles is perhaps due to the influence of the Hellenistic court, where titles were employed in abundance, and of the aretalogies of Greco–Roman gods, recited at religious festivals.

In some Jewish writings one also finds the personification of the attributes of God, especially Logos and Wisdom (=*sophia*). One can find the biblical origins of the Logos in the creative power of God's word (Gen 1), and in the recurring expression 'the word of Yahweh' (*devar Yhwh*), a phrase which encompasses the thought, will, and action of God. In the Greek text of the Bible the *logos* of God creates heaven and earth (Ps 32:6; Sir 42:15; Wis 9:1), is dispatched to man (Isa 2:1; Jer 1:2; Ezek 3:16), and finds expression in the *deka logoi* ('Decalogue' = ten words: Exod 34:28; Deut 10:4) and in the law (Ps 118:9, 16, 17, 25). The personified Logos appears in the retelling of the exodus story in Wis 18:14–16 as the 'all-powerful word' of God that brings death with the sword.[7] The figure of personified Wisdom is clearly attested in Proverbs (1:20–33; 8:1–36), in Sirach (24:1–22), in the Book of Wisdom (6:12–20; 7:22–8:1), and in the Enochic literature (*1 Enoch* 42:1; *2 Enoch* 30:8). It is intimately connected to God, it participates in the creation, it intervenes in the history of salvation, it arouses in man the desire for knowledge, and it upholds the just at the time of the last judgment.[8]

It remains a matter of debate whether the figures of Logos and Wisdom represent the culmination of metaphorical language employed to express in a vivid fashion the action of God, in a kind of literary hypostatization, or actual hypostases separate from God, with autonomous ontological status and subordinate to God.[9] The question is especially acute in the case of Philo, because in his works we find a particularly

---

6 Cf. L. L. Grabbe, *Judaic Religion in the Second Temple Period: Belief and Practice from the Exile to Yavneh* (London 2000), pp. 215–16.

7 The Logos has a prominent role in John 1:1–18. See below, ch. 7, pp. 199–201. In the Targums the phrase '*memra* of God' is used so that anthropomorphic expressions may be avoided and God may be distanced from direct contact with man. The use is not attested in the Targums from Qumran, but seems nevertheless to be ancient; see R. Hayward, *Divine Name and Presence: The Memra* (Totowa, NJ 1981), pp. 1–14.

8 Cf. C. Larcher, *Études sur le Livre de la Sagesse* (Paris 1969), pp. 331–49.

9 For a discussion of this problem, see C. Termini, *Le potenze di Dio: Studio su δύναμις in Filone di Alessandria* (Rome 2000), pp. 18–27.

sophisticated use of the divine attributes, which reaches the point of vivid personification.

It is not easy to summarize the functions of the Logos in Philo's thought. For alongside the philosophical aspects, it is necessary to call attention to the revelatory capacity of the Logos, which is closer to biblical precedents, as well as to the exegetical connection to certain texts of the Old Testament. The Logos has the role of the manifest countenance of God. It is the powerful word that gives solid consistency to the universe (*Her.* 188; *Somn.* 1.241). It is synonymous with due measure and harmony, both in God, reconciling the contrasting attributes of mercy and justice (*Cher.* 27–30), and in the world, bringing together the different elements and neutralizing the forces of chaos (*Plant.* 8–10; *Fug.* 112). Philo makes use of the Logos to explain certain theophanies in the Bible and, in this case, the subordination of the Logos to God serves to safeguard divine transcendence and to express the dialectical tension between the profound mystery of God-as-being and revelation.[10] The Logos plays an important role in the upward journey that brings man to the true knowledge of God (*Conf.* 145–7; *Fug.* 100–5). The human intellect was made in the image of the Logos (*Opif.* 139, 146; *QG* 2.62), and is called to contemplate God, like the Logos, which is called Israel as the prototype of the 'one who sees God'.[11] The salvific function of the Logos is indicated through symbols: the manna, which provides spiritual nourishment (*Leg.* 3.169–70; *Congr.* 173–4), and light, which allows us to see (*Opif.* 30–1; *Leg.* 3.171). The Logos guides men so they do not stumble (*Deus* 182).

The figure of Sophia is less prominent than the Logos in Philo's writings, but it has a legitimate place in the correspondence that one finds in his theology between adjectives that qualify God and the personified attributes. Indeed, it is precisely because God is the only one to be truly wise that he has Sophia beside him. In some cases, Philo links Sophia to a life-giving feminine maternal principle. In union with God, she generates the Logos and the cosmos (*Ebr.* 30–1 with the citation of Prov 8:22; *Fug.* 109). On other occasions Sophia is identified with the Logos and has a filial role with respect to God. It is she that takes delight in the father and is the archetype of earthly wisdom (*Leg.* 1.64–5). With the Logos Sophia enjoys a position of primacy above all

---

10 See Gen 31:13 in *Somn.* 1.227–30 and Exod 24:10 in *Conf.* 96–7 and *QE* 2.37. The Logos may be called *onoma theou* ('name of God'), probably in reference to the angel of God's name in Exod 23:20–1 (*Conf.* 146; cf. *Migr.* 174); it has the title of archangel in *Conf.* 146 and *Her.* 205.

11 *Conf.* 146. In the *Prayer of Joseph* (fr. A: 3), Israel is an angel of the Lord whose name means 'a man who sees God'.

other beings, which is attested by the common titles (*Leg.* 1.43, 2.86). Elsewhere, however, the Logos is the source of Sophia (*Fug.* 97). The fluidity of these schemes reveals the metaphorical orientation of the terminology employed to designate personified Wisdom more than it indicates inconsistency in Philo's theology.

The concept of 'power' (*dynamis*) is also of particular relevance in Philonic thought.[12] In the Jewish religion, omnipotence is an exclusive prerogative of God and for this reason the word *dynamis* (Hebrew *gevurah*) can be used in a periphrastic way to indicate God himself (Mt 26:64). Philo, however, prefers the plural to illustrate the manifold nature of God's power and action. He loves to represent God as the 'Great King', surrounded by an infinite crowd of powers who accompany Him in the manner of loyal bodyguards (*Spec.* 1.45). A term rich with philosophical and religious implications, *dynamis* is well sanctioned in Judeo–Hellenistic tradition, having been employed by Aristobulus to explicate biblical expressions such as the 'hand' or powerful 'arm' of God (fr. 2: 10.1–9). Philo reinforces this tradition and, at the exegetical level, exploits the concept of *dynamis* to explain various biblical phenomena such as the Cherubim in Gen 3:24 (*Cher.* 27–8); certain theophanies;[13] the problematic plural verbs used of God in Gen 1:26 (also 3:22 e 11:7).[14] The most notable of Philo's exegeses, which he himself appears to claim as original in an allusion to a kind of internal inspiration in *De cherubim* 27, relates to an equivalence between the Cherubim and the names of God *kyrios* (Lord) and *theos* (God). The names are explained etymologically as the 'regal power' (*kyrios*) and the 'creative power' (*theos*), and there emerges a tripartite scheme – God and His two highest powers – which we find in many variations. From the two principal powers the beneficent and the legislative/punitive powers take their origin.[15] As for the cosmos, the divine powers serve to establish the order of creation and to act so that the elements will not disperse and be disunited. In the context of the origin of man, Philo resorts to the powers (in the plural and without further qualification) solely to explain the

---

12   For a full study, see my *Potenze*.

13   A key passage is Gen 18:1–15, explained in *Abr.* 107–32 and *QG* 4.2, 8. In this context the powers are defined as the 'measure' of all things, an expression that calls to mind the rabbinic *middot*. Cf. N. A. Dahl and A. F. Segal, 'Philo and the Rabbis on the Names of God', *JSJ* 9 (1978), pp. 1–28.

14   *Opif.* 72–5; *Conf.* 168–82; *Fug.* 68–72; *Mut.* 30–2; *QG* 1.54.

15   In the exegesis of the ark in *QE* 2.68, there are four powers and the Logos. In *Fug.* 94–100, the legislative power is doubled so that there are five powers connected to the Logos, and the total of six corresponds to the cities of refuge in Num 35:12–14. The powers may also be listed without the Logos and without an internal hierarchy, as in *Legat.* 6–7.

plural verb in Gen 1:26. At the religious level, the powers foster progress in one's knowledge of God, beginning from fear and moving toward
friendly commerce, offered by God Himself as a gift (*Fug.* 97–9).

The powers open a unique window through which we can view and
understand the mechanisms of Philonic theology, because they form
a continuous thread that leads us from the manifold aspects of God's
action at the cosmic, historical, and human levels to the depth of the
divine mystery. Philo states on many occasions that the essence of God
is unknowable, but that man can infer His existence from the Logos and
the powers that reveal Him. However, the powers are described by the
same negative adjectives that qualify the essence of God.[16] This means
that while the Logos illuminates the revealed aspect of God, the powers allow at least a glimpse of the mysterious essence of God, which is
power in unity, in as much as God is one and unique. The correspondence between the titles of God (creator, king, legislator, etc.) and the
adjectives that modify the powers (creative, royal, legislative, etc.) is
the clearest literary means by which Philo prevents the powers from
becoming independent hypostases on which to 'unload' an action that
seems unbecoming of God. Philo also safeguards monotheism by continually interchanging the entities of Logos, Sophia, and powers, as well
as their functions and titles. In this way he avoids coming to a binitar-
ian scheme which would result from the concentration of attributes
on only one mediating figure. Philo's theology cannot be understood
by reference to a scheme whereby an ever more extreme divine transcendence requires the presence of lower intermediaries to bridge the
growing distance that separates God from the world. The transcendence
of God does not limit His capacity to act and reveal Himself. God's
omnipotence guarantees that there is no barrier; rather, it is a matter
of safeguarding the *otherness* of God. Revelation does not exhaust the
profound mystery of the divine.

I.3. Angels

Angels are on a different plane than are the personified divine attributes. They are at the service of God and, even though they have a
more perfect nature, they are created beings and are not the object
of worship. Philo admits their existence, but does not devote much
space to a theory of angels, because he remains in line with the tradition of the Pentateuch. In the Persian and Hellenistic periods, angels

16 Cf. *agenetos* (ungenerated: *Deus* 78); *akataleptos* (incomprehensible: *Spec.*
1.47); *akratos* (unmixed: *Cher.* 29; *Deus* 77–8); *aperigraphos* (uncircum-
scribed: *Sacr.* 59); *achronos* (timeless: *Sacr.* 69).

take on more defined characteristics. Many receive a personal name and an individual personality. There also develops a hierarchy with four or seven archangels at the top. They have many duties; they sing praises to God, celebrate the heavenly service, guard certain regions of the cosmos, control the movements of the stars, and supervise atmospheric phenomena. They bring messages to and instruct men; they inform God of what happens; they observe and record human actions; they intercede on behalf of the just; and even in the moment of the last judgment, they take part in the eschatological battle.[17] Typical of some apocalyptic texts is the idea, linked to Gen 6:1–4, that evil did not arise from human sin, but from a disturbance in the domain of the angels. Certain rebellious angels, the 'watchers', lead by Semyaza, united in sexual intercourse with women, fathering the wicked giants and passing on to men knowledge that should have remained secret.[18] According to *1 Enoch* 9–10, God ordered the angels to kill the giants, but their souls, in the form of malevolent spirits, continued to lead men astray. The evil angels take on different names: Mastema in *Jubilees* (10:8); Satan in the *Life of Adam and Eve* (9:1).

In the literature of Middle Judaism, however, there are also texts such as Sirach and Wisdom that devote little space to angels, simply accepting their existence. For his part, Philo comments on Gen 6:1–2 in *De gigantibus* 1–18 and, although he knows of teachings concerning the malevolent angels, he is opposed to such interpretations in as much as they are a source of superstition.[19] Moreover, Philo tends to play down the individual personalities of the angels, not referring to their proper names. They are unbodied souls that live in the air, incorruptible and immortal, akin to the stars. At times they are called *logoi*, which allows us to understand their connection with the Logos-as-archangel (*Conf.* 28; *Somn.* 1.142). They are also defined as servants of the powers.[20] Philo's angelology exhibits points of contact with Greek philosophy in the description of the nature of angelic beings.[21] However, it presents

17   Cf. Grabbe, *Judaic Religion*, pp. 220–5.

18   *1 Enoch* 6–8; *Jub.* 5:1–2, 7:21; CD-A II:17–21; *T. Naph.* 3:5.

19   See the exemplary analysis of V. Nikiprowetzky, 'Sur une lecture démonologique de Philon d'Alexandrie: *De gigantibus*, 6–18', in his collected studies, *Études philoniennes* (Paris 1996), pp. 217–42.

20   *Spec.* 1.66; cf. *Conf.* 174–5.

21   This may confirmed by the equating of angels and *daimones* (*Gig.* 6, 16; *Somn.* 1.140–1) and of angels and heroes (*Plant.* 14). Philo's angelology also reveals its own characteristics. Angels do not have an evil component; they are without passions; they are not a lower kind of god since they are created beings.

typically Jewish components in so far as concerns their function. For example, the angels form a well-organized army in which each member, according to his own rank, performs the task assigned to him in docile obedience (*Conf.* 174). Among the angels, a failure in the performance of the worship and the service of God is impossible. The angels communicate the orders of the heavenly Father to His children and the needs of the children to the Father. Like priests, they celebrate a liturgy in the temple of the cosmos; they have a role in punishing men, but also in granting to them certain secondary gifts.[22]

II. THEORY OF MAN

II.1. The Creation of Man and Sin

Philo does not set out a systematic anthropology. Just as in much of the wisdom and apocalyptic literature of Middle Judaism, his ideas about man take shape from the creation stories in Gen 1–3. That which occurred 'in the beginning' has a paradigmatic and etioliogical significance, and helps us understand God's original design and the reasons for the human condition. That condition is characterized by freedom of choice, but is also disfigured by sin and limited by death.

Within the great variety of created beings, animate and inanimate, man is distinguished by being *methorios*, that is, 'on the border' between the material and the spiritual domains, between time and eternity, and between good and evil.[23] In as much as he has a body endowed with sense-perception and certain biological qualities, man resembles the animals, but he is distinguished from them because he possesses intellectual qualities and free will. Philo describes man's affinity with the divine realm by employing two different models, both founded on the biblical text. On the basis of Gen 1:26 ('Let us make man after our image, after our likeness'), Philo states that man is created after the image of God and that the likeness does not refer to the body, but to the mind, which thanks to its cognitive capacities can raise itself from the cosmos and reach as far as the creator (*Opif.* 69–71). Philo emphasizes the exactness of the image and assigns to *nous* (mind) the function of hegemony over the soul, similar to that which God exercises over the cosmos. There are some important points of contact with this interpretation in the

---

22   *Somn.* 1.141; *Abr.* 115; *QE* 2.13; *Spec.* 1.66; *Virt.* 73–4; *Conf.* 180–1; *Fug.* 66–7. The presence of angels may also be detected in the episode of the burning bush (*Mos.* 1.66–7) and in the cloud that accompanied the Israelites during the exodus (*Mos.* 1.166).

23   Cf. *Gen. Rab.* 8.11.

Book of Wisdom, in which the expression in Gen 1:26 is reinforced, and it is said that God made man 'as the image of his own nature' (2:23). This implies a call to immortality, which is linked to the rightful use of freedom and the achievement of justice in a religious sense.[24] In the *Sentences* of Pseudo-Phocylides 106, on the other hand, the theme of the 'image' is linked to that of God's gift of the spirit. This brings us to the second model which Philo employs to explain the divine property that is present in man.

According to Gen 2:7, God breathes His breath on the 'molded man', that is, the spirit which gives the soul a share in immortality and the capacity to know the good, making it morally responsible (*Opif.* 135; *Leg.* 1.33–42). This liberty confers upon man a dignity that makes him similar to God, but also imposes upon him the burden of free choice (*Deus* 47–8; *Conf.* 177–8). Among created beings, he alone participates in vice and virtue, and this raises the problem of theodicy. Can God, as creator, bear any ultimate responsibility for the ethical wrongs committed by man? Philo regards it as axiomatic that God is the source and initiating principle only of good and that therefore He is totally unassociated with evil. In order to avert from God any possible complicity in human wickedness, Philo states that when He created man, the creator made use of the powers, but the sphere and true scope of their action is left intentionally ambiguous.[25] In this way Philo also solves the difficulty of the plural form of the verb in Gen 1:26 ('Let us make man'), which other Middle Judaic texts interpret by appealing to the presence of Wisdom or of angels.[26]

The ethical condition of man lies in his wavering between good and evil. This condition reflects the dynamic dimension of his being *methorios* ('on the border'), and it emerges for Philo in a paradigmatic way in the fall of Adam and Eve.

On the basis of Gen 2–3, Philo believes that the woman is the starting point or principle of blameworthy life (*Opif.* 151), in that with her appearance the original solitude of man comes to an end. From the mutual attraction love is born and with it physical pleasure, which is

---

24 Cf. C. Larcher, *Le Livre da la Sagesse ou la Sagesse de Salomon*, I (Paris 1983), pp. 266–70.

25 See my *Potenze*, pp. 137–88, esp. 139–52. Cf. also D. Winston, *The Ancestral Philosophy: Hellenistic Philosophy in Second Temple Judaism* (Providence 2001), pp. 128–34.

26 According to Wis 9:2, Wisdom is alongside God, while in 2 Enoch 30:8, the creation of man is entrusted to Wisdom; in 4Q416 fr. 2, III:15–17 and 4Q417 fr. 2, I:17, it appears that angels assist God in the creation of man. In the view of Josephus the creation is the work of God alone (*C. Ap.* 2.192). Cf. also *Gen. Rab.* 8.3–4.

the source of every transgression of the law and leads the human race from a blessed immortality to a mortal and unhappy state (*Opif.* 151–2). Here we find the growing suspicion of human sexuality that is common in Middle Judaism in general. Moreover, the woman, at the instigation of the serpent, the symbol of pleasure, agrees to eat the fruit of the tree of knowledge of good and evil, having disregard for piety and holiness. This sin of hers brings the two first humans in a definitive fashion from a condition of simplicity and innocence into the realm of *phronēsis* (ethical wisdom), which requires the knowledge of good and evil and involves choice and the possibility for error. This is because human freedom does not have an infallible bearing toward the good.[27] On the same plane as *phronēsis* is *panourgia* (cleverness), that is, broad knowledge based on experience and the frame of mind to employ all means, without scruples, to reach the desired end (*Opif.* 155–6).

The fall of the first humans is due, therefore, to an inclination toward pleasure that causes man to bypass the tree of life, which symbolizes *theosebeia* (piety), and a virtuous life linked to God that allows for immortality (*Opif.* 155). After the expulsion of man and woman from paradise, human life progresses in a state of greater distance from God. Woman becomes subject to the pangs of childbirth, and the problems connected to the rearing of children and submission to her husband. Man, for his part, must undertake the toil of labor, because God stops the earth from giving its fruits in a spontaneous manner. For Philo, physical death is not part of the divine punishment; rather, it is 'spiritual death', or the death of the soul to virtue, that makes its appearance because of the choice made by Adam and Eve (cf. Wis 2:24).

Understood in this fashion, the events of Gen 2–3 have paradigmatic significance for Philo, in that they explain the direction that human existence has taken in contrast to an original state of happiness. Nevertheless, the sin did not irreparably damage human liberty, nor did it cause the fall of later generations. As in 2 *Baruch* 54:19, everyone is an Adam in himself. Within Middle Judaic literature, Philo's interpretation of Gen 2–3 stands midway between texts like *Jubilees* (3:17–31) and Josephus' *Jewish Antiquities* (1.40–51), in which only a paradigmatic significance is attributed to the biblical events,[28] and writings such as 4

---

27   Cf. *Opif.* 156, 170; a detailed analysis of these passages is given by M. Harl, 'Adam et les deux arbres du Paradis (Gen. II–III) ou l'homme *milieu entre deux termes* (μέσος-μεθόριος) chez Philon d'Alexandrie', *Recherches de science religieuse* 50 (1962), pp. 321–88. The knowledge of good and evil, which in Sir 17:5–7 and in the Qumran texts is positive, takes on an ambiguous tinge in Philo.

28   Cf. also *Or. Sib.* 1.39–55.

Ezra (7:118) and Paul's Letter to the Romans (5:12). In these latter texts, greater emphasis is given to the consequences of Adam's transgression for later generations in terms of the transference and dissemination of sin and of death.[29] However, it should be stressed that for Philo, the origin of evil takes place at the human level. The Enochic idea of sin on the part of the angels, which then entered the human realm, is alien to him. Also without parallel in Philo is the ethical and cosmic dualism found in Qumran writings, according to which the ultimate origin of evil is attributed to God, in as much as He is the creator of the 'prince of darkness' (1QS III:13–IV:26).

II.2. Salvation: Retribution and Eschatology

Philo has a profound sense of the instability of human existence: man suffers continual ups and downs, and he can easily err and come to ruin.[30] Without divine assistance it is difficult to reach salvation, that is, an intimate relationship with God, which, based on knowledge and contemplation, is accompanied by peace and stability, and lasts for all eternity. One finds in Philo's writings references to the history of salvation, as well as to the hope of a salvific intervention on the part of God in the present, to rescue the Jews from persecution, or in the future.[31] However, the prevailing concept of salvation, which corresponds to Philo's anthropology, lies in the realm of the individual and is based on a kind of panentheism.[32] One reaches salvation by means of the gifts of wisdom and the spirit that provide man with the ability to enjoy communion with God and to practice a life of virtue. The restoration of Israel (or a remnant), in a historical and eschatological sense, is for Philo secondary, as is the notion of covenant. From the time of creation each man has in himself, in his mind, an image of the Logos, and on the basis of the spirit that was breathed into him, is able to know the creator and to remain in contact with Him. It is up to man to care

29 Cf. also *LAB* 13:8–9 (death); *Apoc. Mos.* 32 (sin). The theme is discussed by T.H. Tobin, 'The Jewish Context of Rom 5:12–14', *StPhAnn* 13 (2001), pp. 159–75.
30 *Opif.* 151; *Gig.* 28–9: cf. Harl, 'Adam', pp. 338–9, 372–3.
31 *Legat.* 3–4, 196. In Judaism there are many notions of salvation, beyond that related to the nation: the purgation of sins by means of sacrifices, healing of sicknesses, eschatological liberation, martyrdom. See G.W.E. Nickelsburg, *Ancient Judaism and Christian Origins* (Minneapolis 2003), pp. 61–88.
32 Cf. D. Winston, *Logos and Mystical Theology in Philo of Alexandria* (Cincinnati 1985), p. 55; C. Bennema, *The Power of Saving Wisdom: An Investigation of Spirit and Wisdom in Relation to the Soteriology of the Fourth Gospel* (Tübingen 2002), pp. 71–83.

for and develop this gift or to debase it, and his own efforts are just as important as divine grace in achieving ethical and spiritual progress. Man must forsake pleasure and the other bonds that keep him tied to the material world (*Opif.* 161–6). He must recognize that everything comes from God, and he must live according to His word (*Migr.* 127–8). For His part, God comes to meet the soul that seeks Him out (*Conf.* 93). He aids its efforts in the struggle against the passions (*Post.* 31, 156–7; *Her.* 60, 271–4), He unites it to Himself with His power (*Abr.* 59; *Migr.* 124), and He infuses it with light, sowing seeds of virtue and tending to their growth (*Cher.* 43–4, 49–50). Philo finds the models for his ethical and religious ideas in the biblical *personae*, who live with hope and progress toward the good by means of repentance and virtue, or become alienated from God by the failure to repent and the persistence in vice.

Philo's view of the path to salvation has some points of contact with the Old Testament. Following the prophets, he believes that divine action is necessary to transform the heart of man and make him capable of living according to the dictates of justice.[33] He has inherited from the wisdom tradition the individualistic and universalistic view of salvation, with its focus on man's knowledge of God and his internal relationship with Him, and its emphasis on human effort for the attainment of happiness.[34] Like Philo, Sirach (chs. 44–50) and the Book of Wisdom (chs. 10–19) read the Bible as a story of the triumph of its heroes whose lives have paradigmatic value. Even in some texts from Qumran we find the mechanism of a communication between God and man, that has salvific significance, written into the plan of creation.[35] Man is called to struggle against the forces of darkness and of evil by purifying himself and searching for wisdom. He is sustained in his efforts by the divine spirit and illumination, which lead one on the path of knowledge, correct interpretation of the law, and right conduct.[36] In contrast to Philo, however, the mechanism of salvation at Qumran is to be understood within the context of a sectarian ideology, because the illumination from God is given only to those who adhere to the select community and, first and foremost, to the teacher of righteousness.

In the Hebrew Bible, divine retribution for those who observe or transgress the law is effected during one's earthly life, since only a sad and shadowy existence awaits the dead in the underworld (*sheol*). Reward and punishment are determined by God's judgment on the basis

---

33   Cf. Isa 32:15; Jer 31:31–4; Ezek 11:19–20, 36:24–7; Joel 3:1–5. The prophets, in contrast to Philo, have more of a group perspective.
34   See Bennema, *Power*, pp. 51–71.
35   Cf. 1QS III:17–19; 4Q417 fr. 2, I:16–18; 1QHᵃ IX:15.
36   Cf. Bennema, *Power*, pp. 83–92.

of fidelity to His covenant, or are brought about as a result of one's own just or unjust actions, an idea reflected in the wisdom literature. In Middle Judaism, however, there develops the idea of life after death, understood as immortality of the soul or as resurrection of the body or as some combination of the two. Divine retribution takes place in some scenarios immediately after death; in others after the dissolution of the cosmos and a final judgment.[37] In any case, the existence of a life after death allows for the reaffirmation of divine justice, which sometimes seems in doubt because of the suffering of the just. Within this general context, Philo's view has its own particular characteristics. In tune with other Judeo–Hellenistic texts from Alexandria, Philo makes no reference to resurrection of the body, and he also de-emphasizes the ideas of hell and a last judgment.[38] In fact, he spiritualizes the very notions of life and death, and minimizes the importance of physical death.[39] A truly authentic life consists in practicing of virtue and in being in communion with God. For this reason, the wise man lives already in this life in a kind of immortality, which will take on a perfect form after his death (*Opif.* 154; *QE* 2.39). In corresponding fashion, true death is that of the soul, and it is caused by living a life of vice and in subjugation to the passions. This brings about distance from God, and abandonment by Him. The base person has already killed his own soul during this life and will meet a destiny of ongoing death.[40] In this way Philo resolves the difficulty that arises from the premature and violent death of a just man. For whoever puts God at the center of their own life, death is only the beginning of a renewed life, whereas the unjust who appear to have been triumphant are in reality already dead. This idea of an immortality that is already present in inchoative form during one's earthly existence is also attested in the Book of Wisdom and in *Joseph and Aseneth* (15:2–5).[41] It allows Philo to establish a continuity between one's terrestrial and post-terrestrial life. This continuity is based on the power of virtue to bestow immortality. The result, however, is not 'natural' in such a way that divine intervention is not involved. Even if there is a causal link between virtue and immortality, the role of grace

37   For a survey of the main themes, see Grabbe, *Judaic Religion*, pp. 257–70.
38   This does not mean that God does not take on the role of judge during a man's lifetime, and at times God's judgment may be salvific. See *Plant.* 108; *Her.* 271–4; *Mos.* 2.217–18; *Spec.* 3.52, 4.171–2.
39   See D. Zeller, 'The Life and Death of the Soul in Philo of Alexandria: The Use and Origin of a Metaphor', *StPhAnn* 7 (1995), pp. 19–55.
40   Cf. *Leg.* 1.105–7; *Det.* 48; *Her.* 45, 292; *Congr.* 57; *Somn.* 1.151; *Praem.* 152; *QG* 1.16, 51.
41   Note also the following Qumran texts: 1QHᵃ XI:19–23, XIX:3–14; 4Q417 fr. 2, I:11–14. Cf. Nickelsburg, *Ancient Judaism*, pp. 128–9.

and divine justice remains indispensable. Virtue is a necessary precondition for immortality, but it is not sufficient in itself to attain it. For contrary to the Platonistic perspective, the *nous* or rational part of the soul does not possess immortality as an inherent property, but only in as much as it received the vital breath from God. The last things mirror the first things, and after death there is a rebirth. By the same word by which He created the world, God raises the virtuous man to Himself, removing him from the earthly setting (*Sacr.* 8). Philo describes in a somewhat imprecise and inconsistent fashion the destiny of the soul after the dissolution of the body (*Cher.* 113–15). It appears probable that in his view, the soul retains its individuality and is not absorbed into a greater whole.[42] In favor of this suggestion is the fact that in the hereafter we find a kind of scheme of ranking based on different levels of ethical advancement. Commenting on the deaths of the patriarchs, Philo says that Abraham and Jacob 'were added to the people of God' (Gen 25:8; 49:33), taking this to mean that they became equal to the angels;[43] Isaac is translated into an imperishable and perfect race.[44] Moses, for his part, is simply uplifted by God, by means of His word, into communion and a position of special intimacy with Him. At the time of his translation he was filled with God (*Sacr.* 8–10; cf. *QE* 2.40), and his dual make-up of soul and body was transformed into a unity and became pure mind (*Mos.* 2.288). It appears that God makes those who are true to Him similar to Himself, restoring the original 'image of God' (Gen 1:26).

II.3. Messianism

The question of a national or cosmic eschatology in Philo, linked to the coming of a messiah, is much debated among scholars.[45] The most important texts are found in the final part of *De praemiis et poenis*

---

42 See F. W. Burnett, 'Philo on Immortality: A Thematic Study of Philo's Concept of παλιγγενεσία', *The Catholic Biblical Quarterly* 46 (1984), pp. 459–62, who argues against E. R. Goodenough, 'Philo on Immortality', *HThR* 39 (1946), pp. 101–3.

43 *Sacr.* 5. One may compare this text with those passages where Philo speaks of a return of the soul to the heavenly region (*Conf.* 78), to the ether (*Her.* 283), or to the stars (*Her.* 280; *QE* 2.114). Cf. Winston, *Logos*, p. 38.

44 *Sacr.* 6–7 (on the basis of the term *genos* [race] in Gen 35:29); cf. also *Her.* 280; *QG* 1.86.

45 According to Winston, *Logos*, pp. 55–8, any form of Davidic messianism would be held in check so as not to antagonize the Romans. For U. Fischer, *Eschatologie und Jenseitserwartung im hellenistischen Diasporajudentum* (Berlin 1978), pp. 187–213, Philo denationalizes and spiritualizes the messianic hope. On the various kinds of Messianism in Second Temple Judaism, see Grabbe, *Judaic Religion*, pp. 271–91

(esp. 93–7, 162–72) and in the *De vita Mosis* (1.289–91, 2.43–4), but to evaluate them correctly, we need to clarify our terminology. If by eschatology we mean a theory of the 'last things', which relate to the end of history or a future age, and by messianism we mean the expectation of an earthly or celestial figure who is to annihilate the enemies of Israel and the forces of evil and establish a glorious reign, then both are absent from Philo's writings. We do find, on the other hand, the hope for a better 'near future', a utopia within history, characterized by observance of the law. This may include the figure of a historical messiah, who has Moses-like traits. One may discern here the traditionalist bent in Philonic thought, because the ideas he expresses are rooted in a deuteronomic/istic theology of retribution and in the message of the ancient prophets. One does not yet find in Philo that tragic outlook on the present that is typical of the apocalyptic literature written around the juncture of the first and second centuries CE. According to that outlook, man is powerless in the face of hostile forces and satanic powers. It becomes necessary to disassociate the present from the future and to project salvation into a new era, beyond this one, that is the result of the action of God and of His messiah.[46]

Philo was aware that the national life of the Jewish people had been for some time in a somewhat depressed state, and that this had contributed to a lack of appreciation of its laws and traditions. He thought, however, that if the fortunes of the Jews should improve, the Mosaic law would overshadow all others, and all peoples would abandon their own institutions to follow it (*Mos.* 2.43–4). This is Philo's ultimate hope, but it is not put off to some eschatological age and the final part of *De praemiis* makes clear that it is dependent on human choices. It would be among the blessings that await those who respect the law with their thoughts, words, and actions. Loosely following Deut 28 and Lev 26, Philo claims that the first reward given by God to those who are faithful is victory over their enemies (*Praem.* 85–92). There are two kinds of war waged by man: the most ancient is that against animals, who are hostile to the human species because of their different nature; the more recent kind of war is that waged against other men for reasons of greed or desire for power. No mortal can placate the hostility that exists between the human and animal worlds; only God has the power to grant this privilege to certain peaceful persons who have tamed their internal beasts, namely, the passions in the soul (*Praem.* 87). Wild animals will be tamed when man succeeds in taming the vices within himself, and Philo hopes to see the day when this will happen. Although a utopian ideal, it is not beyond all hope, because

46   Cf. E. Schürer et al., *The History of the Jewish People in the Age of Jesus Christ (175 B.C. – A.D. 135)*, II (Edinburgh 1979), pp. 492–7.

it corresponds to God's original design (*Praem.* 88). At that point, wars will also cease, because men will be ashamed to show themselves crueler than savage beasts. The enemies of a person who has virtue and justice as his allies will not dare to attack him. Or, if they do, by reason of insanity, they will not prevail against the just and the pious. Miracles like those of the exodus will again take place: the adversaries will be stricken by panic, or will be pursued by swarms of hornets. God will send a warrior who will lead the army of the just to victory. The citation of Num 24:7 in *De praemiis* 95 points to a messianism of Mosaic coloring,[47] but this is only one of the possibilities envisaged in the text. Philo's more profound hope is in a human soul at peace with itself on the inside, which, with the sanction of divine blessing, is able to transform the realities in both the natural and the political worlds.

Philo interprets in a literal fashion the blessings set out in the Pentateuch: wealth and prosperity, honor and power, fertility of the soil, progeny, long life and health (*Praem.* 98–126). The misfortunes that befall those who transgress the holy laws of justice and piety are described in a similarly concrete manner: poverty, horrifying diseases, cannibalism, slavery, destruction (*Praem.* 127–51). Philo maintains the powerful rhetoric, meant as a deterrent, of the biblical curses, but he leaves open a window of hope. Those who have been taken in by polytheism and have abandoned the ancestral teachings will understand that such punishments are sent by God not to destroy them, but to make them change their ways. If they confess their sins and repent, they will again find favor with God, a merciful savior. He will free them from the state of exile and slavery, He will reassemble them from the ends of the earth, and He will turn His wrath against their enemies; cities lying in ruin will be rebuilt and prosperity will return.[48] Philo employs the scheme from the exodus to describe the salvation that awaits those who repent. It may appear to be an eschatological scheme, but in reality it is best understood within the system of divine retribution, based on reward and punishment. The operation of the system depends on human decisions and is ongoing within history. It is not a definitive divine action of the 'end of days'.

III. THE LAW

The excellence of the Mosaic law is one of the pillars of Philonic thought. Despite the variations in historical circumstances through the centuries, the Torah has remained unchanged because it carries with it

---

47 Cf. J. Lust, *Messianism and the Septuagint* (Leuven 2004), pp. 69–86.
48 *Praem.* 162–71. Philo's hope is short-term. The phrase *pro mikrou* ('just a while ago') appears often (*Praem.* 165, 168, 170, 1/1).

the seal of nature (*Opif.* 3; *Mos.* 2.14–15). It is inspired, it does not derive from human convention, and it contains the truth unadulterated by mythical fictions and vain rhetoric (*Det.* 125). It allows one to achieve happiness, to live in harmony with reason, and to extend communion with God.[49] The superiority of the Jewish law is based both on divine authority and on the exceptional qualities of Moses (*Mos.* 2.12). He was chosen by God because of his virtue, and he carried the law engraved in his soul before he even became a *nomothetēs* (= lawgiver: *Mos.* 1.162; 2.8–11). Alone among men he enjoyed the constant presence of the spirit that sharpens his intellectual capabilities (*Gig.* 47, 53–5), and was empowered to receive divine revelation without mediation (*QE* 2.29, 40). Philo takes care to emphasize that the Jews are distinguished from all other peoples for their reverence and scrupulous observance of the law. He expresses the hope that one day all humanity will adopt the Torah for themselves, not because of compulsion, but because of admiration for the Jewish way of life.[50]

According to Philo, the law of Moses may be divided into three parts: the account of creation, the stories of the patriarchs, and the normative section.[51] This structure is not haphazard; it reveals the profundity of the lawgiver's wisdom. For Moses, as contrasted with other legislators, placed a preface to his laws concerning the creation. Its purpose is to demonstrate that God is both creator and legislator, and that therefore the Jewish law corresponds to the order of nature (*Opif.* 1–3; *Mos.* 2.46–52). The patriarchs, by their lives and their actions, attest to the fact that it is possible to fulfill the law completely before the Sinaitic revelation, by following the Logos, which is the true law of nature (*Abr.* 3–6). They constitute archetypes of the written laws. This emerges especially in the biography of Abraham, which is centered on *eusebeia* (piety) and philanthropy (*Abr.* 60–207, 208–61), the two virtues that encapsulate the two tables of the Decalogue. The two tables, for their part, form the basis for the taxonomy of the other laws of the Torah, the particular laws.[52] Although the law of nature and the written law are mirror images of each other, it is the former that is the archetype. The Torah points in the direction of a broader wisdom, and in this fashion Philo goes beyond a 'Torah-centric' perspective. Philo's thought

---

49 See R. Weber, *Das "Gesetz" bei Philon von Alexandrien und Flavius Josephus* (Frankfurt am Main 2001), pp. 42–68, 78–114.
50 *Mos.* 2.17, 25–7; cf. also Josephus, *C. Ap.* 2.178.
51 *Praem.* 1–2; cf. *Mos.* 2.46–7, and above, ch. 3, pp. 73–7.
52 On this theme, see C. Termini, 'Taxonomy of Biblical Laws and φιλοτεχνία in Philo of Alexandria: A Comparison with Josephus and Cicero', *StPhAnn* 16 (2004), pp. 1–29.

here has something in common with the wisdom tradition. We see his universalism and his openness to the culture of Hellenism and to the Roman world, but also his pride in being Jewish and having been born and educated in a religious tradition that sees in the Torah the best formulation of the law of nature.

In this manner, Philo gives philosophical dress to an idea attested in different forms in many Middle Judaic texts, namely, the tendency to project the validity of the Sinaitic Torah backward, to the time of creation. In Sirach, Wisdom as a principle of cosmic order brings the Torah into its own sphere (24:1–23); knowledge of good and evil belongs to man from the time of creation (17:7–8) and Abraham observes the law of the Most High (44:20). In *Jubilees*, the content of the 'heavenly tablets' is revealed in a progressive fashion to the patriarchs and is transmitted in written form.[53] An allusion to the knowledge of the Mosaic Torah is present in the historical review in the *Damascus Document*, and it has also been pointed out that in Qumranic exegesis, the patriarchs are punished more or less severely according to their level of awareness of the commandments.[54] That there is a relationship between the nature of the cosmos and the Mosaic law is implied in 4 Maccabees 5:25. On the subject of the dietary laws, it is said that God, the creator of the cosmos, is at one with men by nature when He prescribes a law. Josephus also holds that everything in the Torah has been set out in accord with the nature of the universe.[55]

In Philo's exegesis, the notion of a correspondence between the law of nature and the Mosaic commandments leads to a tendency to emphasize the 'rationality' of each commandment by means of a moderate use of allegorical interpretation. In his treatment of legal texts, however, Philo never annuls the literal sense, because for him, maintaining the practice of the law solidifies the identity of the Jewish community. Accordingly, on the one hand, Philo criticizes the literalists,

---

53 The heavenly tablets include the pre-existent Torah, the book of destiny, the calendar, the register of good and evil, and the *halakhot* or legal traditions; see *Jub.* 3:10, 31, 4:5, 32, 15:25, and F. García Martínez, 'The Heavenly Tablets in the Book of Jubilees', in M. Albani et al. (eds.), *Studies in the Book of Jubilees* (Tübingen 1997), pp. 243–60.

54 Cf. CD-A II:14–III:17 and esp. III:1–6, with G. A. Anderson, 'The Status of the Torah before Sinai: The Retelling of the Bible in the Damascus Covenant and the Book of Jubilees', *Dead Sea Discoveries* 1 (1994), pp. 1–29.

55 *AJ* 1.21–4: cf. Weber, *Gesetz bei Philon*, pp. 287–92, 339–42. In the view of the Rabbis the patriarchs knew the Torah, but their explanations of the phenomenon are not homogeneous: cf. H. Najman, *Seconding Sinai: The Development of Mosaic Discourse in Second Temple Judaism* (Leiden 2003), pp. 128–9 n. 44.

accusing them of being 'micropolitans' (citizens of a small community; *Somn.* 1.39), incapable of understanding the depth of Mosaic philosophy. Yet on the other hand, he disapproves of the 'extreme allegorizers', who are willing to neglect the material observance of a commandment and fulfill only its spiritual sense. In *De migratione Abrahami* 89–93, Philo reproaches them for living in a solipsistic fashion, by breaking social bonds with the Jewish community and not taking thought for good repute.

At the theoretical level, it remains a debated question whether there is any correspondence between Philo's notion of 'unwritten law' and the 'Oral Torah' of the Rabbis.[56] The formal concept of 'Oral Torah' is not attested in any source prior to 70 CE. It seems to be a typically rabbinic theological construct, the intention of which is to bestow the authority of revelation on interpretations of legal material not directly linked to the biblical text. Before 70 CE the traditions of the Pharisees are designated in Greek with the term *paradoseis* (traditions). They were probably transmitted orally, but were not viewed as 'revealed' and were subject to criticism by their opponents.[57] In the Philonic corpus, the closest expression is *agrapha ethē* or *agrapha nomima*, which is best translated 'unwritten customs'. They complement the written laws and are taught within the family.[58] In *De specialibus legibus* 4.149–50, it is said that these customs were established by men of old, not by God, and have been transmitted by means of an *agraphos paradosis* ('unwritten tradition'). For Philo, however, these are common to Judaism as a whole, and are not the specific heritage of a sectarian group.

A related but different issue is whether Philo had any knowledge of the actual content of Palestinian halakhah.[59] A comparison of the content of the Philonic texts and the literature of Middle Judaism demonstrates that Philo has knowledge of Jewish traditions, both common

---

56 The correspondence was denied by I. Heinemann 'Die Lehre vom ungeschriebenen Gesetz im jüdischen Schrifttum', *HUCA* 4 (1927), pp. 149–71, and he has had many followers. Others have taken the opposite view, most recently, N. G. Cohen, *Philo Judaeus: His Universe of Discourse* (Frankfurt am Main 1995), pp. 256–77. For a brief presentation of the issues, see J. W. Martens, 'Unwritten Law in Philo: A Response to Naomi G. Cohen', *JJS* 43 (1992), pp. 38–45.

57 See A. I. Baumgarten, 'The Pharisaic Paradosis', *HThR* 80 (1987), pp. 63–77.

58 *Spec.* 4.149–50; *Legat.* 115; *Hypoth.* 7.6. The unwritten law, on the other hand, is to be equated with the law of nature personified in the patriarchs (*Abr.* 5, 16, 275–6; *Decal.* 1).

59 For this question, see the detailed discussion below, ch. 9, pp. 247–51.

and more specific (proto-Tannaitic, Pharisaic, Essene, Alexandrian).[60] Of these he is not only a tradent, but especially an interpreter, because he is more interested in explaining the sense and basis of Jewish law than in defining how it needs to be applied in praxis.

III.1. Circumcision

Among the prescriptions of the law, circumcision, Sabbath observance, and the dietary rules command our attention, because they constitute factors in Jewish identity. As such, they are known in the Greco–Roman world and are often a cause for sarcasm and accusations of particularism and misanthropy.[61] They afford a good opportunity to examine Philo's halakhic knowledge and to get a sense of his hermeneutic, which seems to follow two basic guidelines. At the cosmic level the Mosaic laws reflect the principles that direct the regular harmony of celestial and terrestrial phenomena. At the anthropological level, they lead one to the virtues, which represent the true expression of human nature; they promote health, thus maintaining the appropriate equilibrium in mind and body.

In the Old Testament, circumcision is the distinctive sign of the covenant that God established with Abraham whereby He promises to him many descendants and a land (Gen 17:1–14). Within the priestly code, however, the rite is prescribed in a context that relates to ritual purity, and there is no specific reference to the covenant (Lev 12:3). The metaphorical use of the term is well attested, especially in the prophetic literature, where the circumcision of the heart indicates one's internal readiness to do the will of God. Obedient submission to the law is proclaimed as a divine gift, that may renew one's faith.[62] In the Maccabean period, after a ban on the rite was imposed by Antiochus IV, circumcision seems to have become a kind of *sine qua non* of Jewish identity.[63]

---

60   Cf. S. Daniel, 'La Halacha de Philon selon le premier livre des Lois spéciales', in R. Arnaldez et al., *Philon d'Alexandrie* (Paris 1967), pp. 221–40; L. Doering, *Schabbat: Sabbathalacha und -praxis im antiken Judentum und Urchristentum* (Tübingen 1999), pp. 383–6.

61   See P. Schäfer, *Judeophobia: Attitudes toward the Jews in the Ancient World* (Cambridge, MA 1997), pp. 66–105.

62   Cf. Deut 10:16, 30:6; Jer 4:4, 9:25; R. Le Déaut, 'Le thème de la circoncision du coeur (Dt xxx 6; Jér. iv 4) dans les versions anciennes (LXX et Targum) et à Qumrân', in J. A. Emerton (ed.), *Congress Volume: Vienna 1980* (Leiden 1981 = Vetus Testamentum: Supplements 32), pp. 178–205.

63   1 Macc 1:15, 48, 60, 2:46; 2 Macc 6:10; 4 Macc 4:24–6. In *Jub.* 15:11, 25–34, circumcision is a sign of the covenant; it is an eternal law, written in the heavenly tablets. There is a reference to metaphorical circumcision in

Nevertheless, within Middle Judaism, views of the importance of circumcision are more nuanced. In some propagandistic writings directed toward Greek readers, circumcision is not viewed as an indispensable requirement for conversion to Judaism. More stress is placed on embracing the faith in the one God, abandoning idolatry, and adopting high ethical principles that are widely shared.[64] A similar viewpoint emerges in the speech of Ananias, who, according to Josephus, spoke to King Izates of Adiabene when he desired to convert (*AJ* 20.34–48). Even more radical are the 'extreme allegorizers', described by Philo in *De migratione* 89–93, who look only to the symbolic value of circumcision and neglect the physical rite.

Philo does not minimize the importance of physical circumcision and grants it a position of privilege within his treatment of the laws, discussing it at the beginning of the first book of *De specialibus legibus* (§§ 1–11).[65] His intention in doing this is apologetic, and his broader objective is to tone down Jewish particularism. He states that other great peoples, like the Egyptians, held to be ancient and wise, practice circumcision (*Spec.* 1.2). This statement is somewhat surprising, because normally the Egyptians are depicted in Philo as a degenerate nation, given to the worst vices, not the least of which is the worship of animals. Philo focuses only on the meaning of circumcision, without treating any of the halakhic details (what? when? how? who?). He adduces four reasons for the rite from tradition. Among other things, circumcision helps prevent certain genital diseases (*Spec.* 1.4; *QG* 3.48). The ancients also desired to assimilate the physical generative organ to the heart, the principle of generation of invisible things (*Spec.* 1.6; *QG* 3.48). On his own authority, Philo adds two symbolic explanations: circumcision is the sign of elimination of superfluous pleasures, not only of the sexual variety, and it helps to stem human pride, serving as a reminder that God is the true cause of procreation (*Spec.* 1.8–11; *QG* 3.48; *Migr.* 92). To confirm this, in *De specialibus legibus* 1.303–6, virtuous men, chosen by God, are contrasted with those who are uncircumcised in heart (Lev 26:41; Deut 10:16), who have not cut out the overgrowth of arrogance from their minds, and refuse to obey the laws

---

Jub. 1:22–5. Cf. S.J.D. Cohen, *The Beginnings of Jewishness: Boundaries, Varieties, Uncertainties* (Berkeley 1999), pp. 39–49, 135–9.

64   Cf. J.J. Collins, 'A Symbol of Otherness: Circumcision and Salvation in the First Century', in J. Neusner and E.S. Frerichs (eds.), *To See Ourselves As Others See Us: Christians, Jews, Others in Late Antiquity* (Chico 1985), pp. 163–86.

65   See esp. A. Blaschke, *Beschneidung: Zeugnisse der Bibel und verwandter Texte* (Tübingen 1998), pp. 193–223.

of nature. Linking the physical act closely with its symbolic meaning, Philo shifts the import of circumcision from the covenant toward the law. It is not the sign of the promise and the divine grace that sanctifies Israel and separates it from other peoples, but rather, it signifies certain ethical and religious values that man is called upon to choose. Accordingly, the function of circumcision with respect to the Mosaic law, symbolized by the opening section of *De specialibus legibus*, is protreptic: circumcision is the entryway to the law, because it signifies two fundamental principles of the Mosaic Torah, the repudiation of pleasure, which is the chief cause of moral error, and faith in God, the true source of every good thing.

III.2. Sabbath

The Sabbath, because it is included in the Decalogue, constitutes the paradigm for all Jewish festivals according to Philo's hermeneutic (*Decal.* 158).[66] He usually designates it by the phrase *hē hebdomē hēmera* ('the seventh day') or simply *hebdomas* ('the number seven'), and in this fashion highlights the numerical value of seven, which is well-documented in Pythagorean and Middle Platonic philosophy. For Philo the Sabbath is a holy, public, and universal holiday that celebrates the birthday of the world.[67] He does not, in contrast to *Jubilees* (2:19–20), view it as distinctive of Israel, or as linked to the covenant or to the liberation from slavery in Egypt, as in the Bible (cf. Exod 31:16–17; Deut 5:15). Rather, he states that already in ancient times, humanity had forgotten the weekly calendar, perhaps because of recurring natural disasters. Only Moses, during Israel's wanderings in the desert, re-established the exact reckoning of the seventh day, thanks to a divine oracle, which was confirmed by the double portion of manna given on Friday (*Mos.* 1.205–7, 2.263–9). Other peoples, however, do celebrate the Sabbath, though often in a partial or incomplete fashion (*Decal.* 96), whereas the Mosaic legislation provides the authentic instructions. Any Jewish priority is based not on the fact of Sabbath itself but on the correct manner of observance.

The Bible speaks of the sanctification of the Sabbath and abstention from work in Exod 20:8–11. Although Philo lists some of the activities prohibited on the day, he prefers to focus on its positive elements. In *De migratione* 91, Philo lists as prohibited activities lighting fires, working the land, carrying loads, instituting legal proceedings, acting

---

66 See Doering, *Schabbat*, pp. 315–86; J. Leonhardt, *Jewish Worship in Philo of Alexandria* (Tübingen 2001), pp. 53–100.
67 *Opif.* 89; *Mos.* 1.207, 2.209–10; *Spec.* 1.170, 2.59, 70.

as a juror, and asking for the restitution of deposits or loans. In addition to those things prohibited in the Old Testament, we find here judicial and economic activities of the public sphere.[68] As in Exod 20:10, the Sabbath rest is granted to servants and to animals (*Spec.* 2.66–70). Philo, however, adds even plants.[69] The lessening of physical exertion and the cares of normal business days is not to be understood as a provision for laziness,[70] or as an occasion for cheap entertainment (*Mos.* 2.211). Rather, it allows for time to be dedicated to the soul. For this reason the Jews assemble in synagogues on the Sabbath and listen in silence to the reading and explanation of the Scriptures. They reflect on their lives, undertake an examination of conscience, and turn to the contemplation of nature.[71] Philo does not indicate whether these regular assemblies on the Sabbath have liturgical significance. He does, however, mention songs and prayers in his discussion of the Sabbath as celebrated by the Essenes and the Therapeutae (*Prob.* 81–2; *Contempl.* 30–2). The rites and sacrifices performed in the temple of Jerusalem on the Sabbath, in accord with Num 28:9–10, are described in *De specialibus legibus* 1.170–2.

The symbolism of the number seven is essential for understanding the significance of the Sabbath in Philo. The long and elaborate discussion in *De opificio mundi* 89–128 shows that the seal of the septenary scheme is impressed upon the cosmos, both corporeal and incorporeal, at all levels.[72] The number seven is indicative of a value that precedes creation, because of the relationship that exists between the hebdomad and the monad (*Post.* 64). It reveals that which is uncreated; it is true festivity and joy (*Cher.* 86; *Mos.* 2.211), peace (*Abr.* 28), and contemplation (*Decal.* 97–8), realities that belong fully only to God. The hebdomad leads from the order of created being toward God, it reveals something of the divine and unites one to God. The Sabbath, therefore, entails a kind of *imitatio Dei* (*Decal.* 100). One should try to reproduce in this

---

68 Buying and selling and doing business are activities mentioned in Amos 8:5; Isa 58:13; Neh 10:32; cf. *Jub.* 50:8. Judicial activities were prohibited by Jewish tradition, as is confirmed in decrees cited by Josephus (*AJ* 16.163, 168; cf. Doering, *Schabbat*, pp. 301–2). The reference to deposits and loans has some analogy with CD-A X:18, but it is possible that this prohibition comes from Alexandrian tradition. It does not conform to rabbinic rulings.

69 *Mos.* 2.22; cf. CD-A X:22–3; Mark 2:23. This prohibition as well is more severe than rabbinic rulings.

70 Contrast Seneca, *GLAJJ* I, no. 186.

71 *Opif.* 128; *Abr.* 28–30; *Decal.* 98–101; *Mos.* 2.211–12, 215–16; *Hypoth.* 7.10–14.

72 See D. T. Runia's commentary on Philo, *On the Creation of the Cosmos according to Moses* (Leiden 2001), pp. 260–308.

world the rhythm of work and rest, of activity and contemplation that is typical of God, and to participate in His peace and in His joy. In *Jubilees* it is said that the angels celebrated the Sabbath with God before man did (2:17–18). In the writings of Qumran, the adherents of the sect take part in the Sabbath liturgy in communion with the angels, in anticipation of eschatological times (11Q17 = 11QShirShabb). And according to the Letter to the Hebrews, the believers are called upon to enter the divine rest (4:3–11). In as much as the Sabbath is the birthday of the world, it teaches that power originates from the uncreated, whereas created beings are passive, they receive that which they possess and are called upon to thank the creator (*Migr.* 91; *Her.* 170). Finally, the Sabbath provides an important lesson in social justice, because a master must perform by himself his small everyday tasks, while a servant is allowed to have a taste of liberty. This arrangement temporarily creates a situation of equity, re-establishing the original harmony of nature.

III.3. The Dietary Laws

According to the Bible the food laws were issued at Sinai (Lev 11) and again repeated in the code of Deuteronomy (14:3–21). They came to be a key element of Jewish identity, so much so that, during the persecution of Antiochus, the forced consumption of swine's flesh was employed as a means to provoke sacrilege (2 Macc 6:18–20, 7:1). The problem of the unusual and apparently irrational nature of these injunctions is well formulated in the *Letter of Aristeas*, where it is asked why, if there is a single source for all things, some are considered impure for food and some even to the touch (§ 129). The same question echoes through the centuries and even modern exegetes remain perplexed when attempting to find a rationale for the distinctions between pure and impure animals in the biblical text. In any case, in contrast to the view that the food laws are to be respected despite their 'irrationality' because they are an expression of the divine will, Judeo–Alexandrian exegetes generally tried to provide rational explanations for the laws by means of symbolic or allegorical interpretation. This is first attested in the *Letter of Aristeas* and is based on the assumption that impurity and sinful behavior may be contracted by contact and association. The Torah functions as a fence, a barrier to maintain purity (*Let. Aris.* 130, 142). For this reason Moses, although he knew that all things by nature are equal, set down the food laws with rational principles in mind, principles based on a kind of linkage between animal behaviors and human ethics (*Let. Aris.* 143, 147). Birds of prey are forbidden to encourage human behavior that follows the dictates of justice and is removed from brute force and violence (*Let. Aris.* 145–9). By contrast, it is permitted to eat quadrupeds that have a split hoof and ruminate, because they symbolize discernment of just and unjust actions and memory of God, the provider of man's physical and mental capacities (*Let. Aris.* 153–7).

Philo takes up the same type of interpretation, but gives it a different orientation, because he inserts the food laws under the general rubric of the tenth commandment, 'thou shalt not covet' (Greek: 'desire').[73] In the biblical text (Exod 20:17), the prohibition is directed against desiring the property of a neighbor, but in Philo it takes on a more general meaning. 'Desire' is viewed as the source of every sort of base passion. This is usually a desire for something falsely regarded as a good: wealth, glory, power, physical beauty. But the primal form of desire is connected to the stomach, because that is the seat of the 'desiring' or 'appetitive' part of the soul (called *epithymētikon* according to Plato's threefold division).[74] Philo finds confirmation of this Platonic conception in the fact that the substantive *epithymia* ('desire') appears in the LXX in the episode of the quails (Num 11:4, 34, 35), to stigmatize the desire for meat that comes upon the Israelites in the desert, and is portrayed as an act of rebellion against God (*Spec.* 4.126–31). Moses regulates the consumption of food by mean of a series of laws that would encourage the virtue of *enkrateia* (self-control) and improve relations between men. He indicates a middle path between the austerity of the Spartans and the hedonism of the Ionians or the Sibarites. This emphasis on frugality and temperance is in accord with the ethical ideals articulated by many writers in the early Roman Empire.[75]

Philo's discussion begins with a reference to the offering of the first fruits. A part of the agricultural products and livestock is given as a sacrifice to God as a sign of thanks and a part is given to the priests as compensation for their services. The act of setting apart the first fruits, besides having a religious basis, promotes self-control, and teaches us not to regard everything as being at our disposal (*Spec.* 4.98–9). With regard to pure and impure animals, Philo mentions the pig and fishes without scales. They are forbidden because the tastiness of their meat

---

73 *Spec.* 4.78–131. Other passages on the dietary laws include *Leg.* 2.105–8; *Post.* 148–9; *Agr.* 131–45; *Migr.* 64–7. For discussion see J.N. Rhodes, 'Diet and Desire: The Logic of the Dietary Laws according to Philo', *Ephemerides Theologicae Lovanienses* 79 (2003), pp. 122–33.

74 *Spec.* 4.84, 92–4. The other two parts of the soul according to Plato are the rational part and the 'irascible' or emotive part.

75 Cf. M.R. Niehoff, *Philo on Jewish Identity and Culture* (Tübingen 2001), pp. 94–110, esp. 105–6. The virtue of temperance, defined as control over desires of the body and the soul, is extolled in 4 Macc 1:31–5. Cf. also 4 Macc 5:23–6, where it is stated that the food laws given by God have their basis in human nature.

excites the pleasure of the belly, provokes gluttony, and, in general, leads to negative effects on one's health. The injunctions may be understood in an ethical sense to encourage a temperate life style (*Spec.* 4.100–2). Philo then goes on to consider other land animals. It is prohibited to eat wild beasts that attack man as well as other carnivorous animals in general. The rationale given is more subtle than that found in the *Letter of Aristeas*. Man must avoid being incited by bestiality and anger so as to go after man-eating animals in a spirit of retaliation (*Spec.* 4.103–4). Ten species of quadrupeds are appropriate for human consumption, those that have a split hoof and ruminate. The first characteristic symbolizes the capacity to distinguish the good from the evil, whereas the second alludes to learning, which entails a long process of exercise, memory, and assimilation (*Spec.* 4.105–9). Reptiles and insects that move along on their belly or have four feet or more are unclean. For the belly is tied to pleasure, and the passions, from which all kinds of vices derive, are four in number. Insects that jump, however, are clean, because they represent allegorically men who are able to resist the pull of earthly weight and elevate themselves toward heaven (*Spec.* 4.113–15). Philo also mentions an injunction against eating animals killed by hunting (*Spec.* 4.120–1). This detail seems to be in contrast with the biblical text (Lev 17:13–14), and is not paralleled in other Middle Judaic texts. Philo concludes his survey with the prohibition on blood and fat. The former is to be poured on the sacrificial altar because it is the essence of life and belongs to God, and the latter must be burned because of its richness (*Spec.* 4.122–5).

In reviewing Philo's explanations of the dietary laws, we get a sense of the breadth of his exegetical system, with its attention to both letter and allegory. Considerations of health are coupled with those of spiritual therapy, and ethics with religious lessons.

IV. ISRAEL

In Deuteronomistic theology Israel emerges as the chosen people, separated from other peoples because the Israelites do not pollute themselves by following other gods (Deut 7:6). The election of Israel is not based on merit or greatness, but exclusively on God's love (Deut 7:7–8), which is an act of grace. The election reinforces the covenant and entails an obligation for the people to consecrate themselves in worship and observe the Torah. The prophets, however, bear witness to the infidelity of Israel, and constantly exhort the people to return to God. Although the breaking of the covenant and rejection by God are not the last word, the restoration of Israel's chosenness has a restriction. Only a small remnant, comprised of those who stayed faithful, will be saved.[76] In the wisdom texts of the Hellenistic age, Israel's election tends to coincide with the gift of wisdom granted to her, and the ethical and religious quality of who is chosen takes on greater importance as the basis for God's choice.[77] In some apocalyptic texts we find a kind of determinism: Israel's election is projected back to the first days of creation. According to *Jubilees*, God sets apart and sanctifies Israel on the seventh day (2:19–20). Thus, the election of God's people precedes her historical existence and guarantees her salvation, in spite of the sin with which she will stain herself. In the writings of Qumran as well, Israel's election is part of God's eternal plan and is removed from the historical plane, but it becomes a matter for the individual. Only the person who belongs to the community represents the true Israel, which is an assembly of elect individuals who have proved themselves free from the sin and the impurity that pollute human nature. They are separated from the 'sons of darkness' and with them God renews His covenant and unveils the mysteries of His words so that they might fulfill the law in an irreproachable fashion.[78] A differentiation within Israel is also apparent in *1 Enoch*, where the election is given an eschatological coloring. The elect are the just, the holy, and the pious, those who stay faithful and separate themselves from the sinners. They will be chosen by God on the day of judgment.[79] Somewhat different is the perspective of Paul, who states in Rom 9:6: 'not all descendants of Israel are Israel.' The distinction is not based on physical ancestry, marked by circumcision, but on faith and obedience to the will of God in Jesus Christ, and it allows for the inclusion of the Gentiles within the 'true Israel'.

For Philo as well, the categories 'the Jews' and 'Israel' do not perfectly overlap.[80] The term *Ioudaios*, which does not occur at all in the *Allegorical Commentary*, has a connotation that seems to be primarily historical and sociological. It defines the Jews as an *ethnos* (nation) or *laos* (people), that have Abraham as their forefather (*Virt.* 212) and Moses as their legislator (*Mos.* 1.1). Jerusalem is their mother city, but they are spread all over the inhabited world (*Flacc.* 45–6). Faith in the true God is a prerogative of the Jews, and it finds expression in excellent cultic practices and in the observance of

---

76   Isa 10:20–3; Zeph 3:12–13. The scheme sin-punishment-restoration of a remnant is also found in the *Psalms of Solomon* (2:6–8, 33–5, 14:5–10) and in the *Testaments of the XII Patriarchs* (*T. Levi* 15:1–4; *T. Dan* 7:3; *T. Asher* 7:5–7).

77   Cf. S. Grindheim, *The Crux of Election: Paul's Critique of the Jewish Confidence in the Election of Israel* (Tübingen 2005), pp. 35–40.

78   See Grindheim, *Crux*, pp. 44–8, 55–69.

79   *1 Enoch* 38:1–4, 93:1–10; cf. Grindheim, *Crux*, pp. 40–4.

80   A detailed analysis may be found in E. Birnbaum, *The Place of Judaism in Philo's Thought: Israel, Jews, and Proselytes* (Atlanta 1996).

laws and customs that are austere and promote virtue (*Spec.* 4.159; *Virt.* 65). They are a people that God loves, they belong to Him and are beneficiaries of a special providential care on His part (*Legat.* 3–4). Interpreting the oracle of Balaam in *De vita Mosis* 1.278–9, Philo states that the souls of the Hebrews are sprung from divine seeds, and are akin to God.

The term 'Israel', on the other hand, is an honorific title, which has symbolic significance and more shades of meaning. It appears almost exclusively in the allegorical treatises and, according to the etymology connected to Gen 32:30(31), it means 'the one who sees God'. For Israel is the name that Jacob receives during his night fight with some kind of messenger of God, after which he said 'I have seen God face to face'. Philo makes clear that the sort of contemplation that Israel is able to gain is not the result of a rational process that takes the created cosmos as the point of departure, but is the gift of God to His suppliants. It is a seeing of God through God, a seeing of light by light (*Praem.* 43–6; *Mut.* 81–2). Philo cites the classic passages from Deuteronomy that emphasize the election of Israel, but in his allegorical exegesis the special bond that unites Israel to God is elevated beyond history and is transformed into the wise soul's belonging to God.[81] In the same fashion, the notion of covenant loses its historical dimension to become a sign of divine grace and of the perfect gift of virtue.[82] It must be stressed, however, that the best way to reach this level of perfection remains closely joined to the Torah and to Jewish religious tradition. Who therefore is Israel, the race of seers, the holy people that has royal and priestly honors (*Abr.* 56)? In *Legatio ad Gaium* 4, Israel is identified with the Jews. Normally, however, Philo leaves Israel's identity less clearly defined and speaks more generally, at times of a *genos* (race) and at times of an *ethnos* (nation). In fact, it appears that belonging to Israel is not linked to ethnic or sectarian factors. Israel is an elite group of sages who achieved perfection in virtue and have reached the apex of spiritual progress. In Philo's vision of things, human merit and divine grace meet in synergy and his elitism retains an inclusive quality. If the Jews, or at least some of them, have reached the ultimate objective by virtue of the excellence of their laws and traditions, it is not impossible for others to reach the same goal by means of the teachings of philosophy (*Virt.* 65; *Praem.* 43–4).

(Translated from the Italian by Adam Kamesar.)

---

81 Cf. Deut 7:7–8 in *Migr.* 60–1; Deut 32:7–9 in *Post.* 89–92 and *Plant.* 58–60; cf. also Exod 4:22 in *Post.* 63.

82 *Sacr.* 57 with the citation of Deut 9:5. One cannot define the Judaism of the Second Temple period as 'covenantal nomism', because the category of covenant plays a significant role only in part of the literature of the period.

5 Philo's Theology and Theory of Creation

I. GOD

In glancing at the titles of Philo's works, it might appear easy to define the nature of God and the cosmos. This is because two of his works, *Quod Deus sit immutabilis* (*On the Unchangeableness of God*) and *De aeternitate mundi* (*On the Eternity of the World*), have titles that are quite pertinent to these topics, and might lead one to believe that these works provide complete and definitive information. But this is not the case. The *Quod Deus* deals essentially with the constancy and irrevocability of divine judgment, and does not treat the question of God's nature. The *De aeternitate* on the other hand appears to be a kind of scholastic work in which two opposing theses are contrasted with each other, not in order to set out the views of the author but rather to put on display his competence and erudition in the philosophical disciplines. However, the work seems to have been handed down in incomplete form, and the part that survives contains a thesis that is irreconcilable with the thought of Philo taken as whole.

Therefore, to follow the path indicated by the titles of his works will not bring us to heart of the subject of this chapter, and it might even lead us astray. For Philo never formulated a theology that was independently forged, or a systematic and autonomous physics. There is a good reason for this, as will become immediately apparent.

To discuss God while taking the world as a point of departure is a well-established method in philosophical study. It is enough to consider the path taken by Aristotle who, starting from the dynamic character of the cosmos, arrives at the idea of God as unmoved mover, or, starting from the imperfection of the world, arrives at the perfection of God conceived as final cause. But to proceed in the opposite direction, that is, to discuss the world while taking God and the divine as the point of departure, is an equally legitimate method and can be understood to correspond to the Platonic (and latter Middle Platonic and Neoplatonic) position. According to this way of thinking, the phenomenon of the world may be understood and deduced from a set of first principles. Between these two approaches one may place Stoic theory, which emphasizes the presence of God in the world and expresses what is essentially a pantheistic perspective.

In basic terms, these are the three philosophical approaches that were dominant at the time of Philo, yet it must be stated that Philo's approach is identical to none of them and, strictly speaking, is not even philosophical. It is rather 'allegorical' or 'exegetical'.[1] This means that Philo does not follow the logical sequence of the problems; for example, instead of asking the question of whether God exists or what He is, he rather takes for granted that God exists and that His nature is that of a creator. This kind of certainty obviously cannot be the result of philosophical reflection, but is a matter of faith, and is derived from the Bible, an absolutely infallible source, even if its language may be obscure. However, God is the source of this revelation, as well as the cause and guarantor of human intelligence and autonomous philosophical knowledge. Accordingly, human thought, if it proceeds correctly, does have the capacity to decipher the symbols of the Bible and to reconstruct their pristine and original sense, which is of a rational variety. Therefore, interpreting the Bible allegorically allows one to gain access to philosophical truths that are certain and absolute. Needless to say, this presupposes that God has expressed His will and thought in the Holy Scriptures. But for Philo it makes no sense to question this. Indeed, when he introduces the account of creation according to the Book of Genesis, he does not even regard that account as the focal point of his concerns, as we might expect. Rather, he sees it as a preamble to the law itself. Moreover, he does not characterize the account of creation as a theological or cosmological tract, but as the preface to a document of ethical and religious content. The purpose of the preface is to show that 'the world is in harmony with the law and the law with the world, and that the man who observes the law becomes thereby a citizen of the world, in that he makes his actions conform to the will of nature, according to which the entire world is governed' (*Opif.* 3).

From this perspective, if the leading ideas of Philo's theology and cosmology are found in the revealed writings, we would have as many 'theories' of God and the cosmos as we have passages of the Bible that speak of God and of His relationship with the world. Accordingly, we find that many of Philo's fundamental ideas are subject to vacillations that are determined by his reliance on different biblical passages, and at the

---

1   This proposition has been advanced by V. Nikiprowetzky in his work, *Le commentaire de l'Écriture chez Philon d'Alexandrie* (Leiden, 1977); see esp. p. 7.

same time, on philosophical influences. The following survey of Philo's primary ideas about God will be set out in terms of these vacillations.

The first issue, which is relevant to all of Philo's theology, is the question of the knowability of God. In fact, if God were completely unknowable, it would be impossible to think about Him or express ideas about Him. Yet Philo appears not to be so far removed from such agnostic tendencies, when he states: 'In searching for God, truly philosophical thought encounters two main problems: does the divinity exist ... and secondly, what is its nature? Now, to answer the first question is not so difficult; the second, however, is not only difficult but perhaps impossible to answer' (Spec. 1.32). But for Philo, abstract philosophical thought is not the only way to arrive at the truth about God. There exists also the way of revelation, which God initiates Himself to respond to man's thirst for knowledge.[2] It is precisely through revelation that man may ascribe to God the attribute of existence (Mos. 1.75). However, as far as God's nature is concerned, one is not limited to what God Himself reveals. God's goodness at least can be deduced in a purely rational fashion, as it was, for example, by Plato from the existence and the beauty of the cosmos. Therefore, man should not desist from the search for God. Even if God is 'ineffable, inconceivable, and incomprehensible' (Mut. 15), one may progress in gaining knowledge of Him, but this knowledge is proportionate to the upward movement of the soul of the individual.

A second problem in the determination of the nature of God concerns His personal or impersonal character. This problem is especially important for defining the relationship between faith, which reaches for a personal God, and philosophical reason, which strives to attain an impersonal and abstract concept of God, such as the unmoved mover of Aristotle. Philo seems to be open to both perspectives. On the one hand, he speaks of man in the image of God[3] and therefore of a God with a personal character, but on the other hand, he regards anthropomorphic descriptions of God as the product of crude and improper understanding. As he puts it, 'in the laws ... there are two supreme principles concerning the cause: one is "God is not as a man", and the other is "God is as a

---

2 Cf. the work attributed to Aristotle, De mundo 6, 397b13, where the author speaks of 'an ancient doctrine, for all men, transmitted from father to son' as a source of knowledge of God. Philo also alludes to a mystic way to knowledge of God, or to a 'theology of silence', which has its source in the biblical commandment, 'keep silent and listen' (Deut 27:9). For this, see Her. 11.

3 This notion is also important for Ps.-Phocylides, an Alexandrian Jewish author who lived in the time of Philo or perhaps slightly before. See his Sentences, line 106, with P. W. van der Horst in his edition and commentary (Leiden 1978), p. 67.

man". The former is a matter of absolute truth, the latter is introduced for the instruction of the masses.[4] Most probably, Philo's true position lies somewhere between the two poles. He would recognize a certain 'personality' in God, in analogy to man, only as regards noetic function. God would be like man, although much greater than man, so far as concerns His thought, but He would be completely different from man as concerns His physical aspect.

Connected to this instance of vacillation is another one concerning the transcendence or immanence of God. Philo's tendencies in this regard are often determined by whether he is dependent on a biblical or a philosophical model at any given point in his exegesis. In Philo one finds innumerable expressions that seem to emphasize the transcendence of God. This notion is encouraged by the Bible itself, which asserts that God has no name.[5] But Philo does not see it as a question only of names, but of metaphysics. That is, he attributes the innominability of God not just to the limitations of human language, but to God's infinite ontological superiority with respect to man and the world.[6] God is in every sense 'the other' with respect to everything that is known to us. As Philo puts it, there is nothing that is similar to God (*Leg.* 2.1; *Somn.* 1.73). This theme of the ineffability of God is very important because it leads Philo to introduce in a systematic fashion the kind of negative theology that would have great influence on later thought, especially that of the Neopythagoreans of the imperial age and Plotinus. It may be acknowledged that some significant antecedents of the idea of the innominability of God may be found in Pythagorean circles at an earlier time (fourth to second centuries BCE). However, in the sources in question, the idea has a sense different from the one it has in Philo, and usually alludes to the irrational nature of the material principle.[7] We

4 *Deus* 53. Cf. A. Kamesar, 'Philo, the Presence of "Paideutic" Myth in the Pentateuch, and the "Principles" or *Kephalaia* of Mosaic Discourse', *StPhAnn* 10 (1998), pp. 34–65.
5 See Exod 3:13–14, as interpreted by Philo, *Mos.* 1.75: 'there is no name that can properly designate me.' Cf. *Mut.* 11.
6 See esp. *Contempl.* 2, where Philo says that God is 'superior to the good, purer than the One and more primal than the Monad'; and *Somn.* 2.28, where he refers to God as 'in his essence disjunct from all creation' .
7 In a fragment of *On First Principles* attributed to Archytas we read as follows: 'There are necessarily two principles of beings: the one which has the series of objects ordered and defined, the other which has the series of objects disordered and undefined. The former is capable of being expressed by name and has a rational nature. It holds together the things that are and also determines and sets in order the things that are not. ... On the other hand the principle which is irrational and not capable of being expressed by

should probably attribute to Philo and to his allegorical interpretation of the Bible the change in significance of 'having no name', so that it indicates something positive or good.

On the other hand, there are passages where Philo seems to understand God in highly material terms. Especially important is *Legum allegoriae* 1.44, where God is described as follows: 'He is in himself, he fills himself, and is sufficient for himself. Indeed, he fills and contains all other things which are insufficient for themselves, isolated, and empty. But he cannot be contained by any other being, because he himself is one and the whole.' This passage (and many others like it could be cited), in which the concepts of 'contain' and 'being contained' are employed to describe the superiority of God over the cosmos, has been inspired by Stoic thinking.[8] Philo uses the concepts, however, not so much with purely theological connotations, but with an exegetical intention, namely, to exclude the possibility that God may be found in some place in the cosmos. In any case, the vacillation between materiality and transcendence is in a certain sense inevitable, because both the transcendence of God and His providential activity in the world are irrevocable dogmas for Philo.

A fourth sphere of ambiguity in Philo's thought is that which relates to the oneness or primacy of God. Is God the only God or the 'first God'? As we shall see, Philo resolves the antinomy of transcendence and providence by means of a series of hypostases or intermediate beings that take their places in a kind of ontological hierarchy between God and the world. Within this hierarchy itself, the differences are not

name does damage to ordered beings and dissolves objects which come into being and essence. As it comes into contact with things, it assimilates them to itself' (ed. H. Thesleff, *The Pythagorean Texts of the Hellenistic Period* [Åbo 1965], p. 19). A similar contrast between *rhētē kai logon echousa* and *arrēton kai alogon* is found in Damippus, with reference to *eutychia*, perhaps in the sense of 'imponderable', that is, unpredictable and irrational (*De prud. et beat.*, fr. 1 Thesleff; cf. Eurytus, *De fort.*, p. 88 Thesleff). One needs to go to a text attributed to Lysis of Tarentum, probably later than those just cited, to find an apparently non-Platonic use of *arrētos*. In a fragment preserved in Athenagoras, God is defined as *arithmos arrētos* (Thesleff, p. 114). This is just a fleeting reference, however, and the term is probably not used in a technical sense, but just indicates a number of unspeakable size. Accordingly, in the period from the 4th to the 2nd centuries BCE, in Pythagorean circles, the term *arrētos* is used primarily in a negative sense, in tune with a Platonic viewpoint.

8   For further detail and bibliographical references, see R. Radice, *Allegoria e paradigmi etici in Filone di Alessandria* (Milan 2000), pp. 137–8 note f.

always clear-cut.[9] Because Philo usually focuses his attention on difficulties that arise in the biblical text, called *zētēmata* or *quaestiones*, he therefore hardly ever confronts problems of this sort in a general way or from a purely theological perspective, and statements that are not consistent with one another are found throughout his writings. That God is one is for Philo a dogma of faith and tradition.[10] He repeats it in many passages. In *Legum allegoriae* 3.82 we read: 'God, being one, "is in the heaven above and on the earth below, and there is none other besides him" (Deut 4:39)'. In *De virtutibus* 214, he defines God with the epithet 'the one' and, in *De opificio mundi* 171, he states emphatically that 'God is one' and that this doctrine is set forth to combat the error of polytheism. Nevertheless, in a few passages he implies that even the stars are gods, 'manifest and perceivable gods' (*Opif.* 27; cf. *Spec.* 1.209, 2.165). Here he aligns himself with Platonic and Aristotelian thought.[11]

One might be tempted to consider Philo's statements of this latter sort to be a concession to popular usage, or a display of philosophical knowledge to adorn his work. However, at least in the case of the Logos and even more in that of Wisdom (= *sophia*), these powers seem to be hypostases coeternal with the creator and collaborators in creation (if God is the father of the world, Wisdom is the mother), so that they would share the same essence with Him. Moreover, from a philosophical perspective, the term *logos* may sometimes mean the mind of God, and in this case the Logos would be essentially equivalent to God.

A final instance of vacillation that may be discerned in Philo's theology is that relating to the infinitude or finitude of the nature and power of God. Regarding the infinitude of the nature of God, Philo does not seem to have any doubts – the being of God cannot be circumscribed (*Her.* 229). But concerning the infinitude of God's power the question is more complicated. In *De sacrificiis Abelis et Caini* 59, he addresses the issue explicitly and states, 'God is infinite, and also infinite are

---

9   The ambiguity here is heightened by the fact that Philo uses the word 'God' to indicate both the supreme being, which is transcendent and ineffable (*Somn.* 2.28), and His creative power (*Plant.* 86). For this reason, everything that is said of God could be attributed to the former entity or to the latter, with the result that there emerge serious inconsistencies concerning the ontological status of God. For further detail on this, see G. Reale and R. Radice in their introduction to the volume of Philonic treatises entitled *La filosofia mosaica* (Milan 1987), pp. CXXIII–CXXIV.

10 Already by the end of the 3rd century BCE, in Alexandrian circles, the ideal of monotheism had been proudly proclaimed and identified as distinctively Jewish in the *Letter of Aristeas* 134.

11 For further discussion and bibliography see my commentary on *Opif.* 27 in *La filosofia mosaica*, p. 247.

his powers.' This affirmation is not insignificant, because it indirectly poses the philosophical problem of God's relationship to evil. Indeed, if God is omnipotent there arises the question of whether God is able to will evil, or more simply, whether he is able to allow evil because, in the latter case, one would need to admit the existence of a part of reality – if not an actual principle – different from or antithetical to God, over which God would have no power. Such a question would hardly be alien to Philo. In *De opificio* 46 we read: 'like a charioteer taking the reigns or a helmsman the tiller, God guides all things according to law and justice, in whatever direction he desires, without the need of anything else. For all things are possible to God.' In this passage we find not only the idea of infinite divine power, but also that of infinite divine freedom. The phrases 'in whatever direction he desires' and 'according to law and justice' are not synonymous, for the creator seems to have the freedom to 'transgress' His own law, by means of miracles for example, and His own justice, by ordering the sacrifice of a child. Of course, such actions would reveal Him to be the conveyer of a greater law and justice.[12] The idea of the infinitude of God as expressed in Philo's writings entails a complete transformation of the Greek concept of the infinite, which, on account of its Pythagorean heritage, was defined more in a negative than in a positive fashion. In Philo, the idea of divine infinitude is characterized by the principle of infinite divine power, as expressed in *De sacrificiis* 59: 'God has infinite powers.' This principle makes for considerable philosophical progress, because it introduces into Greek thought the idea that there can be an infinitude that is not spatial (determined by an absence of boundaries) nor logical (determined by a lack of definition), but rather relating to power, force, and action. The idea is of Stoic origin and may be expressed succinctly in the following form: 'in the order of the universe there is an active cause and a passive cause, and the active cause is the intellect of the universe,' in other words, God (*Opif.* 8 = *SVF* II.302). Even more explicit is this affirmation: 'For God never ceases to create, but as it is the property of fire to burn and snow to chill, so it is the property of God to make. Indeed, this property belongs to him more than it does to others, in as much as he is the source of action of all other beings' (*Leg.* 1.5; cf. *Mut.* 27–8). The 'dynamic' infinitude of God ('dynamic' is here used in the etymological sense of having *dynamis*, 'power') has the double sense of 'able to do everything' and of 'never ceasing to act'. This concept of divine infinitude goes beyond the use of that notion in contemporary Greek philosophy but it anticipates in many ways the Neoplatonic and especially the

12 Cf. H. A. Wolfson, *Philo: Foundations of Religious Philosophy in Judaism, Christianity, and Islam* (Cambridge, MA 1948), I, p. 436.

Plotinian conception of the principle. Nevertheless, as stated, when one attributes this kind of absolute power to God, there arises in a particularly acute fashion the problem of His relationship to evil. In the face of the dilemma of having to choose between the goodness of God and the infinitude of His power, Philo, who did not possess an adequate concept of human will and freedom, does not hesitate to select the first option. He states: 'one should not mix and confuse things by representing God as the cause of all things indiscriminately, but one must distinguish, and attribute to him only the good things' (*Agr.* 129; cf. also *Mut.* 30). In short, just as one reads in *De specialibus legibus* 4.187, even if, from a theological perspective, God has the power to do both good and evil, from an ethical perspective He neither wills evil nor has responsibility for it, because He is good in an absolute sense.

II. CREATION

But what about this activity that seems to be the very essence of God, or at least as far as man may be aware of it? Of what does it consist? Does it involve, as is the case with the Platonic demiurge, the contemplation of the world of the Ideas, or, as in the case of Aristotle's God, the sheer thinking of itself?

Neither the one nor the other appear to have satisfied Philo, who in this instance turned to the Bible, and especially Genesis, to establish that the principal and essential action of God is that of creation and nothing else. And it is in his allegorical exegesis of the cosmology and the anthropology of Genesis that Philo forms the key elements of his philosophical characterization of God and many of the elements of his characterization of man.

As we endeavor to set out Philo's exegesis of the creation narrative, at least in its main points, let us affirm at the outset that the key element is his negation of creation in time. When he states, in a comment on the first verses of Genesis, that the creator did not have need of any extension of time in order to create (*Opif.* 13), he transforms the chronological order of the biblical text into a logical order and transforms the physical beauty of the creation into a beauty in the realm of Ideas. This means that the first creative act cannot be understood with reference to the material cosmos, which always exists within time, but only with reference to an immaterial or noetic cosmos, which by its very nature exists apart from time. One sees immediately that Philo's philosophical source is Plato, who had postulated the existence of a world of Ideas existing beyond the world but determining its nature. But Philo's further comments in *De opificio* 13 change the framework of the issue, because he specifies that 'God creates everything simultaneously, not only in the phase of giving an order, but also in that of conceiving it.' He explains as follows, 'when God wanted to create this visible world, first he forged the intelligible world, so that he might have use of an incorporeal, completely God-like model' (*Opif.* 16). These statements, although expressed in Platonic terms, go beyond the Platonic horizon. This is because the great Athenian philosopher never said, nor could he have with the presuppositions he held, that his demiurge first came up with an ideal plan of the world and only at that point undertook its material realization. He only said that the demiurge established the world 'according to the exemplar' of the world of the Ideas (*Tim.* 31a). The Ideas did not have their origin in the mind of the demiurge, indeed they had no origin at all, as they are eternal and ungenerated. Only the Philonic God can be called 'architect' (*Opif.* 20) of the world, because only He is *creative* in the phase of planning. We find here for the first time the doctrine of the Ideas as the thoughts of God, and, in close association with it, the doctrine of the double creation, that is, the creation of 'conceiving' and that of 'giving an order', as attested in *De opificio* 13. This latter doctrine, because it is in part philosophical and in part exegetical, carries, as it were, the trademark of Philo.

Philo finds a confirmation of this philosophical insight in the fact that in Genesis the first day is not called 'first day', but 'day one', that is, it is explicitly and intentionally differentiated from the other days that are indicated by ordinal numbers. Moreover, the earth created on that day is said to be 'invisible' (Gen 1:2), which from Philo's perspective would indicate that it is earth not perceivable with the senses, but only with the mind.[13] It would be, therefore, the Idea of earth. And if this is true of the creation of the earth, so Philo thinks, it would also be true of all the other parts of the world that are mentioned in connection with that day (heaven, light, air/void, water, *pneuma*).

One should note that this bold and complicated conception of creation finds considerable support in the fact that the account in Genesis is not linear but recapitulative, that is, it presents the creation of the same entities on different occasions and on different 'days'. Thus, for example, the fact that Genesis speaks of the creation of the heavens on the first day, and again on the second day and on the fourth leads Philo to a sophisticated exegesis of the account of creation. In his view, the creation can be seen as taking place in three phases, which can be described as follows: (1) creation of the Idea; (2) creation of the physical

---

13 Cf. M. Schwabe, 'Philo, *De opificio mundi* § 15', *StPhAnn* 11 (1999), pp. 104–112.

(general); and (3) creation of the physical (particular). These phases can be represented on a chart as follows:

	Creation of the Idea	Creation of the perceivable as a whole	Creation of the perceivable in its parts (= embellishment)
I	Idea of heaven: day 1	Creation of the heaven as a whole: 2nd day	Creation of the heaven in its parts: 4th day
II	Idea of earth: day 1	Creation of the earth as a whole: 3rd day	Creation of the earth in its parts: 3rd day
III	Idea of light: day 1	Created as 'universal brightness': perhaps 2nd day	Creation of the light of the sun and stars: 4th day
IV–V	Idea of air/void: day 1	absent	Creation of the air in its parts (birds): 5th day
VI	Idea of water: day 1	Creation of water as a whole: 3rd day	Creation of water in its parts (fish): 5th day
VII	Idea of pneuma: day 1	Creation of the pneumatic/psychic beings: 6th day	

If we examine the scheme set out in the chart, we see that the heaven is created as an Idea on day one, in material form as a whole on the second day, and in material form in its particular parts on the fourth day. The earth is created as an Idea on day one, in material form as a whole on the third day, and in its material parts also on the third day. The air/void is created as an Idea on day one, there is no reference to a general material creation, but it is created in its particular parts on the fifth day. The light is created as an Idea on day one, it is created in material form as 'universal brightness' on a day which is not specified, and it is created in material form as the light of the sun and the stars on the fourth day, in association with the adornment of the heaven. Finally, *pneuma* is created as an Idea on day one, it does not appear to have a general material creation, but it does have a material creation in its particular parts on the sixth day, with the creation of the living things.

This ingenious scheme was developed by Philo no doubt for apologetic reasons, so that he might maintain the overall structure of the creation account in Genesis. It is also a direct consequence of his denying that a chronological order is indicated in the text, and claiming that the order is only logical or philosophical. There arises a difficulty, however, in the progression from the first to the second day, that is, from the sphere of Ideas to the sphere of the physical. Why would God advance to the creation of a material and imperfect world, after he had created the world of the Ideas, which is in perfect harmony with His own nature? One need not forget that Aristotle had maintained the transcendence of God by keeping Him within the sphere of thought alone and isolating Him from the world.

But Philo could not do this, because an Aristotelian approach would have entailed a denial of creation and of the veracity of the biblical account.

Accordingly, Philo is forced to follow a Platonic path and resort to the principle of divine goodness. Plato had affirmed that the demiurge 'was good ... and desired that all things would be as far as possible similar to himself' (*Tim.* 29e). Philo, employing the same reasoning, affirms as follows: 'God decided that it was necessary to confer rich benefits, without limit, on the nature that without divine gift could not obtain even a single good thing by itself. Nevertheless God confers benefits not in proportion to the greatness of his own bounty, which is infinite and without limit, but in proportion to the capacities of those who receive the benefits' (*Opif.* 23).

At this point, the principle of divine goodness, although it explains the creation of the material cosmos, necessitates *de facto* the introduction of a negative principle, matter, corresponding to the *chōra* of Plato. This principle entails a deterioration from the ideal creation, yet at the same time it cannot be attributed to divine activity, because of its negative nature. An option would have been to postulate matter as uncreated, coeternal and even set opposite to God, on the basis of the Platonic theory of first principles.[14] But Philo could not pursue this option because he would have needed to jettison the doctrine of monotheism, which for him was a matter of religion as well as of theology. In a certain sense he leaves the question of the origin of matter unresolved, although we will see later to what extent.

Up to this point we have dealt with the topic of the creation of the world. However, both the text of *De opificio*, and in parallel, the text of Genesis, continue with the creation of man. The creation of man appears to be completely in line with the creation of the cosmos, in as much as it is 'double'. Indeed, it appears to be even more evidently so than the creation of the cosmos, because it is mentioned two different times in the text, once in Gen 1:26 and again in Gen 2:7. And because the two accounts are represented as referring to, on the one hand, a man 'after the image', and on the other hand, a 'molded man', the notion of an ideal creation followed by a physical creation comes easily to the fore. The scheme already set out regarding the creation of the cosmos is easily adapted to the account of the creation of man, even if a number of problems arise. In any case, just as the creation of the cosmos determines for Philo both the nature of God and that of the cosmos, as well as the relationship between the two, so the creation of man determines

---

14   In Middle Platonism (Alcinous), the three first principles are God, Ideas, and matter.

the (even personal) nature of God and that of man, and the basic relationship between the two. In short, the account of the creation of man re-emphasizes the absolutely central importance of the theory of creation in Philo.

III. THE NATURE OF THE POWERS AND THE LOGOS

The problem of matter leads to another important theological problem: that of the relationship between God and matter, which is a negative principle. This problem emerges in the context of the discussion of creation in *De opificio*, and Philo looks to solve it by introducing the theological figures that are the 'powers' (=*dynameis*), and especially the power Logos, which is the most philosophically significant of all of them.

But what are the powers for Philo? The term *dynamis* is one that was of some consequence in Stoic physics, in which God Himself or His providence are thought to be powers of matter.[15] The Stoics probably took over this term and the concept from Aristotle, because already in Aristotelian circles, as represented by the author of *De mundo*, *dynamis* was connected to the theological sphere.[16] We have already referred to the passage in question, but it is necessary to cite it in full here because of its extraordinary similarity to what we find in Philo: 'Some of the ancient philosophers went so far as to affirm that all things that appear to us through our sight, hearing, and other senses, are full of Gods, setting forth a reasoning that might fit the divine power, but not the divine essence' (6, 397b16–20). The distinction postulated between the essence and the power of God, which was no doubt taken over by Philo, was also taken over by his most significant predecessor and the only one whose work survives, at least in some significant fragments. This is Aristobulus, a Judeo–Alexandrian exegete who lived in the second century BCE. Aristobulus employs this distinction as the basis for his interpretation of anthropomorphism in the Bible: 'in our law hands, arm, face, feet, and movement are used to denote the divine power [*dynamis*].'[17] The position of Aristobulus reveals clearly that the theological function of the powers, here in perfect tune with

---

15 For God as 'power', see *SVF* II.1047, for providence, see *SVF* I.176.
16 For the view that the *De mundo* is an authentic Aristotelian work, see G. Reale and A. P. Bos in their edition of the text, *Il trattato Sul Cosmo per Alessandro attribuito ad Aristotele*[2] (Milan 1995). I myself have defended this view in R. Radice, *La filosofia di Aristobulo e i suoi nessi con il De mundo attribuito ad Aristotele*[2] (Milan 1995).
17 Aristobulus, fr. 2: 10.1; cf. fr. 2: 10.8. For more on Aristobulus' notion of *dynamis*, see my *Aristobulo*, pp. 69–95.

Stoic thought, is especially that of making possible God's action *upon the world* (creation) and *in the world* (providence) without compromising His transcendence. At the same time, this tendency was also favored by the canons of allegorical exegesis, which had been codified in Stoic circles but are also attested in an Aristotelian setting, and were universally accepted in Alexandrian Judaism. These canons depend in essence on the principle that God, 'although he is one has many names, because he is named from the many effects that he continually renews' (*De mundo* 7, 401a12–13). Accordingly, the philosophical doctrine of the powers worked in synergy with the exegetical principle just cited, and allowed Philo to maintain both the oneness of God despite His many names and epithets,[18] and the transcendence of God despite His action in the world.

III.1. The Logos

Having said this about the general function of the powers in Philo, it is necessary to add that the Philonic doctrine of the *dynameis* as a whole may be understood with reference to the concept of Logos. From the start, that is, from the allegory of creation in *De opificio*, the Logos is established as a kind of screen between a transcendent God and the sensible world. At the same time it plays a role as an instrument of creation, by means of which God, while having no direct contact with matter, is able to act upon it.

It is therefore natural to ask about the source of this figure of the Logos. For it is so important for Philo that it proves even more efficacious for him than the philosophical doctrine based on Platonic theory. This emerges quite clearly from *De opificio* 24–5, where we read: 'If one were to use more direct terms, one might say that the *intelligible world* is nothing other than the *divine Logos* already engaged in the act of creation. … and this is the doctrine of Moses, not mine.' This passage leads us to believe that Philo was able to choose between two different interpretations of creation, substantially the same, but differing in clarity and in efficacy. One interpretation would be philosophical, the one based on the concept of the intelligible world, while the other would be the doctrine of Moses, based on the Logos. It behooves us to ask in what

18 It may be noted that even the principal powers have a variety of names. See esp. *Conf.* 146: the Logos 'has many names: he is called "beginning", "name of God", "Logos", "man after the image", "the seeing", "Israel" '; also *Leg.* 1.43: 'The sacred text referred to the sublime and heavenly wisdom with many names, since it has many names. It is called "beginning" and "image" and "vision of God".'

sense the theory of the Logos 'is the doctrine of Moses', or rather what connection does it have with the biblical writings.

It appears that the answer to this question lies in the fact that for every act of creation as given in the account in Genesis, the text employs the phrase, 'And God said ... and there was.' This formula, in the eyes of the Alexandrian exegetes, came to give particular emphasis to the relationship that exists between the word of God (*logos*), and the act of creation. However, it must be said that the term *logos* does not appear at all in the Greek text of the creation account in Genesis. Moreover, it was not the only term available to Philo to indicate the 'word' (of God), for he uses the term *rhēma* in *De decalogo* 47 and in many other passages.[19] Thus, while it was hardly obligatory for Philo to employ the term *logos* to indicate 'word' or 'divine word', it was precisely that same term that was used by the Stoics to indicate the chief rational principle, the principle responsible for the creation of the cosmos. This circumstance allows us to appreciate the extraordinary philosophical affinity between two first principles: the creative word in the Bible and the creative *logos* of the Stoics. And this explains why in the middle of Philo's Platonically oriented reconstruction of the relationship between God and the world there appears a Stoic concept.[20]

But here again, a new insight, although it solves some problems, creates others. Indeed, the Stoic Logos is a creative force, but one that is immanent in the world and a constituent part of the world, as emerges clearly from the following passage: 'They [sc. the Stoics] think that there are two principles of the universe: one active and one passive. The passive principle is ... matter; the active principle is the Logos which is in it, that is, god' (*SVF* I.494). Philo, however, would not be able to accept the pantheistic implication of such a statement, and he 'corrects'

---

19 See *Abr.* 112 and esp. *Leg.* 3.173 and *Migr.* 80, where there seems to be a kind of distinction between *rhēma theou* and *logos theou*.

20 The themes discussed in the preceding paragraphs are also attested in Middle Platonic sources from the period after Philo: the problem of having to safeguard the transcendence of God and obviate His contact with matter; the insertion of intermediary beings between the first principle and the cosmos; and the philosophical terms employed, like God, Ideas as the thoughts of God, matter. However, the use of *logos* as a hypostasis is not paralleled in the Middle Platonic texts. By contrast, it is consistently present in a Judeo–Hellenistic setting, for example in the prologue of the Gospel of John, even if there may be significant semantic differences (on this, cf. M. Azkoul, *St. Gregory of Nyssa and the Tradition of the Fathers* [Lewiston 1995], pp. 103ff.). This fact, in my judgment, is proof of the biblical origin of Logos as a hypostasis, a notion that could not have been shared by thinkers outside the Mosaic tradition.

the Stoic view in the following sense. While God is the cause of the world and its material is the four elements, 'the Logos is the instrument through which the world has been created' (*Cher.* 127). In this manner Philo reorients the Stoic Logos in a Platonic sense, since Plato had entrusted to the demiurge, as instruments of the creation of the world, the mathematical and geometrical forms (*Tim.* 53a-b).

Nevertheless, in the context of the account of creation in *De opificio* the Logos is presented only as the location of the ideal plan of the world, that is, as the object of thought of the creator in 'the moment of creation'. However, elsewhere the Logos appears to take on more and more functions, so that one might distinguish (1) a 'Logos in God', identical to God in having the function of His mind, and distinct from God in being the object of His thought; (2) a 'Logos in itself', as the instrument of God; and (3) a 'Logos in the world', as the bond of the world.[21]

It is interesting to note that the Logos is able to redeem the world itself from the negativity that association with matter inflicts upon it. This is because the Logos not only provides order to the world, but it also actively and constantly dominates and controls it, or even, when necessary, props it up internally. In fact, Philo goes so far as to say that 'the most venerable Logos of the one who is puts on the world as a garment' (*Fug.* 110). In this fashion the Logos comes to take the place of the Platonic 'world soul' in an extraordinary integration of philosophical notions and concepts.

III.2. The Powers

III.2.A. SOPHIA If the Logos has origins that are in large measure philosophical, those of Sophia are scriptural. It is in particular in the Book of Wisdom that Sophia has the role of a hypostasis that is at least in part distinct from God.[22] Of great importance is Wisdom 8:1–4: 'Wisdom extends, with power, from one end of the earth to the other and governs the entire universe with goodness ... she makes display of her nobility, because she lives with God, and she is the beloved of the Lord of all things. For she is the master of the knowledge of God, and presides over the works of the creator.' It is easy to recognize in this passage many similarities with Philo's descriptions of the Logos, and there are many more, when one examines the many attributes that Sophia takes on in

---

21   Comparable to this plurality of functions of the Logos in the divine realm is the plurality of the functions of *logos* in man.

22   Behind the figure of Wisdom one might see the remnants of a feminine divinity (Asherah, Maat, Isis), reconfigured so as to be compatible with Jewish Yahwism.

Philo's own allegorical interpretations. He even identifies the two (e.g., *Leg.* 1.65). There seem to be essentially five characteristics shared by the Logos and the figure of Sophia: (1) a role in the creation of the world (*Fug.* 109); (2) the status of principle, image, or vision of God, and the possession of many names (*Fug.* 146; *Leg.* 1.43); (3) a position of dominance and also as focal point with respect to the other powers (*Leg.* 2.86); (4) a noetic function, especially as connected to the image of noetic light (*Opif.* 31; *Migr.* 40–2); and (5) influence on the ethical sphere, especially as a source of the virtues (*Leg.* 1.65). One can generally say that the Logos and Sophia are equivalent for Philo, although there are occasions where he subordinates one to the other.[23] It should also be added that Sophia almost never acts as a power immanent in the world, whereas the Logos does this in abundance.[24] However, the near equivalence of the two could be seen as a proof of the truth of the Bible in its relationship to philosophical knowledge, because an essentially biblical entity appears to correspond to an essentially philosophical entity. The equivalence finds expression in a very clear form in *Quis rerum divinarum heres sit* 133–229, where the theory of the 'Logos-cutter' is presented, which complements the account of creation in *De opificio*. One finds here the hypothesis that the world is the result of continuous division, from an indistinct nature to single individual things. The hypothesis owes something to Plato (*Soph.* 218c–222e), to the treatise *De mundo* (5, 396a33ff.), and relies on Stoic terminology (the word *logos* among others). It also has a biblical basis, in that even in the beginning of the creation on 'day one', there is a division between the light and the darkness and the day and the night.[25] The essential characteristic of this doctrine relevant for our present concerns is the fact that there is no distinction between the noological and cosmological aspects of creation. That is, there is an emphasis on the fact that the 'logic' of the divine intellect in the moment of creation is not distinct from the 'logic' that governs the world in a physical sense. This same logic is the content of Wisdom, and according to the same treatise, it belongs as an inheritance to the wise man. Philo says as much at the conclusion of *Quis heres*: 'The wise man, therefore, is presented as the legitimate heir of the knowledge of the things here mentioned. Scripture affirms: "On that day God established a covenant with Abraham, saying, 'to your descendants I will give this land.'"' What land is indicated, if not the one mentioned before, to which Scripture now makes reference?

23 See *Leg.* 2.86; *Agr.* 51; *Conf.* 146; *Ebr.* 3.
24 Cf. B.L. Mack, *Logos und Sophia: Untersuchungen zur Weisheitstheologie im hellenistischen Judentum* (Göttingen 1973), p. 146.
25 On this matter, see the more detailed discussion in R. Radice, *Platonismo e creazionismo in Filone di Alessandria* (Milan 1989), pp. 90ff.

The fruit of this land is the firm and certain apprehension of the wisdom of God, by which he, through his powers which divide, separating all things, keeps the good things away from evil ... ' (§§ 313–14). In this manner, Sophia and Logos are viewed as both subject and object of the mind of God. It is from this circumstance that one can understand the essential identity between them.

III.2.B. ANGELS–DAEMONS   Angels take on a mediating role that is rather limited, and for the most part they have little autonomy as compared to the Logos, to which they are often assimilated. We see this, for example, in *De cherubim* 35, where the angel represents the Logos of God. In the same treatise (§§ 27–8), the Cherubim represent the two principal divine powers, sovereignty and goodness. In *De confusione linguarum* 28, on the other hand, the angels represent the thoughts and words of God. In this fashion nearly the entirety of the semantic edifice that is the Logos may be expressed by the figure of the angel: the Logos in the broad sense, the powers, and the Ideas. To these significations one may add that of conscience, which has the effect of giving angels an importance also on the ethical–anthropological plane (cf. *Fug.* 203; *Deus* 182).

On the other hand, Philo also interprets angels as the equivalent of the 'daemons' (*daimones*) of pagan thought, souls without bodies, or heroes (*Gig.* 12; *Plant.* 14). They may function as ministers and ambassadors of God (*Abr.* 115), and as intermediaries for the benefit of the human race, which cannot come into direct contact with God (*Somn.* 1.143).

In general, it should be pointed out that in Philo's angelology, ideas of Greek origin play an important role but not a definitive one. Moreover, even the elements taken over from the Hellenic conception of daemons have a different significance in the context of his creationistic theology. The role of the angel is not reduced to that of ambassador of God among men or of co-agent of his providence. In as much as angels are equated with the Ideas, they appear also to participate in the make-up of the world on an ontological level.

III.2.C. THE OTHER POWERS AND PNEUMA   Not all of the powers – which in any case are infinite in number – have their own specific designation (Logos, Sophia, angels, *pneuma*, etc.). Some are denoted simply on the basis of their function. If we pay heed to Philo's own statements, it is possible to identify five key powers: 'the first is the creative power, by means of which the creator created the world with his word (*logos*); the second is the royal power, in virtue of which the creator governs that which was created; the third is the gracious power, through which the great artificer takes pity on and shows mercy for his own work; the fourth is the legislative power, by means of which he orders what we must do; the fifth is that part of the legislative power by which he forbids that which we should not do' (*Fug.* 95). This fifth power is called elsewhere the 'punitive' power.[26]

In any case, above and beyond the vacillations and ambiguities that characterize Philo's statements about the powers, and even his terminology, the important point is that the various powers are closely linked among themselves so as to form a single fabric. The continuity serves the function of reconciling God's transcendence with His creative providence,[27] and His oneness with the multiplicity of His functions and His names. Moreover, the complex of powers, in a general way, is included within the 'super-power', the Logos, which not only is the subject of the most fully articulated treatment on the part of Philo, but is also the power that rests on the firmest philosophical foundations.

We may devote a brief separate treatment to *pneuma* (spirit or breath), which has a distinct importance. As in the case of *logos*, Philo found the term *pneuma* employed both in a philosophical setting (again Stoic), and in the narrative of Genesis. The double precedent, as we have seen, has the effect of confirming Philo's faith in Scripture as a source of philosophical truth, and of heightening the relevance of any given concept in his theology.

In Stoicism, *pneuma* is the principle of all reality, the cause of all things (*SVF* II.340). It is an emanation of Logos, in as much as it is warm breath that breaks away from the fire-Logos and is not differentiated from it in terms of substance (*SVF* II.1051). It is therefore also divine (*SVF* II.1033, 1037). Moreover, according to the Stoics *pneuma* permeates all things, holds them together, and as an emanation of Logos maintains order and harmony. More specifically, *pneuma* is present in the world of inanimate objects as a force of cohesion (*hexis*), in the animal world as the principle of life (*physis*), and in man as the principle of the soul and the mind (*SVF* II.716; I.484). This classification of the different manifestations of *pneuma* corresponds in part to the threefold presence (in God/in the world/in man) that Philo attributes to almost all of the powers, in order to give coherence and unity to his own theology. The importance of this conceptual construct was no doubt heightened in the eyes of Philo because of the confirmation that it appeared to receive in the biblical narrative of the creation. In that account, we learn that

---

26 *Her.* 166. From the same passage we learn that it is also designated 'Lord' (*kyrios*), whereas the gracious or creative power is called 'God' (*theos*). Cf. *Leg.* 1.96.

27 Cf. L.A. Montes-Peral, *Akataleptos Theos: Der unfassbare Gott* (Leiden 1987), p. 164.

'the spirit of God moved over the waters' (Gen 1:2), that animals had the 'breath of life' (Gen 1:30, with the reading *pnoēn*), and that God breathed His own 'breath of life' into the face of man (Gen 2:7). In general, there are innumerable passages in Philo where one finds the term *pneuma* employed in some Stoic sense, be it in the context of his allegorical interpretation or in the broader structure of his theology.[28] In general, one gets the impression that Philo, although he never explicitly denies the incorporeal nature of *pneuma*, has conceded much to Stoic materialism, in the attempt to take full advantage of the unifying force of this concept.[29]

III.3. The Ideas

It may appear somewhat surprising at first glance that Philo views the Platonic theory of Ideas as an indispensable truth, comparable to the fundamental doctrines of his religion. In *De specialibus legibus* 1.327 he states as follows: 'Of men who are impious and sacrilegious, there is not one type but many. Some of these maintain that the incorporeal Ideas are only an empty name, without true reality, eliminating in this manner from things that exist that which constitutes their essential reality, that is, the archetypal pattern of all essential qualities, according to which each thing receives its form and dimension.'

Why does Philo attribute so much significance to this doctrine? The answer to this question probably lies in the theory of creation as articulated in the *De opificio*, which, as we have asserted many times, is the nucleus of Philo's philosophy. According to that theory, the Platonic Ideas are the archetype or perfect forms of the physical world, set to leave their imprint, or rather, to project their image, onto matter. However, while according to Plato the Ideas are eternal and ontologically autonomous, Philo, as we have seen, feels they are created by God-as-architect and are in some sense His thoughts concerning the creation of the world (and later of man and moral values). They have their seat in God's mind,

---

28 For the cohesive power of *pneuma*, see *Opif.* 131; for its presence in God, *Opif.* 30, 135; *Leg.* 1.31ff.; for its biological force, *Praem.* 144; for its constitution of man's mind, *Fug.* 134. Further references may be found in Reale and Radice in *La filosofia mosaica*, pp. CXI–CXIII.

29 One should note that Philo also speaks of a prophetic *pneuma*, which does not have a place in the Stoic scheme. The significance of this concept can be gleaned from the following description of Balaam, where *pneuma* is connected with ecstasy: 'When he went outside he became suddenly possessed, as there came upon him a *prophetic spirit*, which banished the entirety of his art of divination outside of his soul; for it was not legitimate that tricks of a magician dwell together with a most holy presence' (*Mos.* 1.177).

that is, in the Logos. Therefore, if there were no Ideas, two fundamental consequences would follow. The creation would be deprived both of its incorporeal dimension and God would lose His transcendence, one of the attributes that Philo regards as most characteristic of God. This latter point is given particular emphasis by Philo, when he indicates that, according to the theory of the Ideas, 'God created the universe, but *without being personally involved* in this task, because he, being perfectly blessed, could not enter into contact with indefinite and confused matter. He made use of his *incorporeal powers, the true name of which is "Ideas"*, so as to allow each category to take the form that was appropriate to it' (*Spec.* 1.329). Now this passage, and especially the phrase 'without being personally involved', allows us to discern a nuance in the term 'Idea' that is beyond its conventional Platonic meaning. Indeed, according to Philo, the Ideas are not simply a static model that God followed in giving form to the world, but rather, once created, they themselves set to work in order to bestow on each thing the form that was appropriate to it. In short, they would be an active cause, and not just an archetype of creation.[30] They would be productive powers that take the place of God in the process of creation, and for this reason it is possible that He need not be 'personally involved' in the formation of matter. This is not the case in Plato, nor could it be if one adheres to his presuppositions. This interpretation of the Ideas is possible for Philo, however, because it is inseparably linked with his conception of the Logos, concerning which there is an ambiguity that Philo never took the trouble to resolve. It may be put as follows: Is the Logos the world of Ideas contained within the mind of God, or is it the mind of God itself, the cause of the ordering of the world? In other words, is the Logos a part of the project or a part of the architect?[31] Because either answer is possible, it follows that in the one case the Idea would be the *content* of God's thought, and in the other it would be an *act* of God's thought. But in Philo the acts of God's thoughts become words, and the words become creative actions. This circumstance explains why the Ideas could be regarded as incorporeal powers, that is, active forces that execute the work of creation, to a certain degree 'in place of God'. Despite a certain obscurity in this interpretation of the theory of Ideas, one should recognize its importance, because in it one finds an anticipation of an important step taken by Plotinus. For the latter the Ideas, in as much as they are of the second hypostasis ('Intellect'), are

---

30 This is another innovation in the theory of Ideas, in addition to the notion that the Ideas are the thoughts of God, mentioned just above.

31 This ambiguity is present in *Opif.* 20, and in *Opif.* 146, where the human mind is interpreted as a fragment of the Logos.

not just objects of thought, but thinking entities or 'intelligent powers' (*Enn.* 4.8.3). The possibility that Plotinus is dependent on Philo for this adjustment in the theory of Ideas is high.

IV. CONCLUSION: ON THE RELATIONSHIP BETWEEN GOD AND THE WORLD

V. Nikiprowetzky employed the happy phrase 'exegetical constraint' in referring to the problem that faced Philo as a writer and confronts those who read him.[32] He was not in a position to pursue freely the thread of a philosophical theme, but needed to follow and always take into account the biblical text that he was interpreting. As a result, we do not possess from his pen treatises on theology or cosmology, nor even a systematic presentation of his thinking on these topics. Nevertheless, even if the solutions Philo had in view are without an organic unity, the problems or *quaestiones* that he set for himself and tried to resolve are well founded from a theological perspective.

For example, on the assumption that God is one and is transcendent, and that He is continually active and continually creative (*Leg.* 1.18), how does one explain the imperfect and finite nature of the world? Following the lead of Plato, Philo answers this question by pointing to the existence of a negative material principle, which in some manner 'corrupts' God's work. But would not such a principle run the risk of perverting the absolute perfection of God? And what is the position of God with respect to evil? God, responds Philo, does not have contact with matter, neither in the creation nor in the direction of the world, but rather makes use of His powers, which for those same purposes take on a substantial, that is, hypostatic and autonomous character in relationship to God. What then becomes of the oneness and the unity of God? And especially, what becomes of His goodness, which has so much importance in Philo's theory of grace?[33] As we see, for as many *solutiones* as Philo can put forward, new and more pressing *quaestiones* continually emerge at different levels.

But perhaps we can give greater coherence to Philo's thought if we ask ourselves a more general question. What kind of creation did Philo have in mind when he was reading and interpreting the Bible? There are many possible responses to this question.[34] However, let us simplify the matter and put it as follows: Did Philo believe in creation *ex nihilo* or in

32   *Le commentaire*, p. 7.
33   See esp. *Her.* 31, where God is called 'the one who loves to give'.
34   For a more detailed discussion, see my *Allegoria e paradigmi etici*, pp. 95ff.

a kind of *demiurgic* creation, even if more advanced than that described by Plato? Although the positions scholars have taken on this question are anything but unanimous, I believe Philo must have had in mind a mixed type of creation. There was a direct and *ex nihilo* creation of the constructive principles of the world, that is, of the noetic cosmos, of man, and of morals. These, as realities in the realm of Ideas, come into being in the moment they are conceived, and are therefore created *ex nihilo*. On the other hand, there was an indirect and demiurgic creation of the physical cosmos, namely, a molding and formation of matter by means of the powers.

It must be noted, however, that when Philo thinks in terms of Ideas versus matter, good versus evil, virtue versus sin, he is always under the influence of a Platonic vision, according to which *matter and the evil connected with it are non-being and only the Ideas and the sphere of the Ideas are true being*. In this sense Philo could have understood creation as an *ex nihilo* creation of all being, or of all *true* being, because whatever was not created *ex nihilo* was non-being. Oddly enough, however, one almost never finds in Philo a negative conception of the material cosmos, as one finds in Plato. To the contrary, despite its material components, the cosmos appears to Philo to be the greatest, most perfect, most holy and most beautiful of created things.[35] It is not far from the divine, but rather close to it, and would most properly have a reverential posture toward it. In the words of Philo himself: 'The life-work that befits the world consists in rendering thanks continually and without cessation to its father and creator, and in almost reducing itself to its elemental form, in order to show that it reserves nothing for itself, but gives itself as an offering, in its entirety, to God its creator' (*Her.* 200).

(Translated from the Italian by Adam Kamesar.)

---

35   The Stoic influence is here manifest.

6 Philo's Ethics

To speak of the ethics of Philo of Alexandria is obviously not to presuppose that his works should be structured according to the tripartite division of philosophy (logic, physics, ethics) inherited from the Hellenistic period. Philo is well aware of this division but his way of thinking is far too fluid, far too dominated by the requirements of his biblical exegesis to bear such a rigid framework.[1] On the other hand, his interest in ethics is certainly fundamental in his works, although it finds expression in a complex manner. For he relies on the Bible as his first source of inspiration, as the interpretation of the 'special laws' shows, but also refers to a great variety of philosophical themes, the unity of which we shall need to examine. We shall treat the following points in succession: (I) the philosophical principles of ethics, (II) the virtues, (III) the passions, (IV) moral progress, and (V) politics.

I. THE PHILOSOPHICAL PRINCIPLES: *OIKEIŌSIS* AND *HOMOIŌSIS*

Philo was a complex thinker who lived in the age of Middle Platonism, which itself is considered as a turbulent transition period between the Hellenistic and Neoplatonist systems.[2] However, in the way that Philo thinks about morality, although it is a line of thought often difficult to pin down, one point comes out very clearly: he rejects the grounding of ethics on the dogma of *oikeiōsis*, or 'appropriation'. It is a rejection that is all the more remarkable because the dogma of *oikeiōsis* is a fundamental idea of Stoicism, from which he borrowed so much. To appreciate the essence of the dogma, one need but turn to the opening of the speech of the Stoic, Cato the Younger, as reported by Cicero in his *De finibus* 3.16–19: 'Every living being is at birth immediately appropriated

1 For Philo and the tripartite division of philosophy, see the Introduction above, p. 3.
2 On these matters, see G. E. Sterling, 'Platonizing Moses: Philo and Middle Platonism', *StPhAnn* 5 (1993), pp. 96–111.

to itself and wishes to preserve its constitution. It therefore seeks those things that are salutary to it and flees those that are harmful.' The initial motive is thus the love one has for oneself and, paradoxically, this is where wisdom begins. This is because the man who is moving toward self-realization, after having sought instinctively the objects which are beneficial to his constitution, gradually becomes aware of the existence of a universal harmony which appears to him more precious than his first objects of choice. It is also the case that *oikeiōsis* is at the origin of society. For it is the affection of parents toward their children that, through concentric circles, gives rise to cities, to nations, and finally to the *cosmopolis*, the universal city which is formed by humanity. Let us add finally that *oikeiōsis* had become the general framework within which the philosophic doctrines of the Hellenistic schools came to be presented.

Why did Philo, at least implicitly, consider the dogma of *oikeiōsis* to be unacceptable? Probably because being both a Platonist and a Jew, it was impossible for him to admit that ethics had their root in an instinctive impulse common to both man and the realm of all animated beings. As is Hellenistic Judaism generally, Philo is imbued with the biblical idea (Gen 1:26–7) that man has been created on a level superior to that of animals.[3] Stoicism also strongly differentiated between man and animal. For only man, together with the gods, had a share in *logos*. But because the Stoics needed to preserve the unity of nature, they imposed the common standard of *oikeiōsis*, a single structure of life, on both the human and animal realms. For Philo, on the other hand, as K. Berthelot has very rightly put it, 'nature has a normative value only insofar as it is the expression of the divine will (and it is thereby that nature is endowed with rationality). Referring to nature is not, in this context, referring to instinct; in actual fact, nature makes manifest a transcendence.'[4] The Stoic approach was to postulate a kind of continuity, going from the most primitive vital impulse to the most perfect forms of reason. Yet this is what Middle Platonist thinkers rejected, as we see especially in the anonymous *Commentary on Plato's Theaetetus*. The dating of this text remains disputed, but it is not impossible that it falls rather close to Philo chronologically.[5]

---

3   This does not prevent him from advocating an attitude of kindness towards animals; see K. Berthelot, 'Philo and Kindness towards Animals (*De virtutibus* 125–147)', *StPhAnn* 14 (2002), pp. 48–65.

4   *L'humanité de l'autre homme' dans la pensée juive ancienne* (Leiden 2004), p. 119.

5   The *Commentary on Plato's Theaetetus* has been edited by G. Bastianini and D.N. Sedley in F. Adorno et al. (eds.), *Corpus dei papiri filosofici*

However, in contrast to the author of the *Commentary*, Philo refers only rarely in an explicit manner to the Stoic dogma. He prefers to undermine it by attributing to it a meaning different from the one it had in Stoicism. In *De confusione linguarum* 82, he comments on Exod 2:22, where Moses says, 'I am a sojourner in an alien land.' On the basis of this verse, Philo affirms that the situation of the soul in the body is not even comparable to that of a sojourner (= 'metic' or 'resident alien'). The latter, he says, stays provisionally in a place, whereas the presence of thought in the body is a matter not of appropriation (*oikeiōsis*), but rather of alienation (*allotriōsis*). For a Stoic like Seneca, *conciliatio* (the Latin translation of *oikeiōsis*) is, from birth, a permanent movement of the living being to adapt itself to itself (*Ep.* 121). On the contrary, Philo mentions childhood on many occasions but he never considers it as the starting point of an itinerary of which the natural end should be wisdom. For him, 'sin is congenital to every created being, even the best, just because they are created' (*Mos.* 2.147). Therefore, not only does his philosophical belief in transcendence prevent Philo from accepting the dogma of *oikeiōsis*, it is also biblical theology that prevents him from doing so, because it entails a negative determinism that weighs on a human being at his birth, on account of a kind of original sin.

It is also the case that Philo uses the term *oikeiōsis* in a sense that is very close to *homoiōsis*, that is, 'becoming like [God]'; this is a phrase taken from Plato's *Theaetetus* 176a-b, which had become dear to the thinkers of Middle Platonism.[6] Thus, in *De opificio mundi* 145-6, Philo says that the first man, that is, the archetypal man, is in kinship (*suggeneia*) with the divine Logos. This kinship, he explains, is nothing but an *oikeiōsis* of man to divine power, of which he is an imprint, a fragment, a reflection. While in Stoicism, *oikeiōsis* is an impulse that orients the whole life of an individual, what matters to Philo is not the movement but the state of proximity. What then does the resemblance of man to God mean for him?[7] Essentially, it means man's domination of the world, his access to intelligence and knowledge, and his participation in *logos* that enables him to get closer to God and endows him

greci e latini, III (Florence 1995), pp. 227-562. One may find there a meticulous analysis of all the aspects of this problem.

6   The passage is quoted by Philo in *Fug.* 63.
7   On this question see also D. T. Runia, 'God and Man in Philo of Alexandria', *JThS* 39 (1988), pp. 48-75, and W. E. Helleman, 'Philo of Alexandria on Deification and Assimilation to God', *StPhAnn* 2 (1990), pp. 51-71, who rightly emphasizes that the process of identification with God, in Philo, is described in terms of imitation rather than of participation in the divine nature.

with a sort of immortality.[8] Should we therefore conclude, as Berthelot does,[9] that this resemblance has only limited ethical consequences for Philo? True enough, from a concrete point of view, these consequences seem to be limited to the fact that murder is forbidden in *De decalogo* 133 because of the common resemblance of all men to God. Homicide is thus comparable to the pillage of a temple. Nevertheless, this general orientation is rich in potentialities, because ultimately any form of violence toward another human being is a transgression of this fundamental resemblance. At the same time, it is impossible to truly love humanity without loving God. Moses is the quintessential philanthropist as he loves God and is loved in return by Him (*Virt.* 77). Philo does not exploit all the possibilities of this concept within his social ethics, but this does not necessarily imply that the importance of this general framework should be underestimated, especially with regard to the dynamic force to which it gives rise.

Furthermore, one may recognize two levels of kinship between man and God: the level intended by providence through the process of the creation, and the level reached by the human being who, in his search for rationality, consciously takes the resemblance upon himself. The virtuous man, the final product of this quest, thus finds himself in a spiritual kinship with God. This raises the issue of the status of the Jews, the only people to have with God collectively 'a kinship most vital and a far more genuine tie than that of blood' (*Virt.* 79), and the only people to be able to see Him, in accordance with the etymology of Israel often employed by Philo.[10] This does not mean that 'assimilation to God' is possible only for the Jews. For it is certain that 'all who practise wisdom either in Greek or barbarian lands' (*Spec.* 2.44), who neutralize the passions in order to thrust their souls toward the divine powers, and whom Philo defines as 'an ember of wisdom' (*Spec.* 2.47), share, in their own way, the same desire of assimilation to God. The use of the expression 'our species' in the latter passage proves that these righteous men of the nations are also responsible for the ethical destiny of the whole of humanity. It is simply that the election of Israel orients this movement toward God on the basis of the Mosaic law and gives it the dimensions of a collective experience and not just an individual one. The epistemological question about whether it is possible to imitate God without knowing Him is answered once it is God Himself that has turned toward man.

---

8   See *Spec.* 4.14, where Philo speaks of man as being 'akin to God ... on account of his participation in *logos*, which renders him immortal, although he appears to be mortal'.
9   *L'humanité'*, p. 191.
10 Israel = 'one who sees God'. See esp. *Abr.* 57.

II. THE VIRTUES[11]

Philo devoted a treatise to this philosophical concept, which is among the most solidly codified in ancient philosophy, because after Plato the schools usually take up one and the same classification. The difficulty in following Philo's line of thought on virtues is that, in his works, there are three different factors that exert influence, often in a combined fashion:

(1)   the philosophical tradition such as it had been expressed especially by the Stoics;
(2)   biblical virtues alien to Stoicism which transform this classification; and
(3)   allegorical interpretation in which biblical characters are presented as living symbols of virtues

We shall not discuss the first factor in great detail insofar as Philo often follows the tradition fairly closely without adding any original contributions. Let us merely say that all the main themes of the Socratic–Stoic tradition with regard to the virtues are present in Philo. Here are a few examples. The Platonic notion of the unity of virtue, so often taken up by the Stoics, is taken up by Philo when he writes that to have one virtue is to have them all (*Mos.* 2.7). Similarly, the idea that virtue is both theory and practice is developed in the *Legum allegoriae*, where Philo uses terms that correspond to those of orthodox Stoicism (*Leg.* 1.57). In the same work (1.63), the exegesis of Gen 2:10–14 on the four rivers of paradise enables him to recall the four traditional virtues: *phronēsis* (prudence), *sōphrosynē* (temperance), *andreia* (courage), *dikaiosynē* (justice). All of this bears witness to Philo's solid philosophical education to which he refers himself when he evokes his training in the liberal arts. These are presented as a preparation for philosophy, which is described as the servant of wisdom, defined by the Stoic formula as follows: 'the science of that which is divine, that which is human and of the causes of these' (*Congr.* 74–9). In addition, the importance granted by Philo to self-control (*enkrateia*) is a sign of his immersion in the Cynic–Stoic tradition inspired by Socrates.[12] As a force that opposes pleasure, *enkrateia* is defined by the Stoics as a 'science one cannot go beyond, of that which appears in line with right reason' (*SVF* III.264). *Enkrateia* appears in Philo as a variation on the cardinal virtue of temperance, and

---

11   On this topic, see N. G. Cohen, 'The Greek Virtues and the Mosaic Laws in Philo: An Elucidation of *De Specialibus Legibus* IV 133–135', *StPhAnn* 5 (1993), pp. 9–23.
12   See É. Bréhier, *Les idées philosophiques et religieuses de Philon d'Alexandrie*[3] (Paris 1950), pp. 261–6.

'holds out to the soul health and safety for life' (*Agr.* 98). The wish to appear – most probably in the eyes of hypothetical Greek readers – well informed on different aspects of the philosophical tradition leads him to an ample rewriting of the sophist Prodicus' famous tale of Heracles at the crossroads (*Sacr.* 21–45). According to the tale, Heracles is meditating in solitude, wondering which way he should take, when he is approached and addressed by two women, who symbolize virtue and vice (pleasure in Philo's version).

Philo's eagerness to appear well informed can also be of no small consequence for appreciating the coherence of his line of thought. Taking up the Stoic paradox according to which only the wise man is free and all other men are slaves, he relies on Exod 7:1 ('I have made you a god to Pharaoh'), and emerges with the dogma of the very same school according to which the wise man is not a man anymore but a god (*Prob.* 43). True enough, from the fundamentally Jewish perspective that he takes, the idea that the virtue of a man can render him a god is simply unacceptable. And yet, Philo speaks as though Jewish faith and Stoic philosophy shared something in common, probably because he feels protected by the very wording of the biblical text which speaks 'a god *to Pharaoh*'. On the other hand, in *Quis rerum divinarum heres sit* 121, he expresses what was probably his true position: 'No one reaches perfection in any of his pursuits, but undoubtedly all perfection and finality belong to One alone.'[13]

Another interesting aspect of Philo's writings is the coexistence of the Stoic and Peripatetic conceptions of virtue, which are usually incompatible: The first is characterized by its radicalism, and the second is more sensitive to the environment of the moral action. When Philo defines the virtues, in the manner of Aristotle, as 'means' (sc. between two extremes), he does so by referring to a 'mild and social form of philosophy' (*Migr.* 147), a reference well suited to the Peripatetic way of thinking. We must, however, beware of taking him as adhering to that school. In fact, elsewhere, Moses is presented as the champion of an 'unadorned' philosophy (*Prob.* 43). This allows us to conclude that Philo's adherence to Aristotelian ethics will never be but a relative adherence, while his absolute adherence is to the ethics of ascetic and mystic detachment.

The presence in his works of all of this philosophical knowledge makes it all the more interesting that Philo, not satisfied with using the pre-established categories, reformulates them so as to make his biblical exegesis possible. Thus, in *De specialibus legibus* 4.135, the

---

13 In *Mut.* 181–5, where Philo speaks of the hesitation of Abraham when he learns that he will have a child, he indicates that the human soul cannot have the virtues of God, but only the images of those virtues.

four principal virtues are not those of the philosophical tradition: Philo speaks of 'the queen of virtues', piety/sanctity, then wisdom, temperance, and justice. About the first, he says that it formed the subject of an earlier discussion, perhaps a now lost *Peri eusebeias* (*On Piety*), and he says the same concerning wisdom and temperance. The latter two he may have considered to be included within his preceding interpretation of the second table of the law, that is, the second five of the Ten Commandments. As to justice, he deals with it in the subsequent paragraphs both as a religious ideal of submission, as the establishment of a just 'mean', as well as from a Neopythagorean perspective, as a principle of equity in the organization of the world. Courage, the virtue of the soldier, is dealt with in *De virtutibus* 1–50, in line with the Socratic tradition, since it is said to be founded not on rage but on knowledge, although Philo's attention to the details of situations brings Aristotle to mind.[14]

However, it is *metanoia* (repentance) and *eugeneia* (nobility) that hold a central place in the *De virtutibus*. The first is strongly rooted in the Jewish notion of *teshuva* and is attributed to proselytes (*prosēlytoi* or *epēlytai* in the Philonic text), that is, those pagans who sympathized with Judaism. Philo is probably also speaking to those Jews tempted by paganism, as was his own nephew Tiberius Julius Alexander, to whom it had to be told that the community remained open and that such persons would be received in it as 'our dearest friends and closest kinsmen' (*Virt.* 179). Philo's concept of *metanoia* is, as M. Alexandre has rightly emphasized, in contradiction with Stoic teaching, in which *metanoia* is considered as 'an unhappy and seditious passion'.[15] Philonic *metanoia* is inseparably theological and moral: 'As in the sunshine the shadow follows the body, participation in the whole company of the other virtues follows the honor of the true God' (*Virt.* 181). *Metanoia* is the sign of the finitude of the human condition because 'absolute sinlessness belongs to God or possibly to a divine man' (*Virt.* 177), but also of its openness to transcendence.

As to nobility (*eugeneia*), Philo's argumentation is inspired by a Cynic–Stoic line that takes up some Socratic themes and is in opposition to Aristotle's positions concerning the excellence of lineage set out in his treatise *On Nobility*. Philo declares that 'we must give the

---

14   On the issue of courage in Philo, see W. T. Wilson 'Pious Soldiers, Gender Deviants and the Ideology of Actium: Courage and Warfare in Philo's *De Fortitudine*', *StPhAnn* 17 (2005), pp. 1–32.

15   'Le lexique des vertus: Vertus philosophiques et religieuses chez Philon: μετάνοια et εὐγένεια', in C. Lévy (ed.), *Philon d'Alexandrie et le langage de la philosophie* (Turnhout 1998), p. 22.

name of noble only to the temperate and just' (*Virt.* 189). From this perspective, it is Abraham, who, though a son of a Chaldean astrologer, emigrates from the errors of polytheism toward the truth of monotheism and thus becomes the model of true nobility. With regard to the episode of the golden calf, the argument used to justify the massacre perpetrated by Moses and the Levites against their closest relatives and dearest friends consists in the claim that they maintained the love of God as their only friendship and their only kinship (*Spec.* 3.126).

Allegorical exegesis enables Philo to understand the matriarchs as figures symbolizing virtues. One of the most interesting aspects of this exegesis is the consideration of the differences between the sexes. Virtues have feminine names, but they possess, says Philo, 'powers and activities of consummate men'. The opposition between the way pleasure is represented in the shape of a courtesan and the noble vigor of virtue was already present in Stoicism, but Philo gives a specific explanation of the exterior femininity of virtue. Because the virtue of a human being comes after divine perfection, God used a feminine appearance as a sign of the inherent imperfection in the most perfect of humanities (*Fug.* 51). In the most frequent Philonic descriptions, woman symbolizes all that is related to sensation and custom, whereas all that is in the realm of reason is masculine: 'for nature is the law of men, and to follow nature is the mark of a strong and truly masculine reason' (*Ebr.* 54–5). What is characteristic of Sarah, who symbolizes virtue, is thus no longer having anything in common with the world of women, a conclusion Philo arrives at through his exegesis of Gen 18:11. From Gen 20:12, he concludes that she is born from the father (something which she has in common with Athena), cause of all that there is (*Ebr.* 60–1). Furthermore, as if Philo were implicitly answering Seneca (*Vit. beat.* 7.3), he affirms that she 'will count as a matter for laughter those anxious cares of men that are expended on human affairs, whether in war or peace', which, for the Alexandrian, are the concern of education, symbolized by Hagar (*Ebr.* 62–4). According to the *De congressu eruditionis gratia*, Sarah, who is sterile with regard to that which has no value and fertile for the good, unites with Abraham to give birth to Isaac, joy, which Philo qualifies as 'the best of good emotions'.[16]

In the same treatise, the distinction between the rational and the irrational parts of the soul leads to a distinction between two aspects of virtue, symbolized by Leah and Rachel. The first, whose name (in Greek, Leia) means 'smooth' or 'soft', is the adjective used by the Epicureans

---

16 *Congr.* 36. The 'good emotions' are the *eupatheiai* of Stoic teaching. For these, see F.H. Sandbach, *The Stoics*[2] (London 1989), pp. 67–8, and just below, pp. 156–7.

to describe pleasure. Philo, because of exegetical necessity, but also no doubt as an act of provocation toward his main philosophical opponents, applies it to the virtue of the rational part of the soul, whereas Rachel embodies the fight against the senses and all in us that is irrational. Leah is the great way of reason toward virtue, while Rachel is the necessary instrument to engender self-control in the soul, *enkrateia* (*Congr.* 25–32). Fundamentally masculine because of the necessarily masculine character of *logos*, virtue remains nevertheless 'gentle and sociable and kindly' (*Congr.* 71). Indeed, virtue is the benevolent concern one has for the other.

As for Rebecca, V. Nikiprowetzky has shown how the virtue of constancy (*epimonē* or *hypomonē*) that she symbolizes has different meanings in the pagan Greek tradition and in the biblical Greek tradition. In the former, it simply means endurance (in a manner similar to *karteria*), whereas in the latter it also may include the nuance of hope.[17] In Philo, Rebecca personifies the intellectual virtue of Isaac (the self-taught race, which reaches happiness immediately), with whom she unites in his mother's tent (*Post.* 77). The examination of the passages in which Rebecca is mentioned has enabled Nikiprowetzky to show that Philo never uses the term *hypomonē* with a meaning different from the one understood by Greek philosophers.

III. THE PASSIONS[18]

Philo's treatment of the passions seems to be particularly rich in contradictions and has given rise to a great diversity of interpretations. Four points need to be examined in turn: the various Philonic conceptions of the soul; the classification of the passions and the description of passion; the problem of healing the passions; and finally, what seems to be a paradox in Philo, passion transcended by madness.

III.1. The Structure of the Soul

Every conception of passion goes back, directly or indirectly, to a conception of the soul. 'The question of the parts of the soul is one of the areas in which Philo's competence in matters of Greek philosophy

---

17 'Rébecca, vertu de constance et constance de vertu chez Philon d'Alexandrie', in his collected studies, *Études philoniennes* (Paris 1996), pp. 145–55.

18 For further detail, see C. Lévy, 'Philon d'Alexandrie et les passions', in L. Ciccolini et al. (eds.), *Réceptions antiques: Lecture, transmission, appropriation intellectuelle* (Paris 2006), pp. 27–41.

manifests itself in the most clear way,' J. Bouffartigue has written.[19]
The problem is that almost all of the ancient theories on the nature of
the soul are found in Philo's works, with a distinct predominance of
the Platonic and Stoic doctrines. As an example of the Platonic division, we may quote from *Legum allegoriae* 3.15, where Philo writes:
'Our soul consists of three parts, and has one part given to reasoning,
a second to high spirit, a third to desire. Some philosophers have distinguished these parts from each other in regard to function, some in
regard also to the places which they occupy.' This passage shows that
Philo has a perception of Platonism that is enlightened by subsequent
discussions. The allusion to the differentiation being only in function
is probably a reference to the Stoic Posidonius. However, in other texts,
we find the Stoic division of the soul with the commanding faculty,
the *hēgemonikon*, at the center and the seven other parts originating
from it. But there are passages in which Philo completely changes the
spirit of this division, the most striking example being the passage in
which the commanding faculty is compared to a puppeteer who, by
means of strings, commands the other seven (*Opif.* 117). This is an
obvious reference to Plato, *Laws* 644d. In this metaphor as reworked
by Philo, there coexists an active element with mere material instruments, a conception contrary to the Stoic spirit, which always insisted
on the living unity formed by the commanding faculty and the senses.
Moreover, Philo represents a philosophical culture imbued with skepticism with regard to the possibility of even having any certainty about
the nature of the soul. In his words, 'who knows the essential nature of
the soul, that mystery which has bred innumerable contentions among
the sophists who propound opinions contrary to each other or even
totally and generically opposed?' (*Mut.* 10). Because Philo does not
adhere to any dogma in the domain of psychology, he expresses himself
sometimes in Platonic terms and sometimes in Stoic terms, depending
on the biblical text he needs to discuss and on his convictions, which
hardly ever coincide exactly with a specific philosophical doctrine.[20] At
most, we can say that he never employs the Epicurean conception of
the soul. His acknowledgment of ignorance as to the nature of the soul,
however, does not prevent him from having an original and structured
line of thought concerning the passions.

19 'La structure de l'âme chez Philon: Terminologie scolastique et méta-
    phores', in Lévy, *Philon d'Alexandrie et le langage*, p. 59.
20 On the relationship between skepticism and eclecticism in Philo, see
    J. Mansfeld, 'Philosophy in the Service of Scripture: Philo's Exegetical
    Strategies', in J. Dillon and A. A. Long (eds.), *The Question of "Eclecticism"*
    (Berkeley 1988), pp. 70–102.

III.2. The Classification of the Passions

Philo shows originality in this domain in two ways:

(1)   he pretends to accept the Stoic classification of the passions, while he more or less blatantly changes it according to the biblical texts, and

(2)   he makes use of complex procedures in order to evoke what under-lies passion.

It is customary for Philo to refer with apparent academic rigidity to the Stoic division of the passions, the bad ones and the good ones. We know that in Stoicism there are four bad passions: desire (*epithymia*), fear (*phobos*), sadness (*lupē*), and pleasure (*hēdonē*), and there are three good passions (*eupatheiai*): joy (*chara*), caution (*eulabeia*), and wishing (*boulēsis*), each of them being the contrary of a bad passion. Philo uses this classification both as a tool for exegesis and as an instrument for communication with the literate public for whom such classifications were, so to speak, elementary cultural facts. We may consider it as normal that a person such as Philo, who was imbued with Greek culture but did not completely identify himself with it, should have felt a certain freedom with regard to concepts that did not have the same value for him as for a Stoic. In a more subtle way, he uses these notions as conveyors in order to pass on, under the appearance of Stoicism, notions which are foreign to Stoicism and even in contradiction with it. In *Quod deterius potiori insidiari soleat* 119–20, the words in Gen 4:12 that describe Cain as 'groaning and trembling upon the earth', lead the commentator to see in him the allegory of the unhappy life to which 'have been allotted the more grievous of the four passions, fear and grief'. 'For such a life', Philo adds, 'some evil thing must either be present or on its way. The expectation of that which is on its way begets fear, the experience of that which is present begets grief.' These definitions are canonical in Stoicism, but that which follows is much less so. Indeed, Philo refers to the two good passions that in his view are the positive equivalents of fear and grief, and he defines them by changing their object. When we have the good, he says, there is joy, which seems from this perspective to be the contrary of grief, and when we expect the good, there is hope. But in Stoicism, joy is the contrary of pleasure. Hope was never considered by the Stoics as a 'good emotion', because the future for the Stoics, as V. Goldschmidt correctly put it, is 'the scene of the passions'.[21] Actually, Philo carries out a real transformation of Stoicism all the more efficiently in that this transformation respects

---

21   *Le système stoïcien et l'idée de temps*[4] (Paris 1989), p. 171, where the Platonic origin of this idea is emphasized.

the general appearance of the very thing into which it instills a new meaning. To affirm that there exists hope that does not coincide with fear or with an interested concern for the future, both of which are typical of the common man, is an innovative philosophical position, rich in potentialities. It indicates, in any case, just how mistaken the thesis is that Philo unconditionally adheres to Stoicism when it comes to the question of the passions.

A second example is found in *Quaestiones in Genesim* 2.57, which deals with Gen 9:3: 'Every reptile that lives shall be to you for food.' In his allegorical interpretation of this verse, Philo sets out in systematic fashion the bad passions in contrast to the good passions: 'Alongside sensual pleasures there is the passion of joy. And alongside the desire for sensual pleasure, there is reflection. And alongside grief there is remorse and constraint. And alongside desire, there is caution.' We see here that remorse and constraint are set out as the contraries to grief. It is therefore the past, in the form of repentance, that comes to be integrated into the theory of the 'good emotions'. Hope and repentance, biblical virtues, are appended to the Stoic theory of the passions and utterly transform its rationale.

There remains the problem of the definition of passion, which is dealt with by Philo with an inventiveness that has not as yet, it seems to me, been fully elucidated.

It so happens that Philo speaks of the passions in a way that a Platonist would not disclaim. Such is the case in *Legum allegoriae* 1.73, where we read: 'Whenever, on the other hand, high spirit and desire turn restive and get out of hand, and by the violence of their impetus drag the driver, that is, the rational faculty, down from his seat and put him under the yoke, and each of these passions gets hold of the reins, injustice prevails.' Paradoxically, this Platonizing description does not entail a rejection of the Stoic theory, but serves as a means to link Platonism and Stoicism through a variety of approaches. Most often, Philo proceeds by reflecting on the number four. If indeed, as we have mentioned, he scrupulously retains the Stoic four-part classification of the passions, it is precisely because it enables him to connect the Stoic theory of the passions to the Platonic description of the soul. The four passions are the four legs of the horse, the animal that in Plato symbolizes the irrational part(s) of the soul.[22] Plato's use of this symbolism was an aid to Philo in his allegorical interpretation of the Bible, where there are a great number of allusions to horses. In *De agricultura* 82–3, Philo comments on Exod 15:21, where we read, 'Let us sing unto the Lord, for gloriously has he been glorified; horse and rider he threw

---

22 See esp. the description of the winged team of horses in *Phaedr.* 253c–e.

into the sea.' The interpretation is as follows: 'No one who looks into the matter could find a more perfect victory than one in which that most doughty array of passions and vices, four-footed, restless, boastful beyond measure, has been defeated.' There follows a long metaphorical passage about the breeding of horses, which ends in a description of good horsemen who 'are able by applying bit and bridle to the irrational faculties to curb the excessive violence of their movement' (§ 94). We thus find a number of passages in which, on the basis of a biblical allusion to a horse, Philo takes up and develops the theme of the four-legged passion.[23] He is perhaps dependent on Posidonius, who had imported into Stoicism a certain amount of metaphors from Plato. These were able to serve as important exegetical tools for Philo.

But what is the origin of passion? Let us begin with *De congressu* 81, which is the most complete passage of those in which we find a real 'genealogy' of passionate impulses. In this text, as in a number of others, we find the idea that passion is the natural state of man at the beginning of his life: 'In the first stage of our coming into existence, the soul is reared with none but passions to be its comrades, griefs, pains, excitements, desires, pleasures, all of which come to it through the senses, since the rational part of the soul is not yet able to see good and evil and to form an accurate judgment of the difference between them, but is still slumbering, its eyes closed as if in deep sleep.' This is one of the ideas by which Philo distinguishes himself strongly from Stoicism and reveals himself as a distant predecessor of Freud: childhood is not a period of innocence but truly it is 'Egypt, that is, passion'.[24] What comes first is insanity: Esau, who is the symbol of insanity, has the right of the firstborn, whereas Jacob, the reasonable, is born second: 'Folly is congenital to us from our earliest years, but the desire for moral excellence is a later birth' (*Sobr.* 26).

However, Philo seems to say the exact opposite of this in another passage, where the text under discussion is Gen 2:18: 'And the Lord God said, It is not good that the man should be alone, let us make for him a helper corresponding to him.' Philo explains in his comment that man is the symbol of reason and woman symbolizes sensation and passion, which come after reason: 'the commanding part of the soul is older than the soul as a whole, and the irrational part younger' (*Leg.* 2.6). Should we therefore conclude that because of his dependence on biblical texts, Philo the exegete contradicts himself? Actually, the two passages are

23 *Leg.* 2.99; *Agr.* 73; *Spec.* 4.79; *Mos.* 1.26; *Her.* 269; *Congr.* 172; *Abr.* 236ff.
24 *Congr.* 85. On this point see C. Lévy, 'Éthique de l'immanence, éthique de la transcendance: Le problème de l'*oikeiôsis* chez Philon', in Lévy, *Philon d'Alexandrie et le langage*, pp. 153–64.

not necessarily in contradiction. In the passage from *De congressu*, it had not been claimed that reason was absent during childhood but that it remained 'asleep'. There is therefore perhaps a coherence between the two texts, a coherence that is both biblical and philosophical. From the biblical point of view and within Philo's exegetical system, the sleep of reason in the child may represent the sleep of Adam in Genesis. Each man has an individual process of development during which the sleep of reason favors the appearance of passion. From the philosophical point of view, it is a way for Philo to avoid the Stoic conception of a reason that is too dependent on the senses. Reason, for Philo, is not formed through the organization of notions that come from sense-perception. Rather, reason is present in us at birth, not as a mere potentiality but as a reality. It is only that the activation of that reality is postponed.

III.3. The Healing of the Passions

What are we to do with these passions? In some texts, the answer is clear and seems to coincide completely with the Stoic doctrine of the radical extirpation of the passions.[25] According to *De migratione Abrahami* 92, circumcision represents allegorically 'the excision of pleasure and all passions'. The same doctrine is presented in *Quod Deus sit immutabilis* 67: 'Now the lawgiver, thereby being now approved as the best of physicians for the distempers and maladies of the soul, set before himself one task and purpose, to make a radical excision of the diseases of the mind and leave no root to sprout again into sickness which defies cure.' Is such an absence of passions possible? Philo seems to claim so in *De sacrificiis Abelis et Caini* 110–11, where he takes up an important point in Stoic doctrine, namely, that wisdom is possible but extremely rare to attain in perfect form. Elsewhere, he confirms this view by indicating that moral perfection is embodied in Moses. As Philo sees it, 'Moses ... thinks it necessary to use the knife on the seat of anger in its entirety, and to cut it clean out of the soul, for no moderation of passion can satisfy him' (*Leg.* 3.129). In contrast to Moses, the 'person making progress' (= the Stoic *prokoptōn*) must be satisfied with trying to tame passion by a *logos* of clarity and truth.[26] In this fight against the passions, *enkrateia* and *karteria* (self-control and endurance) obviously play an important role together with the four traditional virtues (*Leg.* 3.11, 156, 239, 240). We also find in Philo the idea that passion cannot

---

25 The Stoic metaphor for the treatment of passion is a surgical one; see Seneca, *Ep.* 75.6–7.

26 *Leg.* 3.128, 140. For the *prokoptōn* in Stoicism, see Sandbach, *The Stoics*, pp. 47–8, and just below, pp. 165–6.

be contested when it is in a phase of maximal outburst. Rebecca, who symbolizes patience, on one occasion advises her son Jacob to flee to his uncle Laban in order to escape from Esau. Philo interprets this as an attitude of wise prudence that consists in not confronting passion when it is in a phase of outburst (*Fug.* 23f.). Similarly, according to Cicero, Chrysippus forbids the treating of the inflammations of the soul when they are recent (*Tusc.* 4.63 = *SVF* III.484). All of this seems to form a block of perfect Stoic orthodoxy, but this is a false impression. For at the same time as Philo's thought appears to be well rooted in Stoicism, he reveals his originality in many ways, as we shall see presently.

First of all, as W. Völker has shown, the perfect serenity (*apatheia*) of the wise man in Philo is not the outcome of a natural process through which man fulfills his own nature, but rather it is the result of divine grace.[27] In *De somniis* 1.173, in commenting on the words 'do not fear' which God addresses to Jacob during his dream about the ladder (Gen 28:13), Philo explains that God is a weapon which frees man from fear and all other passions. It is mainly the character of Abraham, however, that enables us to better understand what exactly 'apathy' means for Philo. When he receives the order to sacrifice his only son, Abraham obeys without the slightest emotion: 'he admitted no swerving of body or mind' (*Abr.* 175). He is literally 'apathetic' and yet his apathy is a false one insofar as it is not an acceptance of a natural order but rather the serenity that results from an unwavering hope. Abraham has the belief that God will find Himself a victim even in the huge desert where there seems to be no living creature at all. The apathy of Abraham is thus, despite appearances, poles apart from the apathy of the Stoic wise man. In Abraham, apathy is not the acceptance of nature but the negation of it as inevitable causality, and it is based on the belief that there exists a transcendence that can be free of the laws of nature. Now, Philo notes that at the death of Sarah, Abraham does not remain apathetic. His mind gives him the following advice: 'he should not grieve over-bitterly as at an utterly new and unheard of misfortune, nor yet assume an indifference (*apatheia*) as though nothing painful had occurred, but choose the mean rather than the extremes and aim at moderation of emotion, not resent that nature should be paid the debt which is its due, but quietly and gently lighten the blow' (*Abr.* 257). It seems, therefore, that for Philo there is a bad apathy and a good apathy. The former entails an indifference that borders on inhumanity; the latter entails the absence of excessive and bad passions and for this reason can border on what was called *metriopatheia*, 'moderation of emotion'. We must therefore

27   *Fortschritt und Vollendung bei Philo von Alexandrien* (Leipzig 1938), p. 266.

specify here the nature of the difference between Philo and Stoicism. In contrast to the Stoics, who think that passion is always bad, in Philo there is the idea, probably of Peripatetic origin, of a unity of passion, which is given to man in order to help him, and which he can turn into the instrument of his ruin or of his perfection. This idea is expressed in *Legum allegoriae* 2.8, where Philo says that anger, for example, can be a defensive weapon. We find it again in *De migratione* 118–19, where Philo comments on God's words to Abraham in Gen 12:3: 'in you all of the tribes of the earth will be blessed.' He takes the words to refer allegorically to the transformation of the bad passions into good ones: 'If the mind continues free from harm and sickness, it has all its tribes and powers in a healthy condition, those whose province is sight and hearing and all others concerned with sense-perception, and those again that have to do with pleasures and desires, and all that are undergoing transformation from the lower to the higher emotions.'

It thus appears that the whole of Philo's line of thought about the passions, which is so manifestly influenced by Stoicism, retains a profound autonomy. This emerges still more clearly with reference to the topic of madness, the consideration of which should indicate well the rift between Philo and Stoicism.

III.4. Ecstasy and Madness

Let us note from the outset a significant point. In the Philonic corpus, vast as it is, the occurrences of *melancholia* (literally = 'atrabiliousness') and the related verb are rather rare.[28] This is a sign that Philo does not take the Peripatetic approach to madness, which is based on medical considerations, namely, the idea that the derangement may be due to an imbalance of bodily humors. The words he uses to designate madness are mainly *aphrosynē* (folly), *lutta*, which designates a kind of rage, and *mania*. It is on this last term that we shall focus our attention, leaving aside the problem of *phaulos*, the 'non-wise' person of the Stoics, who is automatically considered by them as a madman – an extremist position that Philo does not share. As for *mania*, it would be fruitless to look for occurrences of this term with a positive meaning in the Stoic school. By contrast, for Philo, there are two types of *mania*, one which corresponds to an outburst of passions and the other which is defined as an ecstasy of divine origin.

The first type is mentioned in *De agricultura* 37: 'Gluttony is naturally followed by her attendant, sexual indulgence, which brings on extraordinary madness (*mania*), fierce desire, and most grievous frenzy.' It also appears in the description of the damaging effects of drunkenness in *De*

---

28   *Leg.* 2.70; *Cher.* 69, 116; *Conf.* 16; *Her.* 249; *Somn.* 2.85; *Plant.* 177.

vita contemplativa 40. With regard to madness as linked to excessive desires, drunkenness plays a particularly important role. The reasons for this are cultural (the important role in Greek society played by the banquet or drinking party[29]), biblical (the drunkenness of Noah), and philosophical (the theme of the drunkenness of the wise man is a *topos* in Stoicism). There is an elaborate treatment of this last theme in *De plantatione* 142–8, where Philo presents conflicting opinions. The first is the opinion of those who hold that the wise man will not drink to excess and will not act foolishly. Others hold that the wise man can drink but will not get drunk because his wisdom will constitute a barrier against the effects of wine. Finally, still others claim that if the wise man drinks to excess, he will be unable to control himself. These three positions are then reduced to two: 'The argument obviously admits of two positions: one establishing the thesis that the wise man will get drunk, the other maintaining the contrary, that he will not get drunk' (*Plant.* 149). The presentation of the arguments brought forward in favor of each of these two opinions attests to Philo's in-depth knowledge of the discussions taking place within Stoicism, as a comparison with Seneca's *Letter* 83 reveals. Both Seneca and Philo cite the syllogism by which Zeno claimed to demonstrate that the wise man will not get drunk.[30] The two texts share many aspects in common, but there is a wide gap between the attitude of Seneca and that of Philo. The former tries to go beyond the theoretical approach to the problem by making use of *exempla*, while Philo, although he claims that he is reproducing scholastic discussions, lingers over the allegorical meaning of drunkenness, that deep joy inherent in wisdom.[31] It is most probably this sort of allegory that was developed in the second book of the *De ebrietate*, lost today, while the first book deals at length with the damaging effects of drunkenness.

A reading of the *De plantatione* shows that Philo knows Stoic literature on the passions in great detail. This only makes more significant the existence, according to him, of a salutary madness that in its very essence is completely contrary to the teachings of Stoicism. In *De fuga et inventione* 167–8, Isaac, who symbolizes joy and grace, is described as one of those men belonging to a race that is above *logos* and that arises not out of human conceptions but out of divine madness. In *Quis heres*

29 Note the extremely critical references to the Alexandrian banquet in *Leg.* 3.156 and *Plant.* 160.

30 Compare *Plant.* 176 with Seneca, *Ep.* 83.9.

31 *Plant.* 168–9. On this question see the classic work of H. Lewy, *Sobria ebrietas: Untersuchungen zur Geschichte der antiken Mystik* (Giessen 1929), p. 38f., and R. Goulet, *La philosophie de Moïse: Essai de reconstitution d'un commentaire philosophique préphilonien du Pentateuque* (Paris 1987), p. 218.

249, Philo is even more precise and, referring to the word 'ecstasy', he says it can have four different meanings: pathological madness brought on by senility or by melancholy; amazement in the face of an unexpected event; the calm of intelligence; and the possession and delirium of divine origin. This madness, a kind of departure of the soul out of itself, often described in Platonic terms, is the possession by God of the soul of the wise man, whom He invisibly strikes as His plectrum (*Her.* 259). We are literally at the antipodes of Stoicism. Indeed, man's objective is no longer a wisdom defined as 'living in harmony with oneself as a rational being', but rather the loss of oneself, which is the only way to make possible the coming of the divine spirit: 'The mind in us is evicted when the divine spirit arrives, but when it departs, the mind returns once again' (*Her.* 265). This does not mean that there is any fatalism in Philo. On the contrary, in this entire passage, he rather loyally presents the Stoic theory of the four passions. But he does so in order to assert that the task of struggling against them allows God to undertake the work proper to Him, that is, to proclaim the emancipation and liberation of the souls that come to Him as suppliants (*Her.* 272–3). Stoicism thus becomes the preparation for a Platonic undertaking that itself is the philosophical expression of biblical transcendence.

Is it possible to discover any linkage, seemingly improbable, between the madness that comes from the exacerbation of the passions and the madness that is defined by God's entry into us? The only passage in which such a linkage is made is, as far as I know, *De specialibus legibus* 3.99. Here Philo speaks of punishments suitable for poisoners and he declares that, among poisonings, the most serious are those that reach the soul: 'Fits of delirium and insanity and intolerable frenzy swoop down upon them, and thereby the mind, the greatest gift which God has assigned to human kind, is subject to every sort of affliction, and when it despairs of salvation, it takes its departure and makes its home elsewhere, leaving in the body the baser kind of soul, the irrational, which the beasts also share. For everyone who is left forsaken by reason, the better part of the soul, has been transformed into the nature of a beast, even though the outward characteristics of his body still retain their human form.' In this passage, Philo does not take up explicitly the dichotomy between good and bad madness. He does appear to imply, however, that all madness involves a departure of reason, which can either propel itself toward God or debase itself somewhere, abandoning the soul to irrationality. In the same fashion, although passion is bad, it has nevertheless been conceived to help man. The Philonic starting point is not fundamentally different from that of Stoicism, namely that God has provided for man. What makes the difference is not so much the provision as the status of the provider. We could be led to think, as

R. Goulet does, that Philo has disturbed by his religiousness the perfect rationality of the Stoics.[32] It seems to me that on the contrary, by moving the pivotal point from the inside to the outside, from immanence to transcendence, Philo gave rise to phenomena of intense disorganization and of paradoxical reorganization that are his own way of interpreting the orientation of the search in a Platonic fashion. In this manner he substituted for the Stoic paradigm of abiding or residence, or *oikeiōsis*, that of a movement outward that is not exile but exodus.

IV. MORAL ITINERARIES: THE PROGRESS TOWARD PERFECTION

Philo expresses a certain negative outlook in *De fuga* 63–4, where he cites Plato's *Theaetetus* 176a-b, to the effect that because evils can never pass away from the earthly sphere, one must become like God as far as it is possible, so as to fly to the heavenly realm. The biblical confirmation of the first part of this statement lies in the allegorical interpretation of the fact that Cain's death is never attested in the Pentateuch (cf. § 60). Cain will not die because he symbolizes the presence of evil on earth. The body itself is often presented as the source of the inevitable passions and of the troubles inherent in the condition of the created being. However, contrary to pessimistic versions of Platonism that interpret life on earth as a fall of the soul, Philo is also imbued with the Stoic notion of providence – the Jewish believer that he is can discern the philosophical expression of the benevolence that guided creation. The body is a given, which it is impossible to completely disregard. It is rather the high estimation of the body that is a mistake, and hence the fight against Epicureanism, the doctrine of the validation of pleasure and of the body. Nevertheless pleasure itself is given a function, in the same way as sensation (*Leg.* 2.6–8; *Cher.* 62), because it is what enables procreation. Pleasure, as A. Le Boulluec has put it, 'seems to be willed by the creator, as if it were necessary for the completion of the created or molded man'.[33] The error lies in giving preference to the 'bodily mass' over the soul.[34]

Thus, for Philo, the human being will inevitably be subject to the passions and other evils that beset created beings. Yet God will

---

32 *La philosophie de Moïse*, p. 566.

33 'La place des concepts philosophiques dans la réflexion de Philon sur le plaisir', in Lévy, *Philon d'Alexandrie et le langage*, p. 146. For the notion of the 'molded man', see *Opif.* 134–5.

34 *Leg.* 2.77. The 'bodily mass' in this passage, as in many others, is symbolized by Egypt.

'accomplish the work that is proper to him in proclaiming redemption and liberty to the souls who are his suppliants' (*Her.* 272–3). It remains to define how to live in the least imperfect way in the world as it is. One of the most frequent answers to this question is the distinction, made paradigmatically in the *De Abrahamo*, among three types of men who strive toward the good. The first, Abraham, is characterized by the effort to know; the second, Isaac, by the simple fact of his happy nature; and the third, Jacob, by the practical struggle against everything in human nature that involves the senses and the passions. However, Philo hastens to add that each one of these three types participates in the other two and takes its name from the feature that happens to be present in the greatest amount (*Abr.* 52–3). This trichotomy is of Platonic/Pythagorean origin, as the first lines of the *Meno* show. Its apparent clarity somewhat hides the complexity of the question of the path toward virtue. Abraham is the archetypal figure of the moral itinerary, and at the instigation of his father Terah (compared by Philo to Socrates in *Somn.* 1.58, because he would be representative of the very idea of self-knowledge), leaves Ur, the town of his ancestors. By doing so he takes his leave of Chaldean astrology, and goes first to Haran (the allegory of the journey to the realm of sense-perceptible reality), and then to Shechem (the allegory of the journey to the realm of the soul as detached from the body). The itinerary is summarized in this way by Philo: 'the soul migrates from astrology to real nature study, from insecure conjecture to firm apprehension, and to give it its truest expression, from the created to the uncreated, from the world to the maker and father of the world' (*Her.* 98). Jacob, who, like Abraham, changes his name and takes up the name of Israel, flees on the orders of Rebecca and from fear of Esau to go to Laban. He then leaves the house of Laban, who is the symbol of a materialist vision of the world, to go toward Isaac (*Fug.* 7–14; *Migr.* 26–30). Only Isaac, precisely because he has his knowledge from himself and because he belongs to 'the new race, superior to reason and truly divine' (*Fug.* 168), is not subjected to these journeys. All of this enables Philo to associate biblical exegesis with the recommendation of Plato in *Theaetetus* 176a-b: one should escape out of the world in order to be become similar to God as far as that is possible.

As scholars have noted, the figure of the 'person making moral progress' (= the *prokoptōn*), so important in the Stoicism of Panaetius of Rhodes and his successors, constitutes one of the major models for understanding the moral itinerary as Philo portrays it.[35] Philo gives a specific description of the itinerary of the *prokoptōn* of which we find

---

35 See esp. D. Winston, 'Philo's Ethical Theory', *ANRW* II.21.1 (1984),
    pp. 409–14.

elements in Seneca.[36] Three stages are distinguished: in the first, the *prokoptōn* is compared to a suitor who hopes to marry *paideia* (education); there follows the stage of progress, properly speaking, compared to the work of a planter of trees; finally, perfection, 'in the form of the building of a house, which has been completed but has not yet acquired solidity' (*Agr.* 158). At each stage of this itinerary, we are told, the soul must protect itself.

One should note, however, the absence in Philo of an essential figure found in the Stoicism of imperial times: the master without whom moral progress is not conceivable. The specific quality of this master has been illuminated by M. Foucault.[37] It seems that such a figure is superfluous or at least secondary in Philo, since everything happens in the face-to-face encounter, so to speak, of man with God. It is not difficult to cite the names of the masters of Seneca, of Epictetus or of Marcus Aurelius, but we would be at a loss, in the vast Philonic corpus, to find the name of even one of those who taught him philosophy. Education, *paideia*, is obviously an essential stage in the path to virtue but it is an early stage with a kind of anonymity, in which the intersubjective relationship, so important in imperial Stoicism, is never explicit. When Philo speaks of the Greek and Barbarian 'ascetics' of wisdom, he insists on the fact that they avoid all public places but at no point does he mention their loyalty toward those who enabled them to go toward wisdom (*Spec.* 2.44).

These ascetics are described as Stoic sages, utterly indifferent to passions, who consider that the 'world is a city, having for its citizens the associates of wisdom, registered as such by Virtue, to whom is entrusted the headship of the universal commonwealth' (*Spec.* 2.45). Here Philo appears to distance himself from Peripatetic ethics, which is more attentive to the body and to the external goods such as wealth and honor. In other passages, however, he seems to take a different line. He seems to get closer to Aristotle, for example, when he says that happiness will come 'when there is welfare outside us, welfare in the body, welfare in the soul, the first bringing ease of circumstance and good repute, the second health and strength, the third delight in virtues' (*Her.* 285). How can we explain this contradiction, in which D. Winston saw, and rightly so, a tension between a very strong ascetic vocation and an ethical realism more inclined to accept the constraints of the body and of the external world?[38] There are of course the requirements of biblical exegesis, which lead Philo to favor one tendency on some occasions and the other

36 Compare *Agr.* 157–60 with Seneca, *Ep.* 75.9.
37 *L'herméneutique du sujet* ([Paris] 2001), pp. 149–50.
38 'Philo's Ethical Theory', pp. 412–14.

tendency on other occasions. However, there is also the fact that within the philosophical tradition itself, the Neo-Academics and Antiochus of Ascalon had claimed that the differences between the Old Academy and the Lyceum on the one hand, and the Stoics on the other were merely formal differences. The Stoa had been accused of having instituted, by the creation of neologisms, a theory of 'indifferents' that allowed it to recognize bodily and external advantages in a kind of roundabout fashion.[39] This could have reassured Philo if he held that there was no essential contradiction in making use of the two systems.

Moreover, the fact that Philo was not completely satisfied with the Stoic theory of moral values is revealed by another passage, the significance of which does not yet seem to have been fully appreciated. In *Legum allegoriae* 3.125–6, Philo speaks of Aaron when he enters the holy place. Philo sets in contrast to the moment when the entire being of the high priest is focused on the 'holy resolutions' (*agiai gnomai*), the 'holy and purified opinions (*doxai*)', which are, however, mere human opinions. He includes in these the *kathēkonta* and the *katorthōmata*, terms used by the Stoics to indicate 'intermediate' and 'perfect' moral actions.[40] It appears, therefore, that in Philo's view Stoic moral doctrine is constituted on the basis of holy opinions, but they remain human opinions. The idea here seems to be that to enter into the presence of God, to rid oneself of all the impurities of one's soul, is an experience that transcends the doctrines and systematic constructions of philosophy. This is what Philo means when, in *De Abrahamo* 268, he says that 'the only good that is infallible and firm is faith in God'. This faith in God (= *pistis pros theon*) can entail certain aspects of philosophy and in particular of Stoic philosophy,[41] but it can never be reduced to a self-sufficient human reason.

V. POLITICS[42]

Philo, as we know, did not look at the great changes of history with detachment. He played an important role in the Jewish *politeuma* (institutionalized community) of Alexandria, and he himself has given

39 See J. Dillon, *The Middle Platonists* (London 1977), pp. 70–4.
40 For *kathēkonta* and *katorthōmata* in the Stoic system, see A. A. Long, *Hellenistic Philosophy: Stoics, Epicureans, Sceptics*[2] (Berkeley 1986), pp. 199–205.
41 See B. Besnier, 'Migration et *telos* d'apres le *De migratione Abrahami*', *StPhAnn* 11 (1999), p. 76 n. 4.
42 On this topic, see, see R. Barraclough, 'Philo's Politics: Roman Rule and Hellenistic Judaism', *ANRW* II.21.1 (1984), pp. 417–553; F. Calabi, *The Language and the Law of God: Interpretation and Politics in Philo of Alexandria* (Atlanta 1998).

ample evidence of what such a commitment involved.[43] His advice is to engage in political affairs before coming to the contemplative life: 'It is good to fight out first the contest of the practical life (*bios praktikos*) before proceeding to the contemplative life (*bios theōrētikos*), for the former is a prelude to the latter, which is a more advanced contest.' The Levites, entrusted with carrying out their normal tasks until the age of fifty (Num 4:3ff.), but directed after that age, according to Philo's interpretation, toward the contemplative life, appear as the symbols of what should be the linkage between the *bios praktikos* and the *bios theōrētikos* (*Fug.* 36–7). Thus we find in Philo, alongside the exaltation of the ascetic ideal, an in-depth consideration of all the aspects of the political side of life. We can only examine a few of these aspects here.

On which issues does Philo join the Stoic philosophers? As they do, he asserts that human beings are united in a natural community (*physikē koinōnia*), which has as one consequence, for example, that the restitution of lost property is a fundamental rule of life in society (*Virt.* 96). Man, because he is rational, is defined as the gentlest of created beings, despite the existence of misanthropes and of people like Judah's son Onan.[44] The existence of this natural community has as a consequence a relationship of kinship among human beings, which Philo describes in the clearest way when he speaks of the Essenes' refusal to possess slaves. In their view, slave owners are impious men who 'annul the statute of nature, who mother-like has born and reared all men alike, and created them genuine brothers, not in mere name, but in very reality'. This kinship would end in friendship if 'malignant covetousness' were not to engender hatred (*Prob.* 79). The same notion of a common natural origin leads Philo to encourage man to pursue philanthropy toward his 'natural kinsfolk' (*Spec.* 1.294–5), which is a response to the accusation of misanthropy constantly made by the Greek opponents of Judaism. But it is also the expression of a universalism that for Philo is both of a philosophical and theological nature, because nature never exists for itself but is always to be seen in connection to divine transcendence. Thus, to kill a man is always an act that causes a stain. Philo probably goes further than Seneca in his critique of slavery, because he is not content with demanding humane treatment of slaves. He goes so far as to advocate their emancipation when he says, 'grant freedom to him who is naturally free' (*Spec.* 2.84), although this universalism is perhaps somewhat tempered by the priority accorded to the Jewish slave. The difference

43   See above, ch. 1, pp. 19–31.
44   See *Decal.* 132; *Post.* 180–1; *Deus* 16–17; *Ebr.* 78; and Berthelot, *L''humanité'*, p. 108.

between Philo and the Stoics, as has been emphasized by Berthelot, lies in the fact that Philo puts at the center of man's social concern not the love of parents for their children but the love of children for their parents. This does not correspond to the Stoic dogma of *oikeiōsis*, but to the biblical commandment of respect for one's parents.[45] Furthermore, Philo hesitates to call the whole of humanity a family when he says that our goods should be shared with all, as with 'kinsmen and brothers by nature' (*Virt.* 140). He transfers here to a metaphorical level that which, at least in Stoicism, is supposed to be the description of reality.

The same use of Stoic themes, but from a non-Stoic perspective, is seen in connection with natural law. This natural law is the foundation of ethics in the Stoa, and is defined by Zeno, the originator of the doctrine, as 'that which commands to do what is just and prohibits the actions that are contrary to justice' (*SVF* I.162). Not to be confused with any particular legislation, natural law is the law of the single *polis* that is formed by the world. But, if we believe what Cicero writes, the concept of natural law is problematic, in that natural law is efficacious for the righteous people but has no hold on the dishonest (*Resp.* 3.33). Hence the proliferation of contradictory laws that are the expression not of reason but of particular desires. It is the same Cicero who, in his *De legibus*, put forward an idea unthinkable in Greek philosophical circles but which anticipated Philo's approach in some respects. He claimed that certain features of Roman legislation coincided with natural law, a claim that would make Rome not a city among others, but a privileged location for the manifestation of law in the absolute. However, the enterprise of the Roman was easier insofar as such an assimilation was the result of his observation of the natural growth, so to speak, of Roman power. Philo, on the other hand, had to reckon with the transcendent character of a law given by God to a specific nation, albeit 'His own' people. This idea involves, as H. Najman has indicated, some formidable obstacles.[46]

That Philo knows the Stoic doctrine of the 'law of nature' (*nomos physeōs*), whenever that doctrine may have been first formulated, appears clear from *De Josepho* 28–31. This passage is often considered, and rightly so in my view, as one of the most complete presentations of the idea. Philo's discussion is linked to the explanation of the name of Joseph, taken to mean, 'addition to the Lord', by which he reaches the idea that individual political regimes are 'additions' to the one natural regime. Philo asserts that the world is a *megalopolis* governed by a single law which, according to the canonical Stoic expression,

45 Berthelot, *L''humanité'*, p. 112.
46 'A Written Copy of the Law of Nature: An Unthinkable Paradox?', *StPhAnn* 15 (2003), pp. 54–63.

'commands what should be done and forbids what should not be done'. But he also reports that humanity is dispersed, and lives in a great many cities which are governed by very different laws. The reason for this must not be looked for, he says, in the diversity of geographical circumstances, but in the presence within the human soul of passions that make a harmonious coexistence of nations impossible. According to Stoic theory, each human being, *qua* rational individual, is potentially a god but in reality, with the exception of the wise man, he amounts to an aggregation of passions destructive for himself and for others so that humanity can form only a 'virtual' city. From the same perspective, we know that only the wise man is king, a circumstance that transforms this Stoic 'kingship' into a virtual government almost never to be realized.

Paradoxically, Philo seems to be more of an immanentist than the Stoics on this issue, because Moses, whose existence no one can doubt, is at the same time a philosopher, a sage, a legislator, a high priest, and a prophet (*Mos.* 2.2–7). Precisely because he combines wisdom and political power in himself, Moses is not only a legislator, he is the incarnation of the law (*nomos empsychos*), as are the patriarchs (*Abr.* 3–5). In his person, he prescribes what is good and forbids what is bad, just as the law of nature does. The best proof of this, according to Philo, is the fact that Jewish law has remained unchanged. The commandments decreed by Moses, he says, 'are in accord with the system of eternal nature'.[47] From this point of view, the kingship of Moses cannot be limited to Israel, and it necessarily has a universalist dimension. The Jewish laws, in contrast to the Greek laws, says Philo, 'attract and win the attention of all' (*Mos.* 2.20).

In contrast to Moses, the figure of the philosopher–king who is the constant object of Philo's admiration, the appreciation of Joseph is much more restrained, a fact that has led to differing interpretations.[48] We know that the name was interpreted by Philo, from the Hebrew, as meaning 'addition to the Lord', which is a contradictory expression because there is nothing that can be added to God. What is more, in his definition of natural law, Philo describes the particular laws as useless and dangerous additions.[49] In the *De Josepho*, however, Joseph represents

---

47 *Mos.* 2.52. See H. Najman, 'The Law of Nature and the Authority of Mosaic Law', *StPhAnn* 11 (1999), pp. 55–73.
48 See F. Frazier, 'Les visages de Joseph dans le *De Josepho*', *StPhAnn* 14 (2002), pp. 1–30.
49 *Jos.* 28–31. The etymology is given in a slightly different form in *Somn.* 2.47. For the rendering of the name 'Joseph', which allows for different options, see V. Nikiprowetzky, 'ΚΥΡΙΟΥ ΠΡΟΣΘΕΣΙΣ: Note critique sur Philon d'Alexandrie, *De Iosepho*, 28', *Revue des études juives* 127 (1968), pp. 387–92.

a sort of ideal politician. In addition to his ancestry and his natural gifts, he had all that he needed to be a good ruler (*Jos.* 54). He was initiated into the pastoral or ruling art at the age of seventeen, his duties as the bursar of Potiphar trained him in economics, and his capacity to control his passions was brought to light in the episode with Potiphar's wife. In short, as has often been noted, he represents the good Hellenistic administrator who also proves to be the healer of society when the famine breaks out.

Joseph's assets, however, are not enough to allow him to confront without ill effects the empirical reality that his multicolored coat symbolizes, a world of infinite variety, fluid and thus impossible to grasp. Even the best politician, when he has the sensible world as his point of reference, can only be an 'interpreter of dreams', although his interpretation is concerned not with the dreams of individuals but with the 'general and public dream' (*Jos.* 125–6). In the *De somniis*, in contrast to the *De Josepho*, the image of Joseph appears to be considerably more negative without, however, there being necessarily any contradiction between the two texts. It is not the paradigmatic Joseph that constitutes the focus of attention, the one whose virtue so impressed his jailer that the latter gave him authority over all of the prisoners (*Jos.* 85). In the *De somniis* there emerges rather the politician thirsty for glory, against whom his brothers are right to rebel. The ambivalence of the character of Joseph shows that, in Philo's view, immersion in the world of politics, even if it does not necessarily lead to perversity, permanently entails such a risk.

VI. CONCLUSION

Is it at all possible to systematize Philo's ethical teachings? Without minimizing the contradictions that they contain, it is possible to characterize them by saying that they are the result of two movements, which in the dynamic line of his thought are contradictory only in appearance. It is necessary to flee from the world in order to come face to face with God, but also to deepen one's insertion into the world in order to experience a relationship with God through meeting others. In this sense, the ethics of Philo are inseparably both transcendent and immanentist.

(Translated from the French by Ada Bronowski.)

III. Philo's Influence
and Significance

7   Philo and the New Testament

To get a sense of the diffusion of Philo's ideas between his own time and the emergence of a literary *corpus Philoneum*, we must rely on Christian sources. In the first two centuries CE, these are the only sources that tell us anything about the possible influence of his teachings on the Greek world. The innumerable Greek-speaking synagogues of the Roman Empire, and especially those in the big cities, will have served as relay stations. They must have been places of learning in one way or another, and they did serve as the setting of one of Judaism's most important innovations, public sermons on Holy Scripture. If we assume that more than one teacher like Philo was active in the urban synagogues of antiquity, the diffusion of Philonic language and ideas can be explained by an appeal to oral forms of transmission.

All clues to Philo's earliest influence on the Greek-speaking world are hidden in the literary corpus of what was to be called the New Testament. To state this is not a 'canonical' approach. For the present chapter, Christian writings contemporaneous with the New Testament, such as the *Epistles* of Ignatius of Antioch and the *Shepherd of Hermas*, are of little interest, because they are devoid of philosophy. And, as regards the documents of early Gnosticism cited by Irenaeus and Hippolytus or contained in the Nag Hammadi library, they have relevance for the question just raised but are chronologically later.

The writings of the New Testament that reveal the clearest evidence of at least indirect Philonic influence are the Epistle to the Hebrews and the Gospel of John. It is possible to explain this influence by reference to known historical circumstances. The author of Hebrews is likely to have been a Jewish Christian from Rome, and may have heard or met Philo in that city, or have had contacts with others who did. For Philo came to Rome in 38 or 39 CE, and remained there for perhaps two years.[1] The Gospel of John was written at Ephesus, and a representative of Alexandrian Judaism, Apollos, was very active in the formation of

---

1   For Philo's stay in Rome, see above, ch. 1, p. 12.

the Christian community there.[2] He and others like him may have been
responsible for the appearance of Philonic ideas at Ephesus. Apollos was
also present at Corinth, and it has been suggested that his influence
may be behind some ideas of Paul's Corinthian correspondents.

In a lesser degree of concentration, points of contact with Philo may
be found in the Pauline corpus as a whole, in Luke, and in the deutero-
pauline writings. Accordingly, we will begin our survey with Hebrews,
the document to which perhaps even Philo himself is closest, and conclude with the latest relevant writing, the Fourth Gospel, the Logos theology of which may be seen as the culmination of the reception of Philo,
at least as regards philosophical depth. Thus we shall consider:

I.   The Epistle to the Hebrews (Rome)
II. The Pauline Corpus
III. The Special Case of 1 Corinthians (Corinth)
IV. Luke; The Pauline School
V.   The Gospel according to John (Ephesus)

These five sections are not meant to cover all of the New Testament. It
will not be possible to treat Matthew or James, even though the latter
gives the only reference in the whole New Testament for the thesis
that God is immutable (1:17; cf. the Philonic treatise *Quod Deus sit
immutabilis*).[3] It is in other writings that the key Philonic themes
appear. We will see that it is the very reception of Philo's ideas that
enabled Christian thinkers to develop what came to be called 'theology'
and what procured for John the evangelist the title 'the theologian'.

As to topics, the sections will be arranged according to the following
scheme:

- Formalities: Literary Genres Employed, Specialized Language,
  Metaphors
- Scripture and the Methods of Its Interpretation
- Knowledge of God, Natural and Revealed
- Secrets of the Divine Name
- Wisdom and Eternal Torah; Angels; the Heavenly Realm

2   For the activity of Apollos, see Acts 18:24–19:1; 1 Cor 1:12, 3:4–6, 22, 4:6,
    16:12; Titus 3:13. He is the only intermediary between Alexandrian Judaism
    and the New Testament who can be named, and is the only Alexandrian we
    hear of in the New Testament.
3   For Matthew, see P.L. Shuler, 'Philo's Moses and Matthew's Jesus:
    A Comparative Study in Ancient Literature', *StPhAnn* 2 (1990), pp. 86–103.
    For James, see C. Siegfried, *Philo von Alexandria als Ausleger des Alten
    Testaments* (Jena 1875), pp. 310–14.

- The Divine Logos
- Creation and Duality; the Two Powers
- Freedom of Choice; Evil and Sin; Grace and Salvation
- Man; Man and Woman
- Sacred History: From the Patriarchs to Moses
- The Exodus: Passover; Revealed Torah
- The Commandments; Concrete Ethics
- Cult, Prayer, Rites, and Holy Places
- Eschatology

In general, we will focus our attention on the facets of a very rich Torah theology that is Philo's, and find its multiple repercussions in early Christian literature. For there is little doubt that 'of all the non-Christian writers of the first century A.D. Philo is the one from whom the historian of emergent Christianity has most to learn.'[4] In this chapter we may confirm this, adding one more perspective: For Philonic scholarship, too, the New Testament writings offer unique opportunities for learning how Philo's teachings were first received, understood, and transformed.

I. THE EPISTLE TO THE HEBREWS (ROME)

The epistle *To the Hebrews* (i.e., to Jewish Christians)[5] is a treatise of both a paraenetic (hortatory) and an exegetical or midrashic character, as is much of Philo's writing. Its destination seems to have been Rome; some of the oldest manuscripts transmit it together with Paul's Letter to the Romans. Its author seems to be temporarily separated from his audience (13:24), or so he writes.[6] His purpose is to strengthen the community's adherence to Christian doctrine – obviously in a situation where it seemed attractive for Jewish Christians to return to the synagogue (6:4–6, 10:26f).

The very rhetorical character of this Epistle hides the fact that it is one of the earliest Christian documents. It is cited already in *1 Clement* 36.2–5 (written in Rome before 96 CE). As there is no trace of the tensions

---

4 H. Chadwick, 'St. Paul and Philo of Alexandria', *Bulletin of the John Rylands Library* 48 (1965/1966), p. 288, quoted with approval by D. T. Runia, *Philo in Early Christian Literature: A Survey* (Assen 1993), p. 64.

5 There was no other term for Jewish Christians in antiquity except the cumbersome 'those of the circumcision' (Gal 2:12; Col 4:11), which was not fitting for a solemn address.

6 He or she: among the persons who have been named as possible candidates for authorship is also Prisca (Rom 16:3; 1 Cor 16:19).

or even of the shock of the Judean war, we may confidently date the composition of the Epistle before 68 CE.[7] This best explains how the treatise can speak of the Aaronite priesthood as an ongoing institution. It also explains the very embryonic state of Christian theological reflection and the imprecision in terminology. The highly rhetorical character of the text by no means remedies these defects, and it even partially accounts for them. So a near-to-perfect form stands in tension with a rather tentative treatment of its topics.

If all these observations, to which the occurrence of Latinisms should be added, are correct, Hebrews may be one of the only literary texts by a Jew – albeit a Christian Jew – from ancient Rome.[8] There is no proof that Roman Jews, who were organized in numerous synagogues, possessed any of Philo's writings, but we may safely assume that Philo was heard in Roman synagogues during his stay in approximately 38–40 CE. There is no direct influence of his writings in Hebrews.[9] However, the author of the Epistle may have learned of Philo's teachings orally, even from hearing him directly.[10]

Formalities

In literary quality, Hebrews is equal to the best of Philonic treatises, using even prose rhythms. This style is also present in James, which shows the elitist literary taste of much of ancient Jewish Christianity (before it became Ebionite).

SPECIALIZED LANGUAGE The Platonic division of the world into an 'intelligible' and a 'perceptible' one, fundamental in Philo (e.g., *Somn.* 1.187f), is reflected in terms like *hypodeigmata* and *antitypa* ('exemplars'; Heb 9:23–4). There is also a 'lower' and a 'higher' level of religious

7 In a forthcoming monograph, to be published in Münsteraner Judaistische Studien, T. Witulski claims that Hebrews is as sophisticated in its general culture as it is rudimentary in its Christian doctrine.
8 It is possible that the author of the treatise *On the Sublime*, probably written in Rome, was Jewish.
9 This has been proved by R. Williamson, *Philo and the Epistle to the Hebrews* (Leiden 1970), who wrote to refute the views of C. Spicq. Cf. K. L. Schenck, 'Philo and the Epistle to the Hebrews: Ronald Williamson's Study after Thirty Years', *StPhAnn* 14 (2002), pp. 112–35. Yet Spicq was right in supposing an ancient, non-Pauline stratum of Christian teaching to be behind Hebrews and the Johannine literature.
10 On Philo and Hebrews in general, see Siegfried, *Philo*, pp. 321–30; J. Daniélou, *Philon d'Alexandrie* (Paris 1958), pp. 210–14; Runia, *Philo in Early Christian Literature*, pp. 74–8.

knowledge, with grades and transitions, which gives room for an ample use of the *teleios* word family (meaning also 'initiate') in both writers. These offer a semantic transition toward *teletē* ('mystery cult'), but neither Judaism (in Philo) nor Christianity (in Hebrews) presents itself as such. Both authors aim at large audiences, and their esoteric language is metaphorical.[11]

METAPHORS In *Opif.* 146, man is called an *apaugasma* ('effulgence') of God's glory by virtue of his share in the Logos; so is Christ in Heb 1:3. This Logos language, however, could already have been learned from Wisdom 7:25f. The synonymous metaphor of an 'imprint' (*charaktēr tēs hypostaseōs autou*; Heb 1:3) seems to be an echo of *Det.* 83 (*charaktēr theias dynameōs*; cf. *Plant.* 18; *Fug.* 12). The Logos is the creator's 'heir' in Heb 1:4 as in *Mos.* 1.145. God's word is called 'heavenly nourishment', especially fitting for those who have passed the age of drinking only milk: *Fug.* 137–40; cf. Heb 5:12, 14 (and 1 Cor 3:2).

Scripture and the Methods of Its Interpretation

Philo's manner of citing each and any Mosaic verse as an oracle is echoed in Hebrews from the opening onward.[12] The books of Moses bear the burden of proof alongside Psalms cited to retell Mosaic history, and there is much emphasis on priesthood and cult. In 12:29, the end of the treatise proper, the author makes use of Deut 4:24 (on God as 'fire'), as Philo does in *De Deo* 7. As a Christian, however, he relies more on the Prophets and the Psalms. Philo does at least recommend them for such a use, however. See, for the Prophets, *De Deo* 6 (on Isaiah); *Cher.* 48f. (on Jeremiah); and for David and Israel's poets as 'sons of God', *Conf.* 149. Likewise it is clear that for the author of Hebrews the words the Psalmist uses are those of the Holy Spirit (Heb 3:7), as are the words of Jeremiah (Heb 10:15). If Philo can treat Jacob's words in Gen 37:10 as an utterance of the *orthos logos* (*Somn.* 1.20), the author of Hebrews can cite Psalms as words uttered by God Himself (Heb 1:5–13), partly addressed to His first-born Son, and partly also as words of the Son (Heb 2:11, 13, 10:5–8). There is no confirmation of scriptural truth outside

11 On this issue, see N.G. Cohen, 'The Mystery Terminology in Philo', in R. Deines and K.-W. Niebuhr (eds.), *Philo und das Neue Testament: Wechselseitige Wahrnehmungen* (Tübingen 2004), pp. 173–87. Cf. below, n. 30.

12 See Runia, *Philo in Early Christian Literature*, pp. 75–8, who compares Heb 3:1–6 and 8:5ff with *Leg.* 3.102–3, where the same scriptural proofs are used.

Scripture itself. God 'swears by himself': *Leg.* 3.203; *Sacr.* 91; cf. Heb 6:13f. (and John 8:13f.).

So much for technicalities. As to content, Philo's Platonism in Hebrews is balanced by an appreciation of history much like that in Paul and in other early Christian literature. It would appear that only the Alexandrian crisis at the time of the governor Flaccus made Philo think of the concrete dangers and changes in world history, especially regarding his people (see above, ch. 1, pp. 19–31); the Christian view of biblical tradition and of its potential to be applied to the present and to the near future, on the other hand, was much more direct. Again, we find typology and not only allegory. As G. Sterling has put it, 'the author [of Hebrews] combined Platonic ontology with a Christian understanding of salvation history.'[13]

Secrets of the Divine Name

For Christ's 'more excellent' name in Heb 1:4, cf. Phil 2:9–11. The creator and his Logos have a common 'name' by which to be invoked (Heb 13:15).

Wisdom and Eternal Torah

In Heb 1:5–14, we hear a kind of heavenly dialogue that echoes the best of Jewish wisdom traditions. In its form, however, it rather contrasts with Philo, who does not cultivate heavenly dialogues (cf. *Conf.* 168–70 on certain biblical plurals). Furthermore, the Hebrews passage is not based on Pentateuchal quotations but on the Psalms and the Prophets.

Angels

According to the angelology of Hebrews, explicit and very Jewish as it is, Christ – in contrast to Philo's Logos – is not an angel, not even the eldest of them (as in *Conf.* 145f): Heb 1:4f.

The Heavenly Realm

In passages like Heb 8:5, 9:11ff, 11:16, 12:22, there is much *hekhalot* speculation adapted for Christian purposes.[14] Heaven in its entirety is God's temple, whereas in Philo God's temple is the cosmos (*Spec.* 1.66, a Stoic thesis), or even the cosmos and the soul (*Somn.* 1.215). There is much

13 'Ontology versus Eschatology: Tensions between Author and Community in Hebrews', *StPhAnn* 13 (2001), p. 210.
14 See L. K. K. Dey, *The Intermediary World and Patterns of Perfection in Philo and Hebrews* (Missoula 1975).

scholarly debate on passages like Heb 8:1–5, and whether its thought relies on a Platonic 'above–below' scheme or on a biblical 'once–then' scheme.[15] It is characteristic of the Epistle to link both schemes and to make one change into the other, as indicated above in the paragraph on scriptural interpretation. There is a future both 'before' and 'above' the believers.

The Divine Logos

Hebrews begins with a reflection on God's speaking (chs. 1 and 2), which shows a somewhat Philonic feature in attributing to the Logos also the function of 'bearing' (*pherein*) or 'supporting' the universe (Heb 1:3, cf. *Her.* 36). In other respects, Logos theology is less developed than in Philo.

The Logos is again personified from Heb 4:12 onward. In this same verse an adaptation of Philo's doctrine of a 'Logos-cutter' (*logos tomeus*, e.g., *Her.* 130–40) may be seen,[16] put even in the comparative (*tomōteros*). In Hebrews, however, the notion is applied to judgment rather than to creation.

The primitive state of the author's reflection on Christ may be seen in a Philonic Logos epithet he adapts, *prōtotokos* ('first born'; Heb 1:6). This term echoes the synonymous *prōtogonos* in *Agr.* 51; *Conf.* 63, 146; *Somn.* 1.215. In Philo, however, the epithet is systematically justified by the qualification of the cosmos as God's 'younger' or 'second' Son (*Deus* 31, etc.). Paul changes this idea in calling Christ the 'first born among many brethren' (Rom 8:29). Both Heb 4:14 and Philo (*Somn.* 1.219, etc.) give the Logos the dignity of being a 'great high priest' in a cosmic sense. The parallelism of heavenly and earthly cult in Heb 8:1–5, even though it is a commonplace of ancient religions, has similarities with *Leg.* 3.102f; *Mos.* 2.74; *QE* 2.82.[17]

Sacred History: From the Patriarchs to Moses

As D. T. Runia has said of the author of Hebrews, 'history, which is to be equated with the history of salvation, is important to him in a way that is not the case for Philo.'[18] Hebrews 11 enumerates all personal

---

15 See esp. G. E. Sterling, '"Philo Has Not Been Used Half Enough": The Significance of Philo of Alexandria for the Study of the New Testament', *PRSt* 30 (2003), p. 265.

16 This is a Stoic concept also taken over by Plutarch, *Quaest. conv.* 6.6, 695b.

17 See G. E. Sterling, 'The Place of Philo of Alexandria in the Study of Christian Origins', in Deines and Niebuhr, *Philo und das Neue Testament*, p. 44 (with further literature).

18 *Philo in Early Christian Literature*, p. 77.

models available from the Hebrew Bible, from the 'just' Abel onward (for him cf. *Det.* 45–8). They must have been known to the audience not only from hearing the books of Moses read in the synagogues, but also from encomia like Philo's *De Abrahamo, De Josepho,* and *De vita Mosis.* Reflections on Abraham's faith in IIcb 5:13–15 and 11:8 are not meant as an alternative to what Paul had said to the Romans in Rom 4 (or 'James' in 2:20–4); they just follow a more traditional viewpoint, much like *Migr.* 43–6 (on Gen 12:1).

Revealed Torah

Very Philonic is the idea of the Decalogue sounded directly from heaven; Hebrews 12:19 quotes Exod 19:16, 19 in a way much reminiscent of Philo (e.g., *Decal.* 33). Hebrews 12:25 also uses oracular language with reference to the Mosaic revelation.

Cult, Prayer, Rites, and Holy Places

Hebrews makes just as much of the Jerusalem cult as does Philo. The kind of 'Platonism' implied already in the Hebrew Bible at Exod 25:9 and 31:1–11, where Moses and Bezalel, respectively, are instructed by God about the 'pattern' of the tabernacle, is expanded in Heb 8:1–5 as in *Somn.* 1.206; *Plant.* 27; *Leg.* 3.96. Both authors' meditations have further details in common, such as the high priest's faculty of empathy (Heb 4:15, 5:2; cf. *Leg.* 3.132). The high priest as interpreted allegorically by Philo is 'not a man but the divine Logos' (*Fug.* 108; cf. *Spec.* 1.116), and is an ambassador on behalf of mankind, as is Christ in Heb 7:25 (and Rom 8:34); cf. *Migr.* 12. The requirement that the high priest be free of sins (Heb 4:15, 7:26) is already present in *Fug.* 109 and *Spec.* 1.230.

Philo's Moses, though he is not an Aaronite, may be called a high priest because he did intercede for his people in crucial moments (Exod 32:9–14; Num 14:10–25). This makes him 'a perfect intercessor towards God' (*Det.* 160; cf. *Somn.* 1.143, etc.), as was Abraham (*Det.* 159). The fact that his intercession takes place outside the camp is noted by Philo (*Det.* 160), as in Heb 13:13 concerning Christ.

Eschatology

In concluding this section, we may state that the author of Hebrews thinks as much in the terms of Philo's spatial scheme and hierarchic world view as he does in the terms of Jewish apocalyptic and early Christian expectations of a near end of the world. This becomes clear

from Heb 1:2 onward. W. Eisele opines that a particularly Middle
Platonic variant of the Christian expectation of a return of the heavenly
Christ may be found in Hebrews, which he links to indirect Philonic
influence.[19] Generally speaking, in Hebrews all spatial conceptions,
especially of salvation (= preservation in Philo) may take on a more
temporal connotation, indicating some transformation of Philonic
notions. Whereas the Sabbath, for Philo, is the birthday of the cosmos
(*Opif.* 89), the 'sabbath rest' that 'still remains' according to Heb 4:9 is
something yet to come. God's people is in motion, and it enters into its
'rest', so it seems, member by member.

II. THE PAULINE CORPUS

Paul of Tarsus, educated 'at the feet of Gamaliel' (Acts 22:3) and 'called
to be an apostle of Jesus Christ' (Rom 1:1, etc.), was surely not a reader
of Philo, but one of those early Christian missionaries who chose to
write in Greek and only in Greek. His general background in the world
of Greek-speaking Judaism, acquired in a number of different locations,
is the most likely explanation for the numerous similarities between
him and Philo.[20]

Formalities

LITERARY GENRES Although Philo wrote tractates and Paul only letters, both use 'homiletical patterns' of oral synagogue teaching, as
P. Borgen has shown.[21] These patterns consist of re-told biblical history
with allegorizing elements that permit one to see it in close parallel
with the present.

SPECIALIZED LANGUAGE Paul makes a conscious and correct use of the
terminology and method of allegorism in Gal 4:21ff. He is the first to
have special expressions for 'typological' interpretation. He employs
the phrases *typikōs synebainen* (1 Cor 10:11: something 'happened

---

19 *Ein unerschütterliches Reich: Die mittelplatonische Umformung des
    Parusiegedankens im Hebäerbrief* (Berlin/New York 2003). Note esp. the
    long chapter on Philo (pp. 160–240).
20 On Philo and Paul in general, see Siegfried, *Philo*, pp. 304–10; Daniélou,
    Philon, pp. 199–203; Runia, *Philo in Early Christian Literature*, pp. 66–74.
21 *Bread From Heaven: An Exegetical Study of the Concept of Manna in the
    Gospel of John and the Writings of Philo* (Leiden 1965), cf. Runia, *Philo in
    Early Christian Literature*, pp. 81–2.

typically');[22] *typoi hēmōn* (1 Cor 10:6: 'types for us'); *typos tou mel-lontos* (Rom 5:14: Adam is a 'type of the one who was to come'). This proves a high awareness on Paul's part of what learned interpreters were doing.

As to theological vocabulary, there are a number of similarities between Philo and Paul. They both qualify God as 'the only wise' (Rom 16:27; cf. 1Tim 1:17; Jude 15; for Philo, cf. *Migr.* 134). The language of 'salvation' and 'perdition', less dramatic as it may be in Philo, yields parallels between Rom 2:7–10 and *Somn.* 1.86. The distinction of a first and a second Adam in 1 Cor 15:45–9 has its parallel in *Opif.* 134; *Leg.* 1.31–8. Paul, however, places the second Adam in the future, whereas Philo uses this expression for mankind as it is in the present.

A typically Greek feature consists in playing with prepositions. Passages like Rom 11:36 ('from him, through him and towards him') can easily be paralleled in Philo (e.g., *Cher.* 125f; *Migr.* 6), who cultivates a formal metaphysics of prepositions.[23]

METAPHORS In a slight variation of biblical language, pious individuals can be called 'heirs' of God: Rom 8:17 (Eph 1:3); cf. *Her.* 68. The simile of the mirror is used in 1 Cor 13:12 as in *Cher.* 115; *Decal.* 105; *Leg.* 3.101. Philo assigns to the soul the aim of being a 'house' or even a 'sanctuary' of God (*Somn.* 1.148–9; *Sobr.* 66, citing Exod 19:6). Paul employs similar language in 1 Cor 3:16f. Circumcision should be interior, as a law-obedient disposition of mind: compare the 'circumcision of the heart' (Rom 2:29) with *Spec.* 1.6–12 and much of *QG* 3.46–52; *QE* 2.2.[24] Philo generalized the Diaspora condition of Jewish life by saying that the Mosaic sage always is a *paroikos* (resident alien) in the world (*QE* 2.2; *Agr.* 64f; cf. Heb 11:13; 1 Pet 1:1, 2:11). He longs for his *patris* (native city) which is heaven: compare *Conf.* 76–8 and Phil 3:20 (cf. Heb 13:14).

22   This is the first time this adverb occurs in Greek literature (a variant has *typoi synebainon*), but it is preceded by the adverb *typōdesteron* in Philo, *Praem.* 67. As to similarities with Philo in content, see Runia, *Philo in Early Christian Literature* 85–6. But whereas Philo is concerned with general culture, Paul's words are about a new event in salvation history.

23   See J. Dillon, *The Middle Platonists* (London 1977), p. 138. This is a feature of contemporary Philosophical teaching. Cf. Sterling, 'The Place of Philo', pp. 49–50.

24   See J.M.G. Barclay, 'Paul and Philo on Circumcision: Romans 2.25–9 in Social and Cultural Context', *NTS* 44 (1998), pp. 536–56. Cf. above, ch. 4, pp. 115–17.

Scripture and the Methods of Its Interpretation

We now come to one of the closest affinities between Philo and the New Testament as a whole. In 1 Cor 9:9 Paul justifies his allegorizing of Deut 25:4 – an extreme case in which the original meaning is completely superseded – by a rule of relevance (or, of *theoprepeia*),[25] that may be found in Philo as well. See *Somn.* 1.102 and especially *Spec.* 1.260 for the rule that 'the law is not about *aloga* (beings without reason, beasts)'.[26] Allegorizing the grammatical number of a given word in Scripture has been noted in Gal 3:16 (the singular *sperma*) as in *Mut.* 145 (the singular *teknon*). First Corinthians 10:4 ('the rock was Christ') is best illustrated in *Det.* 118, where the 'rock' of the biblical text stands for the divine Logos.

Knowledge of God, Natural and Revealed

The thesis of a 'natural' knowledge of God, available to everybody, is cited by Paul in a rather narrow, censorious context in Rom 1:20, 23. It is much more important in Philo's teaching because it has to support the universality of the Torah (*Mos.* 2.171; *Praem.* 31–48). Neither writer boasts of a well-trained intelligence. Instead, they claim divine origin and a special revelation for their most important teachings. One should compare 2 Cor 3:5 with *Mut.* 143 and the very explicit *Migr.* 31–52. Philo hears an inner voice (*Somn.* 2.252), and just as Paul claims to have been called by God Himself through the risen Christ (Gal 1:15f, etc.),[27] Philo claims to have received his doctrine of the two powers through a personal revelation (*Spec.* 3.1–6; *Cher.* 27; cf. *Somn.* 2.252).[28] What had been the Wisdom of creation in older speculation (Prov 8:22ff, etc.) now, in Philo's teaching, comes to be called either Logos (masculine) or powers (plural and feminine).[29] There is much Platonizing convention about all this, and Philo himself says that this way of receiving insights

---

25 'What befits God', a notion underlying much of Homeric interpretation in Hellenistic times, and much of Philonic reasoning as well: *Opif.* 116; *Leg.* 3.26, 203.

26 For more examples, see Siegfried, *Philo* 165–8. Cf. F. Siegert, 'Early Jewish Interpretation in a Hellenistic Style', in M. Sæbø (ed.), *Hebrew Bible/Old Testament: The History of Its Interpretation*, I.1 (Göttingen 1996), p. 184.

27 See S.-K. Wan, 'Charismatic Exegesis: Philo and Paul Compared', *StPhAnn* 6 (1994), pp. 54–82.

28 See F. Siegert, ed., Philon von Alexandrien, *Über die Gottesbezeichnung 'wohltätig verzehrendes Feuer' (De Deo)* (Tübingen 1988), pp. 91–4

29 On the Logos and the powers, see above, ch. 4, pp. 97–101; ch. 5, pp. 135–44.

was 'habitual' for him. It is not linked to mysterious ceremonies and practices (as E.R. Goodenough's generation believed), but simply to an intense reading of the Greek Torah.[30]

The Divine Logos

Much of later Johannine Logos doctrine is already contained in what Paul says of the risen Christ. He is God's 'image' (2 Cor 4:4; cf. Col 1:15),[31] as is the Logos in *Conf.* 97, 147; *Somn.* 1.239. The idea that the Logos or rather Christ 'intercedes' for the believers – here Philo's more or less theoretical 'high priest' comes somewhat closer to experience – is expressed in Rom 8:34[32] (and 1 John 2:1); cf. *Leg.* 3.214; *Gig.* 52; *Migr.*102.

Creation and Duality

In spite of long discourses Philo might offer on this subject, there seems to be no reflection on the human condition as penetrating as is Rom 8. Yet in 1 Cor 4:7 ('What do you have that you did not receive?'), C. Noack finds a type of piety similar to that approved by Philo in his exegeses of Gen 15:9 ('Take for me') in *Her.* 102–11.[33] Just as the Philonic wise man owes all he is to divine grace, so does the believer in Paul.

Freedom of Choice; Evil and Sin

Humans are born 'together with' sin (Rom 5:12 cf. *Mos.* 2.147). Natural man is even a wretch in Rom 7:24; cf. *Leg.* 3.211. The idea of sin as coming from *epithymia* ('desire') in Rom 7:7ff (cf. 1:24ff) may be common to the Judaism of the day, as based on Exod 20:17. James 1:14 (cf. 4:1–3) stresses that it is man's 'own' desire that makes him sin. Philo teaches the same in *Her.* 270; *Decal.* 79–94; *Spec.* 4.79–135. Sin has its root in what is called 'flesh' in a wider or a narrower sense. Note

30 Cf. C. Riedweg, *Mysterienterminologie bei Platon, Philon und Klemens von Alexandrien* (Berlin 1987).
31 It may well be that both references (not only the second) are deutero-pauline and therefore should be given in section IV below. There is no scholarly consensus as to how far 2 Corinthians is made up of genuine Pauline texts. It contains spurious intrusions in more than one place.
32 A few verses before, in 8:26, we find a similar statement about the Spirit, which seems to refer to prayer on earth.
33 'Haben oder Empfangen: Antithetische Charakterisierungen von Torheit und Weisheit bei Philo und bei Paulus', in Deines and Niebuhr, *Philo und das Neue Testament*, pp. 283–307.

Rom 7:5 for the one (human weakness) and *Gig.* 29 with its context for the other (sexuality). Regarding the latter, much of Christian practice and life conduct has tended toward the Philonic rather than the biblical notion, and there were many Christian 'eunuchs' according to Matt 19:12.

Sinful life is described in Rom 1:26–32 much as it is in *Abr.* 135f. Note also *Spec.* 3.37–64, which has a strong emphasis against non-productive sexuality. As in Paul, appeal is made to natural law (*Spec.* 3.46), not to Mosaic ritual.

In both Philo and Paul, however, there is no imputation of guilt prior to the availability of proper information. This comes from the law in Paul (Rom 5:13) and from the Logos (to be gathered, to be sure, from the law) in Philo (*Deus* 134).

Man

Paul's thought relies on an explicit anthropology (Rom 5:12–7:25) which, however, is based less on the creation account of Gen 1–2 than on eschatological and 'soteriological' considerations. It is conceived *ad hoc*, as part of a salvation doctrine, and does not allow for anything divine in man, much as the above-mentioned postulate of a natural knowledge of God does not prevent man from being helpless. Accordingly, the often observed similarities between Philo and Paul with regard to what seems to be a common anthropological terminology have turned out to be parallels of language rather than of thought.[34] Even in cases where the same scriptural texts serve as a basis, the Philonic 'above–below' scheme normally becomes a 'now–then' scheme in Paul, the second half of which takes on greater significance.

As regards human perfection, which is a central concern in most or all of Philo's writing, a shift of emphasis is visible. For Paul, perfection lies not behind but before him. There is a shared link in that Philo hopes that the wise man becomes equal to the 'Son of God', the 'first-born Logos' (*Conf.* 146), and Paul believes Christians to be destined to become 'of equal shape with the image of his Son' (Rom 8:29; cf. Phil 3:21). In Paul, however, this has much more of an eschatological ring.

Another semi-parallel of a similar kind regards the notion of grace. Both authors have much to say on man's entire dependence on God. Nevertheless, 'Philo's views on grace are tied in with his views on

34   See, in much detail, Runia, *Philo in Early Christian Literature*, pp. 68–73, who repeats S. Sandmel's warning against 'parallelomania' in this context.

creation and man's place therein. For Paul grace is focused on the cross of Christ, within an apocalyptic–eschatological framework.'[35]

Another similarity that links Philo with Paul and both with the Stoicism of their day consists in reflections on human conscience, a term for which had only recently been coined.[36]

Man and Woman

There is an oft noted 'modern' feature in 1 Cor 7:3f where Paul declares marriage to be a partnership based on equality. This cannot be found in Philo except, perhaps, in his praise for Sarah who, as regards virtue, is as much of a man as is Abraham (*Mut.* 74–80). But the independence displayed by Christian women, especially Prisca (Rom 16:3f, etc.), was inconceivable to Philo. One prerequisite of such liberty was sexual abstinence, which freed a woman from a mother's duties. There was no room for such an idea in Judaism.

Much overlap may be found, however, in both Philo's and the New Testament authors' recommendation of chastity in general. As to language, no positive use is made of the word *erōs* in the Septuagint nor in the New Testament, whereas Philo's Platonic language is much about philosophical *erōs* or 'longing' for virtue and higher ideas.

Sacred History: From the Patriarchs to Moses

Abraham's life as narrated in Gen 12–25 is a text to be read as diligently as any Torah expressed in commandments. Philo makes him a Torah *avant la lettre* (see above, ch. 4, pp. 112–13). Paul, in turn, makes him a type of the gospel to come (Rom 4, citing Gen 15:6;[37] cf. also John 8:56–8). On the other hand, Jas 2:20–4 wants to return to the use of Abraham as an ethical model.[38]

---

35 Runia, *Philo in Early Christian Literature*, p. 73, summarizing D. Zeller, *Charis bei Philon und Paulus* (Stuttgart 1990). A lengthy treatment of the same subject, with special reference to Eph 2:5, 8, is A. E. Arterbury, 'Abraham's Hospitality among Jewish and Early Christian Writers', *PRSt* 30 (2003), pp. 359–76.

36 For this topic, see P. Bosman, *Conscience in Philo and Paul: A Conceptual History of the Synoida Word Group* (Tübingen 2003).

37 Another text to be cited is Rom 9–11. See K. Haacker, 'Die Geschichtstheologie von Röm 9–11 im Lichte philonischer Schriftauslegung', *NTS* 43 (1997), pp. 209–22.

38 For the patriarchs and other biblical heroes as ethical models, see above, ch. 3, pp. 87–9.

The Exodus: Passover; Revealed Torah

In 1 Cor 10, we find a remarkable midrash on the exodus with some very 'Philonic' liberties. The tradition on the new covenant in 1 Cor 11:23–6 transforms the biblical Passover account. As to revealed Torah, Rom 7:7–13 states its perfection which, however, comes to be limited by the surely non-Philonic midrashic feature in Gal 3:19 (cf. Acts 7:53), namely, that the Torah was proclaimed not by God's own voice, as it is in Philo, but mediated by angels.

The Commandments; Concrete Ethics

There is a Jewish tradition in most of the New Testament from Rom 13:9 onward that cites the Decalogue as a code of universal ethics (cf. Mark 10:19 and parallels; not in John). Properly speaking, it is the second table that is commonly cited. Monotheism and monolatry were taken for granted, and there never was a general obligation for Christians to be circumcised or to observe the Sabbath. Jewish teaching about the Decalogue, however, as it is attested in *De decalogo* and in much of *De specialibus legibus*, made its way into the Christian Church – one reason for the Rabbis to abandon it.

The idea that life is a struggle, expressed in metaphors taken from sports, is common to 1 Cor 9:24–7; *Cher.* 81f; *Praem.* 27.

Cult, Prayer, Rites, and Holy Places

An often expressed principle of 'common Judaism' in the Second Temple period is not to venerate things created (or, even worse, fashioned by man) instead of the creator: Rom 1:23, 25; *Ebr.* 107–10; *Mos.* 2.171; *Virt.* 180.[39] Expressed as a dictate of reason, this claim links up with the thesis of a natural knowledge of God.

Eschatology

In most Christian writings there is ample reception of Judean hopes for a better time and an easy life in a land not dominated by aliens, to which was added one further culminating feature, Christ's return to the world at the end of time (the *parousia*).

There is nothing of this kind in Philo. We shall speak of his highly original ideas, as to the earthly hopes of Israel, in section V below. Suffice it to say that his very Platonic view of the soul gaining immortality by

---

39   Cf. Wis 13:2f; *Let. Aris.* 139; Ps.-Philo, *De Jona* 217.

means of virtue (to which the *nomos* [law] may bring one) finds no great approval among Christian writers.

One more feature needs mention. Paul insists much on the condemnation of sinners and even would-be sinners like Jesus in the Torah (*epikataratos* Gal 3:10, 13, from Deut 27:26 LXX; cf. John 7:49). This comes from a pericope that Philo knows under the name *arai* ('curses'; *Her.* 250) but never explains. Paul's initial Pharisaism seems to have insisted on such texts and was much more pessimistic and fearful than was Philo's religion.[40]

III. THE SPECIAL CASE OF I CORINTHIANS (CORINTH)

In a scholarly interpretation of 1 Corinthians, upheld by G. Sellin and others, a considerable part of that letter has to do with Philonic ideas that were misinterpreted or freely interpreted by some Corinthian believers.[41] If one admits that Apollos, a Jewish Christian from Alexandria and an 'eloquent man' (Acts 18:24) had heard Philo, it becomes plausible that the negation of a bodily resurrection on the part of the believers as reported by Paul in 1 Cor 15:12ff (more correctly in v. 35ff) is the result of indirect Philonic influence. The Corinthian Christians may have drawn their own conclusions from Philo's Platonizing anthropology. According to this, Gen 1 is about an eternal, incorporeal human being (i.e., the 'Idea' of man) and only Gen 2:4ff is about an earthly, corporeal man (*Opif.* 134f; *Leg.* 1.31f, etc.). This could have been a gratuitous and harmless speculation had not Apollos, or rather his hearers, inferred from this that only the heavenly man was fit for eternity, and the corporeal one was destined to complete decay.

The Corinthian episode may receive some more light from Ephesus, Apollos' other and even more important place of activity. He seems to have cherished something like Philo's and later John's 'realized eschatology' (modern phrase), for which the Church of his day was not yet ready. It consists in representing eternity apart from time and from history; that is, the pious soul (so Philo would say) gets in touch with it in some rare and happy moments that foreshadow a condition of eternal

---

40 Cf. T. Seland, 'Saul of Tarsus and Early Zealotism: Reading Gal 1,13–14 in Light of Philo's Writings', *Biblica* 83 (2002), pp. 449–71.

41 For a summary of the issue and the key literature, see Sterling, 'The Place of Philo', pp. 41–3, and the articles by D. Hay, B. Schaller, D. Zeller and G. Sellin himself in Deines and Niebuhr, *Philo und das Neue Testament*, pp. 127–72. Cf. also B. Winter, *Philo and Paul among the Sophists: Alexandrian and Corinthian Responses to a Julio–Claudian Movement*[2] (Grand Rapids 2002).

happiness, to be enjoyed after the death of the body. We shall see that John further developed this idea, which in his edited Gospel became somewhat obscured by glosses.

In 2 Tim 2:18, we find the Corinthians' misguided Philonism expressed in the slogan 'the resurrection has already taken place.' This belief, attributed to a certain Hymenaeus and another, Philetus, and challenged by the Epistle's author, expresses the consciousness of an immortality already acquired (supposing a judgment already passed) much as it is in John 5:19–24.

IV. LUKE; THE PAULINE SCHOOL (INCLUDING 1 AND 2 PETER)

This is a summary section that has the intention of discussing Philonic influences especially on Luke and on 1 Peter, while also acknowledging the Pauline influence in these writings.[42]

Formalities

LITERARY GENRES The longer Pauline pseudepigrapha (Ephesians, Colossians) as well as other products of writers sympathetic to Paul (notably 1 Peter) are treatises rather than letters, and as such are closer to Philo's writings. Luke's work, however, constitutes an exception. In his Gospel, he sticks to the popular way of tale-telling that had already shaped the pericopes of Mark's Gospel. In his Acts of the Apostles, a type of apologetic narration is used that may be loosely compared with Philo's *In Flaccum* and *Legatio ad Gaium*.[43]

SPECIALIZED LANGUAGE Luke's sponsor bears the name 'Theophilus', which was to become a Christian name up to this day. In Philo, *Mos.* 1.255, this adjective, in the plural, characterizes Israel, and from *Virt.* 184 we learn that it means 'beloved by God', whereas *philotheos* has the active sense of 'one who loves God'. Philo's pious men have both

---

42 See esp. the two studies by T. Seland, *Establishment Violence in Philo and Luke: A Study of Non-Conformity to the Torah and Jewish Vigilante Reactions* (Leiden 1995); *Strangers in the Light: Philonic Perspectives on Christian Identity in 1 Peter* (Leiden 2005).

43 See P. W. van der Horst, 'Philo's *In Flaccum* and the Book of Acts', in Deines and Niebuhr, *Philo und das Neue Testament*, pp. 95–105; F. Avemarie, 'Juden vor den Richterstühlen Roms: *In Flaccum* und die Apostelgeschichte im Vergleich', ibid., pp. 107 26.

qualities, whereas Christian usage stresses the former.[44] Luke's use of *metanoia* ('repentance') which implies a turn to monotheism combined with ethical improvement yields some close parallels with Philo, especially *Virt.* 175–86.[45]

METAPHORS Although terms relating to 'begetting' and 'fatherhood' were much favored as theological metaphors in all of antiquity (each Roman emperor was considered to be the 'son' of Jupiter or of Apollo, etc.), there are at least two Jewish equivalents to a virgin birth (Luke 2:34f; cf. Matt 1:18–20) in Philo. Tamar, he says, became pregnant without a man (*Deus* 137), a circumstance which yields some symbolism about 'virginal' virtue whose origin is God alone, but does not seem to involve a historical person of any significance. In *Det.* 123–7, however, Sarah's laughter which gave Isaac his name (Gen 21:6) is interpreted to refer to a pregnancy to which old-aged Abraham had not contributed.[46]

Scripture and the Methods of Its Interpretation

In the New Testament, the strongest and most 'Philonic' expressions of the belief that Scripture is inspired word for word are found in 2 Tim 3:16 and 2 Pet 1:21 (cf. *Her.* 249–66; *Mos.* 2:187–91; *Praem.* 55). Divine words 'resound' in a human mind. In Philo, the Ten Commandments resound directly and without any human help.[47]

Knowledge of God, Natural and Revealed

In Acts, Paul's preaching reflects more of a balanced reliance on both natural and revealed knowledge of God than in the Pauline corpus itself. In Acts 17:22–30, Luke exploits a Stoic commonplace in appealing to natural revelation, and cites Aratus. For a Jewish audience he might have cited Philo.

---

44 The basis, of course, is a Christian theology of grace unmerited, whereas Philo teaches a clear synergism.
45 See Sterling, 'The Place of Philo', pp. 45–7.
46 For a discussion of this and other passages, see Cohen, 'Mystery Terminology'.
47 *Decal.* 33. See F. Siegert, 'Die Inspiration der Heiligen Schriften: Ein philonisches Votum zu 2 Tim 3,16', in Deines and Niebuhr, *Philo und das Neue Testament*, pp. 205–22, esp. for the idea that Moses did not know what he wrote, and that the Decalogue was proclaimed by a physical voice of God without human assistance.

Wisdom and Eternal Torah

According to 1 Tim 6:16, God 'dwells in an inaccessible light'. For this notion, compare Philo, *Opif.* 71; *Spec.* 1.20; *De Deo* 1f. This is a common idea, but if E. R. Goodenough was right, Philo did much to elaborate 'light' mysticism.[48] See below, section V, on the metaphor of 'light'.

The Divine Logos

Runia has shown how much the hymn in Col 1:15–18 uses Philonic language in celebrating Christ as an 'image' (*eikōn*) of God, taking up at the same time a rare use of Platonic language found in Paul (2 Cor 4:4).[49]

Creation and Duality

Regarding the two powers of Philo's speculation, it may noted by way of contrast that the power(s) 'of the air' in Eph 2:2 or 6:12, which indicates something diabolical, foreshadows that kind of dualism and rejection of creation that was to be the basis of Gnosticism.

Evil and Sin; Grace and Salvation

The struggle between *epithymiai* (desires) and the soul in 1 Pet 2:11 is described in very Philonic language.[50] Salvation from sin is a pure gift of God's grace: this Pauline truth is upheld, for example, in Eph 2:5, 8, much more than it would have been by Philo.[51]

Sacred History

There is much theology of (Israel's) history in Luke–Acts, more than is usual in Philo. But a speech like Stephen's in Acts 7, Jewish as it is in most respects, does not resemble what Philo might narrate except for details such as a stress on Moses' education at Acts 7:22.[52]

48 *By Light, Light: The Mystic Gospel of Hellenistic Judaism* (New Haven 1935).
49 *Philo in Early Christian Literature*, pp. 84–5, with further literature.
50 See T. Seland, 'The Moderate Life of the Christian *paroikoi*: A Philonic Reading of 1 Pet 2:11', in Deines and Niebuhr, *Philo*, pp. 241–63, esp. 259, where he points to *Conf.* 21; *Her.* 132; *Leg.* 1.63–73; *QG* 1.13.
51 See J. Whitlark, 'Enabling Charis: Transformation of the Convention of Reciprocity by Philo and in Ephesians', *PRSt* 30 (2003), pp. 325–57; cf. Arterbury, 'Abraham's Hospitality'.
52 Cf. Runia, *Philo in Early Christian Literature*, p. 66. This theme was common in Judeo–Hellenistic literature from Eupolemus (fr. 1) onward.

The Commandments; Concrete Ethics

Philo, just as Josephus and others, believed that the Torah, in spite of its awkwardness especially in ritual matters, was universally valid and infinitely better than any conventional and 'hand-made' set of rules (*Mut.* 26). To keep up with this claim, the Church gave herself statutes and rules, partly imitating the Torah and claiming to rely on the Ten Commandments. On the other hand, domestic codes (*Haustafeln*), such as Eph 5:21–6:9, repeat generalities taken from Greco–Roman convention. From a systematic perspective, there was as much difficulty for Christianity to establish concrete rules of conduct as there was for Judaism to prove the universality of the Torah.

A particular strand of Christian ethics concerns suffering. First Peter 2:19–23 gives a theodicy of suffering that not only echoes Jesus' suffering on the cross (which, theologically speaking, would not need to be repeated), but also Philonic considerations on Abraham (*Abr.* 64).[53] Behind all this is the commonplace of learning by suffering (*pathein – mathein*; cf. Heb 5:8).

Cult, Prayer, Rites, and Holy Places

Whereas Philo avoids pointing to an opposition between the heavenly and the earthly sanctuaries, we find strong criticisms of the temple cult by means of such an opposition in Acts 7:48ff (Stephen's speech) and in Heb 3.[54] Luke sometimes mitigates such criticism, for example, when he avoids attributing the saying against the Jerusalem temple to Jesus (Acts 6:13–14), as the other evangelists do.

Philo was once in Jerusalem 'in order to pray and to sacrifice' (*Prov.* 2.107; note the order of the words). Like him, all New Testament authors pay respect to the temple in Jerusalem, be it still in existence or not. Its importance, however, is reduced to what the prophets already called 'a place of prayer' (Mark 11:17, etc.), and so it remains in Acts 3:1. Ephesians 2:11–22 gives a retrospective on two modes of revelation that should be reconciled (2:17).

---

53 See K.-H. Ostmeyer, 'Das Verständnis des Leidens bei Philo und im ersten Petrusbrief', in Deines and Niebuhr, *Philo und das Neue Testament*, pp. 265–81.

54 The possible Philonic basis of such a criticism is shown by C. Werman, 'God's House: Temple or Universe', in Deines and Niebuhr, *Philo und das Neue Testament*, pp. 309–20.

As to priesthood, the Philonic idea of a common priesthood of the whole people of God (from Exod 19) is revived in 1 Pet 2:5, 9.[55]

V. THE GOSPEL ACCORDING TO JOHN (EPHESUS)

Our last section will be on the writings of the Johannine circle. All of these are traditionally placed at Ephesus, and there is no reason to doubt the information given by Irenaeus and Eusebius. There has been much confusion about the person of the evangelist, who, as we may infer from his very name, must have come from Palestine, something we may easily believe, given his detailed knowledge of the places of Jesus' life.[56] We are also told that he was still alive in Trajan's time (98–117 CE).

There is much secondary editing visible in the Gospel according to John. What can be attributed to the evangelist, a Jewish Christian, is the main layer of the Gospel, that is, its prologue and the chain of narration (interrupted but restorable) that goes up to the end of ch. 20, including parts of ch. 21 and even 8:1–11, which had been left out in the process of (probably posthumous) editing, but should be placed at an earlier point.[57] In 2 John 12, 'the Elder' (this teacher's honorific title), tells us that he much preferred teaching orally.

Looking for Philo's influence on Ephesian Judaism as it is indirectly attested by Ephesian Christianity and especially by John 'the Elder' and evangelist, we are in the comfortable position of knowing by name a learned person who, having become a Christian, was one of two dominating figures in nascent Ephesian Christianity. This was Apollos, who came even before Paul. His influence was greater in this town than in Corinth, as we shall see presently.

John's Gospel, as it took shape two generations later, betrays no knowledge of Philo's actual writings or of Paul's letters, which came to be edited only by that time. The Synoptic Gospels, on the other hand, are all known to the evangelist, even though he never cites them directly.[58]

---

55 See T. Seland, 'The "Common Priesthood" of Philo and 1 Peter: A Philonic Reading of 1 Peter 2.5, 9', *JSNT* 57 (1995), pp. 87–119.

56 The name 'John' is never found in the Jewish Diaspora until Christians came to use it.

57 On the details, see F. Siegert, *Das Evangelium des Johannes: Wiederherstellung und Kommentar* (Göttingen 2008). As to the Johannine Epistles, 1 John, a product of the 'school', is of little interest.

58 Two exceptions, probably due to the editors, confirm the rule: John 5:8 has been taken from Mark 2:9 and John 13:27 from Luke 22:3. This is the manner of the redactors, whereas the evangelist himself never takes over his colleagues' language in a literal manner.

However, John's religious philosophy owes much to the reflections of Philo and his peers.[59]

Formalities

LITERARY GENRES In John's Gospel a Platonic genre is cultivated, dialogue. There are no less than forty dialogues of varying length in the Fourth Gospel, from the calling of the first disciples (1:35–50) onward.[60] Thus the traditional gospel narration receives a more philosophical character, and Jesus becomes a new Socrates.[61] John's Platonism comes from the *Apology of Socrates* and the *Phaedo* as much as Philo's Platonism comes from the mainly monological *Timaeus*.

SPECIALIZED LANGUAGE Here we may anticipate to some extent the paragraph on the Logos. The awkward language in which the Logos is made an 'exegete' of God (John 1:18) is best explained by *Mut.* 15–18 and *Deus* 138, where the Logos is God's 'interpreter and prophet'. What has been called a 'metaphysics of prepositions' in Philo (see section II above) can also be seen in John 1:1–3, where the Logos is 'with' God and is the one 'through' whom everything came to be (cf. *Spec.* 1.81; *Sacr.* 8 [a very close parallel also as to content]). In the same semantic field a difference may be indicated: whereas in Philo 'to beget' and 'to make' are used synonymously and the cosmos also is a 'son' of the creator (*Deus* 31, etc.), Christian language from John 1 onward clearly distinguishes the Father's 'begetting' the Son from his 'creating' the world through the Son.

A 'sending' (*apostellein*) of the Logos as in John 3:17 is also conceivable for Philo (*De Deo* 12; cf. *Her.* 201). The septuagintal term *doxa* ('glory') takes on the specialized meaning of the 'clearness' of revelation in John, with which one may compare Philo, *Spec.* 1.45. In Philo, humans (i.e., human souls or even only minds) may become 'sons of God' (*Conf.* 146), as in John 1:12f. In *Det.* 124, God Himself is considered to be Isaac's father (cf. *Cher.* 44).

59 For earlier treatments, see Siegfried, *Philo*, pp. 317–21; Daniélou, *Philon*, pp. 204–9; Runia, *Philo in Early Christian Literature*, pp. 78–83; Sterling, 'The Place of Philo', pp. 47–51.
60 Only some clumsy additions (e.g., 3:19ff; 6:52–7; 8:37ff, etc.) have obliterated this Socratic feature, thereby creating quasi-Gnostic 'revelation discourses'.
61 This was to become a fruitful comparison from Justin Martyr onwards, whereas Philo rarely names Socrates.

The imperfect tense is used in John 1:1–10 to describe what is timeless truth. Thus it is in *Opif.* 26–35 (day one).[62]

METAPHORS 'God is light', Philo says (*Somn.* 1.75, cf. Ps 27:1), and there was much mysticism around this metaphor in late antiquity, as Goodenough and others have shown.[63] John shares it (1:4ff; 8:12, etc.).

As to the counterpart, darkness, its meaning in the Fourth Gospel depends on whether one takes the Qumran writings or the Philonic corpus as comparative material. Taken on its own, the Johannine prologue (1:1–18) reflects no dualism of conflict or war. Rather, 'darkness' means ignorance of God, as it may in Philo, *Agr.* 162; *Somn.* 1.114; *Jos.* 106. In this respect, the prologue's author, whom we believe to be the primary author of this Gospel, is much more a disciple of Philo than a fellow combatant of the Qumran sectarians.

The Torah, or rather Jesus' teaching or even Jesus himself, is represented as a new manna. Borgen has shown that a traditional midrash scheme pervades much of Philo (e.g., *Fug.* 137–9; *Leg.* 3.169–73) as well as John 6.[64] Even Jesus himself 'feeds' on his Father's will (John 4:31–4), as does the pious soul in *Leg.* 3.152. Another metaphor used by both authors in a similar sense is that of the 'shepherd': John 10:11–16 is similar to Philo's use of Ps 23(22):1 in *Agr.* 50–1 and *Mut.* 115–16.[65] The phrase 'leading the way towards truth' is said of the Holy Spirit in John 16:13 as it is in *Mos.* 2.265 (with a Greek synonym).

Scripture and the Methods of Its Interpretation

In John, Scripture may be explained on the basis of the Hebrew text, as it is sometimes in Paul and in Matthew, which is a non-Philonic feature. His allegorizing of the manna episode (Exod 16 > John 6), however, brings him close to Philo, as we have already said, and so, too, does his allegorizing of the temple.[66] Other similarities have been observed in

62 Sterling, 'The Place of Philo', pp. 48–9, finds the same distinction in Plato, *Tim.* 28b; cf. 29e.

63 See esp. *By Light, Light.*

64 *Bread from Heaven* (cf. already Siegfried, *Philo*, p. 229). On John 6, see Borgen, *Early Christianity and Hellenistic Judaism* (Edinburgh 1996), pp. 177–8.

65 Cf. *Mos.* 1.60–2 on Moses, with R. M. Piccione, 'De Vita Mosis I 60–62: Philon und die griechische παιδεία', in Deines and Niebuhr, *Philo und das Neue Testament*, pp. 345–57.

66 See P. Borgen, 'The Gospel of John and Philo of Alexandria', in J. H. Charlesworth and M. A. Daise (eds.), *Light in a Spotless Mirror: Reflections on Wisdom Traditions in Judaism and Early Christianity*

both authors' use of Gen 1:1–3 and 2:2–3.[67] John's Jesus acts as God's messenger much as does Philo's Moses.[68] There is a common use of the descent motif, which in both authors makes biblical interpretation a kind of a mystical experience.[69]

Knowledge of God, Natural and Revealed

A balance of both forms of knowledge is implied in John 1:9–13, as the Logos is already at work prior to the incarnation. Revelation, of course, has the advantage of *doxa* or 'clarity' (1:14).

Secrets of the Divine Name

There are clear traces of the unpronounceable name in the Fourth Gospel. Jesus says 'I am' much as does the divine voice in Exod 3:14. Note John 4:26, 6:20, 18:5; and the sayings in which 'I am' is completed by metaphors (bread, light, shepherd, resurrection and life, way, truth and life). Jesus' revelation does not consist of a doctrine (this would be a misunderstanding of John's Gospel), but of his own person and the gift of 'life' (*zōē*) that he conveys to those willing to accept it. Everything depends on being in – or coming into – contact with the 'Father', that contact itself being beyond language, except for the use of metaphors. In all such contexts, 'Father' becomes a title of God, in a manner different from Philo.

In Philo, the expression 'the one who is' (*ho ōn*, in the masculine) from Exod 3:14 has its completely Platonic counterpart in the phrase 'that which is' (*to on*, in the neuter), and both expressions occur with equal frequency. The 'being' designated by the neuter lacks any relationship with believers. It is true that one of Plato's later disciples, Plutarch, came to address to his unique deity, Apollo, the prayer 'thou art' (the famous E = *ei* from the Delphic temple of Apollo).[70] But no one, neither the pagan Platonists nor Philo, ever dared to make the Logos speak in the first person by saying 'I am'.

(Harrisburg 2003), pp. 63–4, comparing John 2:13–18 to Philo, *Cher.* 98–107 and *Migr.* 91–3.

67   See Borgen, 'Gospel of John', pp. 48–51.
68   John 1:17 (with no 'but' between both halves of the statement); cf. Borgen, 'Gospel of John', pp. 67–8.
69   See Borgen, 'Gospel of John', pp. 64–6. In John this mysticism is announced from 1:51 onwards. On John the author of Revelation, see Borgen, *Early Christianity*, pp. 309–20.
70   Plutarch, *E Delph.* 17, 392a .

If we take into account the fact that Philo's writing is as much about the Torah as John's is about being in contact with the Father, we are prepared to understand Philo's central passages, too, as improper and indirect speech, destined to stimulate thoughts about what cannot be expressed in words. Thus it becomes understandable that Philo's language shows even less caution and circumspection that does that of the Christians (see below, 'Logos').

Wisdom and Eternal Torah

There is a subtle allusion to Jewish Sabbath theology in all New Testament passages where Jesus heals on Sabbath.[71] The healing of the man born blind in John 9 is one of the clearest examples. For a Jewish reader it must be clear that Jesus' activity is not 'work' as work is forbidden to Israel on Sabbath. Rather, it restores the Sabbath to its full significance in regard to eschatological well-being and effortless plenty.[72] Much of Philo's praise of the Sabbath (e.g., *Cher.* 87–93; *Abr.* 27–30; *Spec.* 2.39–223) can be taken as background, especially because according to Philo the creator does not stop his activity on Sabbath (*Opif.* 13; *Leg.* 1.3–6), whereas for the Rabbis, God may judge on Sabbath but does not create.[73]

The Divine Logos

This very rubric merits a Philonic explanation, because in biblical language there is God, and there is His creation, but there is nothing 'divine' besides God Himself.[74] In John 1:1, however, the Logos is said to be *theos* ('God'), so that the claim might remain within the parameters of biblical monotheism. The best explanation of this is found in *Somn.* 1.227–30, where Philo says that there is no name for 'the one who is'; but improperly He may be called *ho theos* ('God', with the article),[75] as He may be called 'the one who is', where 'is' does not have the same sense as it has when it is predicated of created beings. Now *theos* without the

71 In John 5:1–18 the allusion has become a gross one (in the present writer's opinion this is one of the Fourth Gospel's most reworked passages). Cf. Borgen, *Early Christianity*, pp. 105–57, 163–70, 178–80.
72 Cf. the reference to 'fullness' (*plērōma*) in John 1:16, alongside the mention of Moses in 1:17.
73 *Mekilta* Shabbeta 1 (on Exod 31:17).
74 The adjective *theios* is nearly absent from the Septuagint (see however Exod 31:3 = 35:31 and Hagiographa) and from the New Testament (only Acts 17:29 and 2 Pet 1:3f), but it is common in Philo, and also useful here.
75 See Daniélou, *Philon*, p. 156; Sterling, 'The Place of Philo', p. 48.

article clearly lies one level below, referring (Philo says) to one of two modes of divine action, viz. creation, giving, grace, etc., the other mode being judgment (intimated by the term *kyrios*).[76] In short, it appears that *theos* is another name for the Logos already in Philo, and there is no neglect of monotheism, but rather respect for transcendence.

So far on an important overlap between Philo and the New Testament, especially in John. The creator's 'word' (which, strictly seen, is a metaphor), known from Moses and the prophets, serves as His connection with creation, such as it is and also as it continues to exist.[77] In Heb 1:2 the author had said almost as an aside that 'through' him (His Son) God created the world. John 1:3 says the same thing in a more reflective way, and also avoids calling the Logos a 'tool', as Philo had done (*Sacr.* 8; *Migr.* 6, etc.).[78]

Now Philo's language is even less cautious than was that of the first Christians. Philo calls the Logos a 'second God' (*QG* 2.62; cf. *QE* 2.68).[79] This is something no Christian author had ever said. There is another lack of caution in Philo's calling the Logos the creator's 'first-born Son' and the cosmos the 'second' one, as we saw above. New Testament language more clearly distinguishes the 'begetting' of the Son from the 'making' of the world, and the ecumenical councils insisted on this distinction against the Arians. In the New Testament, the Logos (or Christ) never is a 'sun-like brilliance' in creation, as he is termed in Philo (*Somn.* 1.239). John 1:14 etc., instead, speaks of the Son's *doxa* ('glory').

Yet the fact remains that the Johannine Logos is active in creation as well as in history (of revelation, of salvation), and in the latter sphere it is much more active than in Philo. But even there we may come across a remarkable Platonism: the Son looks at what the Father does (John 5:19), just as the Platonic demiurge and Philo's Logos look at the eternal ideas. These, as Philo hastens to explain, are the creator's own

---

76 For the two principal divine 'powers', see above, ch. 4, p. 100.

77 We agree in this respect with Daniélou, *Philon* 153–63, against H. A. Wolfson. Cf. W. A. Meeks, 'The Divine Agent and His Counterfeit in Philo and the Fourth Gospel', in E. Schüssler Fiorenza (ed.), *Aspects of Religious Propaganda in Judaism and Early Christianity* (Notre Dame 1976), pp. 43–67.

78 Cf. *Spec.* 1.81: 'The Logos is the image of God, through which the whole world was made.'

79 Eusebius does not fail to quote this text in *Praep. ev.* 7.13. See F. Siegert, 'Der Logos, "älterer Sohn" des Schöpfers und "zweiter Gott": Philons Logos und der Johannesprolog', in J. Frey and U. Schnelle (eds.), *Kontexte des Johannesevangeliums* (Tübingen 2004), pp. 277–93; J. Leonhardt-Balzer, 'Der Logos und die Schöpfung: Streiflichter bei Philo (Op 20–25) und im Johannesprolog (Joh 1,1–18)', ibid., pp. 295–319.

thoughts such as they were conceived on 'day one' (Gen 1:5; see *Opif.* 9; *Leg.* 3.101).

What does all this tell us about John's contacts with Philo's teaching? J. Daniélou's answer remains valid: 'The prologue has its point of departure in Hellenistic Jewish theology of the Logos, but in its general form, and it lacks the systematic elements we saw to be Philo's own.' Or again: 'As a common base, there is the text of the Septuagint and especially the creation account where one finds the expression *en archē* and the creation by the word of God. These biblical data had been elaborated in a biblical theology that is the common ground of the Greek Book of Wisdom, of Philo, and of St. John. In as much as Philo is an outstanding representative of this common theology, one can take his teaching as the biblical theology on which the theology of St. John is built, without the further assumption that there is a literal dependence.'[80]

Creation and Duality; the Two Powers

John's prologue is a midrash on creation, as has been frequently stated; John 1:1–5 echoes Gen 1:1–5.[81] The 'cutting' activity of the Logos (in this function called *logos tomeus*; things have to be separated to make up the cosmic hierarchy) is equally evoked when Philo speaks of the two powers. In all this we get close to what shortly afterward became Christian trinitarian theology. Philo prepared it unwittingly in his exegesis of Gen 18:2.[82] The rather visionary three men appearing before Abraham, counting as three or as one in the same context, to Philo symbolize 'the one who is' with His two powers. As noted above, Philo describes this insight as a personal revelation in *Spec.* 3.1–6 and *Cher.* 27. It is the very basis of his theology, as it allows him to systematically reconcile conflicting statements that Moses makes on the Lord's or God's actions.

There was a Christian reception of this exegesis grouping Christ together with two angels (Justin), whereas other authors understood Abraham's vision in the sense that the Father occupied a position superior to the Son and the Spirit (subordinatianism). John's prologue gives a

---

80 Daniélou, *Philon*, pp. 205, 206.

81 See now C.M. Carmichael, *The Story of Creation: Its Origin and Its Interpretation in Philo and the Fourth Gospel* (Ithaca 1996). It has, however, but little basis in concrete texts.

82 See K. Hruby, 'Exégèse rabbinique et exégèse patristique', *Revue des sciences religieuses* 47 (1973), pp. 341–72. We leave aside the more traditional triad consisting of God, Wisdom (as his wife) and the Logos as their 'first-born child' (*Fug.* 108f; *Agr.* 51). This atavism is found in Theophilus of Antioch, *Ad Autolycum* 2.10, together with the first theological use of the Greek word *trias* 'Trinity', but from then on it was abandoned.

balanced account, just as does his way of narrating Jesus' life: Jesus is 'sent' by his Father, but at the same time he executes his mission in a most sovereign fashion. In the end Jesus is not 'resuscitated' (passively, as in the Synoptics), but 'rises' again (actively; John 10:17f; cf. 11:25f). There is complete equality in John 5:19-23.

Such is the trinitarian doctrine underlying the main layer of the Fourth Gospel. After Jesus' departure from this world, there will be another mode of divine presence in the 'Paraclete' (14:26, etc.). Even this language can be explained by reference to *Mos.* 2.134;[83] *Jos.* 239.

Evil and Sin; Grace and Salvation

There is not a great deal of preoccupation with sin in the main parts of the Gospel of John. This is rather a concern of the Pharisees (John 9:16, 24). Tax collectors and prostitutes are absent. In 5:14 and in 8:11 Jesus simply admonishes supposed or alleged sinners to sin no further. John seems to share Philo's view that sin cannot be defeated or beaten as such, but is to be replaced by a superior orientation.

Thus, there is no drama of salvation in John, as there is none in Philo, but rather the offer of a 'new birth' (John 3:1–17).[84] In Philo, even less dramatically, 'illumination' makes humans capable of seeing the divine powers (indicated by the terms *kyrios* and *theos*) at work in creation which is a continuous generation (e.g., *De Deo* 2–3).

Man

An interesting thing about John's anthropology is his definition of what may be eternal in man. In Philo, just as in Plato (and also in first-century Pharisaism as reported by Josephus), it is the soul (viz. of the just). In John it is *zōē* (life), understood in a more abstract sense as something acquired by faith and not merely a gift of God's creation. It may be enjoyed here and now, and it will yield to an enjoyment without end in another world.[85] In Philo, true, the souls are not automatically immortal, and they may die by lack of virtue.[86] The Gospel of John, for its part, is not about virtue, but about receiving the Logos by faith.

---

83 Here 'paraclete' is another title of the Logos, as in 1 John 2:1.
84 The parallels given by Borgen, 'Gospel of John', pp. 61–3 (cf. nn. 42–7 on pp. 74–5), characteristically, point rather to Palestinian than to Alexandrian Judaism. John is acquainted with both.
85 Contrast the more concrete notion of a future life in Josephus, *C. Ap.* 2.218.
86 See above, ch. 4, pp. 108–9.

Man and Woman

Being 'carnal' does not seem to be a major problem for John. The essential is said in 1:13 about a more-than-carnal rebirth. Moreover, 'the flesh [sc. of Jesus' historical descent, supposed to be from David] counts for nothing' (6:63). Even though John himself is said to have lived as a bachelor, as did Jesus, in his text we find the wedding at Cana in a prominent place (2:1–11), as the scene of the very first 'sign' that Jesus performs.

The Exodus: Passover

The English term 'Passover' for the Hebrew *pesah* (or, as the New Testament texts transcribe its Aramaic equivalent, *pascha*) corresponds to the Philonic term *diabatēria*, which Philo and others employed to render *pesah* after the time of the Septuagint. Yet the idea that this can mean an individual's 'passing on' or 'progress' toward perfection (*QE* 1.7f,) also lies behind John 12:23–8 and the whole narrative scheme which has Jesus' public activity spread between two trips to Jerusalem to celebrate Passover.[87] There he becomes a new Passover in his own person, as the tradition in 1 Cor 5:7 also attests. Philo expands much on the 'perfection' of the paschal lambs as described in Exod 12:5. So does John with his *teleios* and *teleioun* language used in connection with Jesus.[88]

Revealed Torah

Pilate calls it 'your (the Judeans') law' in John 18:31, but in the genuine parts of this Gospel Jesus never does call it thus. His attitude towards the Torah is not affected by the tensions he has with the Jerusalem aristocracy. The Johannine Jesus continues what his Father had begun with Israel in giving the law. He confirms the law's intention by replacing it. Philo, of course, would never have admitted this latter conclusion.

The Commandments; Concrete Ethics

In spite of strong pressure in any religious community to define its identity by means of rules of conduct, John's Gospel dares to formulate only one commandment, that of love (*agapē*). This is in some sense new with

---

87 If we put the temporal and spatial indicators of the text back into their former coherence, there emerges a clear and geographically correct itinerary.

88 See C. Schlund, '*Kein Knochen soll gebrochen werden*': *Studien zu Bedeutung und Funktion des Pesachfests in Texten des frühen Judentums und im Johannesevangelium* (Neukirchen-Vluyn 2005), esp. p. 63.

respect to Judaism ('a new commandment', John 13:34), because Lev 19:18 had been but one of 613 commandments of equal weight (especially in rabbinic teaching as it came to be established in that period). There are redactional accretions to the Johannine text that mitigate this radicalism by employing the plural 'commandments', but none of these other commandments is formulated. So Christians are left to determine right and wrong at their own discretion, a highly unusual phenomenon in antiquity.

Cult, Prayer, Rites, and Holy Places

Jesus inaugurates a new type of cult 'in (the) spirit and in truth' (John 4:20–4). His saying against the temple (2:19) opens his activity in Jerusalem, which begins much earlier in this Gospel than it does in the others. Philo's idealizing of the Jerusalem cult and its high priest may imply the same degree of independence from what happens in Jerusalem, but in a completely non-polemical way. There was no conflict about worship in his own life experience.

Eschatology

In the key passages of the Fourth Gospel (leaving out manifest glosses like 6:39f, 44b), hopes for the future are restricted to the resurrection of the dead (especially 11:25, correcting older language in 11:24). This is not conceived as an event in the history of mankind, and no precise timetable for it is given. As to fears, there are none for the believers (3:16–18, 5:21–4, etc.), in a manner not unlike the Epicureans' rejection of religious fear.[89] Similarly, Philo limits his people's political hopes to pacifistic and rather universalistic divine recompenses in the future. Israel is a people destined to have no sovereign apart from God (cf. John 8:33). Philo has a vision of the following kind: Israel will be left free as soon as its visible exercise of virtue will put to shame its foreign oppressors so that they will let it be free (*Praem.* 162–72).

There is a remarkable passage to a similar effect in John (8:32–6; cf. Gal 5:1ff). Freedom is first and foremost freedom from sin and from inner slavery. There are no political conditions to be fulfilled before it happens. This is a conviction most New Testament writers share with Philo against common Jewish apocalypticism.

---

89 The monumental inscription of the Epicurean philosopher Diogenes in Oenoanda (Asia Minor) is evidence of the vitality of Epicureanism in the 2nd century CE.

VI. CONCLUSION: THE MAIN CONTRASTS

One further review of our questionnaire with special attention to contrasts will enable us to see characteristic features of Philonic and of early Christian doctrines as well.

Formalities

Philo is more of a literary author than is any 'author' within the New Testament, let alone writers of intertestamental literature and the Rabbis. His teaching is as literary as that of the others is oral. Much or most of New Testament writing is nothing but an *aide-mémoire* to support oral performance or to overcome a teacher's corporeal absence. So the New Testament writings are quite short and partly anonymous or pseudonymous.

All this is different from Philo. As to literary genres, too, there is no direct comparison between the New Testament, which is not a law code, and Philo, who is the interpreter of a law code. Philo's writing alternates between forms of exegesis (which make up the bulk of his work) and free essays, some of them styled as dialogues. In the New Testament, essays and other types of writing may include exegesis, but are not principally presented as such, with the exception of the midrash-like Epistle to the Hebrews.[90] Some New Testament writings are treatises in a style close to Philo's (Hebrews, James, 1 John), but they are more or less disguised as letters (thus becoming 'epistles'), resting under the spell of Paul's powerful letters. For the rest, simplicity is the seal of truth. One New Testament author (Luke) is a historian of some literary ambition, but he restricts his stylistic skill to framing up traditions of humble folks and to some Septuagint-like, Hebraizing poetry.

Philo, in turn, is not a storyteller. He gives some narration of recent events in his *In Flaccum* and *Legatio ad Gaium*, but its actors, being anti-heroes, have nothing of the importance of Jesus. Philo's accounts always illustrate general ideas, such as providence.

SPECIALIZED LANGUAGE Philo takes over every useful term from Platonism, Stoicism, and other philosophies. There is much more restraint on this level in the New Testament, and also much less syncretism. Paul and John aptly combine a narrow choice of biblical expressions with an even narrower choice of philosophical terms. So

---

90 On midrash in Greek, see F. Siegert, 'Hellenistic Jewish Midrash', in J. Neusner and A.J. Avery-Peck (eds.), *Encyclopedia of Midrash: Biblical Interpretation in Formative Judaism* (Leiden 2005), I, pp. 199–250.

philosophical terms in the New Testament never become metaphorical, as is frequent in Philo.

Scripture and the Methods of Its Interpretation

Philo relies on the Pentateuch as much as the New Testament authors rely on what they call Holy Scriptures (mostly in the plural), that is, the entire canon of the Old Testament. Yet in principle, Philo's canon is the same as that of the New Testament authors; the differences have to do with the theological weight of the different books. In Philo, whose vocation was to be an interpreter of Judaism's law, ninety-eight percent of biblical quotations come from the Pentateuch. This leaves to the scriptural Prophets and to 'David' as author of the Psalms only the role of *claqueurs*. There is not even an allusion to Daniel, in spite of the high esteem in which he was held in other sectors of Judaism.[91] In the Gospels Jesus' reference to himself as the 'Son of Man' is a constant allusion to Dan 7:13, and it is the nucleus of what was to become a 'christology'. Yet the most advanced and most philosophical of all New Testament theologians, John, is remarkable for a most Philonic neglect of apocalypticism.

Knowledge of God, Natural and Revealed

In the New Testament, the thesis of a natural knowledge of God, available to anyone, may be put forth occasionally, but it does not serve as a basis of positive argument. Rather, everything salutary depends on revelation, whereas Philo's thought rests on the pillar of religious philosophy. It is a kind of centaur as opposed to the 'revealed religion' in the New Testament. C. Siegfried may be right in stating that Philo's thinking about God is 'more pagan and philosophical than biblical, whereas that of the New Testament shows the traits of Israel's living God'.[92]

The type of mysticism that underlies the writings of Paul or John is different from that cultivated by Philo. Philo recommends the soul's ascent toward God, and he does so in terms very reminiscent of Plato, whereas the Christian message has the Son of God come down to earth. All effort is attributed to the triune God. Thus we saw that the use of Jacob's ladder (Gen 28:12) is different in John 1:51 and in Philo. One may find references to personal experiences of elevation and *Himmelsreise* in the New Testament (2 Cor 12:2),[93] but nothing is founded upon them.

91 Daniel has a role in the writings of Josephus and in the Septuagint canon he becomes one of the Major Prophets.
92 *Philo*, p. 304.
93 See B. Heininger, 'Paulus und Philo als Mystiker? Himmelsreisen im Vergleich (2Kor 12,2–4; SpecLeg III 1–6)', in Deines and Niebuhr, *Philo und das Neue Testament*, pp. 189–204.

Any 'transport' of the soul based on its own faculties is suspect. Truth only comes from prophetic communication, which means from the outside.

Secrets of the Divine Name

The Sayings Source behind the Synoptics as well as behind John 17:6 deliberately replaces the unpronounceable name by the one Jesus used in praying, 'Father'. If Greek-speaking Judaism had become Philonic rather than Christian, 'the one who is' would be venerated instead of the Christians' 'Our Father' and the Rabbis' *Adonai* or *ha-shem*.

The Divine Logos

Philo's Logos, concretely expressed, is the Mosaic law (*QG* 4.140; *Jos.* 174). Christians transferred this to Jesus as God's voice. Thus revelation became personal, and legislation became secular.

Creation and Duality

John's prologue is a midrash on creation, as we have seen. As a whole, it summarizes Philonic teaching in 1:1–13 (two prose stanzas interrupted by a rejection or limitation of John the Baptist's sectarians), whereas the following part, 1:14–18, adds what is new in Christianity, namely, the incarnation.

The Two Powers

It seems that the New Testament writers could have put to good use the subtle theodicy encoded in Philo's personal revelation on the two powers; but none of them did, not even in a re-defined terminology such as that of the Rabbis. They were not concerned with evil in general, and they had a different concept of salvation. For them it did not consist in an equilibrium of opposites, but in overcoming the sins of individuals.

Man; Man and Woman

Philo writes for pure minds, that is, for readers without an abdomen. He may praise women in as much as they are not flesh but symbolize an idea or a bundle of ideas. In the New Testament, attitudes about sexuality are rather restrained, too, and women may act freely and independently only when they live a celibate man's life. Yet there are unprejudiced passages such as the wedding at Cana (John 2:1–11).

Sacred History: From the Patriarchs to Moses

Philo, true, would use the term 'providence' (*pronoia*) for much of what follows here. This term is absent both from the Hebrew Bible and the New Testament, but it allows Philo to establish a link between the action of the two powers (*De Deo* 12; cf. Plato, *Tim.* 30a), the whole of sacred history, Israel's present experiences, and Rome's rule. In his mind they have to go side by side. In the New Testament no such close associations are made.

To return to a common theme, Abraham is often employed in both corpora to illustrate theological doctrines. Isaac, for his part, gained importance among the Rabbis who came to interpret the *akedah* (Gen 22) as a type of Israel's ongoing experiences. In the New Testament, there is a certain Isaac midrash not only behind Heb 11:17 but also behind passages about God's only Son (John 3:16, 18; cf. Rom 8:32f).

The Exodus: Passover; Revealed Torah

Sacred history, for Christians, includes Jesus' life and death and, to some extent, the origins of the Church. For Christianity, the incarnation of God's Logos in the person of the Nazarene is its primary datum. As Daniélou states, 'For Philo, the Logos did not come in a perceptible form, for it has nothing in common with matter. St. John, on the contrary, says, "He came among his own ... and the Logos became flesh".'[94]

Philo can occasionally play with the idea of something becoming 'embodied' in another. In *Gig.* 6–12 he gives a very traditional account of the angels' seduction of earthly women and begetting giants (Gen 6:2). In *QG* 1.92 on Gen 6:4, he reveals a bit more detail: The angels' 'pneumatic substance' takes on different shapes (shapes, not bodies, let alone flesh). He seems to use a term that must have been in Greek *sōmatoun* ('to embody') at *QG* 2.4 on Gen 6:14. Here 'bodiless ideas' about creation get 'embodied' in Noah's ark. There is nothing personal (and little historical) about it. John 19:5, by contrast, has Pilate proclaim, 'Lo, the man!'

The Commandments; Concrete Ethics

With the exception of Matthew (5:48, 19:21), New Testament ethics are less concerned with perfection than are the ethics of Philo. There is, furthermore, no effort to prove that Moses' commandments are meant for mankind. Certain concerns of Mosaic legislation, however, are taken

94 Daniélou, *Philo*, 206, citing, with reference to Philo, *Deus* 32.

more seriously than in Philo. Luke and the author of James are more social thinkers than is Philo.

Cult, Prayer, Rites, and Holy Places

What has been said in section V can be generalized for all of early Christianity. There are many contrasts regarding temple worship and many affinities regarding worship in the synagogues.

In Philo, as in Judaism generally, there is no particular emphasis on *pistis*, faith. Abraham is its model, of course: *Migr.* 43f (on Gen 12:1) can be compared to Rom 4 (on Gen 15:6). But this and other occasional statements such as in *Her.* 92–5 do not constitute a concrete or even urgent appeal to faith as it is heard in all Christian sources. That faith is counted as one among the virtues (*Abr.* 269f), just as piety is (*Spec.* 4.147), reflects a very Hellenistic perspective. Any New Testament parallels are in late epistles that lie outside the important corpora (e.g., 1 Tim 6:11).

Eschatology

Most of the New Testament remains 'Judean' in that it retains the national hopes of Jewish apocalypticism, but elevates them to a cosmic level. Paul with his school, as well as Hebrews, the Synoptics (Mark 14:62 and parallels, citing Dan 7:13), and the Johannine school (1 John 2:28) await a second, visible coming of Christ 'on the clouds of the sky', that is, in a spatio-temporal world. Few Jewish Christian teachers, it seems, attempted to restrict this would-be knowledge to what can be ascertained by present experience: Apollos (if the hypothesis of section III is correct) and John 'the Elder' (section V). The latter's 'realized eschatology' is about eternal life to be acquired by faith in this world and to be fully enjoyed in the other world – that other world being above us rather than lying in our future. This bears some resemblance to what Philo promises to the wise man's soul, with the exception that what is an exercise of virtue in Philo becomes an appeal to fraternal love in John.

8   Philo and the Early Christian Fathers

I. INTRODUCTION: THE PARADOX

Philo was a child of the Jewish nation, born (we assume) at Alexandria in the Diaspora, but bound to the Jewish heartland in Jerusalem with strong familial and affective ties.[1] He tells us that he journeyed to Jerusalem to pray and offer sacrifices in the temple (*Prov.* 2.107). Thus, it is possible that he was present in the city during those momentous events of the Passover in 29 CE, which laid the foundation for a new world religion, but he most likely would have given them little attention. Reports that he met with the apostle Peter in Rome and that he had contact with the first Christian community in Alexandria are clearly legendary. Yet it was the adoption of his legacy by the Christian Church that ensured the survival of his writings. If this had not happened, the present *Companion* to his writings and thought could not have been written. We are thus presented with a paradox. Philo was neglected by his own people, to whose cause he had shown such strong devotion, and he was rescued from oblivion through the attentions of a group of people of whom he had most likely never heard, and who would later actively oppose his own Jewish religion.

The paradox that I have just outlined will be slightly lessened if we make an adjustment in our perception of the relationship between Judaism and Christianity. It is generally assumed that Christianity as a religion developed from Judaism in a kind of mother–daughter relationship. For our purposes, however, it might be more instructive to adopt the image suggested by A. F. Segal some time ago in his study *Rebecca's Children*.[2] Christianity and rabbinic Judaism can be regarded

---

1   Jerome's report that Philo was of priestly descent (*Vir. ill.* 11) should be taken seriously, though it is not corroborated by any other firm evidence; see D. R. Schwartz, 'Philo's Priestly Descent', in F. E. Greenspahn et al. (eds.), *Nourished with Peace: Studies in Hellenistic Judaism in Memory of Samuel Sandmel* (Chico, CA 1984), pp. 155–71.

2   *Rebecca's Children: Judaism and Christianity in the Roman World* (Cambridge, MA 1986), p. 1.

as siblings, both proceeding from the womb of Second Temple Judaism. It is, of course, a notorious fact that siblings often engage in fierce rivalry and this certainly occurred in the case of Christianity and Judaism after the fall of Jerusalem in 70 CE. The paradox can thus be restated: why did Philo's Christian successors adopt him, but his Jewish successors neglect him?

This chapter will concentrate on the first half of this question. Its aim is to describe and analyse the role that Philo played in the Christian tradition from the second to the fifth centuries of our era. It will build on the previous chapter, in which Philo's relation to the Christian New Testament was discussed, but will not presume on the subject of Philo's relation to the later Jewish tradition, the topic to be investigated in the next chapter. Two main questions will stand at the center of our concerns. First, how did Philo come to be accepted in the Christian tradition? The answer will consist of a narrative that follows a largely chronological trajectory. I shall tell the story of how Philo, though a Jew, came to obtain a position as an honorary Christian. Second, why did this unexpected adoption take place? What were the features of Philo's legacy that appealed to Christians, encouraging them to preserve his treatises and make use of them in their own writings? Finally I shall take a closer look at the fourth century and argue that it was a stroke of good fortune that he came through that difficult period as well as he did.[3]

II. HOW DID PHILO COME TO BE ACCEPTED IN THE CHRISTIAN TRADITION?

The very first clear and uncontested references to Philo by a Christian author are found in the *Stromateis* of Clement of Alexandria. It is generally agreed that this work was written in Alexandria in about 200 CE – the same city in which Philo lived and worked, but nearly a century and a half after his death. Philo is named four times. First he is cited in connection with the etymologies of the names Hagar and Sarah (1.31.1). He is then invoked, together with his predecessor Aristobulus,

---

3   Most of the contents of this article is based on D. T. Runia, *Philo in Early Christian Literature: A Survey* (Assen 1993), which superseded all previous research on the subject. I shall not give detailed references when material discussed can easily be located in this study. The Italian translation by R. Radice, *Filone di Alessandria nella prima letteratura cristiana* (Milan 1999), contains an appendix with text and translation of all patristic texts that refer directly to Philo (pp. 354–445). See also my collection of essays, *Philo and the Church Fathers* (Leiden 1995).

for having demonstrated the antiquity of the Jewish race (1.72.4). A third reference relates to Moses' Greek education as recounted in the *De vita Mosis* (1.151.2). The final time Philo is mentioned is at 2.100.3, in connection with the claim that Plato shares with Moses the same ultimate aim for human life, the quest to 'become like God'. The references, though small in number, cover a broad area of engagement: the allegorical method of interpretation, apologetic history, scriptural exposition, and philosophical ethics. The first mention is particularly interesting because it offers an allegorical interpretation of the Sarah and Hagar story that is quite different from that given by Paul in Gal 4:24–6 and will find later followers in the Alexandrian tradition.[4] In the second and fourth texts, Clement calls Philo 'the Pythagorean', which is, at the very least, a recognition of his learning in the area of Greek philosophy.[5] His Jewishness is not explicitly mentioned, but given the contexts, Clement must have meant it to be understood.

If, however, the corpus of Clement's surviving writings is examined more closely, it emerges that, when it comes to his use of Philo, the four explicit references are merely the tip of a massive iceberg. Centuries of scholarly research have shown that Clement makes much more extensive use of Philonic material. The monograph of the Dutch scholar A. van den Hoek has examined this usage in detail in relation to the *Stromateis*.[6] In four texts – on the interpretation of Hagar and Sarah, the story of Moses, the relation between the Mosaic law and the philosophical virtues, and the interpretation of the high-priestly vestments – Clement uses Philo's actual words in a manner that today would be regarded as tantamount to plagiarism. In other passages the dependence is less literal and extensive, but still very considerable. A fascinating example is found in the famous beginning of the *Protrepticus*, when Clement speaks lyrically about the 'new song of the Logos'. Themes drawn from Philo, such as the cosmological role of the Logos, the music of cosmic and human praise, and the value of newness,[7] are transformed in the new context of Christ the Logos, who came on earth to open the eyes of the blind and reconcile disobedient children to their heavenly Father.

4 Notably in Origen and Didymus the Blind: see A. Henrichs, 'Philosophy, the Handmaiden of Theology', *GRBS* 9 (1968), pp. 437–50.

5 See further D. T. Runia, 'Why Does Clement of Alexandria Call Philo "the Pythagorean"?', in *Philo and the Church Fathers*, pp. 54–76.

6 *Clement of Alexandria and His Use of Philo in the Stromateis: An Early Christian Reshaping of a Jewish Model* (Leiden 1988). Note that this research does not cover the entire Clementine corpus. Similar studies still need to be done for his remaining works.

7 See *Plant.* 3–9 (cited literally at *Protr.* 5.2), 126–31; *Sacr.* 74–6.

Clement must have literally had copies of (some of) Philo's writings on his desk. Otherwise he would not have been able to copy out such large chunks of his Alexandrian predecessor's actual words. This observation neatly illustrates the two paths that we can follow when we investigate how Philo was absorbed into the Christian tradition. We can hunt down references to Philo by name and also uses of his writings that do not credit his name, as indicated by the evidence of intertextuality. But we can also trace the survival and dissemination of Philo's writings in a Christian context. The first path is the intellectual trajectory, the second represents the material aspect. The two are inseparably entwined. Philo's ideas could not have been appropriated if they were not accessible through the availability of his writings, and his writings would not have been available if they were not thought worth preserving. They needed to be kept on the shelves and replaced with new copies when they started to crumble.[8]

Clement's extensive use of Philo points to the first watershed in the transmission of the Philonic heritage. As we saw, one century and a half after Philo's death substantial parts of the Philonic corpus were available to Clement. By this time the Jewish community in Alexandria was only a shadow of what it had once been and Clement, to judge from his writings, seems to have had little or no contact with a living Jewish community. Israel is for him exclusively a theological concept. In the period between Philo and Clement, almost all of the literature of Alexandrian Judaism was lost. Yet Philo's writings were preserved in all their riches and diversity. We would dearly love to know more about how this happened. In the absence of direct evidence it is plausible to conclude that circles close to Clement played a leading role in this process. Eusebius tells us about a 'school' associated with the Christian church of Alexandria, led by the presbyter Pantaenus, Clement's revered teacher. In the scholarly literature this has become the celebrated 'Catechetical school of Alexandria'.[9] Here, we surmise, Philo's writings were preserved because they were considered valuable for the work of scriptural interpretation and theological teaching in the early Church.

But what about the intervening century and a half between Philo and Clement? Unfortunately too little remains of the writings of the

---

8 In normal circumstances texts on perishable papyrus have to be copied out every 60–80 years if they are to survive. As we shall see below, the chances of survival increase dramatically if works are copied onto parchment; see further n. 30.

9 On this school see A. van den Hoek, 'The "Catechetical" School of Early Christian Alexandria and Its Philonic Heritage', *HThR* 90 (1997), pp. 59–87.

controversial Alexandrian theologians Basilides and Valentinus to reach
a firm conclusion on whether they knew Philo, but the probability is
surely in favour of such knowledge.[10] Moreover it would be risky to
assume that Philo's writings were not available elsewhere.[11] As was
noted in the previous chapter, there is no direct evidence to suggest that
New Testament writers were directly acquainted with his works. It is
also not very likely that the Apostolic Fathers would be interested in
Philo. But what about the Apologists? Surely they would be attracted
to Philo's apologetic application of Greek philosophical ideas. The most
interesting case is Justin Martyr. There can be no doubt that there are
affinities between Philo and Justin in the imagery and titles that the
latter uses for the Logos, in the emphasis on the cosmic significance of
the Logos, and in the importance accorded to divine theophanies in the
interpretation of the Old Testament. Recent scholars incline to the view
that these affinities are due to Justin's acquaintance with Hellenistic
Judaism rather than with Philo himself.[12]

Another fascinating case is the work *Ad Autolycum* by Theophilus,
who was elected the seventh bishop of Antioch in 169 CE. There is no
doubt that his doctrine of God in book 1 and his lengthy exegesis of the
early chapters of Genesis in book 2, chs. 11–32, show strong affinities
with Hellenistic Judaism and, in the latter case, may have depended
on a Jewish source. But did he know Philo's work? A striking example
which shows how difficult it is to answer the question with confidence
is the credal statement formulated by Theophilus at 3.9:

We too confess God, but only one, the founder and maker and demiurge of this
entire cosmos. We know that everything is governed by providential care, but by
him alone. We have learned a holy law, but we have as legislator the real God,
who teaches us to practise justice and piety and beneficence.[13]

The resemblances to Philo's famous 'credo' at *De opificio mundi* 170–2
cannot be missed. All five of the doctrines he mentions there are present,

10   See my *Philo in Early Christian Literature*, pp. 123–6. C. Markschies,
     *Valentinus Gnosticus? Untersuchungen zur valentinianischen Gnosis
     mit einem Kommentar zu den Fragmenten* (Tübingen 1992), p. 404, sees
     Valentinus as a bridge between Philo and Clement.
11   Eusebius claims in *Hist. eccl.* 2.18.8 that Philo's works were placed in
     Roman libraries.
12   See O. Skarsaune, *The Proof from Prophecy: A Study in Justin Martyr's
     Proof-text Tradition* (Leiden 1987), pp. 433–4; Runia, *Philo in Early Christian
     Literature*, pp. 97–105.
13   Translation by R. M. Grant in his edition of Theophilus of Antioch, *Ad
     Autolycum* (Oxford 1970), pp. 111–13 (slightly modified); see also his *Greek
     Apologists of the Second Century* (Philadelphia 1988), p. 167.

at least by implication. Moreover the statement that God is a lawgiver who teaches humankind to do justice and practice piety is perfectly Philonic. We note that Theophilus, just like Philo, uses the Platonic epithets *poiētēs* (maker) and *dēmiourgos* (demiurge) for God the creator. The term *ktistēs* (founder), however, may refer to the doctrine of *creatio ex nihilo*, which Theophilus, in contrast to Philo, states explicitly (*Autol.* 2.4). Because Theophilus never mentions Philo by name and verbal resemblances are limited, we cannot be certain that Philo's writings were circulating in Antioch and that Bishop Theophilus was making use of them.[14]

We move on now to the third century, which is dominated by the mighty figure of Origen. In the story of the survival of Philo's writings Origen plays a crucial role. Origen's youth and theological training took place in the same Alexandrian context that we described for Clement. There he would have had opportunity to know the writings of Philo. Through his unparalleled intellectual brilliance, Origen became the pride of the Alexandrian church, but during his middle years he received an offer which he could not refuse and was ordained a priest in the church of Caesarea on the borders of Palestine. We may be certain that Origen took his copies of Philo's treatises with him, for, as we shall see, a generation later they were present in the library of the Caesarean church. Why did Origen go to all the trouble to take them along?

In the vast mass of Origen's surviving writings, Philo is named only three times. Two passages occur in the *Contra Celsum*, his long defence of Christianity (and its Jewish origins) against the pagan Celsus. At 4.51 he cites Celsus' scathing attack on Jewish and Christian allegorizations of biblical stories and comments:

He appears by this to mean the works of Philo or even writers still earlier such as the writings of Aristobulus. But I hazard the guess that Celsus has not read the books, for I think that in many places they are so successful that even Greek philosophers would have been won over by what they say. Not only do they have an attractive style, but they also discuss ideas and doctrines, making use of the myths (as Celsus regards them) in the scriptures.[15]

A little later he discusses the account of Jacob's vision of a ladder reaching to heaven and notes that 'Philo also composed a book about this ladder, which is worthy of intelligent and wise study by those who wish

14   On Theophilus and Philo, see further my *Philo in Early Christian Literature*, pp. 110–16.
15   This passage and the following one are cited according to H. Chadwick's translation of Origen, *Contra Celsum* (Cambridge 1953).

to find the truth' (6.21). The third text is found in the *Commentary on Matthew* 15.3 in an exegesis of Matt 19:12:

And Philo, who enjoys a high reputation among intelligent people for many subjects discussed in his treatises on the Law of Moses, says in the book entitled *On that the worse is accustomed to attack the better* that 'it is better to be made into a eunuch than to rage after sexual intercourse.'

Here Origen actually quotes *verbatim* from *Quod deterius potiori insidiari soleat* 176.[16] All three references are highly complimentary.

As in the case of Clement, however, these three texts are once again just the tip of an iceberg. There are at least twenty other anonymous references to Philo and his writings located throughout the corpus. A. van den Hoek has done a thorough analysis of all the Origenian texts that have been identified by scholars as containing Philonic material, amounting to over 300 in total.[17] Of these, twenty-three refer to him directly (if often anonymously), while another ninety-three exhibit probable dependence on Philo's writings. In the remaining texts dependence is less certain, but many of them reveal at least a Philonic background. Van den Hoek also did an analysis of the content of the 116 texts just mentioned. It emerges that nearly eighty percent of them are concerned with biblical interpretation and the theory of allegory, while the remaining twenty percent relate to philosophical questions and the doctrines of God and creation. The large proportion of these texts that are concerned with biblical interpretation also explains why so many of the references to Philo are anonymous: Origen regards Philo as a distinguished predecessor in the task of expounding Scripture (especially the Pentateuch). He is well aware of the fact that Philo is a Jew, but there was no need to draw special attention to it, except in an explicitly apologetic context such as the treatise against Celsus. It should be noted, however, that the division between exegetical and philosophical texts is far from absolute, because one of the features of Origen's allegorical method is precisely that it allows scope for the use of philosophical

---

16   The passage is of particular interest against the background of Eusebius' report that Origen emasculated himself when young (*Hist. eccl.* 6.8). In this text the act is implicitly repudiated.

17   'Philo and Origen: A Descriptive Catalogue of their Relationship', *StPhAnn* 12 (2000), pp. 44–121. An analysis of these results is given by the same author in 'Assessing Philo's Influence in Christian Alexandria: The Case of Origen', in J.L. Kugel (ed.), *Shem in the Tents of Japhet: Essays on the Encounter of Judaism and Hellenism* (Leiden 2002), pp. 223–39. Most of the anonymous references to Philo are cited in my *Philo in Early Christian Literature*, pp. 161–2.

themes in explaining the Bible, for example through the use of Hebrew etymologies.[18] This he learned from Philo.

Our account of Philo's acceptance in the Christian tradition has now come to a point where two paths diverge. It is possible to remain in Alexandria and Egypt or to follow Origen to Caesarea. We must do both, but will start with the former.[19] Because of its climate Egypt can give us evidence that we are denied elsewhere. Up until now, four Philonic papyri have been found. One of these is quite spectacular. It is a codex of eighty-nine pages, fully preserved with its leather binding, containing the complete text of two allegorical treatises, *De sacrificiis Abelis et Caini* and *Quis rerum divinarum heres sit*. According to the papyrologist C. H. Roberts 'it is beyond reasonable doubt the earliest bound book extant.'[20] It was found in a niche in a wall, where it had been carefully concealed. Because the text contains *nomina sacra* (abbreviations for divine names used only by Christian scribes), we can be certain that it was hidden by a Christian, and it is likely that this occurred during the last wave of persecution at the beginning of the fourth century. A second papyrus found at Oxyrhynchus represents the remains of a much larger codex which contained at least eight treatises. The other two are mere snippets.[21] Three of the four papyri are certainly Christian, and attest to the surprising popularity of Philo's writings in places at a considerable remove from Alexandria. It is remarkable that a Christian, fearing for his life, would go to such trouble to preserve a book of Philo. It should be noted, too, that almost all the treatises represented in the papyri belong to the exegetical and allegorical part of Philo's *oeuvre*.

The turn of the fourth century was a turbulent time for Christianity, not only because of the persecutions, but also for other reasons. The theology of the Alexandrian presbyter Arius caused shock waves that were felt in the Church far beyond Egypt. Little remains of his writings,

---

18 Jerome, in the preface to his *Liber interpretationis Hebraicorum nominum* (Corpus Christianorum: Series Latina 72, pp. 59–60), reports 'on the authority of Origen' that Philo had published a book on Hebrew names which he himself (Origen) used. While Origen's attribution of this book to Philo is almost certainly an error, it can be taken as an acknowledgment of his debt to Philo in the area of Hebrew etymologies.

19 On Philo in Egypt, see D. T. Runia, 'One of Us or One of Them? Christian Reception of Philo the Jew in Egypt', in Kugel, *Shem in the Tents of Japhet*, pp. 203–22.

20 *Buried Books in Antiquity* (London 1963), p. 14.

21 Since I wrote my article cited in n. 19 the fourth Philonic papyrus has been published: H. Harrauer, 'Ein neuer Philo-Papyrus mit περὶ φιλανθρωπίας', *Analecta Papyrologica* 14–15 (2002–2003), pp. 111–15.

so we have no way of knowing whether he referred to Philo in them. In his monograph on Arius' theology, however, R. Williams claims that 'Philo mapped out the ground for the Alexandrian tradition to build on, and ... Arius' theological problematic is firmly within that tradition.'²² He is thinking primarily of the legacy of Origen's theology, which combines an apophatic theology with a strong emphasis on the role of Christ as the Logos and image of God who makes God known to humankind. Both doctrines have strong Philonic roots. It might be expected that the implacable opponent of Arius, the bishop of Alexandria Athanasius, would have exploited this background for polemical purposes, for he also was fiercely opposed to Judaism, but in fact he never mentions Philo in his extant works and it is mainly theological imagery that betrays some Philonic influence in the background.²³

Origen's legacy was carried forward in another way by the great fourth century exegete Didymus the Blind. He continued the work of the Alexandrian Catechetical school, of which he was appointed head by Athanasius. Until 1941 little remained of his writings, but in that year five papyrus codices of biblical commentaries were discovered at Tura in Egypt. As these have been published, it has become increasingly clear how Didymus continues the Alexandrian tradition of exegesis, including the use of allegory and philosophical themes in interpreting Scripture. He refers to Philo by name on six occasions, citing, for example, his allegorical exegesis of the story of Hagar and Sarah and his allusion to Plato's doctrine of philosophers in *De vita Mosis* 2.2, but these texts are only a small proportion of his total debt to him.²⁴ Not surprisingly the largest amount of Philonic material is found in the *Commentary on Genesis*.²⁵

More surprising are the references to Philo in the vast letter collection of Isidore, priest of the church of Pelusium to the east of the Egyptian delta in the early fifth century. In four of his letters Isidore makes extensive reference to Philo.²⁶ He is called *ho theōrētikōtatos* (the master of speculative thought), who 'turns almost the whole of the Old Testament into allegory' (*Ep.* 3.19). The most interesting of the

---

22 *Arius: Heresy and Tradition* (London 1987), p. 123.
23 See my *Philo in Early Christian Literature*, pp. 194–7.
24 References and further details in my *Philo in Early Christian Literature*, pp. 197–204.
25 Covering Gen 1–17:3, edited by P. Nautin (Paris 1976–1978 = SC 233, 244). See now A. C. Geljon, 'Philonic Elements in Didymus the Blind's Exegesis of the Story of Cain and Abel', *VC* 61 (2007), pp. 282–312.
26 Text, translation and commentary on these texts is given in D. T. Runia, 'Philo of Alexandria in Five Letters of Isidore of Pelusium', in *Philo and the Church Fathers*, pp. 155–81; shorter account in my *Philo in Early Christian Literature*, pp. 204–9.

letters gives a long discussion of Philo's doctrine of God in relation to the Christian doctrine of the Trinity, in which he is favorably compared with other Jewish teachers. We shall return to this passage at the end of the chapter. Isidore's letters and the papyri discussed above are evidence that Philo enjoyed a certain level of popularity in Christian circles in Egypt up until the sixth century.

Our account now returns to the bifurcation mentioned earlier and takes the other path that leads to Caesarea. As we saw, Origen had spent the final decades of his life in this city. By 300 CE, his books were in a poor state but they were lovingly restored by the priest Pamphilus, who was in charge of the episcopal library of the Caesarean church. In this task he was assisted by his adopted son Eusebius, who later himself became the church's bishop.

Eusebius is the most famous and influential of the early historians of the Christian Church. Much of his celebrated *Ecclesiastical History* is based on resources that were available to him in the episcopal library. Philo is discussed on two occasions, both in book 2. In the first passage, Philo is introduced as a distinguished scholar of Jewish descent who displayed particular enthusiasm for the philosophy of Plato and Pythagoras (*Hist. eccl.* 2.4.3). He is then cited as a witness to the disastrous events that happened to the Jews soon after the death of Jesus 'on account of what they had perpetrated against the Christ' (2.5.6). Quotations are given from Josephus[27] and the *Legatio ad Gaium* that illustrate Philo's role in events that occurred during the reign of Caligula. These latter passages have been analysed by S. Inowlocki, who concludes that Eusebius, although he quotes verbatim, can be quite 'manipulative … when he wishes to use a text for his own theological and historical views which do not correspond to the ideology of the original author', that is, Philo.[28]

A more extensive account of Philo's role in the history of the early Church is given when Eusebius turns to the beginnings of Christianity in Alexandria. Here he makes his famous claim that Philo's account of the Therapeutae in his *De vita contemplativa* actually describes the first Christians in Egypt who had been converted by the apostle Mark:

They say that this person [Mark] was the first to be sent to preach in Egypt the Gospel which he himself had written, and that he was also the first to establish churches in Alexandria itself. Indeed, so great was the number of men and

---

27   *AJ* 18.257–60, the only time that Josephus mentions Philo.
28   'The Reception of Philo's *Legatio ad Gaium* in Eusebius of Caesarea's Works', *StPhAnn* 16 (2004), pp. 30–49, quote on p. 49.

women who came to believe there at the first attempt and they showed such a philosophic and rigorous asceticism that Philo thought it right to give an account of their practices, assemblies, feasts and all the rest of their way of life (*Hist. eccl.* 2.16).

This claim, inspired by certain phrases in Philo's account (e.g., the term *monastērion* at *Contempl.* 25), was to resonate down the ages and become a standard feature of ancient and medieval accounts of the origins of monasticism. The entire passage (*Hist. eccl.* 2.16–17), which occupies several pages, is cast in a rhetorical mode, seeking to persuade the reader that the account must refer to early Christians,[29] for example, that the weekly feasts of the Therapeutae are a reference to the Eucharist, and so on. At the end Eusebius encourages his readers to look at Philo's account themselves, and this induces him to append a chapter in which he gives a fuller account of Philo's writings. The list he gives is certainly based on the holdings of the episcopal library and mentions all the treatises that are still extant with only four exceptions. A century later Jerome informs us that a later successor to the Caesarean see, Bishop Euzoius, rescued Philo's treatises by having them transferred to parchment codices.[30]

But there is another work of a more explicitly apologetic kind in which Eusebius demonstrates his detailed knowledge of Philo's works. In his *Praeparatio evangelica*, a huge compilation in fifteen books, Eusebius attempts to show that there is an essential harmony between the doctrines of Christianity and what is best in Greek and, to a lesser extent, Hellenistic Jewish culture. On thirteen occasions Eusebius gives literal quotations from Philo's writings, three of which preserve the Greek text that otherwise has been lost. Four topics stand out: (1) the account of the early history of the Jews given in the lost *Hypothetica*; (2) texts on the 'second cause', that is, the Logos; (3) extracts from *De opificio* on the role of the Ideas in the creation of the cosmos, in which a Platonic theory is attributed to Moses; and (4) texts on the role of providence, which Eusebius sees as working on behalf of the Christian Church, just

---

29 See further the detailed analysis of S. Inowlocki, 'Eusebius of Caesarea's *Interpretatio Christiana* of Philo's *De vita contemplativa*', *HThR* 97 (2004), pp. 305–28.

30 See my account in *Philo in Early Christian Literature*, pp. 16–24, where I also discuss the remarkable text in the form of a cross in a Philonic manuscript, which reads: 'Bishop Euzoius had new copies made in codices,' confirming Jerome's report (*Vir. ill.* 113). Euzoius was bishop from about 376 to 379. See also A.J. Carriker, *The Library of Eusebius* (Leiden 2003), pp. 164–77.

as Philo had seen it operating in favor of the Jews.[31] In a manner consistent with this work, elsewhere in his writings Eusebius continues the emphasis on the role of Christ as the Logos, the image of God and the 'second cause' in the work of creation, combining themes from Philo, Origen, and Middle Platonism. Through his teacher, Pamphilus, who had studied in Alexandria, Eusebius continues the Alexandrian tradition, which reserved an honorable place for Philo. What makes Eusebius' treatment of Philo distinctive compared to that of his predecessors is that he is the first to emphasize and articulate the role that Philo played in the continuity existing between Alexandrian Judaism and Alexandrian Christianity.[32]

By the fourth century, therefore, Philo had gained a modest foothold in the Christian tradition. As a Jew his position was tenuous. His contribution could be affirmed, or it could be contested and rejected. Both responses to Philo's work occurred in different parts of the Christian world outside Alexandria.

The Cappadocian brothers, Basil of (Cappadocian) Caesarea and Gregory of Nyssa, did not study in Alexandria. The former got his training in Constantinople and Athens; the latter sat at the feet of his brother. But they were both followers of Athanasian orthodoxy and to some extent they take over characteristic methods and themes of Alexandrian theology. Basil only mentions Philo once, in a text that A. Kamesar has shown to allude to his purported authorship of the Wisdom of Solomon.[33] There is no reference to Philo in his important work, the *Homilies on the Hexaemeron*, often regarded as the beginning of the so-called Hexaemeral literature (exegesis of the creation account in Genesis), but it is clear that Basil had absorbed the contents of Philo's *De opificio* and could draw on this material when preparing his sermons.[34]

The presence of Philo in the impressive *oeuvre* of Gregory of Nyssa is much more extensive. Gregory follows in the footsteps of his brother by incorporating much Philonic material in his two Hexaemeral treatises,

31 Brief analysis in my *Philo in Early Christian Literature*, pp. 222–5; more detailed analysis in S. Inowlocki, *Eusebius and the Jewish Authors: His Citation Technique in an Apologetic Context* (Leiden 2006).

32 The point is well made by Inowlocki, 'Eusebius of Caesarea's *Interpretatio Christiana*', p. 328.

33 'San Basilio, Filone, e la tradizione ebraica', *Henoch* 17 (1995), pp. 129–40. The passage in question is *Ep.* 190.3.

34 See my *Philo in Early Christian Literature*, pp. 236–40, and now the apparatus to E. Amand de Mendieta and S. Y. Rudberg's edition of Basilius von Caesarea, *Homilien zum Hexaemeron* (Berlin 1997 = GCS N.F. 2).

De opificio hominis and *Apologia in Hexaemeron*.[35] But he also explicitly links Philo with the theological views of the Neo-Arian Eunomius, against whom he wrote no less than four voluminous works. Gregory accuses his opponent of stealing material from unwitting earlier authors, including Philo, who is explicitly called 'the Hebrew'. Many pages later Gregory gives an example of what Eunomius took, a statement on Philo's part that 'God is anterior to all beings that are generated'. The relevance of this to doctrinal controversy on the second person of the Trinity is obvious. Puzzlingly no such text can be found in Philo, though the sentiment is Philonic enough.[36] The most interesting text for our purposes, however, is Gregory's *De vita Moysis*, which is the only patristic work to carry the same Latin title as a Philonic work (apart from the *Quaestiones* literature).[37] A.C. Geljon has recently published a monograph in which he makes a full-scale comparison of the two treatises. It emerges that, although Philo's treatise plays a role in the background, Gregory's intentions differ quite markedly. He wishes not so much to give an apologetic presentation of Moses' life as to show how it can function as a model for a life of excellence (*aretē*). For this purpose Philo's allegories, mainly drawn from other works, provide excellent material because of the philosophical language which they speak.[38]

A quite different perspective is gained if we turn to Gregory's younger contemporary Theodore of Mopsuestia. Born in Antioch in about 350, Theodore joined a group of scholars and ascetics in his native city centered around the exegete Diodore of Tarsus. These men developed a distinctive style of exegesis associated with the Antiochene school. Its main distinguishing characteristic was the wholesale rejection of all forms of allegorical exegesis. Preference was given to the literal or 'factual' meaning of Scripture or, in cases where this was insufficient, to typological exegesis. In a fascinating text preserved only in a Syriac translation, Theodore launches an attack on Origen, in which he accuses Origen of rejecting what Christ himself and the apostle Paul teach about biblical interpretation. Instead Origen learned his method from a Jew, that is, Philo, who had been instructed in 'outside learning' and introduced the

---

35 See my *Philo in Early Christian Literature*, pp. 251–6.
36 See further my *Philo in Early Christian Literature*, pp. 244–9; and on the philosophical and theological issues M.R. Barnes, 'Eunomius of Cyzicus and Gregory of Nyssa: Two Traditions of Transcendent Causality', *VC* 52 (1998), pp. 59–87.
37 In reality the Greek titles were almost certainly different; see A.C. Geljon, *Philonic Exegesis in Gregory of Nyssa's De vita Moysis* (Providence 2002), pp. 63–4.
38 Geljon, *Philonic Exegesis*; see esp. the conclusions at pp. 159–74.

allegorical method from the pagans, mistakenly believing that he could use it to defend Scripture, whereas he in fact falsifies it and makes it similar to pagan myths.[39] Theodore appears to have more information about Philo than he could have gleaned from Origen himself, who, as we saw, usually refers to his predecessor only obliquely. His negative view of Philo can be contrasted with the positive view found in Didymus. The two exegetes neatly represent the gulf that separates the Alexandrian and the Antiochene schools of biblical interpretation.

In the western part of the empire there is no evidence for knowledge and use of Philo's writings before the fourth century.[40] But toward its end we encounter the most remarkable case of all. No Christian author ever made more extensive borrowings from Philo than Ambrose, bishop of Milan – they have been estimated as above 600 in number. Yet there is but one single (and in fact rather critical) mention of Philo by name in his whole corpus of writings (and about seven anonymous references). Ambrose thus continues the Clementine practice of quiet plagiarism and in fact takes it to a new height. In five exegetical treatises, mainly on the interpretation of Genesis, his usage is so extensive that the Philonic material can be regarded as the basic framework on which his own exegesis is draped.[41] In a number of letters he uses the same method but on a lesser scale.[42] Unlike the Antiochenes, Ambrose embraces allegorical exegesis and he mines Philo as a valuable exegetical resource. At the same time he is well aware that Philo is a Jew and is ever vigilant in what he takes over. Sometimes censorship is applied; at other times the material is reworked so that it conforms with Christian orthodoxy. The various procedures used by the bishop are expertly analysed by

39 The text is an extract from a brief *Treatise against the Allegorists*, pp. 14–16; it is found in L. Van Rompay's French translation in my *Philo in Early Christian Literature*, p. 267. For its importance see also above, ch. 3, pp. 73, 76, 79–80, 84.
40 Except perhaps the Latin translation of the Muratorian Canon, on which see my *Philo in Early Christian Literature*, p. 276. There are no certain references to Philo in Tertullian.
41 The treatises are: *De paradiso, De Cain et Abel, De Noe, De Abraham* II, *De fuga saeculi*. It should be noted that the Latin translation of *QG* book 6 (in the original numbering) and *De vita contemplativa* was probably made in Italy at about the same time as Ambrose was writing his treatises. The translation is of inferior quality, but was influential in the Middle Ages under the name *Liber Philonis*. See the fine edition of F. Petit, *L'ancienne version latine des Questions sur la Genèse de Philon d'Alexandrie*, I–II (Berlin 1973).
42 See my *Philo in Early Christian Literature*, pp. 293–4.

H. Savon.[43] We shall return to Ambrose's critical attitude toward Philo at the end of the chapter.

Ambrose's slightly younger contemporary Jerome also betrays a considerable acquaintance with Philo and his writings. Indeed he can be regarded as the Latin Eusebius. Jerome includes Philo as one of only three non-Christians in his compendium of famous men, *De viris illustribus* (the other two are Seneca and Josephus). The notice contains biographical details (including the theory about the Therapeutae) and a list of Philonic works based on the list in Eusebius' *Ecclesiastical History*. This raises the question of how much he actually knows about Philo. Scholars have been skeptical about Jerome's claims to polymathic knowledge. But detailed examination of his references to Philo, which refer often to exegetical themes, show that they cannot all be at second hand.[44] Nevertheless it is plain that his interest in Philo is mainly historical rather than exegetical or theological.

The opposite is the case for Augustine, who was impressed by Ambrose's sermons and their use of spiritual exegesis while he was living in Milan (*Conf.* 6.6), before he returned to North Africa. Augustine certainly knows of Philo, because in one of the most interesting patristic passages that refer to him he calls him 'a certain Philo, a man of exceedingly great learning, belonging to the group of the Jews, whose style the Greeks do not hesitate to match with that of Plato'.[45] He then explains Philo's interpretation of Noah's ark in terms of the structure of the human body. This is fine as it goes, but, Augustine claims, when he gets to the openings of the ark, he interprets them as symbols of the lower parts of the body, through which its effluents pass. This interpretation is unworthy of Scripture. The reason Philo goes astray is because he, as a Jew, was ignorant of Christ and did not perceive that the openings indicate the sacraments of the Church flowing from his side. The Philonic text to which Augustine refers is found in *Quaestiones in Genesim* 2.1–7. A huge amount of scholarly ink has been expended on the question of whether this is based on a direct knowledge of that text, perhaps in a Latin translation, or has been derived at second hand, perhaps via Ambrose. On balance direct acquaintance is likely.[46] Elsewhere in Augustine's voluminous works Philonic themes occur, in relation to the doctrine of creation and the interpretation of the early history of humankind, and

---

43 *Saint Ambroise devant l'exégèse de Philon le Juif*, I–II (Paris 1977).

44 See my *Philo in Early Christian Literature*, pp. 312–19.

45 *Faust.* 12.39; full translation in my *Philo in Early Christian Literature*, p. 322. The final part of the quoted phrase refers to the proverb 'either Plato philonizes or Philo platonizes', also found in Jerome, *Vir. ill.* 11.

46 As I argue in *Philo in Early Christian Literature*, p. 324.

also in the theological exegesis of the relationship between the divine pronouncements in Exod 3:14 and 15. It can even be argued that the central insight of the antithesis between the two cities in *De civitate Dei* goes back at least in part to the biblical pairs of Abel–Cain, Sarah–Hagar, Israel–Ishmael in Philo's grand allegorical scheme.[47] But in all of these cases the original themes are thoroughly transformed through Augustine's unrivaled theological genius.[48]

The story could be continued further into the fifth century and beyond. Philo continues to be referred to in the writings of the Church Fathers, but the number of references decreases. Cyril of Alexandria, for example, stands firmly in the Alexandrian tradition, but in all his writings he never refers to Philo. Perhaps his strongly anti-Jewish stance causes him to hold back. Theodoret of Cyrrhus seems indebted to Philo for the method and some of the content of his biblical treatises in the form of *Quaestiones*, but he mentions Philo's name only once.[49] It should not be concluded, however, that the influence of Philonic thought necessarily lessens. In many cases themes from his exegesis and theology have been absorbed into the tradition and authors who use them may not even be aware of their ultimate provenance.[50]

I do not wish to end this account without mentioning three remarkable compilations, each of which use a different method. The first is the *Catenae on Genesis and on Exodus*, a vast collection of exegetical excerpts from patristic authors. The indefatigable editor of these two works, F. Petit, has argued persuasively that they are the work of a single compiler, working in the second half of the fifth century at the earliest, who remains resolutely anonymous behind his collection.[51] In the *Catena on Genesis* Philo stands out as the only Jewish author included (aside from extracts taken from the *Book of Jubilees*); in the *Catena on Exodus*, Josephus is used as well. Nearly one hundred excerpts are included, almost all from the *Quaestiones*. The most striking feature of this work is the way in which it refers to Philo.

47   J.P. Martín, 'Philo and Augustine, *De civitate Dei* XIV 28 and XV: Some Preliminary Observations', *StPhAnn* 3 (1991), pp. 283–94.

48   See my discussion in *Philo in Early Christian Literature*, pp. 324–30; also *Philo and the Church Fathers*, pp. 1–7.

49   See A. Kamesar, *Jerome, Greek Scholarship, and the Hebrew Bible* (Oxford 1993), pp. 92–3; Philo is mentioned at *Quaest. Ex.* 24.

50   Space precludes me from discussing Philo's fate in Byzantium; see the inadequate remarks in *Philo in Early Christian Literature*, p. 271, where it is noted that in the 6th century Armenian Christians, probably living in the capital, translated a substantial part of the Philonic corpus.

51   *La Chaîne sur la Genèse*, I–IV (Leuven 1992–1997); *La Chaîne sur l'Exode*, I–IV (Leuven 1999–2001).

It vacillates between heading the excerpts with the words 'Philo the Hebrew' and 'Philo the bishop', with the latter used more often.[52] The latter epithet, found only here in the patristic tradition, is puzzling. It appears to indicate the total christianization of Philo, yet it is incompatible with the other title. The second work is the *Commentary on the Octateuch* by Procopius of Gaza, compiled around 500 CE. This work is related to the *Catenae*, and it too contains a great amount of Philonic material, but here it is never attributed to him explicitly and is very difficult to extract from the whole.[53] The final work takes us to the eighth century. It is the *Sacra parallela* of John of Damascus, a vast anthology of excerpts from Scripture, patristic authors, Philo and Josephus, organized by subject in three large books on God, the human being, and the virtues and vices. The work has never been fully edited, but according to one report Philo is third on the list of authors most cited, after two of the Cappadocian Fathers.[54] For Philonic scholars, these excerpts have proved a gold mine for research on Philo's text and for lost fragments of his writings. For our purposes it is a final piece of evidence to show how Philo and his writings had been fully absorbed into the Christian tradition.

III. WHY WAS PHILO ACCEPTED IN THE CHRISTIAN TRADITION?

The account given above shows that there are three main reasons for Philo's survival and success in the Christian tradition.

The first is the role that he played as a *historian* and as an *apologist* for the Jewish tradition. Christians were aware that he was a contemporary of Jesus and the apostles, and that his writings recorded events that occurred at that time. In particular Eusebius' use of Philo as a witness for the beginnings of both the Alexandrian church and of Egyptian monasticism was very influential. In a more negative vein, Philo's writings also showed that the troubles of the Jews commenced very soon after Jesus' crucifixion, for example, in the pogrom that afflicted the Alexandrian Jewish community only ten years later. But Philo also provided

---

52 I give a list for the *Catena on Genesis* in my review of Petit's edition in *StPhAnn* 11 (1999), pp. 115–17.

53 A modern edition is lacking; the edition in PG 87 is based on a number of older editions and is incomplete.

54 As reported by J. R. Royse, *The Spurious Texts of Philo of Alexandria: A Study of Textual Transmission and Corruption with Indexes to the Major Collections of Greek Fragments* (Leiden 1991), p. 27 n. 4; see pp. 26–39 for a good introduction to the work (and other anthologies) and Philo's presence in them.

information about the earlier history of the Jewish people, for example, on the patriarchs and Moses. In particular his *De vita Mosis* appears to have enjoyed considerable popularity.[55] This information could be used for apologetic purposes, as for example in Clement's *Stromateis*. The history of the Jews, it is claimed, is ancient and respectable, ante-dating Greek history. Philo's works can also be used to demonstrate that the doctrines of Greek philosophy are already present in Scripture.

The second reason is Philo's value as an *exegete* and *interpreter* of Scripture. Most of his writings are commentaries of one kind or another on Scripture. From the outset Christian authors found them a most valuable repository of scriptural exegesis, in particular for the Pentateuch, the first five books of the Bible on which Philo concentrates. A number of authors such as Clement, Origen, Didymus, and Ambrose make very extensive use of his exegetical material, taking over not only numerous motifs, but also approving of and exploiting his interpretative methods. The allegorical method of interpreting Scripture in terms of an underlying physical, moral, and spiritual sense was introduced to Christianity through Hellenistic Judaism, and particularly Philo. Origen states this plainly in his defense of Christianity against the pagan Celsus. An interesting example of the positive attitude taken by Christian writers in relation to Philo is found in an off-hand comment by Didymus in his *Commentary on Genesis* 5:3–5:

> This is the explanation given of the passage for the moment. But if someone should be interested in the number of the years and in the interpretation of the names of the people born, Philo could give a mystical explanation devoid of pedantry. Consult him, therefore, for it will be useful. (ed. Nautin, II, pp. 13–14)

Philo is a useful exegetical resource, providing material that can help to fathom the deeper meaning of Scripture through the arithmological interpretation of numbers and the allegorical interpretation of biblical names. But not all Christians were so positive. The school of Antioch was strongly opposed to the appropriation of Philo's methods, and Augustine criticizes Philonic exegesis for its lack of christological awareness.

The third reason is Philo's role as *theologian* and *philosopher*. From Clement onward, if not before, Christian writers were well aware of the Platonist coloring of Philo's thought and his positive, if selective, attitude to Greek philosophy in general. They showed their approval through the way that they assumed this same attitude. The chief doctrines in which Philo exerted his influence were the ontological and

---

55 It is the only Philonic work of which we know that it was cited, albeit anonymously, by a pagan author, the late novelist Heliodorus, who paraphrases *Mos.* 2.195 in *Aethiopica* 9.9.3.

epistemological transcendence of God as expressed above all in negative theology, the figure of the Logos as quasi-independent but not separated from God, the creation of the cosmos and of the human being in the image of God, the progress of the virtuous soul and its path toward spiritual perfection and rest in God. Many of these ideas were simply absorbed into the Christian tradition and in time their origin was hardly even noticed. In some cases, however, they remained controversial, particularly in the case of the doctrine of the Logos. On this central point of Christian doctrine it was inevitable that Philo, as a Jew, would be treated with suspicion.

In quantitative terms, by far the greatest number of explicit references to Philo's writings occur in the area of exegesis and allegorical interpretation. It would be an error, however, to separate this usage too strictly from the others. In fact, with the exception of the historical use of his writings, all the other kinds of appropriation are interconnected. Much of Philo's exegesis is regarded as attractive precisely because it offers biblical interpretation with theological and philosophical depth. The tools of allegory, etymology, and arithmology help to make this possible. Moreover, the discovery of theological and philosophical doctrine in the text of Scripture itself was seen as an invaluable apologetic triumph, even if in our historically minded perspective it seems dubious at best. This is the reason that Eusebius also included Philonic material on creation, the ideas and the Logos in his *Praeparatio evangelica*, the most extensive apologetic work that survives from the early Christian period.

IV. CONCLUSION: A JEW IN THE CHRISTIAN TRADITION

In this chapter we have seen how and why Philo's writings were preserved in the Christian tradition. As Didymus, faithful representative of the Alexandrian tradition tells his reader, they are worth consulting because they are 'useful'.[56] This was the fundamental reason that they are still, for the most part, extant. It may seem in retrospect as if the preservation of Philo's writings was an inevitable outcome of the development of Christian exegesis and theology, but I believe that this was not the case. In fact, it can be argued that it took place against considerable odds.

Firstly, it would not have happened were it not for the remarkable dedication of at least five Christians who took care to preserve the material remains of Philo's works from destruction: Pantaenus in the Alexandrian Catechetical school; Origen, who ensured that his library

56   See the quotation above on p. 227.

was taken to Caesarea; Pamphilus, Eusebius, and Euzoius, who cared for the books once they were in the episcopal library, although they could not save them all.[57]

Secondly, we must never lose sight of the fact that Philo was a Jew and was recognized as such, despite some of the wilder speculations of the legend of Philo Christianus. A number of texts show that by the fourth century, as relations between Christians and Jews became ever more contentious, Philo's Jewishness was a source of controversy. As we saw, Gregory of Nyssa associates Philo's theology with the heretical views of Eunomius, although he regards him as an unwitting victim of the latter's plagiarism.[58] In a most interesting little text discovered by Savon,[59] we see how Ambrose adopts a critical attitude toward Philo, in spite of the vast borrowings he makes from his writings:

Philo, *De sacrificiis* 65	Ambrose, *De Cain et Abel* 1.8.32
For God spoke and acted together, placing no interval between the two. But if one should put forward a more truly phrased doctrine, the word (*logos*) was his deed (*ergon*).	God gives swiftly, since he spoke, and action took place, he ordered, and creation took place. For the word of God is not, as someone asserts, his product (*opus*), but is in activity (*operans*), as you find written …

In fact Ambrose misunderstands Philo because he interprets the word *ergon* as 'product', whereas Philo means 'deed'. The reason for the mistake can only be that he is on the lookout for expressions that might be used to support the Arian position that the Logos was created and thus was subordinate to God the Father. In other words, Philo as an author is under suspicion. Another critical voice is that of Theodore of Mopsuestia, who in his polemic against Origen the allegorist explicitly states that he learned his interpretative method from Philo the Jew. A fascinating letter of Isidore of Pelusium, however, explicitly defends Philo:

I admire the truth for the way in which she has induced the souls of intelligent men to combat even the preconceived opinion they have of their own doctrines.

57   In his list in *Hist. eccl.* 2.18, Eusebius mentions a number of books that we no longer possess, including the full text of the *Quaestiones*. The manuscript mentioned above in n. 30 indicates that three books of the *Quaestiones in Exodum* were probably already lost in the 4th century, so were not available to the Armenian translators in the 6th century; see further my *Philo in Early Christian Literature*, pp. 20–2.

58   See above, p. 222. It should be noted that Gregory calls Philo 'the Hebrew'. This epithet has a more positive connotation than 'the Jew', which is first used in our extant sources in the second half of the 4th century; see further D. T. Runia, 'Philonic Nomenclature', in *Philo and the Church Fathers*, pp. 25–53, esp. 39–45.

59   *Saint Ambroise*, p. 120.

For the teaching of the truth has embedded the concept of the holy Trinity so clearly and lucidly, also in the Old Testament, for those who wish to observe it that Philo, though a Jew and a zealous one at that, in the writings which he left behind comes into conflict with his own religion. When he examined the words spoken by God, 'in the image of God I made man' (Gen 9:6), he is constrained and compelled by the truth also to recognize the divine Logos as God. What is the case? Even if he calls him who is coeternal with the Father 'second' and 'higher than number and time', failing therein to reach precision, nevertheless he did gain a conception of another person.[60]

There is thus no doubt that Philo is a Jew, but one who has seen more of the truth of Christian theology than his co-religionists. Isidore stands in the Alexandrian tradition and, instead of criticizing Philo for making statements that are unorthodox and possibly heretical, he commends him for understanding as much as he does.

It may be concluded, therefore, that if the writings of Philo the Jew had first re-emerged in the fourth century, in the contentious anti-heretical and anti-Jewish atmosphere of the post-Nicean Church, there is a good chance that they would have been rejected. But fortunately for us they were first preserved in the second century, at a time when the Christian Church was still building up its intellectual capital. For that purpose, Philo was useful, as Didymus tells us.

60   *Ep.* 2.143; translation in my *Philo and the Church Fathers*, p. 161.

9   Philo and Rabbinic Literature

I. INTRODUCTION

Most scholars agree that there is a significant relationship between Philo and rabbinic literature, yet one looks in vain for an explicit reference to him in that vast corpus of writings. If the Rabbis were aware of his voluminous *oeuvre* and made occasional use of his teachings, the fact remains, nevertheless, that their attitude to this Alexandrian Jewish sage was at best ambivalent. The reasons for this are not difficult to discern, and may readily be glimpsed by examining the evaluation of Philo made by Azariah de' Rossi, the most influential forerunner of the modern science of Judaism, who, in the sixteenth century, redis-covered for the Jewish world the virtually forgotten Philo. Although de' Rossi greatly appreciated Philo's philosophical ability, his highly ambivalent attitude toward him is clearly revealed in a number of criti-cisms that revolve around Philo's ignorance of Hebrew and Aramaic, his belief in the eternity of matter, his allegorization of Scripture, and his deviation from Palestinian halakhah. 'This last charge', he said, 'is weighty enough to sink him like lead into bottomless waters. ... you will not come across any indication that he took upon himself the Oral Tradition alongside the Written Torah.'[1] In arguing this point, de' Rossi cites numerous examples of Philo's adherence to the literal interpreta-tion of Pentateuchal laws in contradiction to the rabbinic understand-ing of them. He thus refused to decide whether Philo's work is 'pure or impure', and although he would not refer to Philo as Rabbi or *hakham*, because he detected sectarian or Essene–Boethusian proclivities in him, neither would he condemn him as a heretic, preferring to call him instead Yedidyah the Alexandrian and treating him merely as one of the sages of the non-Jewish world.

    The lack of explicit rabbinic engagement with Philo has been variously explained. H.-F. Weiss thought that the Rabbis gave Philo the

---

1   *The Light of the Eyes*, translated and annotated by J. Weinberg (New Haven 2001), pp. 140–1.

silent treatment ('Totschweigen'), while D.T. Runia suggested that the Rabbis were encouraged to reject him because his thought had been exploited by prominent Christian thinkers such as Clement, Origen, and Eusebius, a response analogous to their rejection of the Septuagint.[2] However, although the Septuagint began to fall into disfavor among Jews in the second century CE, having been displaced by Aquila's radical revision of it, we nevertheless find it positively evaluated in *b. Meg.* 9a, according to which it was a divinely inspired translation, and in *y. Meg.* 1.17, 71d, where the translators are called 'sages'. With regard to Philo, on the other hand, there is virtually no real response to his meditations on Scripture. The most likely reason for this, it would seem, was due to his writing in Greek, and perhaps more important, his utter reliance on the Septuagint and lack of recourse to the Hebrew original. The Rabbis never mention any of the Hellenistic Jewish writers who wrote in Greek, including even Josephus who had originally composed his account of the Jewish war against the Romans in his 'ancestral language', presumably Aramaic (*BJ* 1.3). They could hardly credit the exegetical work of one who could not read Scripture in the original. Moreover, the Rabbis were essentially uninterested in Philo's philosophical approach, indifferent as they were to all philosophical speculation generally.[3]

In spite of the fact that Philo is never mentioned by name in rabbinic literature, some echoes of his thought are clearly discernible. Numerous scholars have noted the similarity between the image used by R. Hoshaia of Caesarea in *Genesis Rabbah* 1.1 and Philo's striking image of the founding of the city in *De opificio mundi* 17–18. Hoshaia, a Palestinian Amora of the third century, offers the following comment on Gen 1:1:

And I was with him as a nursling (*amon*) [Fox takes *amon* as an infinitive absolute and translates: 'growing up' ('*amoning*', as it were)], *and I was his delight day by day* (Prov 8:30). *Amon* is a craftsman (*uman*). The Torah declares: 'I was the instrument of the Blessed Holy One.' In human practice, when a mortal king builds a palace, he builds it not from his own knowledge alone but uses the knowledge of a craftsman. And the craftsman does not build it from his own knowledge alone, but has rolls (*diphtherai*) and tablets (*pinakes*) so that he may

2 Weiss, *Untersuchungen zur Kosmologie des hellenistischen und paläs-tinischen Judentums* (Berlin 1966), p. 319; Runia, *Philo in Early Christian Literature: A Survey* (Assen 1993), pp. 14–15.

3 On the rabbinic attitude to philosophy, see the perceptive article of W.Z. Harvey, 'Rabbinic Attitudes toward Philosophy', in H.J. Blumberg et al. (eds.), *"Open Thou Mine Eyes ..."*: *Essays on Aggadah and Judaica Presented to Rabbi William G. Braude on His Eightieth Birthday* (Hoboken, NJ 1992), pp. 83–101.

know how to make the chambers and wicket doors. So too did God look into the Torah and create the world, while the Torah says, *In the beginning* (*bereshit*, i.e. with *reshit*) *God created* (1:1), *reshit* referring to the Torah, as in the verse, *The Lord made me as the beginning* (*reshit*) *of his way* (Prov 8:22).[4]

De' Rossi was the first to recognize the close affinity between Hoshaia's midrashic interpretation and Philo's conception of the Logos as the instrument of God in creation. Interestingly, he already connected Philo's conception of the Logos, or the noetic cosmos, with the Kabbalistic doctrine of the world of emanations or *sefirot*. Moreover, W. Bacher, following a lead provided by the pioneering Jewish historian H. Graetz, plausibly suggested that very likely it was the Church Father Origen, who had settled in Caesarea in 231 after being expelled from the church of Alexandria and who was profoundly influenced by Philo, who was Hoshaia's intermediate source.[5]

E. E. Urbach, however, has argued that

R. Hoshaia's homily contains not the slightest reference to the world of Ideas or to the location of the Ideas. In the analogy, 'the architect does not plan the building in his head, but he makes use of rolls and tablets' – a fact that Philo carefully refrained from mentioning, because it contradicted his purpose in adducing the analogy. ... The Torah [in which God looked] ... contains no forms and sketches of temples, gymnasia, markets and harbours, and this Torah is not a concept but the concrete Torah with its precepts and statutes, which are inscribed in letters. Out of those letters and not from numbers ... are the utterances with which the Almighty created the world constructed.[6]

It should be pointed out, however, that the first chapter of Genesis does indeed contain a broad outline of the structure of the universe, which could be seen by the homilist as the intelligible pattern employed by the divine architect. It is perfectly clear from the passage in *Legum allegoriae* 3.97–9, which is generally thought to reproduce material from Aristotle's *De philosophia* (fr. 13 Ross, *apud* Cicero, *Nat. D.* 2.95–6), that the parallel to the entrances, colonnades, and all of the other buildings of the analogy, are the heavens revolving in a circle and containing all things within

---

4   M. V. Fox's translation (modified) in his Anchor Bible commentary on Proverbs 1–9 (New York 2000), p. 286.
5   'The Church Father, Origen, and Rabbi Hoshaya', *JQR* 3 (1890/1891), pp. 357–60. Bacher also points to a dialogue on circumcision that the Rabbi held with a 'philosopher', which 'here and elsewhere (*b. Shabb.* 116a) means a representative of Christianity' (*Gen. Rab.* 11.6). Cf. L. Wächter, 'Der Einfluss platonischen Denkens auf rabbinische Schöpfungsspekulationen', *Zeitschrift für Religions- und Geistesgeschichte* 14 (1962), pp. 36–56.
6   *The Sages: Their Concepts and Beliefs* (Jerusalem 1979), p. 200.

them – the earth, streams of water and air in between, living things, and varieties of plants and crops. As for the Rabbi's obliterating the main object of Philo's analogy – which was to show that, just as the city prefigured in the architect's mind held no place externally but was stamped within, so too the intelligible world could have no other location than the divine Logos – it is quite clear that what had caught the fancy of R. Hoshaia in Philo's analogy was the figure of the architect and his use of a plan for the construction of the city that he was commissioned to design. Philo's polemic with some Middle Platonists, who probably still maintained that the intelligible Forms were independent of the demiurge and were perhaps located in some sort of *hyperouranios topos* or supercelestial realm (so taken by Xenocrates, *apud* Sextus Empiricus, *Math.* 7.147), held no interest for the Rabbi and he therefore ignored that aspect of the analogy. Hoshaia was only anxious to show that the Torah was God's architectural plan, and unlike Philo, writing for fellow Palestinian Jews, he could take it for granted that the Torah was itself a product of the divine mind. Moreover, there is no reference in the Rabbi's homily to God's employment of the letters of the Torah as his instrument of creation. It is only stated that the Holy One looked into the Torah, as an architect consulting his plans, and created the world.[7]

---

7   Runia has suggested that Hoshaia's image tries to correct its model by emphasizing that the architect uses *written* plans, i.e., the pre-existent Torah, and not the mental design placed by Philo in the divine Logos. See his commentary on Philo of Alexandria, *On the Creation of the Cosmos* (Leiden 2001), pp. 154–5. It should be noted, however, that the precise nature of the pre-existent Torah that is identified with God's Wisdom is by no means clear. The context of Proverbs 8 seems to point to its identification with some sort of primordial Torah, i.e. the supernal Wisdom of the deity, rather than the written Torah. But the existence of such a notion in rabbinic literature is only attested in the single statement by Rav Avin (4th century) that the Torah is an incomplete form (*novelet*, literally, the fruit falling prematurely off the tree) or inferior likeness of the supernal Wisdom (*Gen. Rab.* 17.5, 44.12). Urbach, *Sages*, pp. 310–11, has noted that the assertion of R. Simon that the Torah of this world is as nought compared with the Torah of the world to come was referring to Torah as *novelet* in the sense of R. Avin's teaching (*Eccl. Rab.* 11.8). Later it becomes a fundamental concept in Kabbalistic literature, where it is designated by the term *Torah kedumah*. For the frequent occurrence of the identification of Torah and Wisdom in rabbinic texts, see G. F. Moore, *Judaism in the First Centuries of the Christian Era*, I (Cambridge, MA 1927), pp. 265–8; and G. Boccaccini, 'The Preexistence of the Torah: A Commonplace in Second Temple Judaism, or a Later Rabbinic Development?', *Henoch* 17 (1995), pp. 329–50. See also the collection of sources in A. J. Heschel, *Torah min ha-shamayim*, II (London 1965), pp. 3–26; and for *novelet*, III (Jerusalem 1990), pp. 49–53.

II. PHILO'S HEBREW

Many of Philo's biblical interpretations were completely dependent on the Septuagint version, which he invariably cites as his starting point. H. A. Wolfson did indeed insist that, in writing for Greek readers, Philo naturally quoted the translation familiar to them, 'even though his knowledge of Hebrew was such that he could himself without too much effort provide his own translation.'[8] While admittedly there is no positive evidence of his knowledge of Hebrew, the burden of proof, according to Wolfson, is upon those who would deny him such knowledge. Yet, although the evidence for Philo's ignorance of Hebrew is only cumulative, it is all but irresistible. A few examples will illustrate Philo's utter dependence on the Greek version of the Bible. Y. Amir has noted that Philo interprets the biblical description of the earth on the first day of creation as being *tohu va-vohu* (Gen 1:2), rendered in the Septuagint 'invisible and unformed' (*aoratos kai akataskeuastos*), as referring to the 'Idea' of the earth, a part of the Platonic intelligible world. This Hebrew expression, however, cannot designate such a higher level of reality.[9] Similarly, D. Gooding has pointed out that in various places, Philo expounds a passage by playing on the etymology of a word in the Septuagint regardless of whether the Hebrew word that it represents has a similar etymology (*Deus* 103). Moreover, where a Greek word had more than one meaning, Philo will sometimes select one of those meanings, regardless of whether the underlying Hebrew word can have the meaning he insists on (*Deus* 168–71).[10] In any case, one of the strongest arguments once relied on in order to demonstrate Philo's knowledge of Hebrew, namely, the many etymologies of Hebrew names adduced by him, has been effectively removed by the discovery of papyrological evidence that makes it evident that Philo, as some had already conjectured earlier, did make use of Greek *onomastica* that provided him with the information he needed for this purpose.[11]

8 *Philo: Foundations of Religious Philosophy in Judaism, Christianity, and Islam* (Cambridge, MA 1948), I, p. 88.
9 Amir, 'Philo and the Bible', *StPhilo* 2 (1973), p. 2.
10 Gooding, 'Philo's Knowledge of the Hebrew Underlying the Greek', in D. Winston and J. Dillon, *Two Treatises of Philo of Alexandria* (Chico, CA 1983), pp. 120–2.
11 See above, ch. 3, pp. 71–2. For a discussion of Philo's characterization of the Septuagint in *Mos.* 2.37–40, see above, ch. 3, pp. 66–71, and D. Winston, 'Aspects of Philo's Linguistic Theory', *StPhAnn* 3 (1991) pp. 117–22. For some reservations, see D. Daube's interesting paper 'Philo's Hebrew: A Hebrew–Greek Pun', in his *Collected Works*, I (Berkeley 1992), pp. 213–18, and the useful summation of the issues involved by S. Sandmel, 'Philo's Knowledge of Hebrew', *StPhilo* 5 (1978), pp. 107 12.

III. PHILO AND RABBINIC MIDRASH

The vehicle for classical Jewish theology in the ancient world was the literary genre of midrash, and it was therefore only natural that Philo elected to expound his philosophy of Judaism in the form of a vast and hugely expansive midrashic interpretation of Scripture. The tendency to treat Philo's *oeuvre* as pure biblical exegesis thus unduly constricts the nature of his literary enterprise. P.S. Alexander captures the special character of midrashic interpretation in the following remarks:

> Midrash is as much a means of imposing ideas upon Scripture as of deriving ideas from Scripture. It often presupposes a body of tradition which grew up independently of Scripture, and which was then related to Scripture and presented in the form of Bible commentary. ... In the Zohar, a full-blown mystical system can be found presented in the form of midrash, but surely no one would suggest that this system emerged naturally, simply from meditation on Scripture. The system grew up independently, and was then forcibly read into Scripture.[12]

In short, to see Philo primarily as an exegete of Scripture *tout court* is quite misleading. He is a Hellenized Jew who has clearly been intellectually seduced by Platonic philosophy, but who nevertheless remained firmly loyal to his Jewish faith and decided to bend every effort to the task of reconciling the two opposing passions driving his spiritual existence. Since in the Judaism of his day it was not systematic exposition, but the midrashic commentary that was the legitimate form through which the truth could be developed, he chose to Platonize his Jewish heritage through that form of commentary.

The persistent problem that has bedeviled most interpreters of Philo is the question of whether similarities between Philo's exegesis and that of the Palestinian rabbinic midrash are a clear indication of his knowledge of that tradition. Opinions on this matter have been sharply divided. Following in the footsteps of S. Belkin, N. G. Cohen, for example, sought to demonstrate that there was an underlying Palestinian/Alexandrian midrashic tradition, both halakhic and aggadic, on which Philo drew. She notes that 'Geza Vermes posited a chain of haggadic tradition whose embryonic form can already be discerned in the later biblical books. ... [and] cogently argued for the existence of a body of interpretative tradition ... common to the Dead Sea Scrolls and later rabbinic midrashic tradition.' At the same time, Cohen emphasizes

---

12   '3 Enoch and the Talmud', *JSJ* 18 (1987), p. 67 n. 26. The scholar who provided the vital impulse for the view of Philo as primarily an exegete of Scripture was V. Nikiprowetzky in his book *Le commentaire de l'Écriture chez Philon d'Alexandrie* (Leiden 1977).

that the thesis put forth by scholars such as Belkin, Vermes, and
B. Bamberger, is not that there is a direct relationship between Philo
and extant midrashic traditions, but that they are dependent upon a
common ancient midrashic pool.[13] The example she adduces and provides with a detailed analysis is the inference made both by Philo and
the Rabbis from the wording of Gen 7:7 and 8:1 that when Noah and
his family entered the ark, the males and females did so separately, but
when they went out they did so as married couples. The reason given
for this is that it is wrong to create new life while all the earth's inhabitants were being destroyed.[14] Cohen's assumption, however, that the
midrashic theme 'cannot be dismissed as obvious and easily deduced
from the biblical verses but must be read into the text' is questionable,
because the peculiar reading of the scriptural text is glaring and might
well be explained in a similar manner by various exegetes who share
similar homiletical concerns.

The subjective nature of such argumentation precludes the possibility
of its proving Philo's dependence on rabbinic sources. The only way out
of this dilemma is to locate a parallelism between Philonic and rabbinic
midrashic interpretations, where the context makes it perfectly clear that
Philo is reading something into the biblical text that clashes with a fundamental philosophical principle firmly held by him. In such case one may
conclude that he is doing so only under the constraint of a well-known
rabbinic tradition that has become deeply entrenched and is profoundly
rooted in the Jewish psyche. A parallelism of this sort can be found in
Philo's doctrine of repentance, which has many points of similarity with
the analogous rabbinic doctrine. Philo is fully aware that the doctrine of
repentance cannot be harmonized with the Stoic ethical thinking that he
espouses, for we find his exposition of it heavily laden with ambivalence
and ultimately unsuccessful in fully assimilating it into his philosophical
theory of the emotions. Yet he nonetheless reads this doctrine into the
scriptural text even when it is not there, after the manner of a similar
Palestinian tradition (*Mekilta* Shirata 5; *Tg. Ps.-J.* Gen 6:3 and 7:4). Thus,
in response to the question 'why, after their entering the ark, did seven
days pass, after which came the flood,' he answers that it was to grant
them repentance of sins (*QG* 2.13; cf. *QG* 1.91). Here we have a clear

---

13 *Philo Judaeus: His Universe of Discourse* (Frankfurt am Main 1995),
    pp. 34–7. See also P. Borgen, 'Philo of Alexandria: A Critical and Synthetical
    Survey of Research Since World War II', *ANRW* II.21.1 (1984), pp. 98–154,
    esp. 124–6: 'Philo and the haggada and halaka'.
14 Cohen, *Philo Judaeus*, pp. 40–65. The primary sources she considers are
    Philo, *QG* 2.49; *Pirke R. El.* 23; *Tanhuma* Noah 11; *b. Sanh.* 108b; *y. Taan*
    1.6, 64d; *Gen. Rab.* 31.12, 34.7

indication that Philo was in possession of Palestinian rabbinic traditions on repentance and, in spite of the enormous flexibility of his exegetical approach to Scripture, was unwilling in this case to disregard what he considered to be a central doctrine, one that he apparently thought defined the Jewish psyche.[15]

IV. PHILO AND THE RABBIS: SIMILARITIES AND CONTRASTS

Comparisons between Philo and the Rabbis are somewhat complicated by the fact that the Rabbis do not always speak with one voice, nor indeed does Philo himself. The Alexandrian exegete tends at times to express himself ambiguously when the issue involved is particularly sensitive and his own reformulation of it entails a radical revision of traditional Jewish views. Failure to recognize this characteristic of Philo's mode of exposition runs the risk of seriously misunderstanding his true intent. Indeed, much of the charm and fascination of Philo's writing lie in the confident daring he displays in his subtle and at times ambiguous exegesis of the biblical text that both he and the Rabbis so revere.[16]

IV.1 God's Transcendent Immanence

In Philo's hierarchical construction of reality, the essence of God, though utterly concealed in its primary being, is nevertheless made manifest on two secondary levels: the Logos or intelligible world of Ideas, which constitutes God's image (*Somn.* 1.239; *Conf.* 147–8), and the sensible universe, which in turn is an image of that image (*Opif.* 25). Philo further delineates the dynamics of the Logos's activity by defining and describing its two constitutive polar principles: goodness or the creative power and sovereignty or the regent power (*Cher.* 27–8). It is through these powers that God's action within the world is manifest. Philo's choice of adjectives for the powers may readily be traced back both to Stoic and rabbinic tradition. The author of the pseudo-Aristotelian work *De mundo* asserted, after the Stoic fashion, that although God is one, He has many names according to the many effects He Himself produces. Among the many names, He is called God of vengeance (*palamnaios*) and of supplication and grace (7, 401a, 23). Moreover, É. Bréhier has pointed out that the Stoic mythographer Cornutus had allegorized the two mythological

15 A full discussion of this theme will be given below, pp. 251–3.
16 See D. Winston, 'Philo and the Contemplative Life', in A. Green (ed.), *Jewish Spirituality from the Bible through the Middle Ages* (New York 1988), pp. 198–201.

figures Justice (*Dike*) and the Graces (*Charites*), interpreting the former as that power of God which exhorts human beings not to wrong one another, while the latter were the sources of grace and beneficence to them. Philo's frequent references to *Dike* as assessor (*paredros*), attendant (*opados*), and guardian (*ephoros*), and to the Graces as the virgin daughters of God, reveal literary reminiscences of Cornutus' interpretations, and it is clear from Seneca (*Ben.* 1.3) that the allegorization of the Graces, at least, goes back to Chrysippus. In short, Philo found the Stoics referring to the various powers of the Logos and offering an elaborate allegorization of the mythological figures that represented the divine attributes of justice and grace. At the same time he found in rabbinic tradition the frequent coupling of God's attributes of justice and mercy, and even their transformation into self-subsistent powers or hypostases.[17]

Philo also frequently emphasizes that God is above both place and time, but though thus transcendent, He has nonetheless 'filled the universe with himself, for he has caused his powers to extend themselves throughout the universe' (*Post.* 14).

He contains but is not contained (*periechontos ou periechomenou*). To be everywhere and nowhere is his property and his alone. He is nowhere, because he himself created space and place coincidently with material things, and it is against all right principle to say that the Maker is contained in anything that he has made (*Conf.* 136).

A reflection of this Philonic concept is evident in the well-known statement by the renowned disciple of R. Akiba, R. Yose b. Halafta (second century CE):

We do not know whether God is the place of his world or whether his world is his place, but from the verse, 'Behold, there is a place with me' (Exod 33:21) it follows that the Lord is the place of his world, but his world is not his place (*Gen. Rab.* 68.9).[18]

R. Yose's rationalistic philosophical orientation is similarly revealed by his deduction from the verse 'the heavens are the heavens of the Lord, but the earth hath he given to the children of men' (Ps 115:16), that 'neither Moses nor Elijah ever went up to heaven, nor did the Glory

17 For sources and references, see D. Winston, *Logos and Mystical Theology in Philo of Alexandria* (Cincinnati 1985), pp. 19–20.
18 See J. Freudenthal, *Hellenistische Studien* 1–2 (Breslau 1875), p. 73; Urbach, *Sages*, pp. 49, 74–5. For the formula 'containing not contained', see W. R. Schoedel, ' "Topological" Theology and Some Monistic Tendencies in Gnosticism', in M. Krause (ed.), *Essays on the Nag Hammadi Texts in Honour of Alexander Böhlig* (Leiden 1972), pp. 88–108.

ever come down to earth' (*Mekilta* Ba-hodesh 4). As Urbach has noted, the extreme form of this dictum is in keeping with the earlier one cited above, and seeks to negate the view that the revelation of God is connected with ascent and descent.

Philo's conception of God's transcendence, however, goes far beyond what is implied by the formula 'containing but not contained', for he fuses the Jewish insistence on God's transcendence (Exod 33:20; Isa 40:18) with Middle Platonic theories of ineffability. His formula for God's supreme transcendence, 'that which is better than the Good, more beautiful than the Beautiful, more blessed than Blessedness, more felicitous than Felicity itself' (*Legat.* 5), represents the *via eminentiae* of the Middle Platonists, Plotinus, and medieval scholasticism.[19] It was this that led Plotinus to 'condemn the folly of seeking to exalt the One by ascribing it a plurality of attributes, since such additions can only mark a diminution of the One's excellence'.[20] Interestingly, the Rabbis similarly remark that

someone who positioned himself to lead the prayer in the presence of R. Haninah said: God the Great, the Valiant, the Terrible, the Mighty, the Strong, the Tremendous, the Powerful. Thereupon R. Haninah said to him: Have you finished all the praises of your Master? Even as regards the first three epithets [used by you] we could not have uttered them if Moses our Master had not pronounced them in the Law [cf. Deut 10:17] and if the men of the Great Synagogue had not subsequently come and established their use in prayer. And you come and say all this. What does this resemble? It is as if a mortal king who had millions of gold pieces were praised for possessing silver (*b. Ber.* 33b; cf. *y. Ber.* 9.1, 12d).[21]

19 In Alcinous' *Handbook of Platonism* 10.6, we find, as J. Dillon puts it in his commentary on that text (Oxford 1993), pp. 109–10, 'a set of three ways to approach the conception of God, that of negation or abstraction (*aphairesis*) ... that of analogy (*analogia*), and a third to which he does not give a clear title, but for which one may derive a title from his concluding characterization of it as having to do with pre-eminence (*hyperochē*). These are customarily given their later names in Latin scholasticism, the *via negationis*, the *via analogiae*, and the *via eminentiae*.' The strongest pre-Neoplatonic assertions of divine unknowability are found in Gnosticism. See R. T. Wallis, 'The Spiritual Importance of Not Knowing', in A. H. Armstrong (ed.), *Classical Mediterranean Spirituality* (New York 1986), pp. 460–80. See also D. T. Runia, 'Eudaemonism in Hellenistic–Jewish Literature', in J. L. Kugel (ed.), *Shem in the Tents of Japhet: Essays on the Encounter of Judaism and Hellenism* (Leiden 2002), pp. 131–57.
20 R. T. Wallis, *Neoplatonism* (London 1972), p. 59, citing *Enn.* 3.8.11.12–13, 5.5.13.9–16.
21 This rabbinic text is cited by Maimonides in *The Guide of the Perplexed* 1.59 (trans. S. Pines, Chicago 1963, p. 140) where he refers to it as a 'famous dictum – would that all dicta were like it'. It is also cited by Bahya ibn Pakuda, *Duties of the Heart* 1.10 (trans. M. Mansoor, London 1973, p. 142).

Although there are various rabbinic statements that open the door for anthropomorphic descriptions of the deity, there are also others that seek to tone them down, as, for example, the statement in *b. Yevam.* 49b, that although 'all the prophets, who saw through the speculum that does not shine, [perceived some form], Moses, who saw through a speculum that shines (*aspaklaria ha-meirah*), [saw no form].'[22] Significantly, however, Philo's sharp philosophical distinction between God's existence, which is knowable, and His essence, which is not, is, as one would expect, not to be found in rabbinic sources.

IV.2 Two Types of Mosaic Prophecy: Predictive/Ecstatic and Noetic

Inasmuch as the issue of divine revelation is at the core of the Mosaic tradition, it is only to be expected that the ambiguity inherent in Philo's analysis of Mosaic prophecy should reflect his deepest ambivalences. The great divide between the biblical and the Greek philosophical view of revelation is ultimately rooted in the fact that, as Amir has aptly put it, 'for the educated Greek the Godhead does not speak *to* man but *within* man.'[23]

In *De vita Mosis* 2.188, Philo enumerates three kinds of divine oracles: the particular laws, spoken by God in His own person with His prophet as interpreter; revelation through question and answer; and predictive prophecies, spoken by Moses in his own person 'when inspired and of himself possessed (*ex hautou kataschethentos*)'. Philo's description of the first and third categories of oracles yields two types of prophecy, ecstatic and hermeneutical or noetic. The one is mediated through possession, the other through the prophet's noetic response to the divine voice, which is regarded by Philo as a figure for rational soul.

Although Philo has deliberately refrained from drawing out the full implications of the two distinctively different modes of Mosaic prophecy referred to by him, his idiosyncratic bifurcation of the prophetic personality is of fundamental significance for a proper understanding of his concept of divine revelation. In sharp contrast to ecstatic prophecy, divine voice or noetic prophecy does not render its recipient passive. Although no separate account is given by Philo of this mode of Mosaic prophecy, we may discern its nature from his description of the giving of the Decalogue, which must serve us as the paradigm for prophecy through the divine voice. God, we are there told, is not as a man needing

22 For further discussion, see E. R. Wolfson, *Through a Speculum that Shines* (Princeton 1994), pp. 20–8.
23 'Philo and the Bible', p. 4.

mouth, tongue, and windpipe. Rather, He created a rational soul full
of clearness and distinctness that shaped the air around it into a flaming fire, sounding forth an articulate voice. This miraculous voice was
activated by the power of God, which created in the souls of all another
kind of hearing far superior to that of the physical organ. The latter is
but a sluggish sense, inactive until aroused by the impact of the air,
but the hearing of the mind possessed by God makes the first advance
and goes out to meet the conveyed meanings with the swiftest speed
(Decal. 35).

It is important to note that what began in this passage as a description of a corporeal phenomenon, air shaped into a flaming fire, sounding
forth an articulate voice, is suddenly and abruptly allegorized by Philo
into one that is incorporeal, a mind-to-mind communication rather
than the perception of a sense organ (cf. QG 1.42). The very fact, however, that he resorts to a rather intricate description of the miraculous
divine voice in purely physical terms, which is then only diverted to the
intelligible level by a last minute maneuver, is a clear indication that
he was attempting to preserve the literal meaning of the biblical text to
the best of his ability.[24]

For the notion of a mind-to-mind communication in order to explain
the divine voice at Sinai, Philo was apparently indebted to the Middle
Platonic tradition.[25] The Platonists had been exercised by the need to
explain the nature of Socrates' famous *daimonion* or sign, and one of
the interpretations recorded by Plutarch is very similar to that adopted
by Philo to explain the divine utterance at Sinai:

What reached Socrates, one would conjecture, was not spoken language, but the
unuttered words of a daemon, making voiceless contact with his intelligence by
their sense alone (Gen. Socr. 20, 588c-d).

It is essential to note that Philo invokes the notion of ecstatic possession only to explain the ability of the prophet to predict the future,
a talent clearly requiring the exclusive services of the Logos because
no finite mind could enjoy such a power (Her. 61; Mos. 2.6). Moses'
promulgation of the particular laws, however, communicated to him

24 Failing to discern the nuanced phrasing of Philo in *Decal.* 35, Amir takes
    this passage at face value, and considers the 'created voice' of God that is
    described there as belonging to the category of the miraculous. He attempts
    to explain this aberrant motif in Philo as deriving from the fact that the
    notion of the 'created voice' was derived by him from an earlier tradition.
    See his book, *Die hellenistische Gestalt des Judentums bei Philon von
    Alexandrien* (Neukirchen-Vluyn 1983), pp. 77–106, esp. 97.
25 See G. Soury, *La démonologie de Plutarque* (Paris 1942), p. 128.

by the divine voice, is understood to involve the active participation of
the prophet's mind. The same is true of the 'ten words,' which summarize the entire law and required the quickened perception of the entire
Israelite nation. In light of the general thrust of Philo's thought (and
especially *Migr.* 76 and 80), it is very likely that he understands noetic
prophecy to refer to the activation of the intuitive intellect, by means of
which one grasps the fundamental principles of universal being viewed
as a unified whole.[26] In Philo's mystical thought, true prophetic power
is rooted in the special intellectual capacities that God has graciously
bestowed on His chosen ones, and of the latter Moses stands out as a
unique exemplar of unsurpassed excellence.

The rabbinic view of Mosaic revelation, on the other hand, appears
to be diametrically opposed to Philo's understanding of it. We read, for
example, in *Gen. Rab.* 8.8:

When Moses was engaged in writing the Torah, he had to write the work of
each day. When he came to the verse, 'And God said, Let us make man,' he said:
Sovereign of the universe! Why do you furnish an excuse to heretics?' 'Write,'
replied he; 'whoever wishes to err may err.'

In contrast to the supremely creative role assigned to Philo's Moses,
the rabbinic Moses is reduced to a mere scribal functionary, who duti-
fully records the words dictated to him, though he is occasionally portrayed as unhappy with the wording imposed upon him. In rabbinic eyes
even if one asserts that the entire Torah is from heaven, with the exception of so much as a single verse that is not uttered by God but derives
instead from Moses himself, such a one is to be included among those
who have 'despised the word of the Lord' (Num 15:31; *b. Sanh.* 99a).
Philo's customary formulaic references to 'Moses said,' when citing biblical verses, are no less numerous, as Amir has duly emphasized, than
the common rabbinic expression 'the Merciful One (*rahmana*) says.'
On the other hand, Philo not infrequently also emphasizes the oracular
character of Scripture. Yet, inasmuch as prophetic inspiration in Philo's
view is noetic, at least when it is of the non-predictive kind, there is no
contradiction in these passages with those in which the emphasis is
on Moses as author. It should be noted, however, that there are hints
in some rabbinic sources that Moses was considerably more independent than the notion of a mere scribe would indicate. Thus, in *b. Meg.*
31b it is said that the curses in Deuteronomy were offered by Moses of

26 For a detailed analysis, see D. Winston, 'Two Types of Mosaic Prophecy
    according to Philo', *Journal for the Study of the Pseudepigrapha* 4 (1989),
    pp. 49–67; 'Philo and the Wisdom of Solomon on Creation, Revelation, and
    Providence', in Kugel, *Shem in the Tents of Japhet*, pp. 109–30.

his own accord, and according to a narrative in *Midrash ha-gadol* Exod 40:38, Moses independently added the phrase 'even as the Lord commanded Moses,' and because of this he was rewarded by God. But these feeble signs of independence are a very far cry indeed from the supreme philosophical acumen displayed by Philo's Moses.[27]

H. Burkhardt has cited a plethora of passages to demonstrate that, for Philo, the Mosaic authorship of Scripture cannot be detached from his own personality but is rather its fullest expression. Moses is said to have possessed all the virtues without which he could never have composed the Scriptures (*Mos.* 2.11). Indeed, it was Moses' status as a 'living law' (*nomos empsychos*) that qualified him to become the true legislator par excellence (*Mos.* 2.4). In *De vita Mosis* 1.4, Philo calls the sacred books 'the wonderful monuments of his wisdom which he has left behind him'. In *De specialibus legibus* 4.105 we are told that 'as he (Moses) always adhered to the principles of numerical science, which he knew by close observation to be a paramount factor in all that exists, he never enacted any law great or small without calling to his aid and, as it were, accommodating to his enactment its appropriate number.' Even more directly personal is the statement that the prophetic legislator 'used to incite and train all his subjects to fellowship, setting before them the monument of his own life like an original design to be their beautiful model' (*Virt.* 51).[28]

IV.3. Natural Law

Philo's espousal of Stoic natural law theory profoundly shaped his concept of Torah law and his subsequent ability to sing its praises unstintingly and amply justify its controlling influence over his own life and that of his people. Moses, he says, began with an account of creation in order to demonstrate the complete harmony between the cosmos and the law and thus that one who follows the law is acting in consonance with the rational purpose of nature (*Opif.* 3). Within Philo's Hellenistic Jewish context, the identification of natural law with the law revealed by God and transmitted in writing by Moses would probably not have

---

27   See Heschel, *Torah*, II, pp. 294, 345–6; M.B. Shapiro, *The Limits of Orthodox Theology* (Portland 2004), pp. 113–15. *Midrash ha-gadol* is a 13th century rabbinic work on the Pentateuch, emanating from Yemen and consisting mainly of excerpts of older rabbinic texts of the talmudic period. The passage in question may be found in the edition of M. Margulies (Jerusalem 1956), p. 796.

28   See Burkhardt, *Die Inspiration heiliger Schriften bei Philo von Alexandrien* (Giessen 1988), pp. 171–98.

been regarded at the time as particularly surprising. Nonetheless, although J.J. Collins may well be right that according to Ben Sira the law revealed to Moses was implicit in creation from the beginning, and so is an actualization of the natural law, it must be admitted that Philo's exposition of this theory is clearly the first explicit and detailed statement of it.[29] As H. Najman, however, has correctly emphasized, Philo's notion of a written form of the law of nature would have struck his non-Jewish Greek readers as highly paradoxical.[30] Cicero, our main source for the Stoic theory of the law of nature, insists that 'we do not have the firm and lifelike figure of true law and genuine justice: we make use of shadows and sketches (*umbra et imaginibus utimur*). I wish we would follow even those! For they are drawn from the best examples of nature and truth' (*Off.* 3.69; presumably, as Najman correctly remarks, the exemplary lives of those who are virtuous and wise).

Philo's delineation of so sensitive an issue as the identification of Torah law with natural law is, as we might expect, not unambiguous and its precise intent has consequently been much debated. Even a brief analysis of it will clearly reveal the extent to which Philo cautiously avoided spelling out fully the radical implications of his position. What he appears to be saying is that the patriarchs and Moses, the living embodiments of natural law, were sages/philosophers who had a clear and accurate understanding of the Logos structure of the universe and consequently made all their actions to be in conformity with it. For non-sages, who lack that unique insight, Moses formulated rules and precepts that may be derived from the archetypal actions of the sages. He was able to do so inasmuch as he had himself become assimilated to the Logos and therefore could derive from the lives of

---

29 Collins, *Jewish Wisdom in the Hellenistic Age* (Louisville 1997), pp. 54–61, esp. 58. Other formulations of this theory in various degrees of explicitness are found in the *Letter of Aristeas*, Wisdom of Solomon, 4 Maccabees, Ps.-Phocylides, Josephus, and book 3 of the *Sibylline Oracles*.

30 'A Written Copy of the Law of Nature: An Unthinkable Paradox?', *StPhAnn* 15 (2003), pp. 54–63; cf. J.W. Martens, *One God, One Law: Philo of Alexandria on the Mosaic and Greco–Roman Law* (Boston 2003), pp. 1–11, 86–99, 123–30. The sharp contrast between the unwritten natural law and the written law is fully and rhetorically articulated by Philo himself: 'Right reason is an infallible law imprinted not by this or that individual, the perishable work of a mortal, nor on papyrus rolls or stone slabs [a faint echo of the 'tablets of the Decalogue'?], a thing inanimate on materials inanimate, but by immortal nature on the immortal mind, never to perish' (*Prob.* 46, my translation). Cf. Ps.-Aristotle, *De mundo* 6, 400b28–30: 'God is a law to us impartial and admitting no correction or change; he is surely a stronger and more stable law than those inscribed on tablets;' and Plutarch, *Princ. iner.* 3, 780c.

the patriarchs and from his own life the general rules and precepts that these lives exemplified. Thus, the exemplary lives of Moses and the patriarchs actually are or constitute laws of nature. As Aristotle had put it, 'a cultivated or free man is, as it were, a law unto himself' (*Eth. Nic.* 4, 1128a31), and similarly, according to the Hasidic master R. Moses Hayyim Ephraim of Sudylkov, 'the Zaddikim themselves are the laws and commandments.'[31] On the other hand, the enacted laws of Moses cannot be spoken of as embodiments of the laws of nature, but are rather 'copies' or 'memorials' of the natural law embodied by the patriarchs, and as mere copies they can be written down. There is, however, no substitute for the direct insight into the Logos structure of the universe, which unfortunately is available only to the sages/philosophers. No general rules or precepts can serve in its stead, because every situation requiring action differs to a greater or lesser degree from every other. Thus the rules and precepts formulated by Moses are, at best, only general guidelines for what needs to be done. The ultimate criterion for the correct interpretation of the Mosaic law is the unwritten law of nature, the Logos structure of the universe. That this was not simply a Jewish Hellenistic distortion of the nature of Jewish law can be seen from the fact that a great traditional halakhist such as R. Israel Moses Hazzan, who was a member of the high court of Jerusalem, and for a period of five years the chief rabbi of Rome, when dealing with the question of whether the halakhah could promulgate norms that were contrary to reason, held that this was theoretically impossible, because 'the true faith and reason were given by one shepherd.'[32]

Indifference to philosophical speculation foreclosed the possibility of any serious effort on the part of the Rabbis to engage in systematic reflection on their overall philosophy of law and what affinity they might have seen between halakhah and natural law. Nor has any consensus been formed in Jewish tradition on this issue. Certainly there is nothing in rabbinic literature comparable to Cicero's clear-cut formulation of the Stoic theory of natural law in *De republica* 3.33 and

---

31 *Degel Mahaneh Efrayim* (Zhitomir 1850), p. 8. So too, St. Francis of Assisi said: 'I am your breviary, I *am* breviary.' Cf. Rom 2:14: 'When Gentiles who have not the law do by nature what the law requires, they are a law to themselves, even though they do not have the law.'

32 Quoted by A. Sagi, *Yahadut: Bein dat le-musar* ([Tel Aviv] 1998), p. 323. See also pp. 317–34, for a full discussion of Hazzan's halakhic philosophy, and pp. 103–57, for a detailed analysis of the entire question of whether the halakhah recognizes the moral obligation as one that is halakhic. For an excellent discussion of the Stoic theory of natural law, see P. A. Vander Waerdt, 'The Original Theory of Natural Law', *StPhAnn* 15 (2003), pp. 17–34.

De legibus 1.16–19, but neither is there any trace there of the polarized views of the Mutazilites and Asharites that characterized the Kalam on this issue. Although H. Ben-Menahem brushes aside the talmudic dicta that appear to allude to the claim that that which ought to have been commanded is amenable to discovery by human reason (*m. Kidd.* 4.14; *Sifra* Aharei mot 13.10; *b. Yoma* 67b; *b. Eruv.* 100b), inasmuch as this 'by no means establishes its normative standing as a source of law', he does acknowledge that the notion of the Noahide laws is indeed relevant to the idea of natural law (with reference to *t. Avod. Zar.* 8.4; *b. Sanh.* 56a): 'It is relevant to … the proposition that natural laws mirror human nature. The seven Noahide laws (to establish courts of justice; to refrain from blasphemy, idolatry, sexual transgressions, bloodshed, robbery, and eating flesh cut from a living animal) are universally applicable, and as such, point to a universal human nature with which they are in harmony.'[33] In any case, the Philonic notion that the unwritten law of nature is the ultimate criterion for the correct understanding of the Mosaic law is nowhere clearly articulated in rabbinic literature, and is not even unambiguously stated by Philo himself.

IV.4 Philonic Halakhah

As Amir has rightly emphasized, Philo was the first to write a separate treatise on the Decalogue, and his analysis of it reveals a distinctively different approach from that of the Rabbis. Among the 613 commandments catalogued by the Rabbis, we find no special category for the Ten Commandments that would indicate their premier rank; instead, they are distributed among the 365 positive commandments and the 248 negative ones. For Philo the fundamental relationship between the Decalogue and the remaining commandments is that between genus and species, principles and derivatives. He thus transforms the entire mass of the isolated commandments of the Torah into a logically

---

33 'Talmudic Law: A Jurisprudential Perspective', in S. T. Katz (ed.), *The Cambridge History of Judaism*, IV, *The Late Roman–Rabbinic Period* (Cambridge 2006), pp. 882–4. See also Urbach, *Sages*, pp. 315–99; N. Lamm and A. Kirschenbaum, 'Freedom and Constraint in the Jewish Judicial Process', *Cardozo Law Review* 1 (1979), pp. 99–133; D. Novak, *The Image of the Non-Jew in Judaism: An Historical and Constructive Study of the Noahide Laws* (New York 1983). For Islamic views on natural law theory, see G. F. Hourani, *Reason and Tradition in Islamic Ethics* (London 1985); J. Faur, 'The Origin of the Classification of Rational and Divine Commandments in Mediaeval Jewish Philosophy', *Augustinianum* 9 (1969), pp. 299–304; and O. Leaman, *An Introduction to Medieval Islamic Philosophy* (London 1985), pp. 123–65, who includes much of the Jewish data in his discussion.

articulated legal structure, a faithful expression of the divine Logos. This philosophical restructuring is reinforced, as often occurs in his writings, by his invocation of the science of arithmology, whereby he sings the praises of the number ten, which is also the number of the Aristotelian categories in which all existents participate (*Decal.* 30–1).

Wolfson thought he had found a Palestinian text that contained an analogous motif, for we read in *y. Shekal.* 6.1, 49d, that 'between each commandment [of the Decalogue] the sections and detailed interpretations of the Torah were written ... just as in the case of the sea there are small waves between one big billow and another, so between one commandment and another come the detailed interpretations and signs of the Torah.'[34] As Urbach has correctly noted, however, this text only implies that the interpretation and detailed regulations were written down between each commandment of the Decalogue. There is no indication that the Ten Commandments incorporated all the precepts of the Torah. Moreover, as Amir has pointed out, it is not said that the relationship between one big billow and a small one is that of a general principle and its derivatives.[35]

The precise relationship of Philo's halakhah to that of the Rabbis is complicated by the fact that Philo predates the earliest rabbinic compilations by about two centuries. Talmudic sources, however, indicate close ties between the Alexandrian Jewish community and Palestinian Jewry, making it likely that the Oral Law was not limited to the borders of Palestine. Various Jewish Diaspora communities maintained their own synagogues in Jerusalem to serve pilgrims and provide for their needs. A Toseftan tradition (*t. Meg.* 2.17 [3.6]) reports that a

34   This is the source of the *Song Rab.* 5:14 reference given by Wolfson in *Philo*, II, p. 201 n. 8.
35   See the excellent analysis of Amir, *Gestalt*, pp. 131–63. Philo's distinctive structuring of the Torah's laws does appear, however, in late midrashim, beginning with the 11th century. As Urbach, *Sages*, pp. 360–2, has noted, 'it seems that the idea reached these works from R. Saadia Gaon [882–942].' Because Saadia does not rely on any internal source, it seems he derived this from Philo. Although unnoticed by Urbach, our suspicion is strengthened by the fact that Saadia too, in his *Commentary on Sefer Yezirah* 1.1, ed. Y. Kafah ([Jerusalem] 1971/1972), p. 47, connects the Decalogue with the Aristotelian categories. As R. D. Hecht has pointed out, however, Urbach failed to utilize the evidence of the Targums in formulating his argument. The evidence of *Tg. Ps.-J.* Exod 24:12 suggests that there was a Palestinian exegetical tradition that understood the Decalogue to contain all the commandments of the Mosaic law. See Hecht, 'Preliminary Issues in the Analysis of Philo's *De Specialibus Legibus*', StPhilo 5 (1978), pp. 1–55, esp. 14–15. Cf. P. Borgen, *Philo of Alexandria: An Exegete for His Time* (Leiden 1997), p. 61.

first-century synagogue of Alexandrian Jews located in Jerusalem was purchased by R. Eliezer b. R. Zadoq and used for private purposes. The close ties between the Jerusalem temple and the Jews of Alexandria are reflected by the commissioning of artisans from Alexandria to repair damaged temple accessories (b. Arak. 10b), and by the gifts of silver and gold plates for the gates of the temple court, donated by Philo's brother Alexander (Josephus, BJ 5.201–5). When the priests of the house of Garmu refused to instruct regarding the preparation of the Shewbread and those of the house of Abtinas did not wish to teach the preparation of the incense regarding one of its secret ingredients, Alexandrian specialists were brought in, although in the latter case they failed in their mission.[36] Moreover, M.(= E.) Stein suggested that the twelve questions put by the Alexandrians to R. Joshua b. Hananiah (first– second century CE) (b. Nid. 69b) indicated that the Palestinian Rabbis had exerted considerable influence on Alexandrian halakhah, and S. Lieberman went even further, asserting that some of the questions they posed demonstrated that they were indeed great rabbinic scholars and were familiar with rabbinic customs.[37]

In his pioneering work on Philonic halakhah, B. Ritter suggested that the elements in it that were contrary to its rabbinic counterpart were derived from the decisions of local Jewish courts.[38] This was partially accepted by J. Z. Lauterbach, but his most important insight was his demonstration that Philo had often followed an earlier tradition of Palestinian halakhah.[39] Following some hints of I. Heinemann, who had pointed out some passages where Philo seemed to evince an expert knowledge of practical law, E. R. Goodenough made his own collection of such cases and argued that these derived from local Jewish court decisions and that, although they contained Jewish elements, they had their origin in Greek and Roman law.[40] Belkin accepted Goodenough's view, but also demonstrated much more comprehensively the agreement of many of Philo's laws with the early halakhah. Indeed, he characterized Philo as a 'Pharisaic Halakist ... who applied the principles of the

36 Y. Yoma 3.9, 41a; t. Kippurim 2.5–6. See S. Lieberman's commentary on the latter text, Tosefta Ki-fshutah, IV (New York 1962), pp. 761–2; A. Kasher, The Jews in Hellenistic and Roman Egypt (Tübingen 1985), pp. 346–55.

37 Stein, Filon ha-aleksandroni (Warsaw 1936/1937), p. 69 n. 2; Lieberman, Siphre Zutta (New York 1968), pp. 29–31.

38 Philo und die Halacha (Leipzig 1879).

39 S.v. '[Philo Judaeus] – His Relation to the Halakah', The Jewish Encyclopedia 10 (1905), pp. 15–18.

40 The Jurisprudence of the Jewish Courts in Egypt (New Haven 1929).

oral law in interpreting the Bible'.[41] It should be pointed out, however, that the eminent papyrologist, J. Mélèze Modrzejewski, believes that the existence of Jewish tribunals in Alexandria is highly questionable, and that Philo's laws reflect his own interpretation of the biblical laws rather than the actual jurisprudence of Jewish courts. The competence of the Jewish ethnarch in the judicial domain, he thinks, was limited to a kind of arbitration (Josephus, AJ 14.117), and the same applies to the Alexandrian Beth Din cited in rabbinic sources.[42] Under Roman domination, provincial justice became a monopoly of the imperial government, excluding the action of any other autonomous jurisdiction.[43]

A thorough analysis of Philo's halakhah was made by I. Heinemann, a palmary scholar who was well versed in both rabbinic and classical literature.[44] Parallels with rabbinic halakhah, he pointed out, do not prove Philo's dependence on the latter, inasmuch as the Rabbis had themselves absorbed much of Hellenistic culture. Heinemann began with the observation that not enough attention had been given to the parallels between Philo and Greek legal traditions. As P.J. Tomson has correctly observed, however, 'whenever Philo's dependency on sources reflected in rabbinic literature is inconclusive in Heinemann's analysis, as is often the case, he adduces a wealth of Greek and Hellenistic parallels. ... However Heinemann curiously gives precedence to Hellenistic material even where a number of Jewish parallels from different quarters are available.'[45] Heinemann's conclusion that Philo's acquaintance with rabbinic halakha was quite fragmentary, and that much of Jewish tradition was known to him solely from actual practice, appears to be somewhat exaggerated, especially in view of his failure to take sufficient account of early Palestinian halakha. Furthermore, his assessment that Philo's adaptation of Jewish tradition to Hellenistic thought ultimately resulted in the distortion of central conceptions of Judaism, and that his

41 S. Belkin, Philo and the Oral Law (Cambridge, MA 1940); quotation from p. 27. For a list of his writings on Philonic halakha, see Hecht 'Preliminary Issues', pp. 49–50 n. 55. On p. 25, Hecht offers some criticisms of Belkin's methodology.
42 T. Peah 4.6; cf. Lieberman, Tosefta Ki-fshutah, I,1 (New York 1955), p. 182.
43 Mélèze Modrzejewski, 'Jewish Law and Hellenistic Legal Practice in the Light of Greek Papyri from Egypt', in N.S. Hecht et al. (eds.), An Introduction to the History and Sources of Jewish Law (Oxford 1996), pp. 75–99, esp. 81–2.
44 Philons griechische und jüdische Bildung² (Hildesheim 1962).
45 Paul and the Jewish Law (Assen 1990), pp. 37–9. S. Daniel, 'La Halacha de Philon selon le premier livre des Lois spéciales', in R. Arnaldez et al., Philon d'Alexandrie (Paris 1967), pp. 221–40, argues against Heinemann that Philo's exegesis is dependent upon a halakhic tradition in Egypt.

attempt to assimilate Jewish thought to Greek rationalism would have achieved greater success had he possessed a more adequate knowledge of his native tradition, far from being an objective evaluation of the Philonic enterprise, only reveals Heinemann's own particular bias in this matter.

In response to Heinemann, G. Alon decisively demonstrated Philo's use of pre-Mishnaic halakhah. A good example is his discussion of Philo's legitimation of vigilante action against the idol worshipper, in which he pointed out that this was contrary to rabbinic halakhah that required that such a person be tried in court (*m. Sanh.* 7.4). Unlike Heinemann, however, who suggested that Philo formulated his own halakha on the basis of Num 25, Alon correctly noted that Philo was dependent on an early halakhic tradition current in Palestine and the Diaspora in his day, though later abrogated. This can be deduced from *m. Sanh.* 9.6 and is further corroborated by *Jubilees* 30:14–15. Moreover, Philo's use of the Phinehas episode as legitimation for such zealotic action was anticipated by the author of 1 Macc 2:15–28, 49–70.[46]

IV.5. Repentance

The indispensability of repentance is clearly indicated by the rabbinic affirmation of its premundane existence (*Gen. Rab.* 1.4; *b. Pesah.* 54a). Prior to his act of creation, God already laid plans for the acceptance of repentance, for He knew that the world could not otherwise endure, inasmuch as human nature is such that there is no escape from sin.[47] Greek philosophy, on the other hand, had little interest in the feelings of regret or remorse that may at times lead an individual to a complete reassessment of his former life path and his conversion to a fresh course

---

46 Alon, 'On Philo's Halakha', in his collected essays, *Jews, Judaism and the Classical World* (Jerusalem 1977), pp. 112–24. See also T. Seland, *Establishment Violence in Philo and Luke: A Study of Non-Conformity to the Torah and Jewish Vigilante Reactions* (Leiden 1995), p. 69. A number of Philo's Sabbath laws are more severe than their rabbinic counterparts, representing once again the early halakhah. See Y. D. Gilat, 'The Sabbath and Its Laws in the World of Philo', in R. Link-Salinger (ed.), *Torah and Wisdom: Studies in Jewish Philosophy, Kabbalah, and Halacha: Essays in Honor of Arthur Hyman* (New York 1992), pp. 61–73. See also J. Leonhardt, *Jewish Worship in Philo of Alexandria* (Tübingen 2001), pp. 70–3. For a broad overview of Philo's view of Torah law, see also R. Weber, *Das "Gesetz" bei Philon von Alexandrien und Flavius Josephus* (Frankfurt am Main 2001).

47 *Pirke R. El.* 3; *Midrash ha-gadol* Gen., ed. M. Margulies (Jerusalem 1947), pp. 8–9. See S. Schechter, *Some Aspects of Rabbinic Theology* (New York 1936), pp. 313–14.

of existence. Aristotle does indeed note that there is no cure for one who does not regret his error, but not only does he nowhere say that repentance is a virtue, he further asserts that the good man is 'a person who knows no regrets' (*Eth. Nic.* 7, 1150a23; 9, 1166a29). We have already seen, however, how Philo injected the idea of repentance into Pentateuchal verses that made no reference to it whatsoever. Indeed, in the early biblical narratives, repentance plays virtually no role. The generations of the flood and the tower of Babel, the men of Sodom and the Canaanites are not called upon to repent. Nor does Moses avert God's wrath from Israel by rousing them to repentance. Repentance is found in P and D (Lev 26:40–2; Deut 4:29–31, 30:1–10), but there, contrary to the view of the prophets, it can only terminate the punishment but cannot prevent its onset.

In rabbinic literature, on the other hand, the prophetic doctrine of repentance was not only taken over, but was greatly expanded and was to put its indelible stamp on Jewish religious piety forevermore. Because Philo makes only sparing use of the prophetic books in his scriptural commentary, it is clearly the rabbinic conception of repentance that has left its unmistakable mark on him. A brief summary will easily show that virtually all the rabbinic elaborations of this doctrine resurface in his exposition. According to Philo, the effects of repentance are such that sin is expunged, 'the old reprehensible life is blotted out and disappears ... as though it had never been at all' (*Abr.* 19). This was also the prophetic view and it was emphatically repeated by the Rabbis (*Pesikta Rab Kah.* 6.4). The efficacy of repentance, however, depends upon its sincerity, a sure sign of which is that it is marked by bitterness, weeping, sighing, and groaning (*Fug.* 160; *QE* 1.15). Like the Rabbis, however, Philo is concerned that the penitent's sins not be unduly publicized (*Spec.* 1.235–41; *y. Yevam.* 8.3, 9c).

Up to this point, there is nothing in Philo's account of repentance that differs from rabbinic tradition. In analyzing the process of repentance, however, Philo appears to introduce a philosophical mode of description. Especially revealing is his description of repentance at *De fuga et inventione* 159 as 'a restricted and slow and tarrying thing'. The Rabbis, in contrast, emphasize the instantaneousness of the process.[48] Moreover, Philo's assertion that repentance is an irrational emotion (*pathos*) finds no echo in rabbinic literature. In sum, although Philo has not succeeded completely in assimilating the concept of repentance to his philosophical thought, he does nevertheless emphasize its secondary rank in the hierarchy of virtue, explicitly refers to the scars of old misdeeds, and indicates the lengthy intellectual process that precedes conversion to

48 *Pesikta Rabbati* 44, ed. M. Friedmann (Vienna 1880), p. 185a.

a better life. It should further be noted that Philo was undoubtedly aware of a Neopythagorean preoccupation with self-examination that was later taken up by the Roman Stoa, and this may have made it easier for him to incorporate the Jewish emphasis on repentance into his own writings. Philo's treatment of the doctrine of repentance thus further exemplifies the pervasive tensions that characterize much of his writing.[49]

V. CONCLUSION: PHILO JUDAEUS OR PHILO PHILOSOPHICO–MYSTICUS?

Much of the debate about the fundamental character of Philo's thought has unfortunately revolved around resolution of the question as to which side of his psyche ultimately reveals the true nature of the man. The answer should have been apparent to anyone who read his work without any preconceived notions. Philo was fully convinced, rightly or wrongly, that the two traditions he sought to reconcile were really in mutual accord. He would undoubtedly have been quite content to be described as Philo Judaeus *et* philosophico–mysticus. Those who seek an either/or resolution are somewhat reminiscent of those who complained about Spinoza's lack of candor in his use of the famous locution *Deus sive natura*, insisting that the only honest formulation ought to have been *aut Deus aut natura*.[50] But Philo, like Spinoza, would have refused to be put into a box for the convenience of narrow-minded 'micropolitans' (*Somn.* 1.39).[51]

---

49 For a full analysis and discussion, see D. Winston, 'Philo's Doctrine of Repentance', in J.P. Kenney (ed.), *The School of Moses: Studies in Philo and Hellenistic Religion: In Memory of Horst R. Moehring* (Atlanta 1995), pp. 29–40.

50 'Away with this contradiction!,' exclaims Feuerbach. 'Not *Deus sive natura*, but *aut Deus aut natura*. That is where the truth lies;' cited in L.I. Akselrod, 'Spinoza and Materialism', in G.L. Kline, *Spinoza in Soviet Philosophy* (New York 1952), p. 62.

51 For a good survey of earlier views on this problem, see S. Sandmel, *Philo's Place in Judaism: A Study of Conceptions of Abraham in Jewish Literature* (augmented edition; New York 1971), pp. 1–29. For a more recent survey, see Borgen, *Philo: An Exegete*, pp. 1–13. For an excellent discussion of the various labels given to Philo in the ancient sources, see D.T. Runia, 'Philonic Nomenclature', in Runia, *Philo and the Church Fathers*, pp. 25–53. See also my remarks in *Logos and Mystical Theology*, pp. 13–14; 'Philo and the Contemplative Life', pp. 198–201.

CLASSIFIED BIBLIOGRAPHY

Students of Philo are fortunate to have at their disposal some excellent bibliographical resources. The following three contributions are of essential importance:

Goodhart, H. L., and E. R. Goodenough. 'A General Bibliography of Philo Judaeus', in E. R. Goodenough, *The Politics of Philo Judaeus* (New Haven 1938), pp. 125–321, 329–48.

Radice, R., and D. T. Runia. *Philo of Alexandria: An Annotated Bibliography 1937–1986* (Leiden 1992).

Runia, D. T. *Philo of Alexandria: An Annotated Bibliography 1987–1996* (Leiden 2000).

Yearly bibliographies of Philo are published in *The Studia Philonica Annual*, which has been published every year since 1989. These bibliographies represent a continuation of the bibliographies that had been published in *Studia Philonica* 1–6 (1972–1980).

The following classified bibliography is based on the structure of the present volume, and on the works cited in the notes, although it is not all-inclusive of them. The aim is rather to list those works that have Philo as their primary focus, and to supplement them with additional works that have broad relevance to the topics covered in the volume. Each entry appears only once, however, even if it might have been cited under more than one rubric. Needless to say, the bibliography is selective, and an attempt has been made to include some older studies as well as more recent contributions. Additional readings may be found by means of the reference tools just cited, as well as in some of the books and articles cited below under the heading 'Introductory and General Works'.

VOLUMES OF COLLECTED STUDIES CITED IN THE BIBLIOGRAPHY

Amir, Y. *Die hellenistische Gestalt des Judentums bei Philon von Alexandrien* (Neukirchen-Vluyn 1983).

Arnaldez, R., et al. *Philon d'Alexandrie* (Paris 1967).

Greenspahn, F. E., et al. (eds.). *Nourished with Peace: Studies in Hellenistic Judaism in Memory of Samuel Sandmel* (Chico, CA 1984).

Haase, W. (ed.). *Aufstieg und Niedergang der römischen Welt* (=*ANRW*) II.21.1 (1984).

Lévy, C. (ed.). *Philon d'Alexandrie et le langage de la philosophie* (Turnhout 1998).

Nikiprowetzky, V. *Études philoniennes* (Paris 1996).

Winston, D. *The Ancestral Philosophy: Hellenistic Philosophy in Second Temple Judaism* (Providence 2001).

255

INTRODUCTORY AND GENERAL WORKS

Birnbaum, E. 'Two Millennia Later: General Resources and Particular Perspectives on Philo the Jew', *Currents in Biblical Research* 4 (2005/2006), pp. 241–76.

Borgen, P. 'Philo of Alexandria: A Critical and Synthetical Survey of Research since World War II', *ANRW* II.21.1 (1984), pp. 98–154.

Bréhier, É. *Les idées philosophiques et religieuses de Philon d'Alexandrie*³ (Paris 1950).

Daniélou, J. *Philon d'Alexandrie* (Paris 1958).

Goodenough, E. R. *An Introduction to Philo Judaeus*² (Oxford 1962).

Hadas-Lebel, M. *Philon d'Alexandrie: Un penseur en diaspora* (Paris 2003).

Hilgert, E. 'Central Issues in Contemporary Philo Studies', *Biblical Research* 23 (1978), pp. 15–25.

Sandmel, S. *Philo of Alexandria: An Introduction* (New York 1979).

Schenck, K. *A Brief Guide to Philo* (Louisville 2005).

Terian, A. 'Had the Works of Philo Been Newly Discovered', *Biblical Archaeologist* 57 (1994), pp. 86–97.

Thyen, H. 'Die Probleme der neueren Philo-Forschung', *Theologische Rundschau* 23 (1955), pp. 230–46.

Wolfson, H. A. *Philo: Foundations of Religious Philosophy in Judaism, Christianity, and Islam*, I–II (Cambridge, MA 1948).

PHILO'S LIFE AND TIMES

Barclay, J. M. G. *Jews in the Mediterranean Diaspora from Alexander to Trajan (323 BCE – 117 CE)* (Edinburgh 1996).

Etienne, S. 'Réflexion sur l'apostasie de Tibérius Julius Alexander', *StPhAnn* 12 (2000), pp. 122–42.

Fuks, A. 'Marcus Julius Alexander', *Zion* 13–14 (1947–1949), pp. 14–17.

Goodenough, E. R. *The Jurisprudence of the Jewish Courts in Egypt* (New Haven 1929).

Gruen, E. S. *Diaspora: Jews amidst Greeks and Romans* (Cambridge, MA 2002).

Harris, H. A. *Greek Athletics and the Jews* (Cardiff 1976).

Hay, D. M. 'Philo's View of Himself as an Exegete: Inspired but not Authoritative', *StPhAnn* 3 (1991), pp. 40–52.

Kasher, A. *The Jews in Hellenistic and Roman Egypt* (Tübingen 1985).

Mélèze Modrzejewski, J. *The Jews of Egypt: From Rameses II to Emperor Hadrian* (Philadelphia 1995).

'Jewish Law and Hellenistic Legal Practice in the Light of Greek Papyri from Egypt', in N. S. Hecht et al. (eds.), *An Introduction to the History and Sources of Jewish Law* (Oxford 1996), pp. 75–99.

Mendelson, A. *Secular Education in Philo of Alexandria* (Cincinnati 1982).

Pucci Ben Zeev, M. *Diaspora Judaism in Turmoil, 116/117 CE: Ancient Sources and Modern Insights* (Leuven 2005).

Schimanowski, G. 'Die jüdische Integration in die Oberschicht Alexandriens und die angebliche Apostasie des Tiberius Julius Alexander', in J. Frey et al. (eds.), *Jewish Identity in the Greco–Roman World* (Leiden 2007), pp. 111–135.

Schwartz, D. R. 'Philonic Anonyms of the Roman and Nazi Periods: Two Suggestions', *StPhAnn* 1 (1989), pp. 63–73.

'Philo's Priestly Descent', in Greenspahn et al., *Nourished with Peace*, pp. 155–71.

Schwartz, J. 'L'Égypte de Philon', in Arnaldez et al., *Philon d'Alexandrie*, pp. 35–44.

Sijpesteijn, P. J. 'The Legationes ad Gaium', *JJS* 15 (1964), pp. 87–96.

Sly, D. I. *Philo's Alexandria* (London 1996).

Tcherikover, V. A. 'The Decline of the Jewish Diaspora in Egypt in the Roman Period', *JJS* 14 (1963), pp. 1–32.

'Prolegomena', in Tcherikover and A. Fuks (eds.), *Corpus Papyrorum Judaicarum*, I (Cambridge, MA 1957), pp. 1–111.

THE WORKS OF PHILO

Adler, M. *Studien zu Philon von Alexandreia* (Breslau 1929).

Borgen, P. and R. Skarsten. '*Quaestiones et Solutiones*: Some Observations on the Form of Philo's Exegesis', *StPhilo* 4 (1976–1977), pp. 1–15.

Cohn, L. 'Einteilung und Chronologie der Schriften Philos', *Philologus: Supplementband* 7 (1899), pp. 387–436.

Goodenough, E. R. 'Philo's Exposition of the Law and His De vita Mosis', *HThR* 26 (1933), pp. 109–25.

Hay, D. M. (ed.). *Both Literal and Allegorical: Studies in Philo of Alexandria's Questions and Answers on Genesis and Exodus* (Atlanta 1991).

Horst, P. W. van der. 'Philo and the Rabbis on Genesis: Similar Questions, Different Answers', in A. Volgers and C. Zamagni (eds.), *Erotapokriseis: Early Christian Question-and-Answer Literature in Context* (Leuven 2004), pp. 55–70.

Kamesar, A. Review of P. Borgen, *Philo of Alexandria: An Exegete for His Time*, *JThS* 50 (1999), pp. 753–8.

Massebieau, L. 'Le classement des oeuvres de Philon', *Bibliothèque de l'École des Hautes Études: Sciences religieuses* 1 (1889), pp. 1–91.

Morris, J. 'The Jewish Philosopher Philo', in E. Schürer et al., *The History of the Jewish People in the Age of Jesus Christ (175 B.C. – A.D. 135)*, III.2 (Edinburgh 1987), pp. 813–70.

Reiter, S. 'ΑΡΕΤΗ und der Titel von Philos Legatio', in Ἐπιτύμβιον *Heinrich Swoboda dargebracht* (Reichenberg 1927), pp. 228–37.

Royse, J. R. 'Further Greek Fragments of Philo's *Quaestiones*', in Greenspahn et al., *Nourished with Peace*, pp. 143–53.

'The Original Structure of Philo's *Quaestiones*', *StPhilo* 4 (1976–1977), pp. 41–78.

'Philo's Division of His Works into Books', *StPhAnn* 13 (2001), pp. 59–85.

'Reverse Indexes to Philonic Texts in the Printed Florilegia and Collections of Fragments', *StPhAnn* 5 (1993), pp. 156–79.

The Spurious Texts of Philo of Alexandria: A Study of Textual Transmission and Corruption with Indexes to the Major Collections of Greek Fragments (Leiden 1991).

'The Text of Philo's *De virtutibus*', *StPhAnn* 18 (2006), pp. 73–101.

'The Text of Philo's *Legum Allegoriae*', *StPhAnn* 12 (2000), pp. 1–28.

Runia, D. T. 'Further Observations on the Structure of Philo's Allegorical Treatises', *VC* 41 (1987), pp. 105–38.

'Philo's De aeternitate mundi: The Problem of Its Interpretation', *VC* 35 (1981), pp. 105–51.

'The Structure of Philo's Allegorical Treatises', *VC* 38 (1984), pp. 209–56.

Siegert, F. 'The Philonian Fragment *De Deo*: First English Translation', *StPhAnn* 10 (1998), pp. 1–33.

Sterling, G. E. 'Philo and the Logic of Apologetics: An Analysis of the *Hypothetica*', *SBLSP* 1990, pp. 412–30.

Taylor, J. E. *Jewish Women Philosophers of First-Century Alexandria: Philo's 'Therapeutae' Reconsidered* (Oxford 2003).

Terian, A. 'Back to Creation: The Beginning of Philo's Third Grand Commentary', *StPhAnn* 9 (1997), pp. 19–36.

'A Critical Introduction to Philo's Dialogues', *ANRW* II.21.1 (1984), pp. 272–94.

'A Philonic Fragment on the Decad', in Greenspahn et al., *Nourished with Peace*, pp. 173–82.

'The Priority of the *Quaestiones* among Philo's Exegetical Commentaries', in D. M. Hay (ed.), *Both Literal and Allegorical: Studies in Philo of Alexandria's Questions and Answers on Genesis and Exodus* (Atlanta 1991), pp. 29–46.

Tobin, T. H. 'The Beginning of Philo's *Legum Allegoriae*', *StPhAnn* 12 (2000), pp. 29–43.

BIBLICAL INTERPRETATION IN PHILO

Amir, Y. 'Ha-allegoria shel Filon be-yahasah la-allegoria ha-homerit', *Eshkolot* 6 (1970/1971), pp. 35–45.

'Authority and Interpretation of Scripture in the Writings of Philo', in M. J. Mulder (ed.), *Mikra: Text, Translation, Reading and Interpretation of the Hebrew Bible in Ancient Judaism and Early Christianity* (Assen/Maastricht 1988), pp. 421–53.

Blönnigen, C. *Der griechische Ursprung der jüdisch–hellenistischen Allegorese und ihre Rezeption in der alexandrinischen Patristik* (Frankfurt am Main 1992).

Borgen, P. *Philo of Alexandria: An Exegete for His Time* (Leiden 1997).

Burkhardt, H. *Die Inspiration heiliger Schriften bei Philo von Alexandrien* (Giessen 1988).

Carny, P. 'Dimuyim merkaziyim ba-teoryah ha-allegoristit shel Filon', in M. A. Friedman et al. (eds.), *Teuda, III, Studies in Talmudic Literature, in Post Biblical Hebrew, and in Biblical Exegesis* (Tel Aviv 1983), pp. 251–9.

'Ha-yesodot he-hagutiyim shel darshanut Filon ha-aleksandroni', *Daat* 14 (1985), pp. 5–19.

Cazeaux, J. 'Philon d'Alexandrie, exégète', *ANRW* II.21.1 (1984), pp. 156–226.

La trame et la chaîne, ou les structures littéraires et l'exégèse dans cinq des traités de Philon d'Alexandrie (Leiden 1983).

Dillon, J. 'Philo and the Greek Tradition of Allegorical Exegesis', *SBLSP* 1994, pp. 69–80.

Goulet, R. *La philosophie de Moïse: Essai de reconstitution d'un commentaire philosophique préphilonien du Pentateuque* (Paris 1987).

Grabbe, L. L. *Etymology in Early Jewish Interpretation: The Hebrew Names in Philo* (Atlanta 1988).

Kamesar, A. 'The Literary Genres of the Pentateuch as Seen from the Greek Perspective: The Testimony of Philo of Alexandria', *StPhAnn* 9 (1997), pp. 143–89.

'The *Logos Endiathetos* and the *Logos Prophorikos* in Allegorical Interpretation: Philo of Alexandria and the D-Scholia to the *Iliad*', *GRBS* 44 (2004), pp. 163–81.

'Philo and the Literary Quality of the Bible: A Theoretical Aspect of the Problem', *JJS* 46 (1995), pp. 55–68.

'Philo, the Presence of "Paideutic" Myth in the Pentateuch, and the "Principles" or *Kephalaia* of Mosaic Discourse', *StPhAnn* 10 (1998), pp. 34–65.

Katz, P. *Philo's Bible: The Aberrant Text of Bible Quotations in Some Philonic Writings* (Cambridge 1950).

Mack, B. L. 'Philo Judaeus and Exegetical Traditions in Alexandria', *ANRW* II.21.1 (1984), pp. 227–71.

Mansfeld, J. 'Philosophy in the Service of Scripture: Philo's Exegetical Strategies', in J. Dillon and A. A. Long (eds.), *The Question of "Eclecticism"* (Berkeley 1988), pp. 70–102.

Nikiprowetzky, V. *Le commentaire de l'Écriture chez Philon d'Alexandrie* (Leiden 1977).

Otte, K. *Das Sprachverständnis bei Philo von Alexandrien* (Tübingen 1968).

Pépin, J. *La tradition de l'allégorie de Philon d'Alexandrie à Dante*, II (Paris 1987).

Rokeah, D. 'A New Onomasticon Fragment from Oxyrhynchus and Philo's Etymologies', *JThS* 19 (1968), pp. 70–82.

Siegert, F. 'Early Jewish Interpretation in a Hellenistic Style', in M. Sæbø (ed.), *Hebrew Bible/Old Testament: The History of Its Interpretation*, I.1 (Göttingen 1996), pp. 130–98.

'Hellenistic Jewish Midrash', I-III, in J. Neusner and A. J. Avery-Peck (eds.), *Encyclopaedia of Midrash: Biblical Interpretation in Formative Judaism* (Leiden 2005), I, pp. 199–250.

Siegfried, C. *Philo von Alexandria als Ausleger des Alten Testaments* (Jena 1875).

Stein, E. *Die allegorische Exegese des Philo aus Alexandreia* (Giessen 1929).

Thyen, H. *Der Stil der jüdisch–hellenistischen Homilie* (Göttingen 1955).

Walter, N. *Der Thoraausleger Aristobulos* (Berlin 1964).

Winston, D. 'Aspects of Philo's Linguistic Theory', *StPhAnn* 3 (1991), pp. 109–25.

PHILO AND JUDAISM

Amir, Y. 'The Decalogue according to Philo', in B.-Z. Segal and G. Levi (eds.), *The Ten Commandments in History and Tradition* (Jerusalem 1990), pp. 121–60.

Birnbaum, E. *The Place of Judaism in Philo's Thought: Israel, Jews, and Proselytes* (Atlanta 1996).

Burnett, F. W. 'Philo on Immortality: A Thematic Study of Philo's Concept of παλιγγενεσία', *The Catholic Biblical Quarterly* 46 (1984), pp. 447–70.

Goodenough, E. R. *By Light, Light: The Mystic Gospel of Hellenistic Judaism* (New Haven 1935).

'Philo on Immortality', *HThR* 39 (1946), pp. 85–108.

Harl, M. 'Adam et les deux arbres du Paradis (Gen. II–III) ou l'homme *milieu entre deux termes* (μέσος-μεθόριος) chez Philon d'Alexandrie', *Recherches de science religieuse* 50 (1962), pp. 321–88.

Hay, D. M. 'Philo of Alexandria', in D. A. Carson et al. (eds.), *Justification and Variegated Nomism, I, The Complexities of Second Temple Judaism* (Tübingen 2001), pp. 357–79.

Leonhardt, J. *Jewish Worship in Philo of Alexandria* (Tübingen 2001).

Martens, J. W. *One God, One Law: Philo of Alexandria on the Mosaic and Greco-Roman Law* (Boston 2003).

'Unwritten Law in Philo: A Response to Naomi G. Cohen', *JJS* 43 (1992), pp. 38–45.

Mendelson, A. *Philo's Jewish Identity* (Atlanta 1988).

Najman, H. 'A Written Copy of the Law of Nature: An Unthinkable Paradox?', *StPhAnn* 15 (2003), pp. 54–63.

Niehoff, M. R. *Philo on Jewish Identity and Culture* (Tübingen 2001).

Rhodes, J. N. 'Diet and Desire: The Logic of the Dietary Laws according to Philo', *Ephemerides Theologicae Lovanienses* 79 (2003), pp. 122–33.

Schaller, B. 'Philon von Alexandreia und das "Heilige Land" ', in G. Strecker (ed.), *Das Land Israel in biblischer Zeit* (Göttingen 1983), pp. 172–87.

Termini, C. *Le potenze di Dio: Studio su δύναμις in Filone di Alessandria* (Rome 2000).

'Taxonomy of Biblical Laws and φιλοτεχνία in Philo of Alexandria: A Comparison with Josephus and Cicero', *StPhAnn* 16 (2004), pp. 1–29.

Weber, R. *Das "Gesetz" bei Philon von Alexandrien und Flavius Josephus* (Frankfurt am Main 2001).

Winston, D. 'Philo and the Wisdom of Solomon on Creation, Revelation, and Providence', in J. L. Kugel (ed.), *Shem in the Tents of Japhet: Essays on the Encounter of Judaism and Hellenism* (Leiden 2002), pp. 109–30.

'Two Types of Mosaic Prophecy according to Philo', *Journal for the Study of the Pseudepigrapha* 4 (1989), pp. 49–67.

Zeller, D. 'The Life and Death of the Soul in Philo of Alexandria: The Use and Origin of a Metaphor', *StPhAnn* 7 (1995), pp. 19–55.

PHILO'S THEOLOGY AND 'PHYSICS'

Dillon, J. 'Asômatos: Nuances of Incorporeality in Philo', in Lévy, *Philon d'Alexandrie et le langage*, pp. 99–110.

Frick, P. *Divine Providence in Philo of Alexandria* (Tübingen 1999).

Früchtel, U. *Die kosmologischen Vorstellungen bei Philo von Alexandrien: Ein Beitrag zur Geschichte der Genesisexegese* (Leiden 1968).

Mack, B. L. *Logos und Sophia: Untersuchungen zur Weisheitstheologie im hellenistischen Judentum* (Göttingen 1973).

Montes-Peral, L. A. *Akataleptos Theos: Der unfassbare Gott* (Leiden 1987).

Radice, R. *La filosofia di Aristobulo e i suoi nessi con il De mundo attribuito ad Aristotele*² (Milan 1995).

'Observations on the Theory of the Ideas as the Thoughts of God in Philo of Alexandria', *StPhAnn* 3 (1991), pp. 126–34.

Platonismo e creazionismo in Filone di Alessandria (Milan 1989).

Runia, D. T. *Philo of Alexandria and the Timaeus of Plato* (Leiden 1986).

Tobin, T. H. *The Creation of Man: Philo and the History of Interpretation* (Washington, DC 1983).

Weiss, H.-F. *Untersuchungen zur Kosmologie des hellenistischen und palästinischen Judentums* (Berlin 1966).

Winston, D. *Logos and Mystical Theology in Philo of Alexandria* (Cincinnati 1985).

Wolfson, H. A. 'The Philonic God of Revelation and His Later-Day Deniers', *HThR* 53 (1960), pp. 101–24.

Wolters, A. M. '*Creatio ex nihilo* in Philo', in W.E. Helleman (ed.), *Hellenization Revisited: Shaping a Christian Response within the Greco–Roman World* (Lanham, MD 1994), pp. 107–24.

PHILO'S ETHICS

Alexandre, M. 'Le lexique des vertus: Vertus philosophiques et religieuses chez Philon: μετάνοια et εὐγένεια', in Lévy, *Philon d'Alexandrie et le langage*, pp. 17–46.

Barraclough, R. 'Philo's Politics: Roman Rule and Hellenistic Judaism', *ANRW* II.21.1 (1984), pp. 417–553.

Berthelot, K. 'Philo and Kindness towards Animals (*De virtutibus* 125–147)', *StPhAnn* 14 (2002), pp. 48–65.

Besnier, B. 'Migration et *telos* d'apres le *de migratione Abrahami*', *StPhAnn* 11 (1999), pp. 74–103.

Bouffartigue, J. 'La structure de l'âme chez Philon: Terminologie scolastique et métaphores', in Lévy, *Philon d'Alexandrie et le langage*, pp. 59–75.

Calabi, F. *The Language and the Law of God: Interpretation and Politics in Philo of Alexandria* (Atlanta 1998).

Cohen, N. G. 'The Greek Virtues and the Mosaic Laws in Philo: An Elucidation of *De Specialibus Legibus* IV 133–135', *StPhAnn* 5 (1993), pp. 9–23.

Frazier, F. 'Les visages de Joseph dans le *De Iosepho*', *StPhAnn* 14 (2002), pp. 1–30.

Goodenough, E. R. *The Politics of Philo Judaeus* (New Haven 1938).

Helleman, W. E. 'Philo of Alexandria on Deification and Assimilation to God', *StPhAnn* 2 (1990), pp. 51–71.

Jastram, D. N. 'Philo's Concept of Generic Virtue', *SBLSP* 1991, pp. 323–47.

Le Boulluec, A. 'La place des concepts philosophiques dans la réflexion de Philon sur le plaisir', in Lévy, *Philon d'Alexandrie et le langage*, pp. 129–52.

Lévy, C. 'Éthique de l'immanence, éthique de la transcendance: Le problème de l'*oikeiôsis* chez Philon', in Lévy, *Philon d'Alexandrie et le langage*, pp. 153–64.

'Philon d'Alexandrie et les passions', in L. Ciccolini et al. (eds.), *Réceptions antiques: Lecture, transmission, appropriation intellectuelle* (Paris 2006), pp. 27–41.

Lewy, H. *Sobria ebrietas: Untersuchungen zur Geschichte der antiken Mystik* (Giessen 1929).

Najman, H. 'The Law of Nature and the Authority of Mosaic Law', *StPhAnn* 11 (1999), pp. 55–73.

Nikiprowetzky, V. 'Rébecca, vertu de constance et constance de vertu chez Philon d'Alexandrie', in Nikiprowetzky, *Études philoniennes*, pp. 145–55.

Runia, D. T. 'God and Man in Philo of Alexandria', *JThS* 39 (1988), pp. 48–75.

Völker, W. *Fortschritt und Vollendung bei Philo von Alexandrien* (Leipzig 1938).

Wilson, W. T. 'Pious Soldiers, Gender Deviants and the Ideology of Actium: Courage and Warfare in Philo's *De Fortitudine*', *StPhAnn* 17 (2005), pp. 1–32.

Winston, D. 'Freedom ad Determinism in Philo of Alexandria', in Winston, *The Ancestral Philosophy*, pp. 135–50.

'Philo's Ethical Theory', *ANRW* II.21.1 (1984), pp. 372–416.

PHILO AND THE NEW TESTAMENT

Deines, R. and K.-W. Niebuhr (eds.). *Philo und das Neue Testament: Wechselseitige Wahrnehmungen* (Tübingen 2004).

Attridge, H. W. 'Philo and John: Two Riffs on One Logos', *StPhAnn* 17 (2005), pp. 103–17.

Avemarie, F. 'Juden vor den Richterstühlen Roms: *In Flaccum* und die Apostelgeschichte im Vergleich', in Deines and Niebuhr, *Philo und das Neue Testament*, pp. 107–26.

Barclay, J. M. G. 'Paul and Philo on Circumcision: Romans 2.25–9 in Social and Cultural Context', *NTS* 44 (1998), pp. 536–56.

Borgen, P. *Bread From Heaven: An Exegetical Study of the Concept of Manna in the Gospel of John and the Writings of Philo* (Leiden 1965).

Early Christianity and Hellenistic Judaism (Edinburgh 1996).

'The Gospel of John and Philo of Alexandria', in J. H. Charlesworth and M. A. Daise (eds.), *Light in a Spotless Mirror: Reflections on Wisdom Traditions in Judaism and Early Christianity* (Harrisburg 2003), pp. 45–76.

Bosman, P. *Conscience in Philo and Paul: A Conceptual History of the Synoida Word Group* (Tübingen 2003).

Carmichael, C. M. *The Story of Creation: Its Origin and Its Interpretation in Philo and the Fourth Gospel* (Ithaca 1996).

Chadwick, H. 'St. Paul and Philo of Alexandria', *Bulletin of the John Rylands Library* 48 (1965/1966), pp. 286–307.

Dey, L. K. K. *The Intermediary World and Patterns of Perfection in Philo and Hebrews* (Missoula 1975).

Haacker, K. 'Die Geschichtstheologie von Röm 9–11 im Lichte philonischer Schriftauslegung', *NTS* 43 (1997), pp. 209–22.

Heininger, B. 'Paulus und Philo als Mystiker? Himmelsreisen im Vergleich (2Kor 12,2–4; SpecLeg III 1–6)', in Deines and Niebuhr, *Philo und das Neue Testament*, pp. 189–204.

Leonhardt-Balzer, J. 'Der Logos und die Schöpfung: Streiflichter bei Philo (Op 20–25) und im Johannesprolog (Joh 1,1–18)', in J. Frey and U. Schnelle (eds.), *Kontexte des Johannesevangeliums* (Tübingen 2004), pp. 295–319.

Meeks, W. A. 'The Divine Agent and His Counterfeit in Philo and the Fourth Gospel', in E. Schüssler Fiorenza (ed.), *Aspects of Religious Propaganda in Judaism and Early Christianity* (Notre Dame 1976), pp. 43–67.

Noack, C. 'Haben oder Empfangen: Antithetische Charakterisierungen von Torheit und Weisheit bei Philo und bei Paulus', in Deines and Niebuhr, *Philo und das Neue Testament*, pp. 283–307.

Ostmeyer, K-H. 'Das Verständnis des Leidens bei Philo und im ersten Petrusbrief', in Deines and Niebuhr, *Philo und das Neue Testament*, pp. 265–81.

Schenck, K. L. 'Philo and the Epistle to the Hebrews: Ronald Williamson's Study after Thirty Years', *StPhAnn* 14 (2002), pp. 112–35.

Seland, T. 'The "Common Priesthood" of Philo and 1 Peter: A Philonic Reading of 1 Peter 2.5, 9', *JSNT* 57 (1995), pp. 87–119.

Establishment Violence in Philo and Luke: A Study of Non-Conformity to the Torah and Jewish Vigilante Reactions (Leiden 1995).

'Saul of Tarsus and Early Zealotism: Reading Gal 1,13–14 in Light of Philo's Writings', *Biblica* 83 (2002), pp. 449–71.

Strangers in the Light: Philonic Perspectives on Christian Identity in 1 Peter (Leiden 2005).

Shuler, P. L. 'Philo's Moses and Matthew's Jesus: A Comparative Study in Ancient Literature', *StPhAnn* 2 (1990), pp. 86–103.

Siegert, F. 'Die Inspiration der Heiligen Schriften: Ein philonisches Votum zu 2 Tim 3,16', in Deines and Niebuhr, *Philo und das Neue Testament*, pp. 205–22.

'Der Logos, "älterer Sohn" des Schöpfers und "zweiter Gott": Philons Logos und der Johannesprolog', in J. Frey and U. Schnelle (eds.), *Kontexte des Johannesevangeliums* (Tübingen 2004), pp. 277–93.

Sterling, G. E. 'Ontology versus Eschatology: Tensions between Author and Community in Hebrews', *StPhAnn* 13 (2001), pp. 190–211.

'"Philo Has Not Been Used Half Enough": The Significance of Philo of Alexandria for the Study of the New Testament', *PRSt* 30 (2003), pp. 251–69.

'The Place of Philo of Alexandria in the Study of Christian Origins', in Deines and Niebuhr, *Philo und das Neue Testament*, pp. 21–52.

Wan, S.-K. 'Charismatic Exegesis: Philo and Paul Compared', *StPhAnn* 6 (1994), pp. 54–82.

Whitlark, J. 'Enabling Charis: Transformation of the Convention of Reciprocity by Philo and in Ephesians', *PRSt* 30 (2003), pp. 325–57.

Williamson, R. *Philo and the Epistle to the Hebrews* (Leiden 1970).

Winter, B. W. *Philo and Paul among the Sophists: Alexandrian and Corinthian Responses to a Julio–Claudian Movement*[2] (Grand Rapids 2002).

Zeller, D. *Charis bei Philon und Paulus* (Stuttgart 1990).

PHILO AND THE CHURCH FATHERS

Geljon, A. C. 'Philonic Elements in Didymus the Blind's Exegesis of the Story of Cain and Abel', *VC* 61 (2007), pp. 282–312.

Philonic Exegesis in Gregory of Nyssa's De vita Moysis (Providence 2002).

Heinisch, P. *Der Einfluss Philos auf die älteste christliche Exegese* (Münster 1908).

Hoek, A. van den. 'Assessing Philo's Influence in Christian Alexandria: The Case of Origen', in J. L. Kugel (ed.), *Shem in the Tents of Japhet: Essays on the Encounter of Judaism and Hellenism* (Leiden 2002), pp. 223–39.

'The "Catechetical" School of Early Christian Alexandria and Its Philonic Heritage', *HThR* 90 (1997), pp. 59–87.

Clement of Alexandria and His Use of Philo in the Stromateis: An Early Christian Reshaping of a Jewish Model (Leiden 1988).

'Philo and Origen: A Descriptive Catalogue of Their Relationship', *StPhAnn* 12 (2000), pp. 44–121.

Inowlocki, S. *Eusebius and the Jewish Authors: His Citation Technique in an Apologetic Context* (Leiden 2006).

'Eusebius of Caesarea's *Interpretatio Christiana* of Philo's *De vita contemplativa*', *HThR* 97 (2004), pp. 305–28.

'The Reception of Philo's *Legatio ad Gaium* in Eusebius of Caesarea's Works', *StPhAnn* 16 (2004), pp. 30–49.

Kamesar, A. 'Ambrose, Philo, and the Presence of Art in the Bible', *Journal of Early Christian Studies* 9 (2001), pp. 73–103.

'San Basilio, Filone, e la tradizione ebraica', *Henoch* 17 (1995), pp. 129–40.

Martens, J. '*Nomos Empsychos* in Philo and Clement of Alexandria', in W. E. Helleman (ed.), *Hellenization Revisited: Shaping a Christian Response within the Greco-Roman World* (Lanham, MD 1994), pp. 323–38.

Martín, J. P. 'Philo and Augustine, *De civitate Dei* XIV 28 and XV: Some Preliminary Observations', *StPhAnn* 3 (1991), pp. 283–94.

Runia, D. T. 'One of Us or One of Them? Christian Reception of Philo the Jew in Egypt', in J. L. Kugel (ed.), *Shem in the Tents of Japhet: Essays on the Encounter of Judaism and Hellenism* (Leiden 2002), pp. 203–22.

Philo and the Church Fathers: A Collection of Papers (Leiden 1995).

Philo in Early Christian Literature: A Survey (Assen 1993).

'Philo of Alexandria in Five Letters of Isidore of Pelusium', in Runia, *Philo and the Church Fathers*, pp. 155–81.

'Philonic Nomenclature', in Runia, *Philo and the Church Fathers*, pp. 25–53.

'Why Does Clement of Alexandria Call Philo 'the Pythagorean'?', in Runia, *Philo and the Church Fathers*, pp. 54–76.

Savon, H. *Saint Ambroise devant l'exégèse de Philon le Juif*, I–II (Paris 1977).

'Saint Ambroise et saint Jérôme, lecteurs de Philon', *ANRW* II.21.1 (1984), pp. 731–59.

PHILO AND RABBINIC LITERATURE

Alon, G. 'On Philo's Halakha', in Alon, *Jews, Judaism and the Classical World* (Jerusalem 1977), pp. 89–137.

Amir, Y. 'Rabbinischer Midrasch und philonische Allegorie', in Amir, *Die hellenistische Gestalt*, pp. 107–18.

Aslanoff, C. 'Exégèse philonienne et herméneutique midrashique: Esquisse de confrontation dans une perspective linguistique', in Lévy, *Philon d'Alexandrie et le langage*, pp. 265–86.

Bamberger, B. J. 'Philo and the Aggadah', *HUCA* 48 (1977), pp. 153–85.

Belkin, S. *Philo and the Oral Law* (Cambridge, MA 1940).

Cohen, N. G. *Philo Judaeus: His Universe of Discourse* (Frankfurt am Main 1995).

Dahl, N. A., and A. F. Segal. 'Philo and the Rabbis on the Names of God', *JSJ* 9 (1978), pp. 1–28.

Daniel, S. 'La Halacha de Philon selon le premier livre des Lois Spéciales', in Arnaldez et al., *Philon d'Alexandrie*, pp. 221–41.

Daube, D. 'Philo's Hebrew: A Hebrew–Greek Pun', in Daube, *Collected Works*, I (Berkeley 1992), pp. 213–18.

Gershowitz, U., and A. Kovelman. 'A Symmetrical Teleological Construction in the Treatises of Philo and in the Talmud', *The Review of Rabbinic Judaism* 5 (2002), pp. 228–46.

Gilat, Y. D. 'The Sabbath and Its Laws in the World of Philo', in R. Link-Salinger (ed.), *Torah and Wisdom: Studies in Jewish Philosophy, Kabbalah, and Halacha: Essays in Honor of Arthur Hyman* (New York 1992), pp. 61–73.

Hecht, R. D. 'Preliminary Issues in the Analysis of Philo's *De Specialibus Legibus*', *StPhilo* 5 (1978), pp. 1–55.

Heinemann, I. 'Die Lehre vom ungeschriebenen Gesetz im jüdischen Schrifttum', *HUCA* 4 (1927), pp. 149–71.

Philons griechische und jüdische Bildung[2] (Hildesheim 1962).

Kamesar, A. 'Philo, *Grammatikē* and the Narrative Aggada', in J.C. Reeves and J. Kampen (eds.), *Pursuing the Text: Studies in Honor of Ben Zion Wacholder* (Sheffield 1994), pp. 216–42.

Lauterbach, J. Z. '[Philo Judaeus] – His Relation to the Halakah', in *The Jewish Encyclopedia* 10 (1905), pp. 15–18.

Lévy, B. *Le logos et la lettre: Philon d'Alexandrie en regard des pharisiens* (Lagrasse 1988).

Niehoff, M. R. 'Circumcision as a Marker of Identity: Philo, Origen and the Rabbis on Gen 17:1–14', *Jewish Studies Quarterly* 10 (2003), pp. 89–123.

Ritter, B. *Philo und die Halacha* (Leipzig 1879).

Sandmel, S. 'Philo's Knowledge of Hebrew', *StPhilo* 5 (1978), pp. 107–12.

Philo's Place in Judaism: A Study of Conceptions of Abraham in Jewish Literature (augmented edition; New York 1971).

Stein, E. *Philo und der Midrasch* (Giessen 1931).

Stein, M. (= E.). *Filon ha-aleksandroni* (Warsaw 1936/1937).

Treitel, L. *Philonische Studien* (Breslau 1915).

Winston, D. 'Philo and the Contemplative Life', in A. Green (ed.), *Jewish Spirituality: From the Bible through the Middle Ages* (New York 1988), pp. 198–231.

'Philo and the Rabbis on Sex and the Body', in Winston, *The Ancestral Philosophy*, pp. 199–219.

'Philo's Doctrine of Repentance', in J. P. Kenney (ed.), *The School of Moses: Studies in Philo and Hellenistic Religion: In Memory of Horst R. Moehring* (Atlanta 1995), pp. 29–40.

INDEX OF SOURCES

Note: Authors and works of which no specific passages are cited may be searched in the General Index. However, the present index contains the general references to the authors and works listed in it, as well as the specific passages.

Gig. (De gigantibus)

Hypoth. (Hypothetica)

Her. (Quis rerum divinarum heres sit)

Jos. (De Josepho)

Diatr. 4.1   55

Eupolemus
fr. 1   193 n. 52

Eurytus
De fort., p. 88
Thesleff   128 n. 7

Eusebius
general   9, 48, 62–3, 195, 213, **219–21**, 226, 229, 232

Hist. eccl.
general   224
2.4.3   219
2.5.1   54
2.5.6   219
2.6.3   54
2.16   219–20
2.16–17   52, 220
2.18   229 n. 57
2.18.1   39, 65
2.18.2   42
2.18.4   44
2.18.5   50 n. 47
2.18.6   51, 56, 57, 58
2.18.8   54, 214 n. 11
6.8   216 n. 16

Praep. ev.
general   57, 220, 228
7.13   200 n. 79
8.5.11   51
8.6.1–7.20   51
8.11.1–18   51

Eustathius
Comm. ad Il.
I, p. 4 vdValk   78 n. 42, 79 n. 44

Frontinus
Strategmata 1.1.5   15 n. 18

Gregory of Nyssa
general   221–2, 229

Vit. Mos.
general   222
2.204   83 n. 56
2.207   83 n. 56

Ps.-Hecataeus
apud Diodorus,
Bibl. hist. 40.3.4   25 n. 58

Heliodorus
Aethiopica 9.9.3   227 n. 55

Heraclitus the Allegorist
All.
1.3   82 n. 52
3.2   82 n. 52
6.1   79 n. 44
22.1   79 n. 44
26.2   82 n. 52
72.17   71 n. 23
76.4   82 n. 52

Horace
Sat. 2.7   55

Iamblichus
De myst. 7.5   70 n. 20

Isidore of Pelusium
general   218–9

Ep.
2.143   229–30 n. 60
3.19   218

Isidore of Seville
Etym. 1.44.5   79 n. 43

Jerome
general   224

Ep.
57.5.5   68 n. 10
57.5.6–7   70 n. 19
84.12   70 n. 19

dynamis 100, 130, 135; *see also*
  power(s)

ecstasy 161, 162–4
ecstatic prophecy 142 n. 29, 241–2
education
  in ethical advancement 166
  Moses' 66, 193, 212
  Philo's 18, 150
Egypt, Philo's writings in 217–19
election of Israel 121–3, 149
R. Eliezer b. R. Zadoq 249
emotions 237; *see also* 'good
  emotions'; passions
enkrateia see self-control
Enoch 91
Enos(h) 91
Ephesus 175–6, 190, 195
Epicureanism 57, 153–4, 155,
  164, 204
erōs 188
Esau 158, 160, 165
eschatological 102, 119, 122,
  187–8, 199
eschatology 106–11, 182–3, 189–90,
  190–1, 204, 209
esoteric and exoteric works 33,
  47, 77
Essene–Boethusian 231
Essenes 3, 51, 52–3, 56, 118, 168
ethical allegorism 87
ethical models, biblical characters
  as 87–9, 171, 181–2, 188;
  see also exempla
ethnarch 17, 250
etymological interpretation 71–2,
  100, 123, 149, 170, 211, 216–17,
  227, 228, 235
Eunomius 222, 229
Euzoius 220, 229
Eve 104–5
evil 102, 104–6, 113, 121, 130–1,
  144–5, 158, 164
'exegetical constraint' 144, 154,
  166–7
exempla 88–91, 162
exemplar 90, 132, 178, 243

exodus 98, 103 n. 22, 111,
  189, 203
'Exposition of the Law' 33, **45–50**,
  60–1, 77, 80, 85
external goods 166–7
'extreme allegorizers' 14, 25, 28,
  83, 114, 116

faith 126, 167, 182, 202, 209
fall of Adam and Eve 104–6
fall of the soul 164
first fruits 120
Flaccus 13, 53, 180
free will, choice 103–5, 110, 131,
  186–7
freedom (liberty) 55, 119, 151, 168
Freud 158

Gaius 9, 10, 12, 13, 21, 24 n. 52,
  27–31, 53–4, 62
genres/parts of the Pentateuch
  45–6, **73–7**, 84, 112
Gentiles, non-Jews 33, 50,
  122, 149
gerousia 16
Gnosticism 175, 193, 240 n. 19
God
  as architect 47, 132, 142–3,
    232–4
  'containing not contained' 128,
    239–40
  infinitude of 129–31
  innominability of 127–8, 240
  knowability of existence but not
    essence 101, 126, 241
  oneness of 128–9, 136; *see also*
    monotheism
  personal or impersonal 126–7
  transcendent or immanent 97,
    99, 101, **127–8**, 136, **238–41**; *see*
    also transcendence
golden calf 153
'good emotions' 153, 156–7
grace 106–7, 108–9, 121, 123, 144,
  160, 186, 187–8, 193, 238–9
Graces 239
grammar 1, 18